PASSIONATE MOTHERS, POWERFUL SONS

The Lives of Jennie Jerome Churchill and Sara Delano Roosevelt

CHARLOTTE GRAY

Simon & Schuster

NEW YORK ◆ LONDON ◆ TORONTO ◆ SYDNEY ◆ NEW DELHI

Simon & Schuster
1230 Avenue of the Americas
New York, NY 10020

First Simon & Schuster hardcover edition September 2023

SIMON & SCHUSTER and colophon are registered trademarks
of Simon & Schuster, Inc.

For information about special discounts for bulk purchases, please
contact Simon & Schuster Special Sales at 1-866-506-1949 or
business@simonandschuster.com.

The Simon & Schuster Speakers Bureau can bring authors to your live event.
For more information or to book an event, contact the Simon & Schuster
Speakers Bureau at 1-866-248-3049 or visit our website at
www.simonspeakers.com.

Interior design by Esther Paradelo

Manufactured in the United States of America

1   3   5   7   9   10   8   6   4   2

Library of Congress Cataloging-in-Publication Data has been applied for.

ISBN 978-1-6680-3197-1
ISBN 978-1-6680-3199-5 (ebook)

For Phyllis Bruce and Gwendolyn Alice Anderson

CONTENTS

PART 5: THE FINAL YEARS

Jerome-Churchill Family Tree

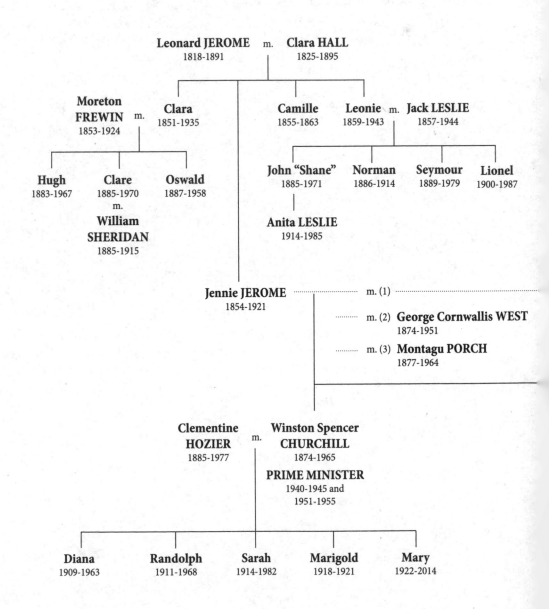

Leonard JEROME   m.   Clara HALL
1818-1891   1825-1895

Moreton
FREWIN   m.   Clara
1853-1924   1851-1935

Camille   Leonie   m.   Jack LESLIE
1855-1863   1859-1943   1857-1944

Hugh   Clare   Oswald
1883-1967   1885-1970   1887-1958
            m.
         William
         SHERIDAN
         1885-1915

John "Shane"   Norman   Seymour   Lionel
1885-1971   1886-1914   1889-1979   1900-1987

Anita LESLIE
1914-1985

Jennie JEROME
1854-1921

m. (1)

m. (2)   George Cornwallis WEST
         1874-1951

m. (3)   Montagu PORCH
         1877-1964

Clementine   m.   Winston Spencer
HOZIER   CHURCHILL
1885-1977   1874-1965

PRIME MINISTER
1940-1945 and
1951-1955

Diana   Randolph   Sarah   Marigold   Mary
1909-1963   1911-1968   1914-1982   1918-1921   1922-2014

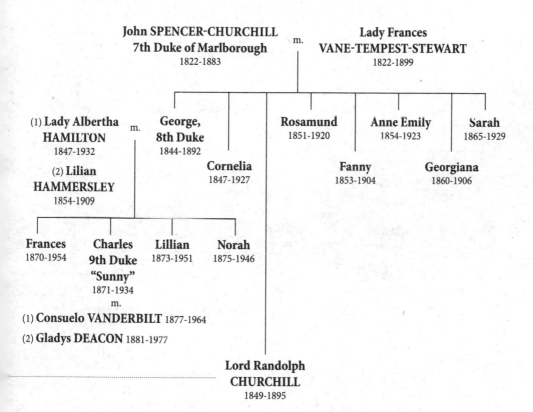

John SPENCER-CHURCHILL
7th Duke of Marlborough
1822-1883

m.

Lady Frances
VANE-TEMPEST-STEWART
1822-1899

(1) Lady Albertha
HAMILTON
1847-1932

m.

George,
8th Duke
1844-1892

(2) Lilian
HAMMERSLEY
1854-1909

Cornelia
1847-1927

Rosamund
1851-1920

Fanny
1853-1904

Anne Emily
1854-1923

Georgiana
1860-1906

Sarah
1865-1929

Frances
1870-1954

Charles
9th Duke
"Sunny"
1871-1934
m.

(1) Consuelo VANDERBILT 1877-1964

(2) Gladys DEACON 1881-1977

Lillian
1873-1951

Norah
1875-1946

Lord Randolph
CHURCHILL
1849-1895

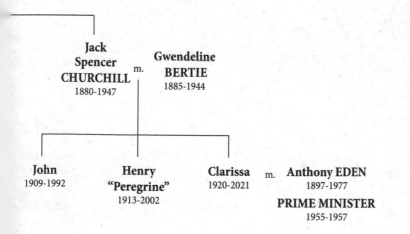

Jack
Spencer
CHURCHILL
1880-1947

m.

Gwendeline
BERTIE
1885-1944

John
1909-1992

Henry
"Peregrine"
1913-2002

Clarissa
1920-2021

m.

Anthony EDEN
1897-1977

PRIME MINISTER
1955-1957

Delano-Roosevelt Family Tree

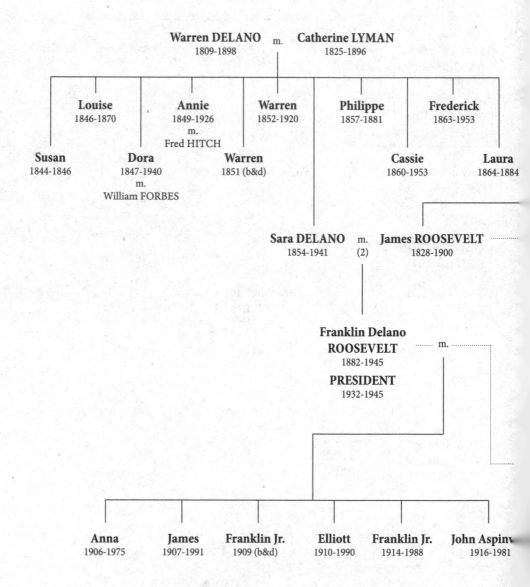

Warren DELANO m. **Catherine LYMAN**
1809-1898   1825-1896

Louise   **Annie**   **Warren**   **Philippe**   **Frederick**
1846-1870   1849-1926   1852-1920   1857-1881   1863-1953
                   m.
                   Fred HITCH

Susan   **Dora**   **Warren**   **Cassie**   **Laura**
1844-1846   1847-1940   1851 (b&d)   1860-1953   1864-1884
                   m.
                   William FORBES

Sara DELANO m. **James ROOSEVELT**
1854-1941   (2)   1828-1900

Franklin Delano
ROOSEVELT   m.
1882-1945

PRESIDENT
1932-1945

Anna   **James**   **Franklin Jr.**   **Elliott**   **Franklin Jr.**   **John Aspinw**
1906-1975   1907-1991   1909 (b&d)   1910-1990   1914-1988   1916-1981

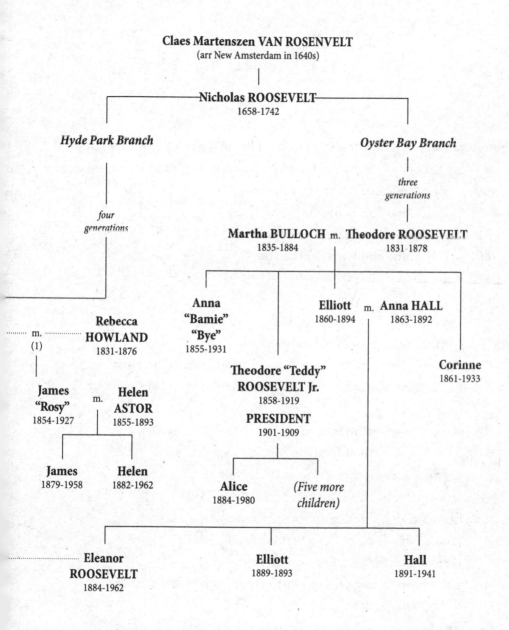

Claes Martenszen VAN ROSENVELT
(arr New Amsterdam in 1640s)

Nicholas ROOSEVELT
1658-1742

Hyde Park Branch

Oyster Bay Branch

three generations

four generations

Martha BULLOCH m. **Theodore ROOSEVELT**
1835-1884   1831-1878

Anna "Bamie" "Bye"
1855-1931

Elliott m. **Anna HALL**
1860-1894   1863-1892

Corinne
1861-1933

m.
(1)

Rebecca HOWLAND
1831-1876

Theodore "Teddy" ROOSEVELT Jr.
1858-1919
PRESIDENT
1901-1909

James "Rosy"
1854-1927

m. **Helen ASTOR**
1855-1893

James
1879-1958

Helen
1882-1962

Alice
1884-1980

(Five more children)

Eleanor ROOSEVELT
1884-1962

Elliott
1889-1893

Hall
1891-1941

TIMELINE

1854: January 9, Jennie Jerome is born in Brooklyn, New York City

      September 21, Sara Ann Delano is born in Newburgh, New York

1861–1865: American Civil War

1862–1865: Delano family lives in Hong Kong

1866–1868: Delano family lives in Paris

1867–1870: Jerome family settles in Paris

1867: Exposition Universelle opens in Paris

1870: Franco-Prussian War

      Delano family returns to the U.S.

      Jerome family moves to England

1874: April 15, Jennie marries Lord Randolph Churchill in Paris

      November 30, birth of Winston Spencer Churchill at Blenheim Palace

1876–1880: Jennie lives in Ireland

1880: February 4, birth of John Strange Spencer-Churchill

      October 7, Sara marries James Roosevelt

1882: January 30, birth of Franklin Delano Roosevelt

1886: Lord Randolph resigns from the Conservative cabinet

1895: January 24, death of Lord Randolph Churchill

1899: Jennie publishes *Anglo-Saxon Review*, vol. 1

      December: Jennie sails to South Africa on hospital ship *Maine*

1899–1902: South African war

1900: Sara temporarily moves to Boston while Franklin is at Harvard

      July 28, Jennie marries George Cornwallis-West

      Winston Churchill is elected Conservative MP

      December 8, death of James Roosevelt

1904: Winston defects to Liberals, appointed to cabinet by Prime Minister Herbert Asquith

1905: March 17, Franklin marries his cousin Eleanor Roosevelt

1906: Sara commissions adjoining homes on East Sixty-Fifth Street, New York City

Winston publishes two-volume biography of his father, Lord Randolph Churchill

1908: Franklin joins a prestigious Wall Street law firm

Winston joins Liberal cabinet, under Prime Minister Asquith

September 12, Winston marries Clementine Hozier

Jennie publishes *Reminiscences of Lady Randolph Churchill*

1910: Sara helps finance Franklin's successful bid for a seat in the New York state senate

1912: Jennie and George Cornwallis-West separate

1913: Franklin becomes assistant secretary of the U.S. Navy

1914–1918: First World War

Winston oversees the Gallipoli campaign, then serves on Western Front

1918: June 1, Jennie marries Montagu Phippen Porch

July, disappointing first encounter in London between Franklin (then assistant secretary of the navy) and Winston (minister of munitions)

Sara deals with crisis in her son's marriage after Eleanor Roosevelt discovers Franklin's relationship with Lucy Mercer

1920: Sara helps finance Franklin's vice presidential campaign when he loses Cox-Roosevelt ticket

1921: June 29, Jennie Jerome Churchill's death, at age sixty-seven

August, Franklin is afflicted by polio; Sara hopes he will leave politics

1928: Sara helps finance Franklin's successful election as governor of New York

1932: Franklin becomes U.S. president and promises a New Deal

1936: President Roosevelt is reelected for a second term in a landslide victory

1939: Sara entertains King George VI at Hyde Park
    September, secret correspondence between FDR and Winston
    Churchill begins (1,700 letters and telegrams)
1940: Franklin is elected for an unprecedented third term as president
    Winston becomes prime minister of Great Britain (aged sixty-six)
1941: August, Franklin and Winston meet secretly off Newfoundland
    and draft the Atlantic Charter
    September 7, Sara's death, at age eighty-six
    December 8, Franklin declares war on Japan after Pearl Harbor
1944: President Roosevelt reelected for a fourth term
1945: Franklin Roosevelt's death, at age sixty-three
1965: Winston Churchill's death, at age ninety-one

A NOTE ON MONETARY VALUES

I have quoted all amounts in the currency and value of the day. In some instances, I have included their value today in order to give the reader a sense of how large some of these sums were, even back then; both Jennie and Sara were born into the very wealthiest level of American society. For these calculations I have used the reliable website measuringworth.com/index.php.

However, while a monetary transaction can be converted into today's dollars or pounds allowing strictly for inflation, its worth at the time may differ dramatically from its worth today. The value of land, houses, and wages has risen by more than a simple inflation calculation would suggest, whereas the cost of manufactured goods has declined relative to inflation.

The Pageantry of Power

1867

Throughout the summer of 1867, the royal carriage clattered regularly along the Champs-Élysées, the imperial crest on its lacquered doors glinting in the Parisian sunlight. The outriders and postilions in green and gold liveries were as impeccable as the four chestnut horses that drew the vehicle. Bystanders stopped to admire the stylish figure sitting in the carriage, her little riding hat set at a jaunty angle and her billowing silk skirts covering the entire width of the seat.

The Empress Eugénie, Spanish-born wife of Emperor Napoleon III, was *the* celebrity of her century. Her glittering jewelry collection, including cascades of diamonds, and her wardrobe of three hundred gorgeous gowns, in silk, satin, brocade, or lace, dictated fashion across two continents.

Among those who watched with awe as the carriage rattled over the cobbles were two savvy young American girls. Neither would ever forget Eugénie's allure. Thirteen-year-old Jennie Jerome, later to become Lady Randolph Churchill and mother of Winston Churchill, would describe Eugénie as "the handsomest woman in Europe." Sara Delano, the future Mrs. James Roosevelt and mother of Franklin Delano Roosevelt, was a few months younger than Jennie, and she too gazed at the carriage, "breathless with admiration." For these two girls, Empress Eugénie's public image epitomized the elegance of France's Second Empire, captured in Winterhalter's flattering portraits and the lighthearted operettas of Offenbach.

The large Delano family, including solemn Sara, with her thick brown hair pulled off her wide forehead, was staying in a grand mansion off the Avenue de l'Impératrice (now the Avenue Foch). Pert, dark-eyed little Jennie was staying with her mother and two sisters not far away, in a spacious apartment on Boulevard Malesherbes. They were part of the extensive American colony that had settled in the most glamorous city in the world. Maybe London ruled a larger empire, perhaps New York boasted more raw vigor. Neither of those cities could compete with Parisian sophistication.

There were many other wealthy expatriates in the French capital that year because the emperor had decided to stage an Exposition Universelle (the second in French history) to promote the glory of the Second Empire and showcase French industrial innovations, artistic talents, and natural resources. This international show of chest-thumping patriotism was Napoleon III's response to the challenge of the 1851 Great Exhibition and the 1862 International Exhibition mounted in London by France's great rival Britain. Seven million visitors had arrived to admire the exhibits in the Grand Palais, and to explore a city radically modernized within the previous decade. On her almost daily excursions down the Champs-Élysées, the Empress Eugénie was deliberately playing to an international audience.

Both girls probably assumed that Eugénie, the beautiful influencer, was doing exactly what was expected of a well-born wife, who could have no official role on her own account. She was being an agreeable asset to her husband. They were still too naive to recognize that many of the women in this period (especially from their own privileged class) played far larger roles than was suggested by the nineteenth-century stereotype of a woman's "natural sphere," as daughter, wife, mother, housekeeper, and submissive helpmeet.

Yet the empress's beauty and elegance had an extra layer—the glimmer of political power, thanks to her sway over her husband, who had ruled France for the past fifteen years. The ruthless Prussian statesman Otto von Bismarck would later call Eugénie "the only man in Paris." Those close to her knew that her husband was guided by her instincts, her arguments. She was proof that, within the constraints of a woman's role in a fiercely patriarchal society, it was possible to exercise one's intelligence and shape one's world.

Since their families knew each other, did the girls ever compare notes on this glitzy figure? Perhaps. There is no record that Sara and Jennie ever met, although their families moved in the same circles. But had they done so they would have agreed that Empress Eugénie was a fascinating woman. They were unlikely to agree on much else.

Jennie Jerome was captivated by the glorious pageantry of the spectacle, because Jennie knew the value of a first-rate performance. Sara Delano would have admired the demeanor of a woman who embodied imperial majesty; Sara understood life in terms of duty. In the future, Jennie would use her charisma to secure her own choices; Sara would shape her destiny through control of her wealth.

There was another parallel in their lives, besides the coincidence of birth and circumstance, and those assumptions about women's roles that they both inherited. One day, each would become the mother of a man of far greater historical consequence than Napoleon III. Their approaches to parenthood were as different as their personalities, yet each developed an unusually intense bond with her son. The examples of resilience, acumen, and loyalty that Jennie and Sara set, the initiatives they took, the impressive support that they provided, and the networks they built, helped mold their sons' characters and careers. Winston Churchill and Franklin Roosevelt adored their mothers and described them as central figures in their lives. The high-level friendship that would develop between the two statesmen reflected patterns of behavior they had learned as children.

I decided to write about these two figures because I'm fascinated by the way that, whatever the restrictions on their lives, women have made choices and shaped the space available to their own purposes. Neither Jennie Jerome Churchill nor Sara Delano Roosevelt would have considered herself a powerful actor in the patriarchal society in which she lived, where financial and political power belonged to men and women were assessed almost entirely through the male gaze. At the same time, neither of these strong-willed women ever considered herself marginal to the society in which she flourished. Because they moved in such privileged circles, both had access to the leading lights of their time in politics and society—and both would use that access. Their forceful personalities and dramatic experiences were in themselves enough to catch my interest.

Sara and Jennie are such delicious opposites—one so relentlessly old-fashioned, the other so daringly nontraditional. Raised with similar values, they made dissimilar decisions as they transitioned from daughters to young wives, to mothers and then to early widowhood. With that, and the fame of their sons, they seemed a natural for a double biography. We may see them as trapped in ridiculous assumptions about women's roles, but that is not how they saw themselves. I wanted to approach each woman through her eyes and words in the moment, using many direct quotations from them so a reader can see the drama of the choices facing them. Twinning the biographies illustrates that women in uber-patriarchal societies could acquire agency through both conventional and unconventional behavior— particularly if they were as forceful as these two were. Their ambitious sons were lucky to have such formidable mothers.

There was a second reason to write about these two women. Their reputations, so different within their lifetimes, have both suffered since their deaths. The influence of each on her son has been minimized; both women have been shoehorned into harmful stereotypes. They (and particularly Sara) have rarely been portrayed in a sympathetic light since their deaths; in fact, their sons' biographers often disparage them—it is as though the Great Men of History must spring, like Athena, fully formed from the head of Zeus, without tiresome interventions from their mothers.

Yet their sons both acknowledged their mothers as key figures in their own lives. Winston Churchill and Franklin Roosevelt clung to the memories of their parents. I wanted to strip away some of the harsher judgments that have been imposed on them since their deaths. I wanted to find the living, breathing human beings under the layers of criticism that historians have lacquered on.

But back to that sunny afternoon in 1867, as two young girls watched an empress ride by. Sara Delano Roosevelt and Jennie Jerome Churchill deserve more than walk-on parts in their sons' biographies. There were bewildering changes in their own lifetimes—a great span of history stretching from the early days of the Industrial Revolution through savage depressions and an era of global war. Thanks in part to the extraordinary confidence each imparted, their sons would help shape the new world. But these women had their own stories, and Winston Churchill and Franklin Roosevelt are only part of it.

PART 1 ◆ A GILDED START

CHAPTER 1

Jerome Flings and Flash

1854–1867

Horse-drawn vehicles were everywhere in Manhattan in the 1850s—carts, carriages, wagons, phaetons. Archival photos of the city capture neither the noise of their jangling harnesses and clattering hooves—the soundtrack of the city—nor the stench of fly-covered horse droppings. Even more alarming was the clatter of a four-in-hand coach hurtling at full tilt down the middle of the newly developed Fifth Avenue. Shocked pedestrians scrambled to get out of the way, then scowled at the flamboyant speedster in a bright green coat as he cracked his whip.

Clutching the arm of the reckless driver was often a gleeful little girl: Jennie Jerome. The middle of Leonard Jerome's three daughters, she was her father's favorite and "tiny mite that I was, I . . . occupied the seat of honor next to him."[1] The horses were trained to rear and prance, and Jennie reveled in the daredevilry as they took corners too fast. She blithely put her faith in her father's horsemanship. Leonard Jerome, part owner of the *New York Times,* had a citywide reputation as a risk-taking financier who rode the fluctuations of the stock market the way he drove his carriage—with dangerous bravado.

Jennie Jerome would spend most of her first thirteen years in New York City, as America's industrial era tipped toward the Gilded Age. The phrase "Gilded Age," which came into popular use some fifty years later, was taken from the title of a novel by Mark Twain and Charles Dudley Warner that described an era of devastating social problems masked by a thin layer of gilt. The Jerome household was entrenched within that creamy gold super-rich crust. Jennie's father was nicknamed "The King of Wall Street." Jennie grew up in a world of lavish mansions, linen tablecloths, and uniformed servants. It was also a world riddled with assumptions about class, race, and gender that make most people today cringe.

Jennie would devote only four pages in her memoirs to her formative years (she was born in Brooklyn), but two themes emerge. First, she was a happy-go-lucky little girl who adored her father. His extraordinary energy and stylish charisma set the mold for most of the men to whom she was attracted as an adult. He instilled in her a passion for horses, and she strove to impress him with her riding skills.

Second, it was her mother, Clara, not her father, who made the key decisions about how Jennie, her elder sister, Clara, and her younger sister, Leonie, would be raised. Leonard Jerome is such a colorful figure that he takes up a lot of oxygen in Jennie's story and has obscured the considerable influence of his more reticent wife. Clara Jerome appears to have been a less conventional, more subtly assertive woman than she is usually given credit for. It was Clara who ensured that Jennie, who was gloriously attractive, would combine American self-possession with European sophistication, and be well educated and accomplished. And it was Clara who ensured that, as Jennie and her sisters matured, they were kept well clear of their father's raffish world.

II

Clara Hall was a shy, dark-haired twenty-four-year-old when she met Leonard Jerome in Rochester, New York. Clarissa, as she was then known, and her two older sisters, Catherine and Caroline, were the daughters of a wealthy landowner and prominent member of the New York State Assembly, but they had been orphaned as children. A pair of elderly aunts raised them in the small town of Palmyra, in upper New York State, then moved them to Rochester, a thriving industrial city on the shore of Lake Ontario. There, Catherine Hall married Lawrence Jerome, Leonard's younger brother.

The Halls had what was then considered a gold standard pedigree: the family was descended from at least two of the passengers on the *Mayflower*'s 1620 voyage, John Cooke and Richard Warren. Catherine, Caroline, and Clara, as she chose to rename herself, were among the most marriageable young women in Rochester's stuffy upper class; they were wealthy and demonstrated exquisite taste in fashion and furnishings. But Clara, an oval-faced beauty, was said by relatives to be unpredictable; one minute she would be a charming flirt, the next minute she would withdraw into a dark mood. Her choice of partner took her contemporaries by surprise. Leonard Jerome, eight years older than Clara, was tall and good-looking, with a walrus mustache and a loud laugh, but he was her social inferior. He and his brother were remembered by a Rochester socialite as "screamingly funny . . . very popular with the ladies owing to the dashing manner in which they rode high-spirited horses."[2] This was not necessarily a recommendation.

Perhaps Clara knew that she would never be satisfied by staid quadrilles in mahogany-paneled drawing rooms, far from brighter lights elsewhere. If so, she must have seen Leonard's large-hearted, noisy personality as her way out. She was mesmerized by Leonard's high spirits. One day, on an expedition to Niagara Falls, thirty-one-year-old Leonard led her away from the rest of the party, then leaned dangerously over the cascading water and shouted, "I won't come back till you've promised to marry me! Look! I'm falling! I'm falling!" Clara gasped in horror, then cried, "I will!"[3] The couple was married on July 5, 1849.

There was more to the Jerome marriage than legal ties. By mutual agreement, the marriage would survive challenges that would shipwreck most alliances. They shared the conventional Victorian assumptions about rigidly gendered roles—Leonard should be the breadwinner, Clara should defer to him while she raised their children. Although Leonard was frequently unfaithful to Clara, throughout their marriage he wrote fond letters to "Clarita" and always took charge in a crisis. They would never risk the stigma of divorce.

So Clara Jerome ignored her husband's wilder behavior and turned a blind eye to his infidelities. However, it seems that soft-voiced Clara had a hidden strength of character that ensured her husband's respect. She saw through the hypocrisy of the age in which they lived. She never challenged the privileges accorded to men that women could never enjoy, but she recognized them and quietly worked her way around them to ensure her own comfort. She took steps to ensure her financial security, at a time when a married woman was assumed to be her husband's dependent.

In 1848, New York had followed the example of several other states and granted women the right to own and control their own property, long before such rights were granted in Europe. The following year, Leonard settled a million dollars—at least $33 million today—on Clara. Was this at Clara's insistence, to protect the capital she had brought into the marriage and Leonard had used to seed his fortune? Perhaps. It was a smart move, since it shielded her and their daughters from his boom-or-bust speculations. Being a man of extravagant gestures, Leonard also presented his wife with a magnificent diamond necklace.

The Jerome marriage would be a model for their daughters, who grew up expecting wedding vows to last a lifetime and men to make extravagant gestures. They noted their mother's financial autonomy, but unfortunately, they also absorbed their father's breezy insouciance about money. Jennie would never appreciate the huge costs of a luxurious lifestyle. Neither she nor her two sisters would marry men who offered either magnificent diamonds or financial stability, but they all assumed that a Leonard Jerome would always be in the background, ready to swoop in to pay bills or help them in an emergency. Jennie's mother passed on to them, and particularly to her middle daughter, a quiet strength in the face of disaster.

Above all, Clara understood the male ego and how to succeed in a world run by men. She instructed her daughters, "Never scold a man, my dears. If you do, he will only go where he is *not* scolded.'"[4] She set them an example of how to secure an unusual degree of independence within a marriage.

III

Clara Jerome had correctly anticipated that Leonard, with his warmth and reckless exuberance, would take her places.

Jennie's father came from respectable but threadbare origins. He grew up in an austere, God-fearing farming family of eleven, in a faded clapboard farmhouse outside Syracuse. Thanks to the generosity of an uncle and an elder brother, he attended Princeton University, but he was suspended after sabotaging test tubes so that they exploded in a chemistry class. He was short on means (he had to switch to the less expensive Union College, in Schenectady, New York) but never of ambition. After training as a lawyer in the same uncle's Rochester law office, he and his brother Lawrence purchased a local paper, the *Daily American*, with funds from Catherine Hall, Lawrence's wife. In addition to tripling the paper's circulation, Leonard championed Republican campaigns to abolish slavery, build libraries, and provide free education.

Rochester was too small a pond for the Jerome brothers, so, after Leonard married Clara, they sold the *Daily American* and moved to Brooklyn, then an independent city of 120,000 only a ferry ride from Wall Street. Leonard was eager to plunge into the macho financial markets of Wall Street and invest in all the new economic ventures spawned by the Industrial Revolution: the steel mills, railroads, oil refineries, factories, and steamships that were making sharp-elbowed speculators rich. Mid-century Manhattan was the perfect environment for an entrepreneur with the brains and drive of Leonard Jerome. Each morning he and another brother, Addison, would catch the ferry across the East River to the Lower Manhattan office from which they ran their brokerage business.

Clara took her time to settle into the new life, and rarely took the ferry to Manhattan. But she began to track the social habits of Manhattan's elite. She shared the aspirations of most wealthy men's wives in the nineteenth century—dressing well, living well, and hoping to rise above her origins. By the time her first daughter was born, in 1851, the Jeromes could afford several household staff members as well as a nursemaid.

The newfound affluence of families like the Jeromes rested on top of a subterranean world of poverty. Within a stone's throw of their handsome four-story Brooklyn brownstone lived the teeming masses who underwrote all that Manhattan wealth. Thousands of immigrants poured into the city. According to the state census of 1845, just over one in three New Yorkers was foreign-born; by 1865, the proportion had risen to almost half. In the Irish tenements on the west side, in Kleindeutschland on the Lower East Side, and within the Jewish and Italian slums to either side of the Bowery, living conditions were often appalling. Immigrants were crammed into overcrowded tenements that lacked heat, ventilation, and adequate sanitary facilities. Whole families lived together in the dim light and endured the fetid smells of single rooms. Typhus and diphtheria were rife; in 1865, smallpox alone killed more than six hundred New Yorkers.

Meanwhile, the city sucked ever more activity into its core. Railroads snaked up the island of Manhattan itself, spreading soot, ash, and noise. Pavements were laid down, dug up, rerouted; tunnels, reservoirs, and sewers were installed to provide cleaner water; the noise was incessant, the dust stifling. New York City was already the largest metropolis in America, with its economic, commercial, and cultural supremacy unchallenged. Unfettered capitalism allowed a handful of men (always men) to make vast fortunes; a few hundred grew very, very wealthy. Leonard Jerome could see opportunities everywhere.

Clara must have felt that her dreams were coming true when, soon after their arrival in Brooklyn, the Republican administration in Washington plucked her husband out of Wall Street and appointed him American consul in Trieste, as a reward for using the *Daily American* as a Republican platform. The cosmopolitan Austro-Hungarian seaport, squeezed between Italy and the Austrian Empire in the northeast corner of the Adriatic Sea, was a mecca for music and literary arts. Welcomed everywhere thanks to her husband's prestigious position, Clara became a fervent Europhile, reveling in white-tie-and-tails dinners, diplomatic receptions, and the frothy Parisian fashions worn by the city's elite.

But after six months, Leonard Jerome had had enough of the froth. He grew tired of Trieste's endless parades of aristocrats who "spoke more languages than I, but none paid for their own education, and surely it is more important to think clearly in one idiom than to chatter in five."[5] He craved the financial jungle of Wall Street and the chance to make a fortune. By 1853 Clara and her family were back in Brooklyn, sharing a house with Addison Jerome at 8 Amity Street. Clara would recall that her husband "did not wait to unpack before he plunged. Every dollar he had not settled on me was in constant use on the market."[6]

Jennie's father now embarked on his swashbuckling career of making and losing fortunes, usually through speculation and shorting stocks. During the day he and his brother followed stock trades in all the emerging industries; in the evenings, he became known as a master of repartee at lively stag dinners. A contemporary recorded that in this fast-paced, tough milieu, he thrived. "I never knew him to take a drink in a bar or public place, yet he belonged to the city with all its garish brilliance. No man ever became more completely a New Yorker."[7]

Money was not the only driving force in Leonard Jerome's life. Musical from childhood, he adored opera. Sometimes he worshipped the divas from afar; other times, he took talented young women under his wing and helped promote their careers. The youngest and most beautiful were more than professional protégées, and were said to adore their dashing and generous Svengali. Clara ignored her husband's affairs.

Leonard's careless presumptions about women were evident when his second daughter was born, on January 9, 1854. Leonard promptly announced that she should be named after his latest passion—the superstar soprano Jenny Lind, the "Swedish nightingale." "Jennie?" exclaimed his wife. "Just Jennie? It's an impossible name." But as usual, Leonard Jerome got his way, and the daughter who would prove most like him in character was named after a celebrity performer.[8]

Clara gave birth to two more daughters after Jennie: Camille, who died in early childhood, and Leonie, in 1859. At the same time, she was busy navigating Manhattan's social scene. From the late 1850s, she took her daughters each summer to Newport, Rhode Island, a small seaside town on the brink of becoming fashionable thanks to families like the Astors and the Vanderbilts. It was the right place to be, although Clara was not yet courting important friends. Jennie's memories of Newport were simple: "We were allowed to run wild and be as grubby and happy as children ought to be."[9] Her father would appear for weekends, often with one of his glamorous young protégées in tow. Jennie trotted around the Rhode Island resort in a dogcart, given to her by one of her father's girlfriends and pulled by two donkeys named Willie and Wooshey.

Although most schools and colleges were exclusively male, wealthy Americans did not consider educating girls a waste of money. Educational activists were starting to establish educational institutions for women—Vassar College in 1861, Wellesley College in 1870, Smith College in 1871, among others. In common with most well-heeled matriarchs, Clara Jerome had no intention of letting her daughters become overeducated (and perhaps unmarriageable) bluestockings, but she did not want them to be ignorant, either. Private tutors ensured that well-born girls were well-read, while the Jeromes' regular trips to Europe instilled respect for classical traditions, Renaissance art, and foreign languages.

The girls attended a small private school that took academic studies seriously. From a young age, they took piano lessons and their mother oversaw their practice sessions rigorously. By the time they reached adolescence, Clara and Jennie were already approaching concert pianist levels. This was a skill much valued in the best drawing rooms.

Jennie's mentions of her education are fleeting. She recalls being taken by her father to opera matinees "to improve our minds." She was always a voracious reader. In a leatherbound volume she owned that is now in the Churchill Archives in Cambridge, there is a hand-written catalogue of the books that Jennie bequeathed to a descendant: the Dialogues of Plato; Montaigne's essays; the complete works of De Quincey and of William Makepeace Thackeray; many volumes of history, including those by Agnes Strickland; plus novels by Walter Scott, Tolstoy, Jane Austen, and several French authors; plus poetry by Yeats and Byron.[10]

Clara also raised her daughters to be as fashion-conscious as she was herself. An early photo reveals three well groomed girls with carefully coiled ringlets, wearing versions of stylish adult gowns. Little Clara and Leonie, with fair hair and bland expressions, are only ordinarily pretty. Jennie, who was perhaps seven at the time, already dominates the threesome, with her glossy black curls, huge dark eyes, and impudent expression as she leans into the camera.[11] In the opinion of Elinor Glyn, a British author of risqué bestsellers in the early 1900s, "The American woman is unquestionably the most beautiful, the best-dressed, best-turned-out and consequently the most attractive of all women." Clara ensured that Jennie Jerome fit the description.

IV

One of the few anecdotes Jennie told about her childhood is about weekly dancing classes during the Civil War years, where "every little Southerner I met at dancing classes was a 'wicked rebel,' to be pinched if possible."[12]

Jennie was six years old in 1860 when Abraham Lincoln, who opposed the expansion of slavery, was elected U.S. president. The following year, the Southern states split from their Northern neighbors and formed the Confederacy so they could continue their vicious practice of slavery—a practice that allowed slaveholders to justify owning, controlling, torturing, lynching, raping, and often killing human beings. For the next four years, a ferocious war raged as the young Republic came close to tearing itself apart. By the time the last Confederate fighter surrendered, President Lincoln had been assassinated and there had been over a million casualties, including as many as 750,000 deaths. The Thirteenth Amendment had been added to the Constitution, outlawing slavery and emancipating the four million African Americans who had been enslaved. But this was only one step in the Black struggle for true equality—a struggle that Black activists had already been fighting for decades. Freed Black peoples' status in the postwar South remained precarious as their legal rights were ignored and racist organizations such as the Ku Klux Klan emerged.

There were many vociferous supporters for the abolition of slavery in New York, including William Lloyd Garrison. The city already had a large population of free African Americans and many more would arrive from the South after the war ended. Concentrated in low-paid jobs, many were employed by wealthy families—the Jeromes had a Black nursemaid called Dobby for years. Yet the brutal battles of the Civil War or debates about how to achieve true equality for Black people barely touched everyday life for much of the New York elite. Moreover, Leonard Jerome had no fear of being conscripted. A Northern plutocrat could avoid the draft by paying a $300 commutation fee (about $9,630 today) or bribing a poor man to go in his place. Soon it was widely believed that the Civil War had become a "rich man's war and a poor man's fight." While thousands of soldiers were killed or wounded at Bull Run and Harpers Ferry and Gettysburg, the hostilities made men like Jennie's father rich.

In 1860, the year before war broke out, Leonard Jerome had purchased a large block of shares in the *New York Times* and was soon in cahoots with the financial editor. The *Times* threw its support behind President Lincoln and his Republican administration. Leonard proved his personal support for the Union side with a check for $35,000 (over $1 million today)[13] toward a ship to catch Southern blockade runners, plus generous contributions toward care of the wounded. At the same time, thanks to its excellent sources within the administration, the paper made itself indispensable to the serious reader with its cool analysis of economic and political issues. Leonard now had a platform for his market tips, and reporters from other papers and speculators hung on his recommendations, especially for various railway schemes. During the Civil War, the newspaper's circulation increased enormously, and Jerome was soon reputed to be worth $10 million—a fabulous sum back then, and equivalent to over $300 million dollars today.

Leonard Jerome's success mirrored the expansionary boldness of his country. While the Civil War would leave the South's economy in shambles, the North was becoming the world's industrial powerhouse. Higher tariffs to protect domestic industries, government subsidies for railroads, and land grants for settlers profoundly shaped the development of the American economy for the rest of the century. Railroad mileage doubled between 1865 and 1873, and increased by a further 50 percent by 1881, boosting demand for iron, steel, and coal. The iron pathways through forests, prairies, and mountains, which funneled immigrants westward in vast numbers, finally reached the Pacific in 1869.

The frenetic activity spawned vast opportunities for bold entrepreneurs to seize. The term "robber baron" entered the American lexicon in 1859 when it was used to describe the ruthless business practices of Cornelius Vanderbilt, who amassed a huge fortune in the shipping industry. Soon the derogatory term was being applied to men who would become some of the richest Americans in history, including Andrew Carnegie, who built a steel empire, and John D. Rockefeller, who made a fortune from oil refineries. In the late 1860s, Vanderbilt recruited Leonard Jerome as an investor in a bold new scheme: the merger of several existing rail lines into the lucrative New York Central & Hudson River Railroad.

Clara must have been proud of her successful husband, but she also watched his rakish reputation spread alongside his wealth. He never did things by halves. He built an extravagant six-story red brick and marble mansion, at the intersection of Madison Avenue and Twenty-Third Street, adjacent to the residence of one of Manhattan's greatest snobs, the redoubtable Mrs. Schermerhorn, and he celebrated his arrival there with a sumptuous ball. At each end of the ballroom stood a fountain—champagne bubbled in one, cologne spouted from the second. Next door to the mansion stood the family's three-story stables, filled with horses, grooms, and carriages. According to the *New-York Tribune,* "Except for the Emperor's Mews in Paris, it is doubtful if any stable in the world is as fine . . . Black walnut, plate glass, carpeted floors and other costly decorations ornamented the place. Above the stable he built a private theatre, handsomely adorned . . ."[14] Leonard Jerome's stage was a launchpad for his young, talented sopranos as he aspired to be a Medici of American music patrons.

Jennie and her sisters would have heard from the servants about some of their father's more extravagant gestures. He once hosted a dinner at Delmonico's, the city's top restaurant, at which, as each female guest unfurled her starched white napkin, a gold bracelet fell into her lap. (Clara does not appear to have been present.) He cofounded the American Jockey Club and established a racecourse just outside the city. As his friend August Belmont, another high roller, said of his good friend, "One rode better, sailed better, banqueted better when Mr. Jerome was of the party."[15]

Leonard Jerome was never sufficiently wealthy to be considered an A-list robber baron, but he was in their ranks. However, Clara had now been in New York long enough to realize that she and her daughters were never going to be acceptable to Manhattan's old guard, despite her *Mayflower* ancestors or her daughters' arpeggios. Her husband's flashy extravagance branded them as nouveau riche, which made the Jeromes marginal to the city's social establishment.

So who belonged to this establishment? The most obvious members were descendants of the original Dutch colonists who had arrived in the New World well before the American Revolution: Schermerhorns, Roosevelts, Schuylers, Brevoorts, Van Rensselaers. Such families gloried in the label Knickerbockers (a term that was either an Americanization of a common Dutch surname or a reference to the early settlers' knee-length breeches), and they deeply distrusted glitter. Pious and personifying the Dutch virtue of thrift, most did not flaunt the fortunes they had made over the years through banking, trade, and real estate. Instead, this self-styled elite preferred to live quietly, manage their country estates in the Hudson Valley, and husband their resources for the next generation.

Old guard friendships were restricted to people who shared the encrusted dignity of established wealth. Their fortunes were as solid as the mahogany furniture and their family ties as sturdy as the drawing room bell pulls in their brownstone houses on Washington Square. They worshipped together at Grace Church (Episcopal) and belonged to the same exclusive network of clubs and cultural associations. Alongside the Saint Nicholas Society, there was the Union Club, the Arcadian Club, the Lotos Club, and the Century Association, each with membership limited to a few hundred men, high entrance fees, and a practice of blackballing unsuitable applicants. John Jacob Astor, the richest man in America, barely qualified for membership in the exclusive Saint Nicholas Society because his family had not arrived in New York until 1784. Jews, Catholics, and Blacks never crossed their thresholds.

Old money families were entirely confident about their place in the world; a sense of superiority was bred in their bones. Despite living in the nation's most boisterous democracy, they fought to protect their exclusivity with elaborate rules and rituals borrowed from European aristocracy. Outsiders like Clara and Leonard Jerome were given the cold shoulder. In 1854, *Frank Leslie's Ladies' Gazette of Fashion* advised readers to go through the formalities of an introduction "with the most bland expression . . . yet insensibly [to] convey to the introduced an impression that a further intimacy would not be agreeable."[16]

Why did newcomers even want to move into these circles, however grand the lineages and refined the manners? In a New World republic supposedly founded on principles of equality, what was the attraction in joining a self-declared aristocracy that seemed determined to establish an Old World class system? Some of the recent arrivals in the city were indifferent to Knickerbocker pretentions. Nothing signaled

Leonard Jerome's disdain for tight-lipped snobbery as much as those spirited rides along Fifth Avenue.

But others, especially the wives of the new class of entrepreneurs, smarted at the sneering condescension of society matrons. Clara knew, for example, that Jerome money was as good as that of Mrs. William Astor (née Schermerhorn), Manhattan's most powerful hostess. Her newly purchased Meissen tea set was just as delicate as those owned by members of the Van Rensselaer clan; her ornate bonnets and elaborate gowns were styled by the same milliners and seamstresses as those sported by wives of Knickerbocker grandees.

Clara Jerome came to dislike Manhattan. After being presented to Emperor Napoleon III and the elegant Empress Eugénie on one of the family trips to Paris, she wrote, "I have found the court I want."[17]

V

In 1867, Jennie's mother announced her intention to sail to Europe with her three daughters, now sixteen, thirteen, and eight years old. According to Jennie, Clara moved for health reasons, to consult a physician in Paris. "Finding that the educational advantages were greater in Paris than in New York, we decided to remain there."

This was only half the story. Up to this point, Clara chose to ignore her husband's infidelities, but Leonard had recently taken up with a New York widow, Mrs. Fanny Ronalds. Diarists who met Fanny gushed about her beauty, her voice, her style. In *Memories of an Old Etonian*, Greville Moore wrote, "Her face was perfectly divine in its loveliness, her features small and exquisitely regular. Her hair was of a dark shade of brown and very abundant."[18] Fanny Ronalds dressed impeccably and sang beautifully, and Leonard Jerome was besotted.

Gossip flared. When Mrs. Leonard Jerome was introduced to Mrs. Fanny Ronalds at a ball one evening, a hush fell on the others in attendance. Clara could have cut Fanny with the curled lip of an Old New Yorker. Instead, as she took her white-gloved hand, she reacted with gentle tolerance. "I don't blame you," she whispered. "I know how irresistible he is."[19]

However, Clara evidently had had enough of her husband's dalliances. Moreover, Leonard's fortune was starting to sag, and her American dollars would go much further in France than they did in Manhattan. She had always wanted her daughters to be multilingual, and she knew that in Paris, where the American colony numbered over four thousand, wealthy Americans were welcomed.

But there was even more to the move than this. The marriage prospects of the Jerome sisters must have worried their mother. The salons of France's Second Empire, where Emperor Napoleon III and Empress Eugénie held court, were easier to penetrate than Knickerbocker circles. In Paris, her daughters could acquire a sophistication to match their American self-assurance, while Clara could carve out a new life for herself, away from Leonard's boisterous triumphs.

The four Jerome women and a retinue of servants, including Dobby, who had looked after the girls since they were small, crossed the Atlantic and settled into spacious, well-furnished lodgings at 70 Boulevard Malesherbes.

Jennie would note in her memoirs that "my mother went out a great deal in French society, where her beauty attracted much attention, *la belle Américaine* at that time having all the charm of novelty."[20] Leonard visited regularly, but for most of the year Clara was on her own, making new friends and sizing up potential suitors for her daughters. If she had stayed in New York, she would have been trapped in a social cul-de-sac. In Paris, she could reinvent herself. She remained a loyal wife and a conscientious parent, as Victorian custom demanded, and she shrank from scandal. But she relished her escape from Manhattan's snobbery.

CHAPTER 2

◇

Delano Decorum and Discipline

1854–1870

While the Manhattan social elite threatened to ignore the nouveau Jeromes, it offered a warm embrace to members of the Delano family. Jennie's contemporary Sara Delano would sail through life with the unassailable poise of someone who knew she belonged. Delanos had the pedigree, connections, and manners to qualify for membership in New York's old guard.

Sara was born on September 21, 1854, nine months after Jennie Jerome, in that playground of old money, the Hudson Valley, half a day's carriage ride north of New York City. This pastoral area had already spawned its own artistic tradition, the Hudson River School, led by Thomas Cole and Frederic Edwin Church, among others. For their wealthy patrons, these painters depicted a dreamily romantic landscape of ancient hills and gentle streams far from the brash exuberance of industrial America. A viewer would never guess there were coal mines up the road, or that many of the landowning gentry owed their fortunes to slavery and other exploitative forms of trade.

Sara's birthplace was the Delano country estate called Algonac, a name appropriated from the Algonquin words for "hill" and "river." Travelers on the road that led 152 miles north from Manhattan to Albany, the state capital, had no chance of seeing the estate, at the halfway point in their journey, thanks to a carefully planted screen of maples, beeches, and flowering shrubs. But passengers on one of the Hudson's puffing little steamships could glimpse the Delanos' forty-room brick and stucco mansion through the trees on the river's west bank, two miles north of the prosperous little river port of Newburgh. Algonac, with its square tower and stone gatehouse, was one of several magnificent estates dotting both banks of the wide, placid waterway. Most of them belonged to wealthy, long-established dynasties, and, to anybody who dared doubt, Algonac announced that the Delano family was part of this privileged class. Although not Dutch Reformed in origin, the Delanos could claim several forebears who had arrived on the *Mayflower* in 1621, plus roots in the ruling Boston clique known as the Brahmins. Sara's grandfather, Warren Delano, had a large estate called Fairhaven, in New Bedford, Massachusetts, where the family congregated for seashore summer vacations and Thanksgiving celebrations. Throughout their lives, Sara and her siblings regarded their grandfather's rambling mansion as a family shrine.[1]

The importance of self-control was drummed into Sara from an early age. When she was four, she fell against the sharp corner of a cabinet and gashed her head badly. Bleeding and frightened, the little girl ran howling to her father, Warren Delano. He calmly washed the cut, then announced that he would stitch the wound shut himself because it would take too long to summon a doctor from Newburgh. Telling Sara to be brave, he held the little girl firmly between his knees as he threaded a sharp needle, then pulled it through her scalp. According to her son's biographer Geoffrey C. Ward, "The pain was excruciating, but Sara never moved or cried out. It was wrong to worry others."[2] Such self-discipline would characterize Sara for the rest of her life.

Stoicism also characterized Sara's mother, Catherine Lyman Delano, the youngest child of a respected Massachusetts judge. Literary and musical, Catherine was a model of the sweet femininity most valued in mid-nineteenth-century upper-class America. Her mother, Anne Lyman, described her as "never out of temper and always ready to oblige to any extent that her friends can claim."[3] One of her sons would note approvingly that she "always had a kind thought, word or deed for friend or stranger."[4]

Slender, dark-haired, and demure, Catherine Lyman was only eighteen when she met Warren Delano in 1843. Fifteen years older than his new bride, Warren radiated the confident authority of a handsome, successful man who was on his way to making a fortune in maritime commerce. He had returned from China, where he represented a major Boston trading house, to look for a wife. Within weeks of their first encounter, Catherine became Mrs. Warren Delano and found herself wrenched away from her peaceful New England life and swept off to China by her new husband. It was an abrupt change. The young bride wrote to a cousin about her fears of disappearing on a long, dangerous voyage to a country on the other side of the globe of which she knew nothing: "I feel that it is my duty to go, but I do feel sad to think of the long separation from all my kind friends . . . When I think of my poor experience, it seems almost dangerous to undertake such a thing and I feel unhappy, and then if I stay home I should not be happy . . . I have determined to go and look on the bright side."[5]

Catherine being Catherine, off she sailed with a brave smile, determined to ensure that all her husband's needs were met. Throughout her life, Sara would follow her mother's conventional example and, like most of her wealthy female contemporaries, make her family her priority, whatever the circumstances. But Catherine's example of wifely deference was one to which her daughter would pay only lip service in the years ahead. In personality, and often in conduct, she would prove to be more her father's than her mother's daughter.

II

Sara was Catherine and Warren Delano's seventh child, and the fifth to survive infancy. In the nine years before Sara's birth, Catherine had proven herself more robust than her family might have expected. Immediately after her marriage, she had traveled with her new husband to the cramped compound in Guangzhou (then called Canton) where foreigners were allowed to live. There she weathered three lonely years, watched her firstborn, a daughter, die before her second birthday, and clung to a second little girl, Louise, whose health was always delicate. But she had also seen her husband's career flourish. He was senior partner in Russell & Company, the largest American firm in the lucrative China trade, and, as he kept reassuring Catherine, he could expect to return to the United States with a "competence"—$100,000, or well over $3 million today.

Judging by the souvenirs of China that Catherine always cherished, she knew that her husband's business encompassed purchases of tea, porcelain, silk, and other luxury items. Did she know that these goods were acquired in exchange for opium? The Chinese government made repeated attempts to stamp out the opium trade, which was dominated by the British, because, thanks to Western traders since the mid-eighteenth century, addiction had become a devastating epidemic within the Middle Kingdom. Estimates suggest that one out of every ten Chinese was an opium addict.[6] But traders like Warren Delano kept importing opium and showed no remorse for the damage the narcotic wreaked on Chinese people and society.

Russell & Company's profits soared. Men like Warren Delano and his brother Edward, who had joined him in the business, regarded the Chinese addicts as moral degenerates rather than victims of coercive and unscrupulous Western merchants.

It must have been a relief for Catherine, now in her early twenties, when her husband announced, in 1846, that he had amassed his competence and they could return to America. The Delanos settled in New York City so that Warren could start investing his fortune in all the exciting new ventures of an industrializing America—property, railroads, copper mines in Tennessee and Maryland, coal mines in Pennsylvania. Soon he was one of the wealthiest businessmen in mid-century Manhattan. He kept his hand in the maritime trade, too, by building and owning several clippers.

The Delanos acquired one of the most prestigious properties in the city—39 Lafayette Place, one of a group of nine town houses known as Colonnade Row. Fronted with massive fluted stone columns, each house had marble mantelpieces and massive mahogany doors hung on silver hinges. However, more important than the

Corinthian columns were the neighbors, who included the writer Washington Irving and several Astors. Sara would later describe Colonnade Row as "the aristocratic center of the city."[7] Two more Delano daughters, Deborah (always known as Dora) and Annie, were born at this address, plus a son who died in infancy.

Warren and Catherine Delano slipped effortlessly into Knickerbocker circles. Although Warren, like Leonard Jerome, had had to make his own fortune, his *Mayflower* ancestry and New England self-possession ensured that he was welcomed into the right clubs, where he shared with other members the distrust of vulgar newcomers who flaunted their money. He deplored the lavish French châteaux, Italianate mansions, and pseudogothic castles that were creeping north on Fifth Avenue and Madison Avenue, erected by the likes of Leonard Jerome.

Warren Delano was prepared to do business with predatory stock speculators, but he didn't want to mingle with their wives and families. And he did not want his children to associate with them, either. He acquired an old fruit farm in the Hudson Valley, named it Algonac, and employed the prominent landscape architect Andrew Jackson Downing to enlarge it. Downing, who had worked in Washington laying out the grounds of the White House and the Capitol, understood the process of gentrification before the term was invented. He converted the farm building into an Italianate mansion with expansive, elegantly curated outbuildings and grounds. It was all superbly opulent and dignified, with its elaborately carved rosewood furniture, Chinese porcelains in display cabinets, and wide, old-fashioned hall hung with pictures, armor, and "quaint devices from China." A large bronze bell from a Buddhist monastery was placed in the garden. Each bedroom had its own tin tub for bathing, plus chamber pots to be emptied by maids.[8] The estate required a staff of at least ten people to maintain it.

Here, in 1852, Catherine gave birth to a son, Warren, and then, two years later, a fourth surviving daughter—Sara, known as Sallie to her immediate family. Another son, Philippe, arrived within three years. The children were educated at home by a succession of French or German tutors and governesses, and rarely mixed with neighbors. Sara's early days were spent in the secluded stability of Algonac, scrambling to keep up with three older sisters and an elder brother. The diaries that Warren and Catherine Delano kept jointly record weather, church sermons, classics read aloud, children's activities. "A beautiful warm day and the children leave off their flannel drawers . . . Children out in the afternoon with Phil in his boat on Mr. Brown's pond . . . The children, Warren, Sallie and Philippe are up early and have their explosions of fire-crackers . . . Warren, Sallie and Phil playing games in the school-room."[9]

Domestic harmony prevailed at Algonac; the children never heard their parents disagree. This was hardly surprising, since Warren Delano was such an imposing man, both physically and psychologically. Tall, with a fierce gaze, bushy side whiskers, and an intimidating glare, he exerted an authority that was rarely challenged. He was an implacable Republican, fond of saying that while all Democrats were not horse thieves, in his experience "all horse thieves were Democrats."[10] If anybody complained about the weather, he would bark, "Nonsense. All weather is good weather." In a biography of Sara Delano Roosevelt entitled *Gracious Lady*, by Rita Halle Kleeman, for which the main (if not only) source was Sara herself, Warren Delano's forcefulness jumps off the page. Kleeman writes that Warren's children gave him "unquestioning obedience . . . due to a firm conviction that their father's opinions and beliefs were absolutely infallible and that he knew best about everything."[11]

Whether Catherine simply ducked conflict or recognized the benefits of allowing her husband to present himself as the only head of the family, she quietly dealt with any disagreements in private. Bad news was never discussed in front of the children. In later years, Sara described her childhood as "tranquil . . . unmarked by adult emotions," and would marvel at her parents' ability to protect their children from "all traces of sadness or trouble or the news of anything alarming."[12] Catherine was likely responsible for this. The carefully wrought stability of the relationship, and the suppression of all un-pleasantness, could not have been a greater contrast to the uneasy ties that bound Clara Jerome to her boisterous husband, Leonard.

Sara Delano firmly believed that her mother "depended on [my fa-ther] utterly, and while at times when they were separated, she showed herself capable of making decisions wisely, it would never have oc-curred to her to make one for herself when he was there."[13] Separation occurred frequently, however, so Catherine Delano was usually in charge of the household. While Catherine gently raised her children in the idyllic Hudson Valley estate, far from New York City's crowded tenements and noisy streets, Warren Delano spent most weekdays conducting his professional affairs from his town house in Manhattan.

The longest separation came when Sara was seven.

In 1857, the American economy went into a tailspin after a rapid period of expansion in which too many banks, merchants, and farm-ers had made risky investments. Hundreds of companies failed; real estate prices collapsed; thousands of people were out of work. Warren Delano, in his late forties, watched his roaring profits turn into stran-gling debts. He noted in the journal that he and Catherine kept, "The monetary situation from New York worse than ever . . . Stocks, bonds and money tighter. Failures abundant and confidence diminishing."[14]

Expenses were cut, the Lafayette Place mansion was sold, but the financial slide gathered speed. By January 1860, Warren decided that if he was to protect his family and avoid bankruptcy, he must act. He took a bold step for a gray-haired man of fifty: he chose to return to the China trade and earn another competence. He took leave of his wife (now pregnant for the ninth time) and children, and set sail for the other side of the world.

For two years, Catherine Delano maintained Algonac routines with quiet skill. A skeleton staff kept Algonac going, and she asked various relatives to help with her growing family, which soon included a sixth daughter, Catherine, known as Cassie. Catherine's cousin Nancy Church gave the older children lessons in the schoolroom. Her sister-in-law Sarah, with her husband, Ned Delano, ensured that the children sat up straight, modulated their voices, and spoke clearly. Sara and her sisters sewed shirts for Union soldiers now fighting the Civil War.

Warren Delano wrote regularly from China, and Sara was the child who was allowed to soak the stamps off the envelopes and carefully paste them into a scrapbook. She was enthralled by her father. All her life she would treasure a small tintype, made just before her father's abrupt departure, which showed her sitting on Warren's lap, enclosed by his long arm. "There was no one like my father," she recalled over seventy years later.[15] She never appears to have spoken of her mother like that: Catherine Delano fulfilled her maternal role with such self-effacing skill that Sara simply took her for granted.

III

The handsome square-rigger, its many canvas sails bellying before the wind, sailed out of New York harbor as the June sun sank in the west. The 183-foot-long clipper was towed beyond the bar by two steam tugs while various friends and relations dined on board and then wished the travelers well. Once the guests departed on the tugs, the captain fired several cannons, and his passengers cheered loudly as the last rays of sunlight glinted on the topsails.

Catherine Delano made sure that her two nursemaids, Davis and Ellen, had firm hold of her three youngest children, including eight-year-old Sara, while the four older ones, aged between sixteen and ten years, hung over the rail, elated by a brisk wind and the prospect of unexpected adventure. From the hold came the faint sounds of a whole menagerie of animals, to ensure a supply of fresh provisions—chickens, pigs, geese, turkeys, and a cow, all secured in pens.

Warren Delano had sent for his family to join him in the British colony of Hong Kong. Once again, Catherine left the comforts of her American home and faced a long journey halfway around the globe. This time, it was even more challenging. With seven children in tow, she was returning to a country where diseases like typhoid were rampant, where she had already lost a child, and where she would have no family support—only local servants whose language she could not speak, and who would rarely show affection for a *fanqui* [foreign devil]. In later years, Sara would reflect that it must have been "altogether terrifying to my . . . mother to give up her beautiful home and its peaceful security for perhaps the rest of her life." Yet in the detailed journal Catherine kept of the four-month trip, she never complained. That evening, she simply began a new diary. "Log of the S.S. *Surprise*. June 25, 1862 to October 31, 1862. New York to Hong Kong" and listed all her family members, plus her cousin Nancy Church, and the two young nursemaids. Then she noted, "We need not say it was sorrowful to leave our friends, but we must look forward to the happy meeting with our husband and father in Hong Kong. Seasickness followed and we were soon all in bed."[16]

It was a daunting voyage, lasting 128 days, through the North and South Atlantic, around the Cape of Good Hope, up through the Indian Ocean and the Malay Archipelago to the China Sea. For the first few days, Catherine recorded how quickly excitement turned to nausea. "Louise and Annie suffering a good deal from sea-sickness. Nancy has a bad head. Davis' head troubles her and Warren seasick. Ellen miserable. Dora not very bright and Sallie uncomfortable . . . None of us present a very brilliant appearance." There were fierce storms, days of endless rain, unbroken horizons, and becalmed seas. Members of the Delano party were the only paying passengers on the clipper.

Delano discipline held. Catherine Delano ensured that they stuck to Algonac routines—lessons in the schoolroom, music practice on the piano that came with them to Hong Kong, games on deck in the afternoons when weather permitted. Dining at sea was not so different from dining at Algonac. Unless the seas were too high, the family sat around a heavy wooden table, covered with a linen tablecloth, and ate off high-quality china. A typical entry in Catherine's journal reads, "Had a good dinner, oyster soup, corned pork, rice, peas and flapjacks, after which the Capt. gave us some brandy, which seems to do one good after eating pork."

"Our lives were regulated as they had been at home," Sara would remember later. Seasickness, heatstroke, chilblains—alongside the boredom and frustration of being cooped up—were among the low points of the journey.[17] In the South China Sea, the temperature soared to 126 degrees Fahrenheit, and Sara's mother noted, "Perspiration falls off one like rain."[18] But Sara Delano and her siblings would never forget singing sea shanties ("Down the river hauled a Yankee clipper!"), learning to identify the stars, fishing for nautilus, and signaling with flags. While Catherine's grandson Franklin Delano Roosevelt was in the White House, a wooden replica of the *Surprise* would adorn a table in the Oval Office.[19]

Four months and six days after leaving New York, Sara and her siblings sighted Hong Kong's harbor. Soon a small craft was speeding toward them, with a tall figure standing in the bow. When the *Surprise* finally dropped anchor, Warren Delano sprang onto the clipper's deck to greet his family. Sara treasured her first glimpse of him: "all dressed in white, very tall and slight and good looking, with his side whiskers and mustache, coming very quickly up the side of the ship on a ladder that the sailors had let down."[20]

Catherine Delano forgot her misgivings as she settled her family into Rose Hill, the luxurious mansion on top of one of Hong Kong's hills that her husband had rented. In this large stone house with a walled garden, Warren Delano had created an Asian version of Algonac's seclusion. While he continued to trade with the Chinese mainland across the Zhujiang River estuary, his children took lessons in the schoolroom with Nancy, and practiced their scales on the piano. On the rare occasions when they stepped beyond Rose Hill's gates, it was to visit other expatriate families.

Although the household was dependent on the work of Chinese cooks, maids, gardeners, stable boys, and watchmen, Sara and her siblings never learned a word of Chinese. Rose Hill was a cocoon, and Catherine Delano quietly carried on as though she still lived in the Hudson Valley. Two more children were born, Frederic in 1863 and Laura in 1864. American national holidays were observed. Sara and her brother Warren decorated their pony cart with American flags when they drove it to the weekly horse races at Happy Valley, the British racecourse.

But after seven-year-old Philippe fell ill with diphtheria, Warren and Catherine Delano decided to ship him and twelve-year-old Warren II and ten-year-old Sara home, under the supervision of their fifteen-year-old sister, Annie. Sara spent the next two years with Aunt Sarah and Uncle Ned in New England. Photographs from this period depict a child of obvious aplomb, with thick brown hair, deep-set eyes, and a determined thrust to her chin. She was already emerging as the most thoughtful of the Delano children, with a strong sense of duty toward her younger siblings, especially Philippe, who was closest to her in age.

Warren Delano recouped his fortune and, once again a very wealthy man, left Hong Kong and turned his back on the China trade, quietly burying his responsibility for supplying opium to thousands of Chinese addicts. One of the very few statements he ever made about these activities came in a letter he wrote to his brothers: "I do not pretend to justify . . . the opium trade in a moral and philanthropic point of view, but as a merchant I insist that it has been . . . fair, honorable, and legitimate . . . liable to no further or weightier objections than is the importation of Wines, Brandies and Spirits into the U. States."[21] Next, he turned his attention back to the booming economy of post-war America.

It is unlikely that Sara knew that her revered father's fortune originated in the nineteenth-century equivalent of fentanyl. Instead, she absorbed the message that her generation of Delanos represented the acme of Yankee bloodlines, not only because she and her siblings could claim thirteen ancestors from *Mayflower* stock but because—as she proudly explained to her respectful biographer—her forebears had played a role in America's political, intellectual, and social history.[22]

IV

The family could not return directly to Algonac, as it was rented out. Besides, Warren was in no rush to return to America, where the Civil

War was just drawing to an end. Instead, he took his family to Paris, where they rented the large apartment off Avenue de l'Impératrice, which boasted wide windows and a balcony.

"Paris was gay with flags and bunting in honor of the foreign princes and rulers" arriving to visit the great 1867 exposition, Sara recalled for Rita Kleeman. Such exotic figures as the Russian tsar, the Ottoman sultan, and the khedive of Egypt as well as major and minor European royals rode past the Delano balcony, as the children hung over it to stare at their brilliantly colored uniforms. But the most unforgettable for Sara was the Empress Eugénie, "quite unconscious of Sallie and Phil and even the more dignified older brother and sister, gazing breathless with admiration."[23]

The Jeromes arrived in the French capital while the Delanos were still there. Given the small world of American expatriates, they probably crossed paths. But unlike the Jerome girls, the Delano children were limited in their visits to the crowded exposition grounds; they spent more time on historic buildings and monuments, museums, and galleries. Every morning, Celestin, the Delanos' butler, walked Sara over to the Avenue de Malakoff, where she was enrolled in classes taught by a Madame Grenfell to a small number of French and American girls. Every afternoon, the Delanos' nanny would arrive with the younger children to pick her up for the walk home through the Bois de Boulogne. When she celebrated her twelfth birthday, in September 1866, her aunt gave her a book entitled *Famous Girls Who Have Become Good and Illustrious Women.*[24]

The Paris sojourn was brief. Warren Delano did not want his children to mingle with American social climbers or continental riffraff. Paris was not his only concern; he found New York's new millionaires "pretentious" and "boasting," and he told his brother Ned that he might settle permanently in Europe. He was considering the purchase of an isolated country estate where he might "organize my household as to combine the real comforts and proper luxuries of life with a system of order and regularity of studies, duties, exercise, and recreation."[25]

There would be no European Algonac, probably because most

of the Delano children had outgrown their governesses. From Paris, the family moved to Dresden for the winter, and Sara, now fluent in French, studied German and music at a local school. When most of her family returned to America, she stayed on in Germany for two more years with two of her siblings, all under the care of Aunt Sarah and Uncle Ned, and attended finishing school.

According to her biographer, Sara relished learning European history and languages, and making new friends; she was certainly too self-disciplined to acknowledge any homesickness. But in May 1869 some sad news arrived from Algonac. Sara's eldest sister, Louise, whose health had been poor ever since her birth in China, had finally but not unexpectedly died. Warren and Catherine now summoned their family home.

Sara, along with her aunt and uncle and siblings, managed to find passage to New York City on the *Westphalia*, the last steamship to leave a German port before the Franco-Prussian War began. During this 1870 conflict, a coalition of German states led by Prussia defeated France, and the subsequent rebellion within France unseated Emperor Napoleon III and left the beautiful Eugénie homeless. The Jeromes would see bloodshed in the streets of Paris and watch aristocratic friends fearing for their lives, but the Delanos steamed safely away, untouched by the traumas of war and revolution. Sara returned to Algonac after an interval of eight years.

Far from the European upheavals, the family mourned Louise's death and then resumed the old routines of daily household prayers, Sunday visits to Newburgh's Unitarian church, and evening card games. Family activities and get-togethers with Hudson Valley neighbors—picnics, musical soirees, skating parties—fill the pages of the family diaries. "Stormy day and we all stayed home with books and work. Sallie and Cassie made caramels"; "Afternoon a party drove on the river, which was thronged by young and old on skates, in sleighs, etc. making quite a gay scene." Few outsiders penetrated this close-knit society, linked together by family connections over several generations and with a low tolerance for unconventional behavior.

For the rest of their lives, the five surviving sisters, along with their three brothers, would find more pleasure in the company of each other, plus their partners and children, than almost anyone else's. At five foot ten, Sara was the tallest of the girls and the most dignified. With her long, graceful neck and firm chin, she was strikingly good-looking and started to receive invitations to evening parties with neighbors. Her eldest surviving sister, Dora, was already married (the wedding had been in Paris), and Annie was entertaining young men. Manhattan's Gilded Age rituals of courtship and marriage—rituals that the Jeromes had fled—seemed the inevitable next chapter for Sara. Unlike Jennie Jerome, Sara Delano had guaranteed access to the elite.

Yet she remained single for some years. Was this her choice? She did not need to marry for money, and perhaps the security of Algonac was preferable to the company of the callow young men she met. Or perhaps she exuded a certain hauteur that potential suitors found intimidating. However, Sara was certainly not averse to the idea of marriage. She would take her family by surprise.

CHAPTER 3

High-Spirited Jennie
1867–1873

Thirteen-year-old Jennie Jerome arrived with her mother and sisters in Paris as the Exposition Universelle was in full swing. There were thousands of other American visitors besides the Jeromes and Delanos, including Samuel Morse, inventor of the telegraph, and the writer Mark Twain (who was disappointed by Parisian women: "I knew by their looks that they ate garlic and onions").[1]

The vast oval exhibit hall on the Champ de Mars was a showcase for French industrialists and artists and proclaimed France's prosperity. How could the Jeromes resist the exhibits? Throngs gaped at a monumental pendulum clock by Eugène Farcot, the Suez Canal dredging machine, a collection of 450 plants from the French West African colony of Gabon, the historical canvases of Jean-Louis Ernest Meissonier. The exhibition's splendor was in tune with the transformation of Paris itself over the previous decade. Thanks to Baron Haussmann, streets had been broadened and now converged on central focal points; slums had been demolished; newly laid water and sewer pipes and gas lines had transformed the lives of Parisians. In the cafes along the Champs-Élysées and in Montmartre, artists and aesthetes discussed the Meaning of It All. The windows of new department stores such as Printemps were filled with tantalizing merchandise. A new line of steam-powered boats called Bateaux Mouches plied the Seine.

France was enjoying the same breakneck pace of economic development as the United States, but its government was spending more on civic amenities than American authorities, and the country was celebrating its cultural heritage and talents as well as its industrial innovations. In the introduction to the exhibition's handbook, the *Paris Guide*, Victor Hugo, the grand old man of French letters, proclaimed, "As Athens became Greece, as Rome became Christianity, thou, France, become the world!"[2]

Like Sara, Jennie was intoxicated by the pageantry and energy. "Never had the Empire seemed more assured, the Court more brilliant, the fêtes more gorgeous. The light-hearted Parisians revelled in the daily sights of royal processions and cavalcades. The Bois de Boulogne and the Champs Elysées, where we were living at the time, were crowded with splendid equipages."[3] She was as blind to the pervasive poverty in the narrow streets behind the boulevards—the crowded sweatshops, filthy stables, cramped housing—as she had been to the slums of New York's Lower East Side. Instead, she was starstruck by the glamor of a society in which princesses and duchesses curated their public images in the same way that celebrities do today. She would soon learn how fragile such celebrity could be, but that did not stop Paris from becoming her favorite city in the world.

II

Once Mrs. Jerome had settled Clara, Jennie, and Leonie and the servants into the spacious Boulevard Malesherbes apartment, she turned her attention to her daughters' education. She paid particular attention to finding the right teacher to further their musical talents. And then she plunged into launching her social life. Charming and healthy, with impeccable manners, the forty-two-year-old started writing her name with accents—Jérôme—and enjoying herself in the society in which she had chosen to settle.

Fifteen years earlier, during Leonard Jerome's brief period as American consul in Trieste, Clara had discovered French fashion design, and now she learned that the Empress Eugénie's favorite couturier was Charles Worth. Soon she was one of the House of Worth's most loyal customers. Her closets rapidly filled with gowns of silk, satin, and tulle that featured the bustles favored by the empress, along with piles of whale-boned underwear to give her the required hour-glass shape. She had grown too plump to aspire to the eighteen-inch waists that her daughters managed, but she was still shapely. Clara, a consummate social strategist, knew that the impact of an eye-catching gown could be incalculable; it suggested not just wealth and style but also talent and significance. Jennie took this lesson to heart; cost would be irrelevant to her if she was trying to achieve a particular effect.

But cost was becoming a problem, although the Jerome sister-hood was barely aware of it. The year after they arrived in Paris, their father made a bold stock play that went sour. After riding high for so many years, Leonard Jerome had invested thousands of dollars in Pacific Mail Steamship stock in order to corner the market in it, and then could not sell it. He lost most of his capital. He faced his cataclysmic loss with characteristic sangfroid, shrugging that he had the remnants of other investments to live on. Then he quietly leased his Madison Avenue mansion and left Manhattan for the Boulevard Malesherbes.

There he discovered that his daughters were growing up a little too fast. The eldest, Clara, was blond, pretty, obsessed with her appear-ance, and attracting too many older admirers. The youngest, Leonie, was simply willful. On one occasion, the Jeromes were having tea in the drawing room when Leonie was teased by one of her sisters for walking in the Champs-Élysées with her toes turned in (toes appar-ently should be turned *out*). Leonie seized the tablecloth, dashed china and cakes to the floor, and disappeared in a rage.[4]

But it was Jennie, dark-haired and mischievous, who made the most extraordinary announcement. She was never going to marry, she declared, because she was going to be a concert pianist. Her musical skills matched her ambition, but her parents were shocked that Jen-nie would consider that a moneymaking profession was preferable to a good marriage, and that she assumed it was her right to make such a choice.

Leonard Jerome was bewildered by these unruly girls. He asked his wife, "Why are [they] so wild?" Mrs. Jerome was amused by the question. "Well dear," she replied. "They are *your* daughters."[5]

The girls had absorbed their mother's fascination with royalty, and the Empress Eugénie was a role model for them all.[6] Mrs. Jerome was awestruck by her social prestige, which put New York's Knickerbockers in the shade. Clara was enthralled by her glittering appearance. For little Leonie, Eugénie was a fairy queen. But for Jennie, the empress demonstrated that a beautiful woman could have behind-the-scenes power. There was a great deal of gossip about the imperial marriage: the emperor was a well-known philanderer, and the couple rarely spent time together in private. Eugénie was the Princess Diana of her day—a radiantly beautiful fashionista adored by the public. But there was more to her than that. She advocated for women's equality, acted as regent when the emperor left Paris, and often attended meetings of her husband's council of ministers.

The Jerome sisters' focus on the imperial court cannot have pleased their robustly democratic father. However, he continued to leave their education and manners to Mrs. Jerome, because he accepted the conventional wisdom of his day: girls must learn to please men in order to attract suitable husbands. He could see that Americans like the Jeromes were welcomed at the imperial court and that nobody cared where their money came from. This meant that access to the circles to which Mrs. Jerome aspired in Second Empire Paris was much easier for Clara and her daughters than it was in rigidly snobbish Manhattan. Besides, Leonard was preoccupied with his friend Fanny Ronalds, who had followed him to France. And he soon returned to the city he had made his own: New York.

In her memoirs, Jennie Jerome rattles off the titles of "all the most beautiful and charming women of Paris, including many attractive foreigners," who spent their days driving around in their carriages, and their evenings swishing around palaces in Monsieur Worth's creations. "Helped by the magnificence of their appearance," she writes, they gave Paris "that air of elegance and distinction which could neither be surpassed nor emulated by any other capital in Europe."[7] She envied her elder sister who was old enough to "go into society," and was invited to one of the emperor's famous hunting parties at Compiègne, outside Paris. For three days, over a hundred guests rode, visited local sites, dined off gold plates, danced and played in the royal château. Ladies were required to change into different outfits at least three times a day. Clara sent home a desperate plea: "I shall need another dress—something white [only foreigners wore bright colors] trimmed with anything you think pretty. I think I must have it—in fact two if possible—for these ladies dress so much and never appear in the same."[8] At the close of the visit, each guest was presented with a gift. Jennie recorded how Clara, "much to my envy, was given an inkstand shaped like a knotted handkerchief, filled with napoleons." Meanwhile, Jennie was stuck in the schoolroom, learning French and practicing her scales.

Leonard, still entangled with Mrs. Ronalds, briefly returned to Europe in the spring of 1870 and swept his two daughters off to Nice for a holiday. Clara's report to their mother in Paris captures both the girls' regard for their swaggering father and also the international company they kept. "Papa was very tired last night when he got here, but this morning he looked so fresh and handsome that we told him the ladies would all be after him . . . He has gone out and said he wouldn't be home till four . . . I suppose Jennie told you what a charming day we passed at Cannes . . . there was Lord-Someone-or-Another and his father, the Earl-of-Something-Else . . . Madame Rothschild, from Vienna, asked me if I knew Mrs. Belmont . . ."[9]

The beautiful Jerome sisters assumed that there would always be a Lord-Someone-or-Other or a wealthy Rothschild hanging around them. Jennie's unorthodox ambition to become a professional pianist gradually faded.

III

At seventeen, Jennie was keenly aware of her beauty and eager to make her debut into society. Shapely and coquettish, she was ready for the "coming out" ceremony—the virginal white dress, the low curtsey to the empress. The Jeromes' lady's maid was already adept at pulling corset laces as tight as possible to achieve a tiny waist. Tight lacing also emphasized the size of a woman's breasts. Some women padded their bosoms with horsehair; Jennie was voluptuous without any props.

But Franco-German tensions torpedoed Jennie's dream of being presented at the imperial court. Rivalry between France and its neighbor had been simmering for months, as Germany nursed territorial ambitions and France feared a shift in the European balance of power. While the Jeromes danced and shopped, Bismarck was redefining the map of Europe, intent on the unification of German states through (as he put it in a famous speech) "blood and iron" rather than long-winded speeches and consensus. A war with France, he calculated, would spur pan-German nationalism. In August 1870, the well-armed Prussian army invaded France, imposed crushing military defeats on French forces, and marched to the gates of Paris.

Everything happened so fast. The Second Empire collapsed, the emperor was deposed, the Third Republic was proclaimed, and a grueling siege of Paris began. Most of the American colony fled, and the crush at the railway stations was overwhelming. From New York, Leonard Jerome fired off a telegram telling his family to flee to London.

But Jennie's mother could not bear the idea of abandoning their charmed life, plus a household of exquisite possessions and gowns. She insisted that a sprained ankle rendered her immobile. "And so we tarried," Jennie would recall. "Our house became the rendezvous of the few of our French friends who had not gone to the front." Jennie finally persuaded her mother to leave with a few possessions tied in tablecloths. She organized her maid Marie to help them to the railway station (Mrs. Jerome was pushed through Paris on a wheelbarrow) and then return to the house. Marie was given orders to pack their trunks and follow them the next day. But Marie and the trunks never came; the Jeromes caught the last train out of the besieged city before the Prussians halted rail travel. From Deauville, on France's north coast, Clara Jerome and her daughters managed to find passage on a cross-channel steamer, but they arrived in England as refugees, with only the bags they could carry.

Mrs. Jerome and her daughters were devastated by their changed circumstances. "Debarred as we were from our bright little house and our household gods [sic] it was indeed a sad time," Jennie would write later. Now, instead of a scintillating season of haute couture and gallant suitors in one of Europe's most beautiful cities, she could look forward to "a winter spent in the gloom and fogs of London . . . our friends scattered, fighting or killed at the front."[10] London was indeed a dismal prospect; it was even more crowded and polluted than New York and had none of the lighthearted charms of the Paris of the Second Empire. Inadequate sewers and constant coal fires had made it into a stinking, squalid city, with regular outbreaks of typhoid and cholera. The rain was incessant; the sulfurous fog, composed of gas and coal dust, was sometimes so thick that boys carrying flashlights had to lead cabs and omnibuses through the streets. Yet London was safer than Paris in 1870, where the human suffering during the siege was terrible. Food hoarded in warehouses was rapidly consumed, and citizens were reduced to eating dogs, cats, rats, and zoo animals. Elephant trunk meat sold for eight dollars a pound.[11] More Parisians (approximately 40,000) died of starvation and disease than of battle wounds during the four-month siege by the Prussians.

Leonard Jerome lived up to his wife's expectations and his daughters' dashing image of him. Summoned from New York by telegram, he swept his family into London and installed them in Brown's, a small but smart hotel off Piccadilly. Their comfortable suite, furnished like an English country house with deep armchairs and chintz curtains, included a music room with two pianos so Clara and Jennie could practice their duets. From outside, the clip-clop of hansom cabs driving down Albemarle Street to clubs such as Boodle's and Brooks's filtered through the windows of the Georgian building. After the initial shock of loss, Mrs. Jerome got back to the serious business of her daughters' education and hired a music teacher and a German governess.

Leonard's finances had shrunk, but he protected his family from the worst of his misfortunes. They must have known that the mansion on Madison Avenue had been let, and there were no more flamboyant dinners featuring gold bracelet amuse-bouches. But there were no constraints on the Jerome clothing bills, reinforcing "Jennie's disastrously optimistic belief that money would always be found," suggests biographer Anne Sebba.[12]

Money was also found for Napoleonic keepsakes. As soon as they dared, Leonard and Clara Jerome and their daughters returned to Paris and found their residence (they had moved to even smarter lodgings, on Boulevard Haussmann) barely damaged. Leonard packed up their valuable collection of Italian paintings. On the grounds of the smoldering Tuileries Palace, Clara chanced upon an open-air auction of imperial possessions. She noticed a gilt-edged dinner service with golden crowns and the initial N (for Napoleon) and immediately decided that she wanted this keepsake of the glorious French court she had loved so much. Her bid was successful, and she hired men with barrows to take the service home.[13] The purchase reflected not only her love of France but also her single-mindedness when she decided she wanted something. (Her grandson Winston Churchill would relish using the service at Chartwell, his home in Kent, six decades later.)

Jennie was heartbroken by the state of the city. "Ruins everywhere. The sight of the Tuileries and the Hôtel de Ville made me cry. St. Cloud, the scene of many pleasant expeditions, was a thing of the past, the lovely château razed to the ground. And if material Paris was damaged, the social fabric was even more so . . . Some of our friends were killed, others ruined or in mourning, and all broken-hearted and miserable, hiding in their houses, and refusing to be comforted."[14]

Many Americans welcomed the collapse of the Second Empire. Elihu Washburne, the American minister, wrote privately, "I am rejoiced beyond expression at the downfall of this miserable dynasty and the establishment of the Republic."[15] But Jennie's sympathies were entirely with the aristocrats among whom her mother had hoped her daughters might find spouses. She was too young and naive to understand the complexities of the crisis from which France would

slowly emerge: the left-wing forces unleashed by the briefly triumphant Paris Commune after the siege was lifted, France's shift to a
Republican model of government, French resentment of a ruthless
Germany that would simmer for the next half century. All she knew
was that the Second Empire's glamorous court life was over.

The challenge for Jennie's mother was to relaunch her daughters
into an entirely different society—the British aristocracy. In London,
the entry point for the Jeromes was through the network of titled
French refugees to whom Mrs. Jerome remained close, and who congregated in the Brown's Hotel suite. It helped that her daughter Clara
had recruited several admirers in Paris salons; it was even more helpful that Jennie and Clara were much in demand to play delightful
duets at elegant drawing room teas. Clara, blond and ethereal, was
overshadowed by her dark-haired, more assertive sister, who used
her husky voice and sooty eyelashes to great effect with potential admirers. Together the two eldest Jerome girls (Leonie had been packed
off to boarding school in Wiesbaden) made a good-looking, talented,
and charming pair.

Thanks to their childhood in New York and Paris, Clara and Jennie were more accomplished and polished than young women with
less education who had rarely stepped onto foreign soil. Growing up
in three different metropolises gave Jennie and her sister an additional advantage. They were social chameleons, fluent in English and
French, with an outsider's antennae for the rules and rituals of each
culture—the table manners, the correct addresses, the seating proto-
cols, and the taboos. Clara would obey the rules in order to "belong."
Jennie would grasp them, but after proving that she had absorbed
them, she liked to flout them.

IV

The Jeromes remained unsettled in London, where Clara had caught
typhus, so in July 1871 Leonard decided to take his family to Cowes,
on the Isle of Wight, off the south coast of England. In some ways,
Cowes was the English equivalent of Rhode Island's Newport, where

the Jeromes had spent summers ten years earlier. It was a modest seaside town that had become a smart resort for the aristocratic circles in which Clara was eager to mingle. But while Newport flaunted palatial "cottages" and American millionaires, Cowes boasted elaborate yachts and British and European nobility. The Royal Yacht Squadron, then the most exclusive yacht club in the world, was housed in a castle built by Henry VIII, and in the 1860s the town liked to style itself as the "Yachting Capital of the World."

Crucial to Cowes's popularity was the patronage of the twenty-nine-year-old Prince of Wales, eldest son of Queen Victoria and a notorious playboy. The future king filled his days and nights with card games and visits to the racetrack. Actively disliked by his mother, now a lonely widow who regarded him as frivolous and irresponsible, he dutifully performed ceremonial functions but chafed at his exclusion from any political power. He and Alexandra, his beautiful Danish-born wife, were intensely social, and both enjoyed being fashion icons. The prince was a stickler for proper dress at any occasion he attended, and his admirers slavishly adopted his fashion choices—his goatee, the silk top hats, and the cuffs on his trousers, his habit of leaving the bottom button of his waistcoat unbuttoned. He traveled with two valets, while two others remained home to maintain his enormous wardrobe in spotless condition.

Bertie, as Prince Albert Edward was known, had already developed both a paunch (hence the unbuttoned waistcoat) and a taste for affairs that his wife tolerated with good grace. During his lifetime he had as many as fifty-five lovers outside the marriage, according to some accounts, and he would be named as an adulterer in several divorce cases.[16] Parties at Marlborough House, his London home, were wild occasions, at which young swells like himself tobogganed down the stairs on silver trays. Intellectuals were unwelcome. As Frances, Countess of Warwick, one of the women who shared his bed, would write years later, "We considered the heads of historic houses who read serious works, encouraged scientists and the like, very, very dull . . . We wished to know as little of them as possible, and our wishes were law."[17]

Despite his reputation as a roué, Bertie's affability and energy made him a popular companion. His attendance at Cowes's annual sailing regatta held each August had transformed it from a lively sporting event into a major society occasion. Each summer, when London's seasonal carnival of balls and luncheons had drawn to an end, an entourage of courtiers would follow the prince and princess to Cowes. Contemporary photos and sketches depict a press of beautifully clad women parading through town and lounging on the wicker chairs artfully arranged on the Royal Yacht Squadron club's lawn.

This was the society into which Clara Jerome now introduced her daughters. Jennie would recall that "it was delightfully small and peaceful. No glorified villas, no esplanades or pier, no bands . . . People all seemed to know one another. The Prince and Princess of Wales and many foreign royalties could walk about and amuse themselves without being photographed or mobbed." Mrs. Jerome was happy to join several of their Paris friends who had taken up residence there, including the deposed Emperor Napoleon III and Empress Eugénie.

The Jeromes rented Rosetta Cottage in West Cowes, a modest Georgian residence overlooking the sea, with a rambling garden and apple orchard behind it. Only a short walk away was the Royal Yacht Squadron clubhouse, where Jennie and her sister could join friends. Even closer was Beaulieu House, where the former emperor and his wife had taken up residence. "We were asked by Their Majesties to go for an expedition round the Island," Jennie recalled in her memoirs.[18] Other guests included several Spanish grandees, but the "expedition was rather a failure, owing to the roughness of the sea, most of the party seeking 'the seclusion that the cabin grants.'" With piercing insight, Jennie described the former emperor leaning against the mast looking old, ill, and sorrowful. "Even in my young eyes, he seemed to have nothing left to live for." Only Empress Eugénie and the two sturdy Jerome girls "enjoyed the breeze." Within a couple of years, the ex-emperor would die in exile, in a modest home in Chislehurst, Kent.

Soon stiff white invitation cards lined the Jeromes' mantelpiece. Society hostesses couldn't get enough of Clara, now twenty, and seventeen-year-old Jennie. Thanks to their mother's careful supervision, they displayed exquisite gowns, charming manners, and melodious duets—yet there was more to their success than sparkling looks and virtuoso playing. There was also their combination of Parisian manners and American vitality.

The Prince of Wales admired American women because "they are livelier, better-educated, and less hampered by etiquette . . . not as squeamish as their English sisters, and better able to take care of themselves," he once remarked.[19] The prince was not alone in the warmth of his welcome to young American women. In the next few years, a wave of sparkling young Gilded Age heiresses would cross the Atlantic Ocean and marry into the British peerage. Between 1870 and 1914, 454 titled Europeans would acquire American brides.[20] One hundred British aristocrats, including six dukes, would marry American women. Unknowingly, Jennie Jerome would be the eye-catching avatar of this phenomenon.

Within weeks, the Jeromes were established within Cowes social life. Leonard Jerome would renew the lease on Rosetta Cottage for each of the next two summers. Throughout these years, Clara Jerome insisted on remaining with her daughters in Paris during the winters, while her husband crisscrossed the Atlantic. Gilded Age Manhattan remained his world, and he continued to play the role of King of Wall Street despite severe setbacks.

Leonard missed his family, who were evidently so busy enjoying themselves that they had little time for letter writing. On a humid New York day in August 1873, he wrote a wistful letter, using his pet names for them:

> Mrs Clit, Miss Clarita and Miss Jennie,
>   Dearly beloved. It is nearly two weeks since I had a letter.
> You must be sure to write the particulars of all that is going on.
> I have no doubt you will see many nice people and will have
> Cowes all to yourselves as far as Americans are concerned . . .
> Don't forget while sitting under your own vine and eating up

your own fig tree that I am awfully disappointed if I don't get
my weekly letters.[21]

The summer of 1873 was a crucial turning point in Jennie Jerome's life; within days, there would be plenty of news for her father. A deckle-edged invitation had arrived at Rosetta Cottage. "To
Meet Their Royal Highnesses, the Prince and Princess of Wales and
Their Imperial Russian Highnesses the Grand Duke, Cesarewitch
and Grand Duchess Cesarevna, Captain Carpenter and the officers
of H.M.S. 'Ariadne' request the honour of the Company of Mrs. and
Misses Jerome on board, on Thursday, August 12th, from 3.30 to
7.30 p.m. Dancing. Boats will be in attendance at the RYC Landing
Place. R.S.V.P."[22]

That afternoon, the three Jerome women delicately stepped into
a launch at the Royal Yacht Squadron landing stage. They held onto
their hats and scarves as they were ferried over to the *Ariadne* in the
light breeze, under a cloudless blue sky. Despite the length of their
flimsy white tulle dresses and the constrictions of their tightly laced
corsets, they climbed onto the cruiser with agility. The ship was
draped with the national colors of Britain and of imperial Russia, and
the deck was already occupied by couples dancing stately quadrilles
to the accompaniment of the Royal Marine Band. Clara and Jennie,
bare-shouldered and beautiful, were immediately surrounded by admirers. A slight, pop-eyed young man with a bushy mustache and an
arrogant expression watched from the deck rails.

This was Lord Randolph Churchill, the twenty-four-year-old
second son of the 7th Duke of Marlborough, who was a member of
the Prince of Wales's "Marlborough House set." He had recently
left Oxford University and spent some months traveling through
Europe. Lord Randolph disliked dancing, but today he decided to
brave the dance floor with one of the two young women who were the
center of attention. Soon he and nineteen-year-old Jennie had joined
the quadrille.

Jennie probably bestowed one of her most bewitching smiles on her partner as she suggested that they sit out the next dance, sip champagne, and chat. The truth was that Lord Randolph was a clumsy dancer, and she had tired of having her feet trodden on.[23] Yet there was an instant chemistry between them. They discovered shared interests in horses and travel. Randolph was impressed by Jennie's fluency in several languages and her sophistication; Jennie was amused by Randolph's wit and intrigued by his closeness to the heir to the throne. She had watched her mother maneuver from the margins toward social respectability, and she knew that access to power and to the upper echelons of society required strategy as well as charm.

The lights of other yachts were flickering in the dusk before Mrs. Jerome finally found her daughter with this new acquaintance, and suggested that Jennie was being improper. Her daughter should not let one man monopolize her all evening. Jennie dutifully rose from her seat. However, before Mrs. Jerome had even registered that her headstrong daughter was manipulating her, Jennie had nimbly obliged her mother to invite Lord Randolph to dinner the following evening.

CHAPTER 4

Self-Assured Sara

1870–1880

Initially, Jennie Jerome was an outsider to the privileged societies, first in France and then in England, in which she had found herself, but her mother had shown her how to navigate through the barriers. Sara Delano's early years had been as cosmopolitan as Jennie's, with sojourns in China, France, and Germany, yet she had remained within the opulent Manhattan bubble in which her family was embedded. Like Jennie, she was a self-assured child of the elite. Unlike Jennie, she had never had to develop strategies or come up with ways to behave. She was to the manner born.

Yet there were gradations within the Delano world. To an outsider, the plutocrats of Manhattan's Gilded Age looked like one homogeneous blur of wealth—an early version of today's one-percenters, and often equally oblivious to poverty. But within the city's affluent social elite, the divides between old and new money were steadily widening. The latest generation of millionaires was eclipsing even Leonard Jerome in flash and fortune, and the Knickerbockers did not like it.

While Jennie Jerome and Sara Delano were still in short skirts, a self-appointed tastemaker named Ward McAllister had arrived in the city, and, as one newspaper reporter put it, "devoted himself to the task of social discrimination."[1] Trailing whiffs of European sophistication, thanks to two years spent in France, McAllister dedicated himself to protecting the elite from the worst of the arrivistes. A portly man with extravagantly waxed whiskers, he was an unctuous snob, insisting that "we have to draw social boundaries [on the basis of] old connections, gentle breeding, perfection in all the requisite accomplishments of a gentleman, elegant leisure and an unstained private reputation."[2] McAllister's critics scorned him as a flunky or as New York City's "Head Butler," but they recognized that he knew how to organize the most lavish dinners and the best balls, cotillions, and other exclusive dances.

McAllister's nose for refinement was impeccable. And he acquired a powerful patron: Mrs. William Astor.[3] Caroline Schermerhorn Astor was the reigning queen of Manhattan society, and she was obsessed with the protection of old money traditions and status and the exclusion of pushy newcomers. The supercilious McAllister became her henchman. It was he who would write in a newspaper column that there were "only 400 people in fashionable New York Society." ("If you go outside that number," he warned, "you strike people who are either not at ease in a ballroom or else make other people not at ease.")[4] The number was popularly supposed to be either the capacity of Mrs. Astor's ballroom at 350 Fifth Avenue, her mansion on Fifth Avenue and Thirty-Fourth Street, or the number of people in all of New York society worth inviting to it.

The annual Astor ball in her Manhattan mansion every January was regarded as the climax of the season, and McAllister was the gatekeeper who kept invitations out of the hands of the wrong people: social climbers, swells, tradesmen, Jews, divorcées. Mrs. Astor had a particular aversion to shopkeepers, which meant that Alexander Stewart, who owned a dry goods store and was among the wealthiest men in the city, never crossed her threshold. "I buy my carpets from [the Stewarts]," the hostess remarked while preparing a guest list, "but then is that any reason why I should invite them to walk on them?"[5]

However, McAllister was a sufficiently canny operator to know that he could not keep new money out forever. As the Knickerbocker snobs floundered in the face of the arriviste invasion, he negotiated

the balance between the acceptance of vast new wealth and the pres-
ervation of Mrs. Astor's order. In 1872, he founded the Society of
Patriarchs, which had twenty-five members. Alongside scions of
established families such as the Astors and the Van Rensselaers,
McAllister handpicked a few railroad millionaires and successful
speculators who met his rigid standards of decorum.

Within a few years society members were selecting guests for the
Patriarch Balls, which McAllister designed as "the most brilliant balls
of each winter." His intent, he would explain in his memoirs, was to
make it "extremely difficult to obtain an invitation to them and to
make such invitations of great value; to make them the stepping-stone
to the best New York society."[6] Who was "in" and who was "out" in
the Gilded Age had never been more apparent.

This was the backdrop to the teenage years of Jennie Jerome and
Sara Delano—a wealthy ruling class that each decade grew wealthier
and more entangled in elaborate formalities. Their families would
have had no doubt who would, and who wouldn't, be invited to the
balls, where girls with the right bloodlines might attract the right suitors. It was no wonder that Clara Jerome had decided to take her talented daughters elsewhere. Nor was it surprising that Warren Delano
saw Gilded Age Manhattan as the perfect marriage market for his
daughters.

II

By the time she was sixteen, Sara Delano had emerged as a pillar of
her family. Her father regarded her with pride, especially after she had
plowed through all six volumes of Sir Walter Raleigh's *History of the
World*. For her mother, Catherine, Sara was a reliable helper, joining
her in various acts of local benevolence—distribution of food to the
poor, contributions to money-raising sales, visits to the Newburgh
alms house. Her younger siblings—Cassie, Frederic, and Laura—
found her a little intimidating. Fred recalled that while she was working her way through those six volumes, she would block out their
chatter with her hands and shush them.

Warren Delano continued to prefer that his family remain cloistered at Algonac, socializing with other Hudson Valley families. "Life at Algonac was joyous," according to Sara's admiring biographer Rita Halle Kleeman. "There were visits to be paid and received, there were church sociable and meetings, daylight and moonlight picnics . . . occasional house parties."[7] The Delano family diary describes a musical soiree at Algonac for which fifty guests arrived. "The party continued until twelve o'clock and the dancing was unabated. The oysters were good and all was pronounced a success."[8]

The sisters attracted "an avalanche of young men," according to their father, but Warren Delano kept most of the suitors at bay. He was determined to set standards and control their lives. He rigorously monitored invitations, emerging from the library to prowl through the drawing room, inspect the company, and check on activities. Delano clannishness bordered on xenophobia. As an adult, Sara would describe her father as caring "little for outsiders, but [he] would do anything for his own family."[9] When a suitor arrived to visit one of his daughters, Warren Delano barked, "Who and what are his parents and family?"[10] Young men with the wrong pedigree or prospects were sent packing.

When Sara was twenty-one, the brash nephew of a Hudson Valley neighbor broke through the Delano defenses. Stanford White was "a magnificent-looking boy, with a shock of flaming red hair, full of life, intensely musical," according to Kleeman. He was also a gifted draftsman, a keen sportsman, and a flashy dresser. White worked long hours, slammed doors, and shouted "Thunder and guns" when he got excited—which was frequently.[11] The rather staid Sara was fascinated by this excitable young man, who actively flirted with her. But her father was appalled by White's exuberance and regarded him as a terrible prospect as a son-in-law. When White sent Sara a large bouquet of flowers one day, Warren said, "I suppose that these are from the red-haired trial. Remember that I don't care for that at all."

"That ended it for Sallie," wrote Kleeman, "for she still thought that her father knew more than anyone else in the world and that whatever he said was right."[12] Did Catherine, Warren's wife, speak up for Sara, who had already shown herself to be a sensible young woman? The family diary does not reveal any parental schism; instead, records show that Sara quite suddenly left Algonac in order to accompany her sister Dora, and Dora's husband, Will Forbes, who worked for Russell & Company, on their voyage to Hong Kong. By the time she returned to Algonac nine months later, there was no more talk of Stanford White. Her sense of family duty had weighed more heavily than the giddy excitement offered by her flamboyant suitor. She accepted that the match was unsuitable for someone of her birth.

In this case, her father's instincts were proven correct. White would become a celebrated neoclassical architect, designing palaces for several of the Gilded Age rich. But his personal life was always complicated (he was sexually voracious, and probably bisexual), and in 1906 he was shot dead by the husband of one of his lovers.

Warren Delano might have been overprotective, but he was also confident that any daughter of his belonged on the "best" guest lists. So the "beautiful Delano girls," as they were known, often took the steamer down to Manhattan to attend Patriarch Balls and dinners hosted by Fifth Avenue's fashionable families. They moved in a tight-knit circle of cousins and friends—Roosevelts, Astors—many of whom they had met in Europe. Once one of these young women reached her eighteenth birthday, she would go through the elaborate "coming-out" ritual. With hair elaborately crimped into an adult style and shoulders bared, she would attend her first formal dance wearing a pale, wasp-waisted gown and long white kid gloves and carrying a bouquet of roses or lily of the valley.

Warren Delano wrote to his son Warren in January 1873 that Sara, then nineteen, "attended her first *great* city party" and, according to her chaperone, had looked "very handsome (No doubt of it) and received much attention." Sara's father, for whom such parties were anathema, assumed that Sara must have found the gathering an "ordeal"—but Sara, young and gregarious, does not appear to have shared his distaste. She loved to dance, according to one of her friends, whether it was Strauss waltzes or a popular new step such as the galop, and her height, grace, and elegant gowns ensured plenty of admiring glances.

"Sallie . . . to Mrs Wm. Astor's evening party," her father noted with satisfaction a few weeks later in the family diary, "the largest and finest house in N. Y., beautifully and tastefully decorated."[13] Mrs. Astor's party would have been organized by Ward McAllister and held at 350 Fifth Avenue, a far less lavish residence than the ersatz French château that the architect Richard Morris Hunt would build for her some twenty years later, at Fifth Avenue and Sixty-Fifth Street. That vast mansion would boast a Beauvais tapestry, a Sèvres vase, Louis XIV furniture, and an art gallery filled with expensive but dull French paintings.[14] At the plainer but still imposing 350 Fifth Avenue, Sara Delano and her friends were met at the door by a nearly floor-to-ceiling portrait of Mrs. Astor. Three drawing rooms led to a spacious art gallery that doubled as a ballroom.

Throughout her early twenties, Sara spent much of the winter season in Manhattan, staying with aunts and attending the kinds of balls, cotillions, and dinners at which Jennie Jerome would never have been welcomed, and which would be described with shrewd insight in the novels of Edith Wharton. Wharton was eight years younger than Sara, but the two met and Sara knew her by her family nickname, "Pussy Jones" (Wharton was born Edith Newbold Jones), and thought of her as "a gifted child who wrote poetry."[15] With none of Wharton's icy objectivity about Gilded Age snobbery, Sara took invitations to Fifth Avenue balls for granted and made her nonchalance clear to Rita Halle Kleeman. "When Sallie went back to Algonac from her visits to New York, her friends were always sorry for her," Kleeman wrote. "They could not imagine what she would do with herself in the country. But she was always happy to get back and would say over and over again. 'How much nicer it is here than in New York!' "[16]

The Delanos were an exclusive bunch, pleased with their own company, but it was good company, with solid middlebrow tastes. There were subscriptions to *Punch*, *Cornhill* magazine, the *Illustrated London News*, the *Atlantic*, and *Scribner's*. The girls read and enjoyed the novels of Henry James, William Makepeace Thackeray, and Charles Dickens. They took drawing lessons from Frederick Stuart Church, an illustrator whose work appeared in *Harper's Bazaar*. Sara traveled into Manhattan for singing lessons, symphony concerts, operas, and parties. Throughout her life, she was a keen opera fan. When she went to performances at the Academy of Music, she would probably have seen Leonard Jerome, another opera fan. But she would not have acknowledged him.[17]

III

The years ticked by. Soon Sara was celebrating her twenty-sixth birthday—way past the age that women like her usually arrived at the altar. She was as good-looking and graceful as ever, with her glossy brown hair piled into a chignon and her figure shaped into the requisite S curve by her corset. She radiated cool aplomb. Yet she was now a veteran of seven Manhattan's social "seasons"; her two elder sisters, Dora and Annie, and most of her friends were married; the pool of eligible bachelors was shrinking. Had the broken romance with Stanford White made her mistrust her own judgment? Was she too attached to her family to leave Algonac? It certainly appeared that she had settled into being the compliant daughter, devoted to her father, sharing the running of the household with her mother, and acting as the emotional anchor for her siblings.

What Catherine thought about her daughter's future is unknown, although it might be assumed that she quietly wanted Sara to achieve a partnership as solid as her own. Any difference of opinion between Sara's parents on how their daughter's future should unfold was hidden by their determination to present a united front to both their own children, and the world beyond. Warren Delano was perfectly happy to keep her at home: Sara's cosmopolitan upbringing, fluency in three languages, and impressive education simply made her a more interesting companion for him. Confident in his own place in society, he was more concerned with protecting his children from uncertainty than securing advantageous alliances or independent futures for them.

Both Dora and Annie had married employees of Warren's old firm Russell & Company, but their father had insisted that neither wedding could take place until the grooms' fortunes were secure. Dora had been forced to wait nine years.[18]

At this stage in her life, Sara Delano appeared content with an existence that even her own friends regarded as dull, and which Jennie Jerome would have found suffocating. But Sara obviously enjoyed a placid rhythm. Throughout her life, the word "Algonac" was code for "All is well." When her son Franklin crossed the Atlantic in 1905, upon landing he telegraphed a single word—"Algonac"—back to his anxious mother, to reassure her that he was safe.[19]

Nevertheless, Sara continued to accept invitations to social events in New York City. One April evening in 1880, she joined a small dinner party at the Roosevelt home on West Fifty-Seventh Street given by Martha "Mittie" Roosevelt, whose daughter Anna—known as Bamie—was one of Sara's closest friends. Bamie had three siblings: Theodore Junior (the future president), Elliott, and Corinne. They belonged to the "Oyster Bay" Roosevelts, the branch of the Roosevelt clan that had settled on Long Island.

Mittie Roosevelt introduced Sara to James Roosevelt, a tall man with a high brow, deep-set eyes, and muttonchop whiskers. James was a distant cousin of Mittie's recently deceased husband, Theodore Roosevelt Sr.

James Roosevelt came from a different branch of the Roosevelt clan than Mittie's children. Their common ancestor, Claes Martenszen van Rosenvelt, had left Holland in the mid-1600s and sailed west to the New World. Within a century, his two grandsons, John and James, had put the family on the road to wealth and power, thanks to eighteenth-century investments in Manhattan real estate and trade with the West Indies. Their accumulated fortunes, like that of so many American plutocrats during these years, depended on the sweat and suffering of enslaved Black people who could never themselves gain any wealth from their toil to pass on to their own children.

Between the two brothers, they had twenty-two children. John's family acquired country estates at Sagamore Hill, in Oyster Bay, on the North Shore of Long Island. James's descendants turned north, and became gentleman farmers on the Hudson River. By the time Sara met James Roosevelt, the Oyster Bay Roosevelts were known for their energy and exuberance, and were firm Republicans, while the Hudson Valley Roosevelts, who supported the Democratic Party, were characterized by gravity and decorum. These Roosevelts boasted a family crest that featured roses and plumes, and a deep resistance to change: each patriarch of the Hudson Valley Roosevelts relished being a "gentleman of the old school." In the words of FDR biographer Jean Edward Smith, this branch of the Roosevelt family "avoided flamboyance, moved cautiously, and did not become involved in public affairs unless they had to."[20]

Sara's fellow dinner guest embodied these qualities. Twice Sara's age, James Roosevelt was as courteous and dignified as an undertaker.

The silver-haired widower sat next to Sara. As the polished silverware and cut glass goblets reflected the candle flames, he took an obvious delight in her company. "He talked to her the whole time," Mittie told Sara's friend Bamie after the guests had left. "He never took his eyes off her."[21]

He was also comfortably "One of Us." The Roosevelts were nowhere near as wealthy as the Delanos, but several generations of marital alliances had entrenched the family in the Knickerbocker network. James Roosevelt had a richly furnished brownstone town house on Washington Square (ground zero for Knickerbocker prestige) and belonged to several exclusive clubs in Manhattan, including the Union Club and the Century Association.

James Roosevelt's family had arrived in the Hudson Valley two generations before the Delanos. Twenty-four miles upriver from Algonac, the Delano home, James's grandfather had built a house in the village of Hyde Park, on the east bank of the river, six miles north of Poughkeepsie. That house, in which James himself was born, had burned down in 1865, but James had quickly acquired a nearby property, which he named Springwood. It had 110 acres of land and a magnificent view of the Hudson River from its front veranda. There, he and his first wife, Rebecca, had lived happily with their son, James Roosevelt Roosevelt—the double Roosevelt signaling pride in the name. Over the years, James and his family continued to acquire neighboring properties and eventually accumulated 1,600 acres.

Sara's father had known James Roosevelt for years, as a contemporary, a neighbor, and a fellow investor in various enterprises. A Harvard-trained lawyer, James had nursed ambitions as a young man to become a Gilded Age tycoon through strategic investments in coal mines and railroads. He invested so heavily in the Southern Railway Security Company, which sought control of all rail lines south of the Potomac, that he had been made its president. He also had considerable holdings in Consolidated Coal, where both he and Warren Delano were board members. But James Roosevelt did not have a magic touch or a gambler's luck. Both of these investments tanked, and he had been forced to resign from both in the early 1870s.

However, unlike either Warren Delano or Leonard Jerome, he had never invested more of his capital than he could afford to lose. So after these disasters, he had retreated to his study at Springwood, where he enjoyed a happy marriage and the administration of his estate. Each day, clad in Scottish tweeds and carrying a leather riding crop, he rode around his fields and meadows, inspecting his property. Shepherds, stable hands, and farmworkers doffed their caps as "Mr. James"—as he was known in the neighborhood—rode by. An unkind observer suggested that James aspired to the style of the British politician Lord Lansdowne but that, with his rosy cheeks and leather gaiters, "what he really looked like was Lord Lansdowne's coachman."[22]

James and Rebecca Roosevelt, with little "Rosy," as their son was known, fell into a routine of summers in the Hudson Valley and winters in Europe. While they were in America, they made regular trips into Manhattan in their private railroad car, the Monon, which stood ready on a siding off the main Hudson River tracks. Fitted out in brass and mahogany, with a Black porter-cook to look after them, the

Monon clicked over the tracks of the Delaware and Hudson Railway, in which Roosevelt remained a major shareholder.

It was all so comfortable, so harmonious. But in 1876, James Roosevelt's life fell apart when Rebecca died from heart disease, after twenty-three years of marriage. James, now in his fifties, was grief-stricken. He began to confide his loneliness to his cousin Bamie Roosevelt, who was known in the family as an unusually sympathetic woman.

His affection for Bamie gradually turned into love—although she was younger than his son Rosy. They exchanged letters when he was traveling: "If you knew the pleasure it gave me to sit down . . . to read all that you are doing," he wrote to Bamie from France. "I must confess, however, that it made me fearfully homesick, as I have such a longing to be with you all once more."[23] Mittie Roosevelt, Bamie's mother, tactfully suggested to her cousin that the passion was not reciprocated.

And then James Roosevelt met Sara. For all his public diffidence, he could act fast when he had a goal in mind. Soon after the Manhattan dinner party, the Delano family diary included frequent references to visits to Algonac from "Mr. Roosevelt from Hyde Park." In time, James wrote to Catherine Delano and asked if Sara could visit Springwood in a party that would include Bamie, Corinne, and Mittie.

Catherine must have known where this invitation might lead, but she immediately agreed that Sara might spend a week at Hyde Park. There, James made a point of introducing Sara to his brother, his sister-in-law, and his mother, all of whom lived close by. In addition, there were visits to beautiful local spots, games of croquet on the front lawn, outings on the river, and other diversions. By the end of the week, the two were committed to each other. Where Stanford White had dazzled the intimidating Sara with his boldness, James Roosevelt won her over with impeccable lineage and certainty of security. Roosevelt prepared to ask his friend Warren Delano for his daughter's hand in marriage.

What a shock for Warren Delano! He'd had no idea that when his contemporary had come to call, he had been visiting Sara, not himself—and Catherine had obviously chosen not to enlighten him.[24] He could not object to the alliance between the two families; James Roosevelt not only had his prestigious pedigree but also radiated the invincible belief in his class superiority that characterized old money. But there was the twenty-six-year age gap; and there were other disconcerting differences. James Roosevelt was a Democrat and an Episcopalian—two loyalties of which the forceful Warren Delano heartily disapproved.

Moreover, Sara's father did not share the concern about "marrying off" his daughter that was felt at the time by other fathers, including Leonard Jerome. The Delano fortune would ensure his children's future security. Since Sara had not acquired a suitable beau at Mrs. Astor's smart parties during her early twenties, he was more than content at the prospect of her living at Algonac for the rest of her life as companion to her aging parents and spinster aunt to her siblings' children.

But Sara could be as strong-willed as her father, and she made it clear to her parents that she wanted this match. By late July, only ten weeks after they had met, Sara and James Roosevelt were engaged. Warren Delano now wrote to his son Warren that the engagement "relieved my mind of many anxieties! It leaves my child within comparatively little distance from here . . . and so far as I can know or judge, it assures her of all the comforts and necessary luxuries of life."[25] He also admitted that James Roosevelt was "the first person who has made me realize that a Democrat can be a gentleman."

For her part, Sara had committed herself to a man who closely resembled her beloved father in more than age. Mr. James was wealthy, reliable, and even more conventional than Warren Delano. There would be few adjustments to make as she made the move up the Hudson Valley from the peaceful regularity of Algonac to the equally sedate rhythms of Springwood.

Unlike Jennie Jerome, Sara Delano had never felt the need for adventure or social success. However, despite appearances, she had not relished the idea of staying at Algonac forever; although she loved the lifestyle, she recognized that her existence there could dwindle into monotony. So she had chosen to move up the road while remaining within the insulated world of the Hudson Valley. Toward the end of her life, she confided to her son that, had she not taken up James's invitation to visit Springwood, "I should now be 'old Miss Delano' after a rather sad life."[26] What she could never have expected was that her own son would take both of them far beyond Hudson Valley values.

PART 2 · COURTSHIP AND MARRIAGE

CHAPTER 5

Jennie's "Very Dangerous Affair"

1873–1874

A t this stage in their lives, Sara and Jennie had much in common. They had absorbed the Victorian message that only family and motherhood could give meaning and purpose to their lives, and that a family's material well-being was the husband's responsibility; women were expected to stay at home. Sara enjoyed the quiet cushion of the Delano fortune, but she still preferred marriage, with its built-in assumption of male control, to a lonely spinsterhood.

However, the world was slowly starting to change around them. Thriving industrial economies gave women new opportunities to escape the assumptions that had confined them to domestic roles. In the United States, Susan Anthony and Elizabeth Cady Stanton were traveling around the country, campaigning for women's rights. In Britain, married women were lobbying for an entitlement that American women like Clara Jerome already enjoyed—the right to own their own property. In both countries, women were surging into different forms of activism—championing temperance, suffrage, access to education. Most activists belonged to the rapidly expanding middle class. Upper-class women usually felt greater loyalty to their class than to their gender, while working-class women already employed outside the home rarely had the time or energy to get involved in crusades.

Sara and Jennie were still too young to challenge the status quo, and too focused on their immediate future—betrothal, marriage—to pay much attention to the shifting landscape of women's aspirations and the public battles for women's rights. But like everyone else they read the headlines, and the next few years would reveal their private determination not to submerge themselves into dependence on their husbands.

II

In August 1873, nineteen-year-old Jennie Jerome was acknowledged as one of the most captivating women in Cowes, the Isle of Wight's classy sailing resort. She and her sister Clara had been presented to the Prince and Princess of Wales at the Royal Yacht Squadron Ball during Cowes Week, the regatta, and their mother had allowed them to attend a few exclusive parties. As Jennie's great-niece Anita Leslie would write in her biography of Jennie, "They took it for granted they should head the elite in any country where they chose to alight."[1]

Nothing enhances a beautiful woman's appeal more than her own recognition of the power of her looks, and Jennie's charisma had broken through the patrician hauteur of one of the most cynical young swells in the country: Lord Randolph Churchill. At the party aboard HMS *Ariadne,* the twenty-four-year-old son of the Duke of Marlborough monopolized her all afternoon.

Jennie's new admirer belonged to one of Britain's grandest ducal families. He had been raised, from the age of about eight, in one of Britain's greatest stately homes: Blenheim Palace, Oxfordshire, the monumental 187-room architectural folly built for John Churchill, 1st Duke of Marlborough, after the Battle of Blenheim. The duke's brilliant victory had saved Britain from a defeat by France that would have allowed Louis XIV to dominate Europe. The palace was so splendid that, after a visit in 1786, King George III remarked, "We have nothing to equal this." Randolph was not in line to inherit this stately pile, but Blenheim infected him with the confidence of those born into the loftiest level of political and social power, in a country that at the time ran the largest empire in the world. Just as Algonac symbolized security and comfort for the Delanos, Blenheim symbolized for the Churchills their unassailable superiority.

When he wanted to charm, Lord Randolph was brilliant— sharp-witted and funny, and a lively conversationalist. And on the *Ariadne,* he was determined to charm Jennie even though she was, in British class terms, an outsider. Apart from her elegance, she was a more sophisticated conversationalist than most of the English-women he knew, including his six badly educated sisters. He would come to admire her musical abilities, and they shared a love of horses. She had already caught the eye of the Prince of Wales, and it was most gratifying for the young aristocrat to have the exclusive attention of the belle of the Royal Yacht Squadron lawns.

Jennie's attraction to Lord Randolph is less easy to understand. Granted he was, in the admiring words of his son Winston, "utterly unguarded to his intimate friends, something of a dandy in his dress, an earnest sportsman, an omnivorous reader"[2]—qualities Jennie admired or shared. But he also had an unpredictable temperament. His childhood friend Lord Rosebery mentioned his withering sarcasm along with his wit, and his violent eccentricity alongside his daredevilry. Rosebery, whose tongue could be almost as caustic as Lord Randolph's, described his friend's "philippics" as a "striking combination of the picturesque and the burlesque . . . His laugh . . . in its very weirdness and discordance . . . was merriment itself."[3] High-strung and impulsive, Randolph chain-smoked, "in a diamond-studded holder, forty hand-rolled Turkish cigarettes every day until his tongue was burned."[4] But the arrogance and acerbity were obscured by his repartee as the couple chatted on the *Ariadne's* upper deck and the sunlight sparkled on the waters of the Solent. Jennie was smitten.

Churchill's own parents were less dewy-eyed about their younger son. During a classically aristocratic education at Eton and Oxford, Randolph had established himself as a rowdy rule-breaker who smashed glasses and windows, treated servants badly, and drank to excess. Since then, he had resisted his father's wish that he embark on a political career, and instead outspent his allowance, accumulating considerable gambling debts in the process. He showed no interest in securing his future.

If Randolph's uncertain character wasn't enough to make him poor marriage material, his family's financial situation, despite its lofty social standing, was a serious obstacle. During the 1880s, the wealth and power of Britain's great ducal families were in decline, although few recognized it at the time. After the removal of tariff barriers thirty years earlier, Britain's big landowners (some seven thousand families owned four-fifths of the land in Britain) had watched their incomes slowly collapse as imported meat and grains flooded into Britain, driving down domestic prices. Families like the Marlboroughs relied on the farms on their vast estates to support their opulent lifestyles, but farming no longer yielded enough income. Lord Randolph's father had already been forced to sell thousands of acres in Wiltshire, Shropshire, and Buckinghamshire to pay for the upkeep of his crumbling palace and its eighty-eight servants, alongside the costs of his family's London mansion.

Jennie knew none of this as she stared into Randolph's eyes. She had no idea that Randolph's elder brother George, Marquess of Blandford, was a well-known dissolute, notorious for drinking, drug-taking, and promiscuity, and in no position to restore the family fortune. As she and Randolph fell in love, she was unaware that his parents were hoping he might find a way of making some money (a challenge he was ill-fitted to meet) or find a wife who would bring much-needed capital into the family. And Randolph was equally ignorant of Jennie's situation: despite her apparently infinite dress allowance, she was not a wealthy heiress.

In the summer of 1873, Jennie had not yet decoded Britain's aristocracy, or grasped the mink-lined networks that had connected its progeny for generations. All she knew was that, from birth, she had been groomed to make an advantageous marriage, and this young man's title and ancient pedigree outshone anything that Manhattan's self-styled elite might offer. As one of fewer than thirty dukes, Randolph's father belonged to the very top layer of Britain's 431 hereditary peers in the House of Lords. These were men who took it for granted that they were the natural governors of the realm.

It was an illusion that would soon dissolve. A few years later, a rising young politician called Joseph Chamberlain, a successful Birmingham industrialist, would deride them as members of a class who "toil not, neither do they spin," and which had never contributed "one iota to popular liberties or popular freedom, or done anything to advance the common weal, but . . . has protected every abuse and sheltered every privilege."[5] But in 1873, Jennie was indifferent to such ideas as she started to plan her own future.

III

The evening after the dance on the *Ariadne*, Lord Randolph Churchill arrived as planned at Rosetta Cottage, accompanied by his friend Colonel Edgecumbe.

After her years in Paris, Jennie's mother understood food in a way that was rare among British hostesses, and she had made a point of hiring a French cook. (There was a glut of French chefs on the market, given the collapse of aristocratic entertaining in Paris.) The dinner was delicious. After dessert, Clara and Jennie sat down at the piano and demonstrated their formidable music skills. Colonel Edgecumbe noted what a pretty sight Jennie's dark curls and Clara's golden head made together, and Lord Randolph leaned over to him and whispered that he meant to make "the dark one" his wife.[6] Colonel Edgecumbe was probably taken aback; he had never known his friend to be serious about a woman before. Clara Jerome was equally taken aback when she remarked to her younger sister that she did not care for Lord Randolph's brusque manner or bushy mustache and Jennie replied, "I'm sure you'd like him if you knew him better." Speaking with unusual intensity, she added, "Please try to [like him], Clarita, because I have the strangest feeling that he's going to ask me to marry him . . . and I'm going to say yes." Clara burst into incredulous laughter.[7]

Lord Randolph made his proposal even sooner than expected. He and Jennie had arranged an "accidental" encounter the following day, after church, and Jennie asked her mother to invite Lord Randolph back to Rosetta Cottage for dinner again. Mrs. Jerome hoped for at least a duke as Jennie's suitor, not a second son, and was already concerned that this romance was moving too fast. Jennie had still not celebrated her twentieth birthday; Clara, at twenty-two, was still unmarried. But despite her mother's hesitation, Jennie insisted that an invitation be issued. After dinner, she led her suitor into the garden, ostensibly to take a breath of sea air and to admire the lights of the yachts glittering in the harbor. By the time they reentered the cottage, Lord Randolph had asked Jennie to marry him and Jennie had accepted.

Two days later, when Randolph had left Cowes, Jennie broke the news to her mother. Mrs. Jerome was appalled. Jennie, headstrong and in love, paid little attention to her mother's reservations. She wrote to Randolph, "Although she likes you *very* much, [she] won't hear of it. But I am sure we shall easily get her on our side later on – when we see you in London or perhaps here – God bless you darling." She signed herself with a novel nickname, "Yours Jeannette," then added, "Don't smoke too much."[8] She would soon learn that such strictures had little effect. Lord Randolph shared with his chum Rosebery an ability, as a fellow Old Etonian wrote, to appear to "ascend in a balloon out of earshot every time he is addressed by one not socially his equal."[9]

Randolph was already on his way home to tell the family. In the weeks that followed, volleys of correspondence were triggered between the besotted couple themselves, between each lover and their parents, and within each family. In later years, Jennie shrugged off the dramas of the courtship—in her memoirs, she resorts to the cliché "The course of true love never runs smooth" before skipping ahead to married life. However, she bequeathed to her descendants and biographers a cornucopia of private letters (held in the Churchill Archives at Churchill College, Cambridge, and in Blenheim Palace) that capture a great deal not just of the participants' characters and mutual infatuation but also of the transactional nature of marriage negotiations.

Randolph knew that his parents would not like a match with an unknown American girl to whom he had proposed only three days after their meeting. He knew the strongest opposition would likely come from his father, who was out of town, so he sat down on August 20 and tried to describe on paper his feelings for this young woman.

"I do not think that if I were to write pages I could give you any idea of the strength of my feelings and affection and love for her; all I can say is that I love her better than life itself, and that my one hope and dream now is that matters may be so arranged that soon I may be united to her by ties that nothing but death itself could have the power to sever . . ." Randolph went on to extoll Jennie's virtues, to request a raise in his allowance, and to assure his father that, if married to Jennie, he "might become, with the help of Providence, all and perhaps more than you ever wished and hoped for me."[10] Lastly, he added a few sentences designed to catch his father's eye: "Mr. Jerome is a gentleman who is obliged to live in New York and look after his business. I do not know what it is. He is reported to be very well off, and his daughters, I believe, have very good fortunes . . ."[11]

The Duke of Marlborough was deeply unimpressed and suggested that Randolph's emotions had paralyzed his judgment. Meanwhile, he made a few inquiries about Leonard Jerome and was horrified. A London lawyer reported that Jerome "lives very extravagantly, and it is not unlikely that his income, large as it is, may be absorbed in his expenditures." Another friend told the duke that Jerome was not prominent socially, although he was "a thoroughly respectable person." An American acquaintance was blunter. "Jerome is a well-known man with a fast reputation, has been a large stock speculator, and was a few years ago supposed to be well cleaned out and managed to hold on to some purchases of real estate heavily mortgaged."[12]

"From . . . what I have heard," the duke wrote to Randolph, "this Mr. J. seems to be a sporting, and I should think vulgar kind of man. It is evident he is of the class of speculators."[13] The idea of a marriage outside the British class system shocked the duke: "Under any circumstances, an American connection is not one we would like . . . you must allow it is a slight coming down in pride for us to contemplate the connection."

If the 7th Duke of Marlborough shuddered at the prospect of an American daughter-in-law, in Manhattan Leonard Jerome winced at the idea that his impetuous daughter had been swept off her feet by an equally impulsive young man. He weighed in with a cautionary letter to Jennie. However, his reservations were not about money or English snobbery but about his daughter's emotional intensity. "I fear if anything goes wrong you will make a dreadful shipwreck of your affections. I always thought if you ever did fall in love it would be a very dangerous affair. You were never born to love lightly. It must be *way* down or nothing . . . Such natures if they happen to secure the right one are very happy but if disappointed they suffer untold misery . . ."[14] But as usual he left all parenting decisions to Clara Jerome, telling Jennie that if her mother approved, an engagement was probably fine. His top priority was a forthcoming racing event; "[if] the weather is favorable we shall have a splendid meeting."

Then Leonard heard that the Duke of Marlborough had been doing a few background checks on him, and it stirred all his Yankee prejudices against European snobs. He cabled a withdrawal of his consent but left his wife to handle the fallout. Once again, Jennie soon overrode her mother's concerns.

Jennie and Randolph exchanged long and frequent letters filled with passion and romance.[15] Their parents all continued to express misgivings, but in the face of their children's determination to pursue their affair, they were left with little alternative but to try and delay the marriage until passions cooled.

By the fall, the Jeromes were back in Paris, in their Boulevard Haussmann residence. In October, Jennie received an exultant letter from her beau. He had told his father that he would stand for Parliament in the borough of Woodstock if his parents agreed he could marry immediately afterward, and the strategy had worked. The duke agreed that the marriage could go forward as soon as Randolph was elected. Randolph wrote from Blenheim, "The clouds have all passed away, and the sky is bluer than I have ever seen it since I first met you in Cowes. It is exactly six weeks tomorrow since we met on board the

Ariadne, and I am sure I seem to have lived six years." He insisted he had no real interest in a political career ("public life has no great charms for me, as I . . . hate both bother and publicity") but he was prepared to plunge into it "if I think it will please you."[16]

It would more than please Jennie. She would never have been content to settle down with a placid country gentleman. She embraced the prospect of marrying a man who had all the qualities required— the right pedigree, education, and network—to achieve political eminence. The wives of political players had no public role, but—like the Empress Eugénie—they had front-row seats to national events and the possibility of backstage influence. She determined to be well prepared for the role, even if Randolph was lukewarm in his enthusiasm. She began to read everything about British politics that she could find, especially the speeches of the Conservative leader Benjamin Disraeli, Randolph's hero.[17] She developed strong opinions.

At the same time, Jennie was also still leading a full life in Paris, practicing the piano, attending social events, and watching political clashes between the leaders of the newly established Third Republic and their royalist and Bonapartist opponents. Her meetings with Randolph were brief and infrequent, and Mrs. Jerome (acutely conscious of the proprieties) tried to ensure they were well chaperoned. Throughout the autumn of 1873, the couple was usually separated by the English Channel, and their correspondence (they exchanged letters as often as two or three times a day) simmers with frustration, misunderstandings, and occasional jealous flare-ups. Lord Randolph was possessive and jealous; Jennie was by turns soothing and combative. The passion of all these hastily written missives is extraordinary, given that they had spent barely more than three days in each other's company.

And meanwhile, their fathers locked horns on that vital aspect of upper-class marriages on both sides of the Atlantic: the dowry. Since both men were in financial difficulties, negotiations were tense and prolonged. Relations between the two families deteriorated as lawyers haggled over who should pay for telegrams and postage ($61, about

$1,400 today), property charges, and the charges for preparing the dowry agreements.[18]

The Duke of Marlborough was determined that, if his son insisted on marrying an American adventuress, she should at least bring some cash into the family. The Blenheim estate had been reduced to one-quarter its original size, and the duke was contemplating selling family heirlooms including jewels, art, and the famous Sunderland Library, one of the finest private collections of rare books in Europe, rich in incunabula and early Bibles.[19] Even if Leonard Jerome was no Rockefeller, how much money was he prepared to give the couple?

For his part, Leonard Jerome had never entirely recouped his losses of the 1860s and had suffered further reversals in the American stock market crash of 1873. Nor did he relish the idea of bankrolling Britain's aristocracy, members of which openly sneered at Americans. But he could not withstand his favorite daughter's determination. So he abandoned his objections to the match and made the kind of assurances that Jennie loved to hear: "I want you to have all the dresses etc. that you wish. You ought to have a box at the opera occasionally. You should give parties and live handsomely." He justified these extravagant promises by adding, "you will be more swell than ever now and you will be certain to have a great influence on Clara's future."[20] Nonetheless, he was in no position to endow the couple with a lavish settlement.

The courtship was interrupted in January 1874 when the Liberal prime minister, William Ewart Gladstone, called the long-awaited general election, and Lord Randolph dutifully stood as Conservative candidate for the parliamentary seat of Woodstock. Jennie followed the election avidly. Although her suitor had no idea how to recruit supporters or give a speech, he won the seat by 569 to 404 votes. The following day, loyal Woodstock citizens (most of whom depended on the Marlboroughs for their living) pulled their new representative and his father through the town in a horseless carriage. After that, Randolph wrote Jennie, "there was nothing more to be done except pay the bill, which I let my father do. I was very glad to get away as the place had got on my nerves and altogether I wanted a change of scene."[21] He did not mention that his party had won the election, and that Benjamin Disraeli was the new prime minister.

Within days, Randolph crossed the channel, and during February he spent as much time as possible with the Jeromes. But there was still no date fixed for the wedding, and no agreement on financial arrangements.

Anne Sebba, author of an authoritative biography of Jennie Jerome, has traced the tortuous negotiations, as Randolph's father tried to pressure Jennie's father into the most generous settlement possible. The final bill for Leonard Jerome was £50,000 (£5 million today), derived from various Manhattan rents, railway stocks, and government bonds, which would yield an annual income of £2,000 (close to £190,000 today). Leonard Jerome was outraged when the duke announced that this income would be paid to Lord Randolph, not Jennie, because, he said, it would be without precedent if "Miss Jerome is made quite independent of [my son] in a pecuniary point of view." Steeped in British legal traditions of primogeniture and entail, designed to support aristocratic succession, he grudgingly suggested that Jennie might receive £300 (about £30,000 today) as "pin money." [22]

Leonard Jerome was shocked by the duke's assumption that a wife could not control her own fortune. He finally prevailed over the duke, and they agreed that the £2,000 allowance should be divided equally between Jennie and Randolph. Reflecting the American belief that women should be entitled to some autonomy, he told the Duke of Marlborough, "I can but think your English custom of making the wife so utterly dependent on the husband most unwise."[23] But it would not be until 1882, with a new Married Women's Property Act in Britain, that Jennie's right to have her own income would be protected; until then, she could not legally own property or keep an inheritance. Many British parliamentarians had argued furiously against the new law, on the grounds that the inevitable result would be discord in the home. The 1882 act did not make women equal to men in civil law, but it was a small step toward greater independence.

Jennie's father was unable to extract from Marlborough a commit-ment that, if Jennie died before Randolph, she would have the power to designate the recipient of the £50,000 capital. On this point, Lord Randolph was emphatic. He "told his future father-in-law that unless all the dowry capital came to him in the event of his wife dying child-less 'all business between us was perfectly impossible and he could do what he liked with his beastly money.'" He was offended by the idea that, as the master of his house, he would not have total control of his finances. Leonard Jerome capitulated, glumly noting, "I have ignored American custom and waived all my American prejudices."[24]

While the haggling over the Jerome settlement continued, the Duke of Marlborough quietly settled £20,000 (£2 million today) on his son, plus about £2,000 (£200,000 today) out of which Randolph would have to pay his debts. He also said he would pay Randolph's expenses as MP for Woodstock.[25] Randolph had rented a town house on Curzon Street, in the heart of Mayfair, for £250 a month (£25,000 today), and he now promised Jennie that there was a room in it for her sister Clara.

And then the tempo abruptly quickened. The financial discus-sions were concluded, with settlements that would yield a total an-nual revenue for the couple of £3,100 (£290,000 today)—an amount that barely covered the town house rent. Leonard Jerome agreed with Randolph's demand that, in the event of Jennie predeceasing him, the dowry money should be equally divided between Randolph and Jennie's family. At short notice, the date and place were fixed for the wedding: April 15, 1874, in Paris.

Lord Randolph's older brother George and three of his sisters arrived, plus Jennie's fourteen-year-old sister Leonie from her Ger-man boarding school. Leonie admired Jennie's trousseau and re-ported to a friend that it included twenty-three French-made gowns, seven Paris bonnets, and some "very fine linen." Jennie confided to her sisters that the gowns "will have to last me a long time,"[26] as she considered her budget, and Randolph worried that they would over-flow the closets of the bijou Curzon Street house. With typical brio,

Leonard Jerome arranged a splendid dinner for everybody the night before the event. The Prince of Wales, already charmed by Jennie, signaled his approval of the match by sending his secretary Sir Francis Knollys to be best man.

The ceremony was held at the British embassy, on Paris's grand rue du Faubourg Saint-Honoré, and it was swift and plain. In fact, it was so speedy and unadorned that it raises several questions. Why were Lord Randolph's parents conspicuously absent from their favorite son's wedding, despite having given the union their blessing? Why were the dowry negotiations concluded in a rush, with the final papers being signed on the morning of the wedding? Why did Mrs. Jerome consent to such a simple ceremony, with only family present, when she might have been expected to prefer a lavish event that would demonstrate her newly won social prominence?

Was the wedding rushed simply because the passionate young couple wanted to be united as fast as possible? Or was it because Jennie and Randolph had broken all the Victorian taboos and enjoyed a premarital physical relationship? Mrs. Jerome was a strict parent, but several biographers have suggested that the young couple may have given her the slip back in February, during Randolph's visit to Paris, and enjoyed assignations in his hotel room. After he returned to London, he wrote to his fiancée, "I like to think of you being in my room. You can't think, darling, how I long to be back . . ."

After February, the letters are more ardent than ever. "I almost think I had better not kiss you again till I can for good."[27] Such behavior was particularly hazardous for Jennie—apart from the possibility of pregnancy, she faced scandal if the marriage did not go ahead and any intimacy with Randolph became known.

In April 1874, there was no whisper of speculation. After a wedding breakfast, Jennie changed out of her lace-trimmed white satin gown and into a blue-and-white traveling dress, and the couple went by horse-drawn carriage to a friend's château. Leonard Jerome presented his favorite daughter with a very special gift, a parasol of white Alençon lace, with an exquisite long handle of tortoiseshell ringed with gold. Mrs. Jerome wept as she waved her daughter goodbye. Carefree Jennie, who had won all her battles, told her, "Why, Mama, don't cry, life is going to be perfect . . . always."[28]

Three-quarters of a century later, Jennie's great-niece would discover in her parents' attic the carefully preserved wedding parasol that had framed Jennie's face as the newlyweds drove away. Anita Leslie imagined how Jennie's eyes "must have flashed against the white Alençon lace . . . For Jennie was a very inflammable person—we all knew that."[29]

Inflammable. Never a word used to describe Sara Delano, although she too would demonstrate her single-minded determination by following her heart.

CHAPTER 6

———◇———

Toxic Churchill Dynamics

1874–1880

With her marriage, Jennie Jerome had achieved access to the upper reaches of the British peerage. It was a privileged class in which she had not been raised, where bloodlines counted more than brains, and which was predisposed to eject foreign bodies. She did not know its codes, traditions, sports, clubs, schools, jargon, or loyalties. Merely winning the title Lady Randolph Churchill was not enough; she would need to fit into an upper class that was more rigid than the Astors' in Manhattan, and to adjust to a pageantry less fun than that surrounding the Empress Eugénie in Paris. It was an intimidating prospect, especially at a moment in British history when the political power of the aristocracy was beginning to crumble and its wealth to dissipate.

However, Jennie radiated optimism and American self-assurance, and she had watched her mother navigate social barriers, learning how to assimilate into the right circles. Youth and beauty were a currency useful for purchasing social standing, and her defenses against rejection included a lively intelligence and genuine warmth. She blithely assumed that the passion she and Randolph shared would overcome all obstacles. How could she know that Lord Randolph was a far less stable character than he appeared to her?

"My first visit to Blenheim was on a beautiful spring day in May, 1874," she recalled in her book *Reminiscences*. She and Lord Randolph were met at Woodstock railway station by a party of the duke's

tenants and Randolph's constituents, who took the horses out of the
carriage's traces "and insisted on dragging us through the town to the
house."[1] She was overwhelmed by the beauty of the palace's setting as
they passed through the imposing stone archway and she saw the lake
and the vast park studded with ancient oaks.

But she did not gush to her husband about the magnificence of the
scene. Instead, she resorted to irony, as she quoted poet Alexander
Pope's ridicule of the palace's pretensions:

" 'Thanks, sir,' cried I, ''tis very fine,
But where d'ye sleep and where d'ye dine?
I find by all you have been telling,
That 'tis a house, but not a dwelling.' "[2]

By Jennie's careful account in *Reminiscences*, she was welcomed by
her in-laws. She describes the Duke of Marlborough as "extremely
kind . . . [with] the most courteous and *grand seigneur* appearance
and manner," and her husband's mother, Frances Anne, Duchess of
Marlborough, as "a very remarkable and intelligent woman, with a
warm heart, particularly for members of her family, which made up
for any overmasterfulness of which she might have been accused."[3]
Once settled into Blenheim's daily routine, she observed with an
outsider's astonishment the extraordinary formality of life in a ducal
palace. "At luncheon, rows of entrée dishes adorned the table, joints
beneath massive silver covers being placed before the Duke and
Duchess, who each carved for the whole company, and as this included governesses, tutors, and children, it was no sinecure." During
the regular shooting parties, with dozens of guests, breakfast was "a
ceremonious meal, and no one dreamed of beginning until all had
assembled."[4]

But Jennie had no experience of country life, and after New York,
Paris, and London, the Blenheim schedule was deadly. "So assiduously
did I practise my piano, read, or paint, that I began to imagine myself
back in the school-room."[5] She would read the newspaper for an hour

each morning, so that she could participate in political conversations at dinner, and she filled the long afternoon hours by visiting neighbors or walking in the gardens. Dinner was always a full-dress affair, and then the evening yawned ahead, with reading and card games until the clock struck eleven. Sometimes a family member would surreptitiously move the clock's hands forward, in order to curtail the ennui.[6] Such an ordered life might have suited Sara Roosevelt. For Jennie, it was purgatory. She felt trapped both by the rigid routines and by how little was expected of her.

Accustomed to North American luxury, Jennie Churchill also had to adapt to damp, dark rooms, lack of any indoor plumbing (numerous maids dealt with all the chamber pots), and a domestic hierarchy so rigid that, upstairs and downstairs, no one dared step outside their preordained role. A footman would not perform the job of a housemaid; an outdoor worker would never stray indoors. A future American resident of Blenheim observed, "It is strange that in so great a house there should not be one really livable room."[7]

The Churchills escaped to their four-story rented house on Curzon Street as soon as they could. In their bubble of privilege, they lived well beyond their means. Their household staff consisted of a butler, French cook, footman, valet, lady's maid, and housemaid. Lord Randolph ran up gambling debts while his wife continued to order expensive Paris gowns. Bills were paid late, if at all.

Twenty-year-old Jennie was determined to enjoy her first London season with, as she put it, "all the vigour and unjaded appetite of youth," and she threw herself into the giddy whirl.[8] There were daily rides along Hyde Park's Rotten Row, and endless dinners, parties, and balls, often lasting until dawn. There were expeditions to the races at Derby, Ascot, and Goodwood, and outings to flower shows and pigeon-shooting competitions.

During the summer months, the Prince and Princess of Wales lived at Chiswick House, in West London. The future Edward VII, who had been charmed by Jennie at Cowes, frequently invited the Churchills to dinners and garden parties. Jennie was soon a royal favorite, as her irreverent humor made Bertie roar with laughter. At one dinner, he told her that the American fiancée of a British aristocrat was very lucky because, although the groom was poor, his family had "come over with the Conqueror." Jennie replied, "That's all very well, but if I were the girl, I'd prefer to marry into a family that had done a little conquering on its own account."[9]

Young and glamorous, Jennie Churchill loved the blue-blooded buzz, and enjoyed the admiring glances she attracted, as she sauntered through the park in one of her tight-waisted Worth gowns or demonstrated her equestrian skills. At the same time, she observed that her husband's compatriots regarded American women (a novelty back then) as "strange and abnormal . . . to be viewed with suspicion, if not avoided altogether."[10] Their only raison d'être was their dollars—otherwise, what was the point? If one of her own compatriots behaved as any well-bred woman might, she was saluted with the remark, " 'I should never have thought *you* were an American,' which was intended as a compliment."

Jennie would later recall the derision with lofty amusement:

> No distinction was ever made among Americans; they were all supposed to be of one uniform type. The wife and daughters of the newly-enriched Californian miner, swathed in silks and satins, and blazing with diamonds on the smallest provocation; the cultured, refined, and retiring Bostonian; the aristocratic Virginian, as full of tradition and family pride as a Percy of Northumberland, or a La Rochefoucauld; the cosmopolitan and up-to-date New Yorker—all were grouped in the same category, all were considered tarred with the same brush.[11]

When she wrote this, thirty years after her arrival in Britain, Jennie was firmly established within English society. But the British disdain for Americans would color some perceptions of her son Winston, whom an angry member of Parliament once dismissed as a "Yankee mongrel."[12]

II

The new Lady Randolph Churchill wanted her husband to make his mark on the world and catapult them both into powerful circles. She had never accepted Randolph's insistence, during their courtship, that he was standing for Parliament only so his father would agree to their marriage, and she found the company of politicians stimulating. When Lord Randolph rose in the British House of Commons to deliver his maiden speech five weeks after the wedding, she waited anxiously to hear how he was received.

The news was not good. Nervous and ill-prepared, Randolph objected to a proposed new military center in Oxford, which he claimed would introduce "roistering soldiers and licentious camp followers" to the elite university town. His Tory colleagues winced at his snobbery, and one critic described him as hard to hear and difficult to follow. Only Prime Minister Disraeli, a friend of the Duchess of Marlborough, was kind. He wrote to the new MP's mother: "He said some imprudent things . . . but he spoke with fire and fluency; and showed energy of thought and character, with evidence of resource."[13] The speech was a clumsy start to the political career that would in time consume her husband.

Undaunted, Jennie began to think of ways she might promote her husband's career. She began to give small dinners to which she invited senior members of government. Disraeli was a frequent guest; he was "always kind and talked to me at length," Jennie wrote in *Reminiscences*. The Prince of Wales, a fellow guest, teased his hostess about her intentions. He asked Jennie "what office I had got for Randolph."

In time, Jennie Churchill would establish an amazing reputation for the conviviality of her dinners, the attention to each guest's preferences, the sophistication of her menus. These events would be important tactics in furthering the careers of first Randolph and later Winston. However, in the early days, her housekeeping was erratic. At her first dinner party, the soup arrived with the meat course floating in it, while the poached eggs, which were meant to have been in the soup, were served alongside. Having always left such arrangements to her mother in the past, she had assumed she could leave the gastronomic details to her French chef, who, she recalled, had become "excited."[14] (Presumably she meant that he had gone to pieces when he heard that his dishes were being served to royalty.) But from the start, leading decision-makers came for Jennie's sparkling conversation and the beauty of her gaze. In education and fashion, she outshone other young London hostesses—and thanks to diligent attention to newspapers, she could hold her own in any political debate.[15] Her warmth and wit made up for her husband's impatience and sarcasm.

The dinner parties petered out during the fall because Jennie was pregnant. The duke had purchased a new house for them, 48 Charles Street, near Berkeley Square, for £10,000 (nearly £1 million today),[16] and Jennie was soon writing to her father for money to help furnish it. Once the London season of balls and dinners was over, Jennie moved back to Blenheim with her sister Clara. According to Anita Leslie, Jennie's great-niece, the two Jerome women irritated the Marlborough family. Jennie made her boredom obvious (she yearned to be out on horseback—forbidden, in her condition), while Clara's good looks, wardrobe, and sophistication did not endear them to Lord Randolph's unmarried sisters.

In late November, the Duke of Marlborough hosted one of his elaborate shooting parties. Chafing at the restrictions on her activities, Jennie hauled herself into a pony trap and drove off to follow the guns. After a day of bumping around on country roads, she went into labor and staggered into a small ground-floor room that was the nearest bedroom to the main entrance of Blenheim Palace. Thirty-six hours later, at 1:30 a.m., before there was time for a London obstetrician to reach Woodstock, the baby was born with the help of the local doctor.

In the villages around Blenheim, church bells rang out, and Randolph wrote to Jennie's mother in Paris that Jennie "suffered a good deal poor darling, but was vy [very] plucky & had no chloroform. The boy is wonderfully pretty so everybody says dark eyes and hair and very healthy considering its prematureness . . . We had neither cradle nor baby linen nor anything ready, but fortunately everything went well & the difficulties were overcome." He added that the Woodstock solicitor's wife had lent them a layette.[17]

The *Times* notice of Winston Churchill's birth read, "On the 30th Nov., at Blenheim Palace, the Lady Randolph Churchill, prematurely, of a son." Was the baby premature or was he conceived before marriage? There has been plenty of speculation, since his birth was only thirty-four weeks after the Churchills' wedding in Paris, and most pregnancies last forty weeks. However, it is equally possible that Jennie had short pregnancies (her second son also arrived a month early) or that, as a first-time mother, she had not realized when she had conceived. There was no mention, however, that the infant was underweight, and he was said to be sleeping through the night within five days, so the suggestion that he was premature is dubious.

Winston's birth did not cause Jennie to miss a beat—she does not even mention it in her memoir. There was no thought that she might nurse the newborn herself; a wet nurse was immediately hired. The baby was christened at Blenheim Chapel on December 27: Winston Leonard Spencer-Churchill. "Winston" was to honor the child's ancestor Sir Winston Churchill, who had fought for King Charles I in the English Civil War, and also Lord Randolph's elder brother Winston, who had died aged four; "Leonard" was for Jennie's father.

Baby Winston was handed over to a woman who would become his most reliable beacon of love during his childhood: Mrs. Everest, a forty-one-year-old widow from Kent, who, Winston Churchill would later write, "looked after me and tended all my wants. It was to her I poured out my many troubles."[18] Nannies were ubiquitous in aristocratic British households; in the year that Winston was born, the London *Times* carried an average of twelve advertisements for nannies a day, and more than one hundred thousand nannies were in service in Britain.[19] However, few of these women were given as much responsibility as Mrs. Everest or developed such a close relationship with their charges.

Immediately after their son's christening, the Churchills returned to Mayfair and their life of amusing dinners and trips to the races.

III

Family concerns, in the form of toxic Marlborough dynamics, would dominate Jennie's life for the next few years.

The first challenge to Jennie came when her brother-in-law the Marquess of Blandford showed his liking for her. Blandford's own marriage to Lady Albertha Hamilton (known as "Goosie" within the family) was wretched. During these years, practical jokes—pails of water balanced on top of bedroom doors, rubber spiders in soup bowls, chocolate puddings concealed on dining room chairs[20]—were the delight of London's smart set, and Lady Albertha was an expert in this particular torture. She delighted in serving hunks of soap alongside the cheese at dinner, to make her husband look foolish. More exasperating to her in-laws was the fact that, so far, she had produced three daughters but no male heir to the dukedom. Blandford had grown fond of his beautiful, witty American sister-in-law and he presented her with a ring. Jennie naively displayed it to her mother-in-law.

This lit the fuse of explosive family recriminations. The duchess was outraged that Blandford should have given away a ring that, she said, belonged to Goosie; Randolph told his brother of their mother's fury; Blandford wrote the duchess a blistering letter accusing her of "the intense jealousy that you often display . . . and the mischief you so often make"; the duke plunged in, accusing Randolph of acting "dishonorably and treacherously"; Randolph protested vigorously and broke off communication with his parents.[21]

Jennie's immediate instinct was to offer to return the ring and apologize to all concerned, but it was too late. The duchess, who had never warmed to her American daughter-in-law, was unforgiving, particularly because her favorite son had sided with his wife, not his mother. "It is a bitter sorrow to find both our sons torn against us," she wrote to Jennie. "Randolph has trampled over our affection . . . As for you, dearest Jennie . . . I wished to be more a mother than a mother-in-law and perhaps I was wrong."[22] Jennie soon escaped to Paris and a visit with her own, more placid mother, and she advised Randolph to patch up the quarrel: "Why talk about or occupy yourself with it?"[23]

There were more storms ahead, again triggered by the Marquess of Blandford's behavior and again exacerbated by Randolph. This time, Blandford's behavior sparked a full-blown Victorian scandal and temporarily destroyed Jennie's carefully cultivated relationship with the Prince of Wales.

The cause of this second blowup was Blandford's affair with a married woman, Edith, Lady Aylesford. Lady Aylesford was a doe-eyed beauty who was tired of her polo-playing and rather stupid husband, "Sporting Joe" Aylesford. In the fall of 1875, Lord Aylesford left England for several months on a trip to India with the Prince of Wales, and Blandford promptly took up residence in an inn close to the Aylesfords' home, Packington Hall, in Warwickshire. Then Lady Aylesford sent her husband a letter, announcing that Blandford had asked her to seek a divorce, and had said that he was going to do the same. They would defy society and marry. Sporting Joe was outraged, stopped hunting tigers with the prince, and rushed back to London, where he petitioned for divorce, citing Blandford as corespondent.

Jennie watched with horror. Affairs were tolerated among the Prince of Wales's friends, but any mention of divorce was regarded as a betrayal of the whole social construct. If her brother-in-law's affair became public, it would tarnish the entire Marlborough family. Her husband was heedless of such concerns and resorted to devious strategies to defend his elder brother. Lady Aylesford had entrusted to Randolph some love letters that the Prince of Wales himself had written to her; Randolph wrote a note to the prince, threatening to release them if Bertie didn't stop the divorce proceedings.

The prince was outraged by Lord Randolph's threat. He challenged him to a duel and, when dissuaded from taking such a disastrous step, forwarded Lord Randolph's note to his mother. Queen Victoria stood by her son, insisting that his letters to Lady Aylesford were innocent (a dubious conclusion). Faced with this royal dictum,

Lord Aylesford renounced his divorce plans, his wife retreated to her own family, and the Blandfords went their separate ways. However, the Aylesford affair led to the expulsion of the Churchills from fashionable London life.

Jennie's plans to promote her husband's career and her friendship with the heir to the throne were ruined. The Prince of Wales let it be known that he would not visit any home in which Lord Randolph Churchill and his wife were guests.[24] Winston Churchill included in his admiring biography of his father a partial account of the Aylesford affair, without mention of the word "blackmail." "Powerful enemies were anxious to humiliate him. His own sensitiveness and pride magnified every coldness into an affront. London became odious to him."[25]

Throughout the whole episode, Jennie exhibited unswerving loyalty to her husband, and the behavior of the Prince of Wales's emissaries made her "boil with rage." "My own darling dear Randolph," she wrote from her mother's apartment in Paris.

> I wld give anything to have you here tonight I feel so wretchedly – if we are to have these ennuis – do for Heaven sake lets go through them together – Now don't say 'oh yes that is all very well but you are weeping over yr Marlborough House balls' . . . No darling I assure you it is not so – how can I help feeling sick at heart when you are away from me – in difficulties *et pardessus le marché, avec un 'rhume accablant.'*[26]

Perhaps this setback was a blessing in disguise. Winston Churchill spun the story that way. "Without it, [Randolph] might have wasted a dozen years in the frivolous and expensive pursuits of the silly world of fashion; without it he would probably never have developed popular sympathies or the courage to champion democratic causes."[27] But in the short term, it demonstrated to Jennie her husband's unpredictable nature and the ease with which social success could evaporate. She had gone from being the toast of the town to a pariah.

The episode illustrated the hypocrisy of the aristocratic circle around the prince, which, Victorian conventions notwithstanding, reveled in adultery as long as the participants were discreet, their partners were either ignorant or tolerant, and their children were none the wiser. There was even an arrogant assumption that servants would have no clue about their employers' antics. In fact, the servants always knew what was going on. Jennie's friend Daisy Greville, Countess of Warwick, would recall in her memoirs that servants "would as soon have thought of criticizing their 'betters' as they would have thought of criticizing God . . . It seemed to be a point of honor . . . to cover their employers' misdeeds, and lie for them, and stick by them."[28]

IV

As London doors slammed in the Churchills' faces, Jennie swept Randolph off for a visit to America, where they were "invigorated and refreshed by contact with the alert intellects of my compatriots."[29] When they returned weeks later, she found that she and all her in-laws were effectively banished from England. Prime Minister Disraeli had appointed the Duke of Marlborough viceroy of Ireland.

As Jennie would write, "Lord Beaconsfield had pressed him to accept, thinking that it might distract his thoughts from certain family worries." The duke certainly didn't want the job; it meant he had to sell off yet more of Blenheim's art treasures, since viceregal expenses amounted to £40,000 but the salary was only £20,000. Lord Randolph was to accompany his father as unpaid private secretary, a post he intended to combine with his duties as an MP. Always an optimist, Jennie decided to make the best of the move. "Not being in favor with the Court, from which London society took its lead, we were nothing loath [not unwilling] to go."[30]

The Churchills were based in Dublin for the next three years. They and their young son moved into Little Lodge, a modest white building close to the official viceregal residence. They were accompanied by Mrs. Everest and various servants, a retinue taken for granted as part of any such household and rarely mentioned in Churchill correspondence. Among the staff were Randolph's valet, Jennie's lady's maid, a cook, a chauffeur, a housekeeper, and several maids. Far more staff accompanied the Duke and Duchess of Marlborough, who shuttered Blenheim Palace and now moved into the ninety-five-room Viceregal Lodge. There, with their three unmarried daughters, they held court as imperial plenipotentiaries. The viceregal buildings were within Phoenix Park, an enormous spread of 1,700 acres with woods, deer, and winding paths. (Today, the former Viceregal Lodge is the official residence of the president of Ireland and is known as Áras an Uachtaráin.)

Lady Jennie Churchill tried her best to make a life for herself in Ireland. She relished the wit of Irish leaders, lawyers, and bishops whom she met at her father-in-law's table. "I cannot remember meeting one really dull man."[31] Hunting became her ruling passion; she hunted with almost every pack of hounds in Ireland, recklessly spurring her mount toward high walls and over heavy gates. The hospitality of wealthy English landowners allowed her to enjoy the country's picturesque landscapes (particularly in Galway, Connemara, and Killarney) and trout fishing.

At the same time, both she and Randolph were shocked by the desperate plight of families who ate nothing but potatoes and salt, and who had pawned all their bedding and clothing to survive. Dissatisfaction had been rumbling across Ireland throughout the nineteenth century; regular failures of the potato harvest caused horrific famines. In the previous thirty years, out of a total population of six and a half million, over a million people had died of hunger and two and a half million had fled their hunger-ravaged country. Fed by intense resentment against English landlords and the Westminster government, Irish campaigners for Home Rule were growing vociferous and demanding. But the idea that part of the United Kingdom might have its own parliament was anathema to Britain's Conservative Party, and Randolph's colleagues on Tory benches ignored Irish demands.

In *Reminiscences,* Jennie described how "neglect and misery have rooted the people in their shiftless and improvident habits." She reflected the attitude of her class in observations on the "heartrending poverty of the peasantry, who lived in their wretched mud-hovels more like animals than human beings." Lord Randolph became increasingly sympathetic to the plight of the Irish, although both his father, the viceroy, and his fellow MPs at Westminster were appalled by his attitude.

Lord Randolph spent weeks at a time in London among those colleagues. A pariah within London society, he was now intent on becoming a rising star in the House of Commons—the perfect dandy in his frock coat and walrus mustache. He sharpened his speaking skills and carved his own path within the Conservative Party as someone unafraid to challenge party leaders. His views on social reform at home, particularly on Irish issues, were progressive, even as he upheld established Conservative Party support for the United Kingdom.

Like-minded colleagues drifted toward him, as he needled the Tory old guard and opposition Liberals with his biting humor. Alongside his unexpected ambition was an intolerance of bores. "On one occasion when buttonholed [by an elderly peer] at his club, he listened halfway through an interminable story, then rang the bell for a footman." When the latter arrived, he told him to " 'listen until his lordship finishes' while he himself slipped away."[32]

But his wife, who would have loved to share his triumphs, was not with him. "I don't find [Dublin] dull," Jennie wrote Randolph, "except when I think of London and its amusements."[33] Her relationship with the Marlboroughs, particularly the duchess, remained cool. She missed the liveliness of the London season, the opportunity to follow her husband's career much more closely, and, most of all, him. Although Randolph affected indifference to those around him, Jennie's letters were full of loving expressions. Anita Leslie, Jennie's great-niece, discovered a particularly touching example in the family archives illustrating Jennie's affection for Randolph and her relationship with Winston, now an active four-year-old firmly in the care of his nanny:

Winston has just been with me – such a darling he is – I can't
have my Mama go – & if she does I will run after the train &
jump in, he said to me. I have told Everest to take him out for
a drive tomorrow if it is fine – as it's better the stables should
have more work . . . Goodbye darling. I love you ever so much.
Your J.[34]

Loneliness was not the only challenge within Jennie's marriage.
It was starting to dawn on her that her husband's erratic behavior—
impulsiveness, impatience, frequent absences—might be due to more
than just his personality. Even as a child, Lord Randolph Churchill's
health had never been robust, and as an adult he was notorious for
chain-smoking and excessive drinking. Although he insisted there
was nothing wrong with him, he now suffered crippling headaches
and high fevers for which he consulted London doctors regularly.

Jennie often felt he was deliberately avoiding her. Even when he
was in Ireland, he left her in Dublin while he went shooting with
friends or accompanied his father on official trips. Her letters to him
capture a growing anxiety about her marriage. "Do you know, darling, this is the longest separation since our marriage and I hope the
last," she wrote, followed a few weeks later by the cri de coeur "I don't
think I can stand it much longer without you."[35]

All she got in return were accounts of her husband's political
speeches and conversations. According to Anita Leslie, "Fiercely
egocentric and arrogant as only a Duke's son in Victorian England
could be . . . Randolph Churchill was incapable of loving or noticing
any human being as such. He admired his wife . . . but neither she nor
her sons would ever hear the warm words for which they yearned."[36]

Jennie was in unfamiliar territory, with a husband who ignored her
pleas and was always elsewhere. Mindful of her mother's advice that
a wife should never scold her husband—"If you do he will only go
where he is *not* scolded"[37]—she felt her hands were tied. All that was
left was the tepid companionship of the Duchess of Marlborough and
her sisters-in-law. The occasional visits of Clara and Leonie were her

only reminders of family warmth. Jennie continued to write loving missives to Randolph, expressing her anxiety about his health and their money worries.

Had conjugal relations between them stopped altogether? Given how easily Jennie had conceived her first child, it is surprising that a second pregnancy did not occur within a couple of years (although Jennie would have been aware of the primitive forms of contraception available back then, such as condoms, douches, and vaginal sponges). What is certain is that, as the Churchills grew apart, Jennie continued to crave intimacy and began to look for companionship elsewhere.

One of the most famous descriptions of Jennie dates from these years. It captures her radiance and vitality. The author of this glowing tribute was Edgar Vincent, Viscount D'Abernon, a former ambassador who was making a formal call on the viceroy.

> The Viceroy was on a dais at the further end of the room sur-
> rounded by a brilliant staff, but eyes were not turned on him or
> his consort, but on a dark, lithe figure, standing somewhat apart
> and appearing to be of another texture to those around her, radi-
> ant, translucent, intense. A diamond star in her hair, her favorite
> ornament—its luster dimmed by the flashing glory of her eyes.
> More of the panther than of the woman in her look, but with a cul-
> tivated intelligence unknown to the jungle. Her courage not less
> great than her husband—fit mother for descendants of the great
> Duke. With all these attributes of brilliancy [and] such kindliness
> and high spirits . . . she was universally popular. Her desire to
> please, her delight in life and the genuine wish that all should share
> her joyous faith in it, made her the centre of a devoted circle.[38]

Lord D'Abernon, who enjoyed his reputation as one of the most handsome men in England, would become Jennie's intimate friend in the years ahead. His line "more of the panther than of the woman," with its delicious implication of sexual magnetism, had stuck with Jennie ever since.

Jennie struck up several close friendships with men during the Dublin years, and gossip about her flirtations once prompted Lord Randolph, in a rare departure from his usual disregard, to send her a surprisingly affectionate warning. "I really do think my darling you ought to be more careful in yr manner to men, who are always too ready to take a liberty. I have such confidence in you that I never bother you, but these kind of things are very annoying & vexatious."[39]

Two of Jennie's most persistent admirers were Evelyn Boscawen, the 7th Viscount Falmouth, a hearty, handsome military man whose nickname was "Star," and Lieutenant Colonel John Strange Jocelyn, a friend of Jennie's father-in-law who would become the 5th Earl of Roden. There is speculation that one of these men fathered Jennie's second child, Jack, who was born on February 4, 1880. Jack's full name was John Strange Spencer-Churchill, but Jennie's descendants consider that she was too discreet to have dropped "Strange" into his name in order to indicate his parentage. Falmouth is considered a more likely candidate, as Jennie mentioned "Starman," as she called him, frequently in her diaries and letters to her sisters.

Jack's legal father, Lord Randolph Churchill, showed as little interest in this second child as he did in his older son. But both in childhood and later, Winston showed great affection for his brother. And a photo of Jennie with her two sons shows how much the boys resembled each other, suggesting that they might perhaps have been full brothers rather than half brothers after all.

Within weeks of Jack's birth, Jennie was happy to hear that the Irish exile was over. Prime Minister Benjamin Disraeli called a general election, which to the surprise of most observers he lost to William Gladstone's Liberals. A change of government at Westminster meant a change of viceroy in Dublin. The Marlboroughs packed up and returned to Blenheim, and in April 1880 the Churchills moved into a small town house, 29 St. James's Place, a cul-de-sac that ran south from Piccadilly. But shortage of funds constrained Jennie's social life. She told her mother, "I haven't been to many balls, as I simply cannot afford to get dresses and one cannot wear always the same thing. Money is such a hateful subject to me just now."[40]

Jennie Jerome Churchill was now twenty-six, and the marriage that had begun with such passion was riddled with conflicts, secrets, and money worries. She was too independent and tough-minded to buckle under pressures beyond her control, such as her husband's temperament and ill-health and their debts, but she was also too passionate and sensuous not to stray. For the restless "panther" of Lord D'Abernon's description, divorce was not an option, but neither was fidelity.

During the years of her marriage to Lord Randolph, Jennie hewed to the code by which she and Sara Roosevelt had been raised. She kept up appearances. In fact, she was more than outwardly loyal to her husband; in the short term, she did everything she could to promote his political career, and longer term, she would show extraordinary love and forbearance as his health continued to decline. Jennie Jerome Churchill remained firmly married, and defined herself as Lord Randolph's spouse—in her opinion, a far more interesting role at this stage of her life than her role as mother.

Where did her son Winston fit in the first decade of Jennie Churchill's married life? He was almost out of sight, and often out of mind. It was Mrs. Everest who oversaw Winston's and Jack's daily routines, organized their clothing, and took the boys to visit their grandparents at Blenheim. At this stage, "Oom," "Woom," or "Womany," as Winston called Mrs. Everest, was the most important woman in his life. In *My Early Life,* the adult Winston would describe how Jennie was the "fairy princess" who arrived in the nursery to kiss him goodnight before swanning off to dinner. "She shone for me like the Evening Star. I loved her dearly—but at a distance."[41]

Jennie's maternal conduct was normal within the British aristocratic circles in which she lived. Sara Delano Roosevelt, in contrast, was no fairy princess, but she rarely allowed any distance between herself and her child.

CHAPTER 7

Roosevelt Harmony

1880–1890

Sara Delano married James Roosevelt on October 7, 1880, at Algonac, her family home in the Hudson Valley. Like Jennie Jerome's wedding in Paris seven years earlier, the ceremony was not as elaborate as might have been expected. But like almost everything in Sara's life, this was according to the custom of her class and circumstances. The Delano family was going through the rituals of mourning because Warren Delano's sister Sarah, who had done so much to help Catherine Delano with her large brood, had died a few weeks earlier.

The funeral of this spinster aunt had been James Roosevelt's first exposure to the overwhelming clannishness of his fiancée's relatives. As family members surged toward Algonac in their furs and diamonds, it was also a chance to absorb the immensity of the Delano fortune. Warren Delano slyly reported to his son that his future son-in-law seemed "a little surprised at the luxury and comfort surrounding the old home."[1] The Delanos scorned anybody who flaunted wealth, but they certainly didn't want their own underestimated. In the New World, money was at least as important as class.

Despite the shadow cast by Aunt Sarah's death, which meant a restricted guest list and a gloomy requirement that guests wear black, the Delano-Roosevelt marriage was a splashy affair—much grander than the hasty Jerome-Churchill nuptials in Paris. A New York paper noted that the bridegroom was "a familiar figure in New York circles" and that "the bride's father is one of the largest land-holders in the vicinity of New York."[2] Many of the 125 friends and relatives ("a small number of the best representatives of New York society," according to one New York newspaper)[3] had traveled by steamer up the Hudson River, enjoying a gorgeous boat ride past riverbanks on which autumnal bursts of red and yellow glowed within the dark green foliage.

When the guests disembarked at Newburgh ferry landing, they found a line of Delano carriages, coachmen doffing their caps and horses pawing the ground, waiting to take them to Algonac. According to the *New York World*, "the villagers and residents in the pretty country cottages on the roadside turned out to do honor" to them. The wedding itself took place in the spacious parlor at Algonac, which was filled with color thanks to orchids in huge Chinese vases and a canopy of blossoms.[4]

Observers were struck by the contrast between bride and groom. Sara, tall and radiant with youth, swept into the parlor. Her gown of white brocade showed off her statuesque figure; her thick brown hair was swept up into an elaborate style. Around her neck was the five-strand pearl necklace that James had given her, and which she would often wear in formal portraits for the rest of her life. James, gray-whiskered, round-shouldered, and two inches shorter, took her hand as they exchanged their vows. Years later, a guest recalled several elderly Algonac employees at the back of the room "crying that such a lovely girl should marry an old man."[5] But Sara was happy with the choice she had made for herself.

As the celebrations wound down, the newlyweds emerged from Algonac and James helped his new bride into the Delano carriage waiting beneath the porte cochère. When he himself had taken his seat, the coachman cracked his whip and drove north. After ten miles, the halfway mark between the Delano and Roosevelt properties, the Delano vehicle drew up alongside a Roosevelt coach, waiting there with Mr. James's liveried coachman. Sara dismounted from her father's carriage and climbed into the Roosevelt conveyance, while her new husband took the reins for the rest of the drive to Hyde Park. The carriage rolled on, finally passing through the tall, ivy-covered stone columns that flanked the entrance to Springwood's winding tree-bordered drive.

Once they arrived at Springwood, a more modest house than Algonac, James led his wife into the home where each would live for the rest of their lives. That night, the new Mrs. Roosevelt wrote in her notebook: "Marriage of James Roosevelt and Sara Delano, October 7th, 1880," then described without comment her journey to Hyde Park.[6] Superficially, it was an almost seamless transition from her father's to her husband's authority, and from Delano to Roosevelt routines.

Except the symbolism distorts the reality of Sara's marriage. Sara was far wealthier than her new husband: a share of the Delano millions would someday come her way, and by American law it would be hers to manage. Even if his new wife had been penniless, Mr. James could easily support her in the style to which she was accustomed. What a cushion of security! No wonder there were none of the dowry wrangles that preceded the Churchills' wedding; there were no financial pressures.

Sara, like Jennie, was still deeply immersed in the Victorian belief that a woman's most important roles were as daughter, wife, and mother. She would be known to servants and villagers for the rest of her life as "Mrs. James." However, for all her formal deference to Mr. James's seniority and patrician attitudes, the new Mrs. Roosevelt remained the self-possessed, imperious woman who intimidated her younger sisters. Her strength of character was never in doubt, and it would not take long before James realized that his young wife liked complete control of family life.

II

At first, Sara happily adapted to her husband's deeply ingrained habits. She replaced her Delano allegiance to Newburgh's Unitarian Church with a new loyalty to Hyde Park's St. James Episcopal Church, where James served all his life as a vestryman. When she was in Hyde Park, she would join her husband in his carriage each

Sunday for the short drive to the small brick pseudo-Gothic church. She smiled graciously at neighbors as she walked up the aisle to the third pew on the left, with its red silk cushions and brass nameplate "J. Roosevelt."

A web of local relatives and friends quickly absorbed James's new wife. In a house across the lawn lived Rosy Roosevelt, James's son, his wife, Helen, and their son, known as "Taddy." In a villa a mile away resided James's mother, with a lace cap and perfect manners. Close to her in a splendid new mansion lived James's Uncle John, with his wife and two little girls, Grace and Ellie.

Springwood was smaller than Algonac, and its glass cabinets were filled with European rather than oriental souvenirs, but Sara did not replace the carpets and curtains that had been chosen by her predecessor, Rebecca Roosevelt. The house was run by Elespie (Elspeth), the Scottish housekeeper hired by Rebecca several years earlier. A cook and housemaid carried out Elespie's orders, so that even the menus likely dated from the previous regime. Each morning, Sara accompanied her husband on his daily ride around his land. Each evening, she played bezique with her husband, just as Rebecca once had. She had suggested that he might enjoy the Algonac practice of reading aloud, but the suggestion was quietly rebuffed. He resisted installing a telephone, arguing that it would disturb his peace and quiet. The only innovation Sara managed was in the drawing room, where she replaced Rebecca's gray silk curtains with curtains made from five bolts of rich blue Chinese damask that were a gift from her father.

But Roosevelt ties could not compete with those of Algonac. Sara and James Roosevelt regularly joined the Delano household to celebrate Christmas, Easter, family birthdays, and anniversaries. When Sara's husband took brief business trips into Manhattan, Sara immediately summoned the carriage for the twenty-mile drive south. There she would settle into the big, high-ceilinged rooms of her childhood, with their deep chesterfields and glass cabinets filled with jade and porcelain treasures.

The Roosevelts spent a few days with the Delanos at Algonac in the run-up to the 1880 presidential election. Given their differing party loyalties, it is unlikely that Warren Delano and James Roosevelt discussed the eventual winner, Republican James A. Garfield. James's loyalty remained with the Democratic Party, to which he contributed handsomely. However, he heartily disapproved of the glad-handing slipperiness of politics at which his own son would excel. He had already turned away several invitations to run as his party's candidate for Congress, state senate, or assembly, and he infected both his wives with his distaste. (Rebecca Roosevelt noted in her diary in 1874 that her husband had attended a political meeting and "I was dreadfully afraid he would be nominated . . . but he got home safely.")[7] The only elected office he was prepared to contest was supervisor of the village of Hyde Park. He took a keen interest in local institutions, including schools, jails, and psychiatric hospitals, but his involvement went no further than hefty donations and benevolent leadership.

Five days after the election, Mr. and Mrs. James Roosevelt took the train to Manhattan on the first leg of their honeymoon. At the docks, they boarded the White Star Line's brand-new luxury liner SS *Germanic*, reaching Liverpool a mere eight days later. For the next ten months, Sara and her husband meandered comfortably through Italy, Switzerland, Germany, Holland, and Spain, shopping, attending concerts and operas, and sightseeing. Hopscotching from one luxury hotel to the next, traveling in private carriages, they admired Renaissance treasures and averted their eyes from beggars in the streets.

Their social life was a European version of Hudson Valley routines, with visits to American friends and relatives residing in those countries. In her diary, Sara noted that in Florence they had "lunched with our Consul . . . dined with the John Bigelows, had a pleasant evening with the Charlie Woolseys [cousins of James Roosevelt], walked in the Boboli gardens and did many pleasant things."[8] In Paris, Sara was reunited with her whole family: Warren Delano booked an entire floor of the Hôtel du Rhin and summoned his children for a month of opera, carriage drives, sightseeing, and shopping.

From Paris, the Roosevelts traveled to Holland and then to Germany, where, in Celle, Sara showed her new husband the school she had attended. In Ghent, where Jehun de Lannoye's crest was carved into the wall of the magnificent Gothic cathedral, Sara enjoyed pointing out to James the coat of arms of the remote ancestor from whom her family derived its name and prestige.

In London, they dined with friends and met a Madame Goldschmidt, who was none other than the former Jenny Lind. James had known her years ago at the height of her fame as the "Swedish nightingale"—the nightingale after whom Leonard Jerome had called his second daughter. All those years ago, Sara's husband and Jennie's father had likely attended one of the same Manhattan receptions in her honor. Now, however, Jenny Lind was, in Sara's words, a "plump pleasant-faced little woman in black taffeta."[9]

Occasionally Sara confided a little self-reflection to her diary, judging a Spanish bullfight, for instance, as "a cruel, savage amusement, not a sport." When her husband bought her an old Spanish lace mantilla, she noted, "James too devoted to me." But even Rita Halle Kleeman, Sara's deferential biographer, admitted that the diary was neither introspective nor analytical.[10] It was a bare listing of places, purchases, and events, and reflected its author's emotional restraint and no-nonsense approach to life.

The Roosevelts were in England when Sara began to feel queasy. On a Sunday in late August, she nearly fainted while attending a service in York Minster, "but the feeling passed over." She was four months pregnant, and it was time to book passage home, once again on the *Germanic*. They reached New York after a perfect honeymoon. "James was wonderful in the way he did it all and we have had such happy days," Sara wrote in her diary. "He has been untiring and thoughtful of everything."[11]

Back at Hyde Park, the Roosevelts resumed their routines, as Sara recorded in her diary. "Mother Roosevelt lunched with us . . . James keeps busy. He goes to town at least once a week, and has school meetings etc. . . . . Rosy dines with us nearly every night . . . James to town, I to Algonac." When Sara was not going to Algonac, her siblings were visiting her. "We all drive and enjoy rowing as well." Winter arrived, and soon the Hudson River was frozen and the sycamores, oaks, and pines around Springwood were laden with snow. Sara and James distributed turkeys to "our people around the place" before traveling to Algonac for Christmas. Her advancing pregnancy is never mentioned in the daily entries; well-bred women of her day would have regarded this as too much information.[12]

In late January, the diary entries abruptly stopped. Sixteen months after her wedding, and several days after her due date, Sara Roosevelt went into labor in her bedroom at Springwood. The birth was tough. As the gas lamps flickered and the servants waited anxiously in the kitchen on the floor below, Sara lay on the big mahogany bed, suppressing her screams of pain as Mrs. Carrie Lee, a trained nurse, counted the contractions. The pain continued all night, and at dawn Mr. James sent for Dr. Edward Parker, the local doctor from Poughkeepsie. He urged Sara to push, but the baby wouldn't budge. Sara's mother arrived, and her son-in-law told her that Sara was in trouble. Mrs. Lee worried that the baby would be born dead, and Dr. Parker administered chloroform (too much, it turned out) in order to give Sara some rest.

After twenty-four hours of labor, the baby finally slid into the world. He was large, blue, and floppy. Dr. Parker began mouth-to-mouth resuscitation; once the child had air in his lungs, he gave a thin, high-pitched cry. He was soon thriving, but his mother hovered on the brink of death.[13]

James Roosevelt took over Sara's diary, and on Monday, January 30, 1882, he made the first of several entries. "At quarter to nine my Sallie had a splendid large baby boy. He weighs 10 lbs., without clothes."

Next, he wrote to Sara's father, informing Warren Delano, "Poor child, she has had a very hard time," but assuring him that she had given birth to "a bouncing boy."[14] It was an anxious time for everybody. Her brother Philippe had died a month before she had gone into labor, and twelve days after her baby's birth, typhoid took the life of her four-year-old nephew, Warren Delano IV, son of her older brother.

Sara's recovery was slow; it was four weeks before she left her bed-room and went downstairs. Unlike Jennie Jerome Churchill, she did not spring straight back into her daily routines. Dr. Parker visited frequently, urging her to rest. She had good reason to love this baby, and not just because she had nearly died herself. Roosevelt biographer Geoffrey C. Ward suggests that Dr. Parker advised her that "it would be wisest not to have more children."[15]

We know an extraordinary amount about Sara's child-rearing prac-tices because in 1933, the year her son moved into the White House, a book titled *My Boy Franklin* was published. It was written in the first person, and the author was given as "Sara Delano Roosevelt, as told to Isabel Leighton and Gabrielle Forbush." Leighton and Forbush were two journalists who had interviewed Sara for a lengthy magazine series about her son, then turned their articles into a book crammed with anecdotes about Franklin's childhood.

"At the very outset," Sara (or Leighton and Forbush) wrote in a typical passage, "he was plump, pink, and nice. I used to love to bathe and dress him, although I took the responsibility of lifting and turning him rather seriously. I suppose all young mothers are a little fearful in the beginning of dropping their babies, and in that respect I was no different from the rest. Still, I felt . . . that every mother ought to learn to care for her own baby, whether she can afford to delegate the task to some one else or not."[16] Sara did not hand over her baby to a nanny, as Jennie Churchill had done eight years earlier. Departing from the practice common within her class, she breastfed him for a whole year.

Sara's bond with Franklin was powerful from that tentative first breath onward. Knowing there would be no more babies, she dedi-cated herself to protecting the one she had. From the day of his birth, her son would be the center of her attention.

III

Sara's fierce love for her son began with a quiet but lengthy struggle over his name, which began before his birth. In the Roosevelt fam-ily, there had been a tradition to alternate James and Isaac in each generation. Mr. James had broken that pattern when he named his first son James Roosevelt Roosevelt, and he now decided that the new baby should inherit the name Isaac. Sara detested the name; her beloved baby was *not* going to be saddled with it.[17] In the first months of the marriage, Sara had happily deferred to her husband, as her more accommodating mother had done to Warren Delano. But now her strength of will and Delano loyalty emerged. She wanted to name her son Warren Delano Roosevelt, after her father. Mr. James's choice of name, Isaac, never stood a chance.

Sara's father was delighted. He took a proprietary interest in the child: the baby was "a beautiful little fellow—well and strong and well-behaved—with a good-shaped head of the Delano type," he bragged to his son.[18] But the family decided that it would be too painful to give Sara's new son the same first names as her recently deceased four-year-old nephew. So Sara selected another Delano name—Franklin, after her favorite uncle, Franklin Delano, who had married Laura Astor and who lived up the Hudson River Valley at a magnificent estate near Barrytown, purchased with the help of Laura's lavish trust fund.

Reluctant to entrust her precious boy to others, Sara dismissed the English nurse hired by James Roosevelt because she found her too intrusive. For the next few months, Sara, with the help of her household staff, looked after her newborn son herself, until her sister Dora Forbes found a Scottish nanny named Helen McRorie, and Sara declared that she was "a good and experienced woman and very gentle."[19] McRorie ("Mamie" to her charge, "Ellen" to Sara) managed her employer as skillfully as she managed her young charge. She stayed for nine years, but she was never a mother substitute as Mrs. Everest was for the young Winston Churchill.

By March 20, both mother and son were in good health and Sara was back in charge of the diary. "We arranged the flowers beautifully and papa, mama and Elliott Roosevelt came up. At 11 we took darling Baby to the chapel in his prettiest clothes and best behavior. Dr. Cady christened him 'Franklin Delano.' . . . The whole party came home for lunch."[20] Elliott Roosevelt, James Roosevelt's distant cousin, was one of the godparents. Had he lived, he would also have become Franklin's father-in-law twenty-three years later.

Soon Roosevelt habits were resumed; Sara's neighbors enjoyed watching her trotting off in her dogcart to deliver food to the hungry, flowers to the hospital, and clothing to the poor. She organized a sewing class for local girls. Then there were the numerous carriage rides and calls on family and friends. On most occasions, she recorded in her diary, "Baby went with us."

Every detail of Franklin's development was catalogued—his smile, first teeth, first steps. "He crows and laughs all the time." She kept him in starched white skirts for his first four years, then dressed him in Scottish kilts. He finally graduated to pants when Sara discovered in London a supplier of pretty little sailor suits. He was already five when his mother finally consented to his first boyish haircut, and she wept as she gathered up the blond tresses. They were gently braided, then laid in a silk-lined box.

When Franklin rode next to his father in the Delano carriage through Hyde Park, people doffed their hats to him. With age came confidence—and a mischievous appeal that his large circle of relatives found adorable. At Algonac, his mother's parents, siblings, nieces, and nephews fussed over him. When he was four years old, an aunt commented that he had a "lot of tact." "Oh yes," he replied. "I'm chock full of tacks."[21] It became a family saying, as well as a sign of his precocity . . . and his skill at charming an audience.

Springwood, and Sara's enveloping love, had a profound impact on Franklin, although the Roosevelts rarely spent more than a few weeks there at a stretch. Many years later, he would write, "In thinking back to my earliest days, I am impressed by the peacefulness and regularity of things both in respect to places and people. Up to the age of seven, Hyde Park was the center of the world."[22] And Franklin was the center of Sara Roosevelt's life. She ensured that her son rarely endured a moment of uncertainty about his place in the world.

Franklin's arrival did not disrupt his parents' regular travels. He was only three when they resumed their habit of spending winters in Europe. The Roosevelts were a striking, well-tailored couple as they crossed the Atlantic, then toured the Continent in style. James Roosevelt, now in his late fifties and showing his age, was gracious and dapper as he tipped the steward who showed them to their first-class accommodations. Sara, tall and slim, acknowledged the respect she regarded as her due; although still in her twenties, her demeanor was so haughty that she often seemed as old as her husband. In their wake came their little boy, curls brushed and shoes shined, with his uniformed nanny, various maids, and a pile of cases and trunks. Within the next few years, Franklin traveled extensively through Europe, visiting important capitals (in Paris, his father took him up the new Eiffel Tower) and mingling with European royalty at various health spas.

In 1885, Sara, James, and their entourage enjoyed the usual leisurely perambulation through Europe. But only a couple of days after they had boarded the SS *Germanic* for their return to New York, a savage swell started tossing the liner up and down, and huge breakers crashed against its steel sides. The storm raged all night, and even Sara's Delano sangfroid was shaken. Just after breakfast, "the ship seemed suddenly to drop into a trough in the sea and everything became dark," Sara would record. She said to her husband, "We seemed to be going down," and he replied, "It does look like it," and left the cabin to find out what was happening. As Sara held four-year-old Franklin tight and awaited James's return, she watched water trickle under the cabin door, and heard the screams of steerage passengers trapped on the lower decks.

Soon James returned to report that the captain was missing and that the vessel was foundering. Five lifeboats had been ripped off their davits. Yet as Franklin's parents prepared to abandon ship, both remained extraordinarily cool. "I never get frightened, and I was not then," Sara told her biographer Kleeman. "But when the water was high enough to touch the bottom of a fur coat that was hanging by my berth, I took it and wrapped it around the baby, saying to my husband, 'Poor little boy. If he must go down, he is going down warm.'"

If the ship foundered, Sara would go down too, but her son would be in her arms.

The *Germanic* miraculously righted itself. James Roosevelt immediately went on the bridge and insisted that the captain (who had been temporarily knocked unconscious when the biggest wave hit) turn back to Liverpool for repairs and said that he would take responsibility for this decision with the ship's owners. Franklin never forgot the restraint and courage his parents displayed while others panicked; these were qualities that would characterize his own behavior as an adult.[23] And Sara refused to let the experience dent her enjoyment of travel.

In 1886, Sara, James, and Franklin, now five, took the train to Washington for a few weeks. They moved to the capital because James Roosevelt wanted to enlist the support of President Grover Cleveland for a business venture. Roosevelt had given generous donations to the Democrats. Before long, Sara was cutting a swathe through the capital's society, enjoying "two months of very gay, pleasant life, constant dinner and charming people," she told Kleeman. "Every one has been charming to us and even Franklin knows everybody." The president resisted James's lobbying, then James resisted the president's invitation to become U.S. ambassador to Holland.[24]

At the end of their stay, James Roosevelt took his little boy with him to the White House to say farewell to the president. Grover Cleveland, exhausted by political battles, made an unexpected gesture. He laid his hand on Franklin's blond curls and said, "My little man, I am making a strange wish for you. It is that you may never be president of the United States."[25]

This comment probably pleased Sara Roosevelt, who at the time agreed with her husband that politics was a grubby profession. She carefully noted it in her diary. Much later, she was asked if she had thought her son would become president. "Never, oh never," she replied. "The highest ideal I could hold up before our boy [was] to grow up to be like his father: straight and honorable, just and kind." Why would anybody ever want to leave the Hudson Valley? Her hope was that Franklin would be "a beloved member of the family and a useful and respected citizen of his community."[26]

Two themes dominate Sara's diaries: close ties with Delano relatives, and incessant concerns about the health of her husband and son. Her worst moment came when Franklin was seven and the family embarked on the White Star's luxury liner the *Adriatic* for England. Two days out of New York, the little boy was afflicted with stomach pains and diagnosed with typhoid fever—a potentially fatal disease. It was Sara's greatest fear: the potential loss of her precious only child. The captain immediately surrendered his own quarters to the little boy and his mother. "I sit by him all night and only go to my own room to dress," Sara wrote. Once the *Adriatic* docked in Liverpool, Sir Thomas Ismay, founder of the White Star line and an old friend of Mr. James, sent a special tender with a trained nurse aboard to meet the steamship. The wan youngster was transferred to the home of a doctor, where he remained for several weeks. Sara reluctantly left him in the doctor's care only when she was convinced he was recovering his health.

As Franklin left infancy behind him, Sara continued to enjoy her social and cultural routines. From Hyde Park, there were frequent trips to Manhattan, which pulsed with energy and wealth, and where men like J. P. Morgan were driving the industrialization of America and remaking the economy. James Roosevelt kept a suite at the Hotel Renaissance on West Forty-Third Street, and Sara loved to dip into the city's booming cultural activities—theater, operas, concerts, recitals. In her diary, she carefully noted the stars—singers Nellie Melba and Lilli Lehmann, the pianist Ignacy Jan Paderewski (also a favorite of Jennie Churchill's), the actors Sarah Bernhardt, and Ellen Terry and Sir Henry Irving. She would take music lessons while James went to his club and Franklin visited museums (the Museum of Natural History was a favorite). Together, the threesome went for carriage rides in Central Park and called on yet more Delano and Roosevelt relatives in their lavish new homes on Fifth and Madison Avenues. At dinners, Sara would wear black satin and all her diamonds because, she told Rita Halle Kleeman, "She always felt that there was nothing quite so lovely for formal occasions."[27] And there was nothing that indicated the understated grandeur of old money more effectively, either.

The Jerome Park racetrack, which Leonard Jerome had helped establish in the 1860s in what is now the Bronx, was a big attraction. The Roosevelts would travel there in one of the stylish carriages—a four-in-hand, perhaps, or a phaeton—owned by James's older son Rosy. Eager spectators arriving for the Belmont Stakes, the Champagne Stakes, or less prestigious races pulled up in vehicles of all kind: butcher's carts, drays, barouches, sulkies, light wagons, even farmer's wagons. They could picnic on the grass next to the track and view the races from the three-tier wooden grandstand with seats for eight thousand. But for the Manhattan elite there was The Bluff, a luxurious clubhouse that overlooked the course. For people like the Roosevelts, Manhattan was a village. Rosy Roosevelt and Leonard Jerome, both avid equestrians with a taste for the turf, would have known each other well.

And then there were the summers on Campobello Island, a rocky island in Canadian waters just off the coast of Maine. Several wealthy Americans had built summer cottages there in the mid-nineteenth century and enjoyed sailing in Passamaquoddy Bay. It was a smaller, more rustic summer community than Newport, Rhode Island, but it had its own cachet.

Attracted by the invigorating sea air, beach walks, and congenial social life of picnics and tea parties, the Roosevelts had bought four acres when their son was still a toddler. Their summer cottage took three years to complete, but when it was finished it was exactly what Sara had planned—a simple wooden house with wide porches overlooking a sandy beach and Passamaquoddy Bay. She quickly furnished it, arranged for weekly baskets of fresh vegetables and fruit to be sent from Hyde Park, and organized tea parties with other summer visitors. "Sometimes James sails with some of the gentlemen," she noted. "I work or read German or French aloud with several people here who care for these languages."[28] Before he was in his teens, Franklin had become an excellent sailor who could read the wind like a professional and single-handedly helm the family sailboat, the *Half Moon,* around the rocks and treacherous tides of the Bay of Fundy.

In public, Sara and James Roosevelt gave the impression that their relationship was unsullied by discord. One observer noted, "They are a most attractive couple, so cultivated and refined—and, a thing I love to see, always—devoted to each other."[29] They relished adventures together. James Roosevelt liked to travel incessantly, and his railway investments gave him both justification for inspecting routes and also the luxury of his own private railcar, provided by the Delaware and Hudson Railway. Sara accompanied him because, she confided to Kleeman, she was otherwise "very lonely, in spite of dear little Franklin."[30] One winter they parked their four-year-old son with her sisters and mother at Algonac for three months and went off on a trip through Mexico and on to California. Sara's diary included the usual list of sites seen and friends visited. They were treated as VIPs everywhere.

Yet underneath the image of marital fulfillment, there may have been strains. Sara destroyed her journals for the years 1884–1887; FDR biographers have suggested that she decided to eliminate evidence of marital discord from the otherwise discreet pages.[31] Perhaps it was the age difference between the partners that started to exasperate Sara. She was young, beautiful, and vigorous, and at the New York City balls she attended before her marriage she had loved to dance. Although she insisted that she preferred country living, the city thrilled her. Her idea of heaven was an evening in a Tier 1 box at the opera house, listening to Dame Nellie Melba and graciously waving to acquaintances. Her husband was older and less active. In photos, he seemed happiest sitting in a rocking chair at Springwood, cigar in mouth and book in hand.

James was also rigidly old-fashioned. In 1893, at the Chicago World's Fair, Sara bumped into an old friend, Margaret Carey de Stuers Zborowski. "Maggie," as she was known, was a niece of the late John Jacob Astor III, and when she married Baron Alphonse Lambert

Eugène ridder de Stuers, a Dutch diplomat, in 1875, the wedding was a Knickerbocker society triumph. Sara had been one of Maggie's bridesmaids, and she described her friend's new husband to be "the nicest foreigner I have ever met." But the marriage went off the rails. Maggie fled the marital home and landed up in Sioux Falls, South Dakota, a rough frontier town then known as the Divorce Capital of the United States thanks to its permissive laws. It was, in the words of the *Pittsburgh Daily Post*, "a Mecca for the mismatched,"[32] and those who ended up there were catnip for scandal sheets across the Continent.

Maggie had obtained her divorce and had promptly remarried. Her new husband was William Elliot Morris Zborowski, a dashing New York millionaire and daring equestrian who had been Maggie's beau before her marriage.[33] Now the newlyweds were trying to reintegrate into society, despite being shunned by the Astor family. Sara was delighted to encounter Maggie at Chicago, but James was decidedly frosty; divorce was unacceptable, and he asked his wife not to see her friend again. On this occasion, Sara yielded to her husband's request, but in a rare admission of conflicted feelings, she wrote in her diary, "It is not easy to make up my mind."[34]

Lack of sexual relations may have exacerbated tensions. (The Roosevelts never shared a bedroom, but that was not unusual for couples of their class.) Geoffrey C. Ward suggests that "the Roosevelts had adopted sexual abstinence as the only certain way to avoid a second and possibly fatal pregnancy."

It is poignant to contemplate that both Lady Randolph Churchill and Mrs. James Roosevelt may have abandoned physical relations with their husbands while each was still in her twenties. If they did, each woman dealt with this loss of intimacy quite differently. Jennie Churchill looked for intimacy elsewhere. She moved in aristocratic British circles where extramarital affairs were openly tolerated. For Sara Roosevelt, a straitlaced woman living in the genteel Hudson Valley, extramarital sex was unthinkable. She remained loyal and loving toward Mr. James, but she poured her formidable emotional energy into travel, good works, and shaping the character of her son.

IV

As Sara watched Franklin develop from a shy, chubby toddler into a youngster, she took great joy in giving him what was, in her eyes, the perfect childhood.

Franklin rose at seven, ate breakfast at eight, learned his lessons from nine until noon, and was then allowed to play for an hour until lunch at one. After lunch there were more lessons, supervised play-time, supper at six, and bed by eight. His mother read aloud to him, and supervised his nightly bath. (He was eight and a half before he bathed alone.) When he was naughty, the punishment was chilly dis-approval. "We never subjected the boy to a lot of don'ts," his mother wrote. "And while certain rules established for his well being had to be rigidly observed, we were never strict merely for the sake of being strict. In fact we took a secret pride in the fact that Franklin instinc-tively never seemed to require that kind of handling."[35]

Franklin's upbringing was like his mother's as far as material com-forts and family security were concerned. However, Sara had been the fifth in a family of nine surviving Delano children, and had grown up with the constant sibling companionship and rivalry that Franklin never knew. When the Roosevelts were at Springwood, his mother would invite the offspring of other well-to-do Hudson Valley families to come and play, and depending on the season, the children would climb trees and build treehouses, or skate and have snowball fights. Franklin had inherited his mother's urge to control. When Sara re-proached him for being so bossy, he replied, "Mummie, if I did not give them orders nothing would happen."[36]

Most days, Franklin was alone. Sara would play games with him, but according to her own memoir, she wasn't much fun. One day, when he was only four, she was playing a board game called Steeple-Chase with Franklin, and she won twice in a row. He demanded that they trade horses because he was convinced hers was better. She gave it to him, rolled the dice—and won again. "This crowning humilia-tion was not to be borne, and he sulked in furious silence. Quietly, I picked up the toys and told him in as firm a tone as I could muster that, until he learned to take a beating gracefully, he could not play any games again. I dare say I was thought rather a hard disciplinarian at that time, but it was the last indication anyone ever saw of a lack of sportsmanship in Franklin." It was typical of Sara that she told this anecdote with such assurance—confident that her strictness was justified, even with such a young child, and that Franklin's subsequent sportsmanship was thanks to her.

Mother and son frequently read books together. Sara particularly remembered one book they read twice—*The Swiss Family Robinson*. As far as she was concerned, this classic story of a shipwrecked family whose survival depends on the virtue and omniscience of its patriarch offered her son the perfect template for their own family life.

At some point, Franklin grasped both the difference between the fictional Robinson family dynamic and the Roosevelts', and the oppression of the rigid daily schedule that Sara imposed. His mother described in *My Boy Franklin* how she noticed one day at Campobello that his spirits were low.

A little alarmed, I asked him whether he was unhappy. He did not answer all at once, and then said very seriously, "Yes, I am unhappy."

When I asked him why, he was again silent for a moment or two. Then, with a curious little gesture that combined entreaty with a suggestion of impatience, he clasped his hands in front of him and exclaimed, "Oh, for freedom!"

. . . I was honestly shocked. For all he was such a child, his voice had a desperate note that made me realize how seriously he meant it.

That night I talked it over with his father . . . We agreed that unconsciously we had probably regulated the child's life too closely. Evidently he was quite satisfied with what he did with his time but what worried him was the necessity of conforming to given hours.

So the very next morning I told him that he might do whatever he pleased that day. He need obey no former rules nor report at given intervals, and he was allowed to roam at will. We paid no attention to him, and, I must say, he proved his desire for freedom by completely ignoring us. That evening, however, a very dirty, tired youngster came dragging in. He was hungry and ready for bed, but we did not ask him where he had been or what he had been doing. We could only deduce that his adventures had been a little lacking in glamor, for the next day, quite of his own accord, he went contentedly back to his routine.

By now, Franklin had begun to pursue hobbies, including bird-watching and stamp collecting, that let him create his own small worlds. By the end of his life, his philatelic collection would include well over a million stamps, in 150 matching albums. But Sara was close by, sometimes intruding on his privacy. During an afternoon when he was rearranging his stamp collection, she decided to read to him. He seemed so absorbed in his stamps that she reproached him for not listening to her. She recorded with satisfaction that he looked up, then repeated word for word the paragraph that she had just read. But soon he preferred to read to himself, choosing books of naval history.

And how did Mr. James fit into this intense family dynamic? "Franklin never knew what it meant to have the kind of respect for his father that is composed of equal parts of awe and fear,"[37] Sara Roosevelt wrote. Mr. James, or "Popsy," as his son called him, was a much less powerful presence than Warren Delano had been. Instead, he was a careful and sympathetic listener. "His father never laughed at him. With him, yes—often. They were such a gay pair when they went off on long rides together." James Roosevelt taught his son all the outdoor skills he had enjoyed—rowing, sailing, skating, sledding—and groomed him to be a country gentleman like himself, with a serene trust in divine providence and his place in the world.

Occasionally, father and son entered into a conspiracy to sidestep Sara's authority. On the rare occasions when she asked her husband to reprimand Franklin, James would take the boy out of her sight, then say quietly, "Consider yourself spanked."[38]

Had James Roosevelt been a younger, healthier man, that relaxed father-son alliance might have balanced the suffocating mother-son bond. But when Franklin was ten, his sixty-two-year-old father began to complain of back pains and indigestion. His doctors attributed the pains to kidney trouble, and Sara carried on with her usual commitments. On November 1, 1890, the Dutchess County Hunt was scheduled to have its annual breakfast at Springwood. Sara's new English butler, Charles Anderson, had supervised the large buffet laid out on the sideboard in the dining room: oatmeal, baked potatoes, mutton chops, muffins, coffee, and tea. Forty riders pounded up to Springwood's front door, sweaty and elated from the morning's chase. While Roosevelt grooms looked after their horses, Sara greeted her neighbors.[39]

The whole tableau must have looked like something out of a Currier & Ives print—the gracious hostess at the door, the champing horses. No one would have known that anything was wrong. But upstairs, James Roosevelt lay in bed, too ill to greet his guests. He had suffered a mild heart attack and would never regain his full health.

From now on, there was no question that Sara was the most important parent in Franklin's life, and he flourished within her enfolding love. At the same time, Sara enlisted her son's collusion in her determination to preserve Mr. James's well-being. As a child, Franklin fell in with his mother's plans to reduce any source of stress in his father's life. However, as he approached adolescence—a time to separate himself from his parents—he began to build up subtle defenses to keep loved ones at arm's length. A sunny smile and agreeable manner would, he discovered as an adult, be an effective way to hide his thoughts and intentions. Sara would be one of the few people who could sometimes see beyond the facade.

PART 3 · MATERNAL BONDS

CHAPTER 8

Jennie's Dream Crumbles

1880–1886

There was little that was either calm or routine about Jennie Jerome Churchill's years as a young wife and mother. Now that she was back in England, she was captivated by British politics, with its constantly shifting alliances and the brilliant cut and thrust of Westminster debate, and eager to encourage her husband's growing ambition. If she knew there was going to be an important vote in the House of Commons, she would join a handful of other wives in the Speaker's Gallery. "Next to speaking in public oneself, there is nothing which produces such feelings of nervousness and apprehension as to hear one's husband or son doing so."[1]

By now, politics had become a blood sport for Lord Randolph, and he had honed his style. When he rose to speak in the House of Commons, his thumbs hooked into the sleeves of his perfectly cut waistcoat and the ends of his mustache extravagantly curled, his fellow Conservatives crowded the opposition benches to hear his vicious jabs and caustic wit. His party needed this jolt of adrenaline; it had been demoralized by electoral defeat and the loss of its charismatic leader, Benjamin Disraeli. Even though Lord Randolph was a mere opposition backbencher, the *Times* printed his speeches verbatim.

Most of these speeches skewered Liberal prime minister Gladstone's resolve to allow the Irish to have their own parliament. Randolph was a classic Victorian imperialist, as his son would be. But he was also a maverick within Tory circles, keen to bait the leaders of the Conservative Party on their inadequate response to Irish famines and their aristocratic disdain for demands for electoral reform.

Jennie admired her husband's outspokenness. There was no way that she could have a political career herself: women didn't have the right to vote or run for public office. Only men could be center stage. The only woman who might be seen wielding power was Queen Victoria herself. So Jennie sublimated her own hunger for public recognition (which had partly inspired her childhood ambition to be a professional pianist) into support for her husband. She set out to enhance his career in as many backstage ways as possible.

II

One way that Jennie knew she could have an impact was through useful social connections. "Our house became the rendezvous of all shades of politicians . . . Randolph's growing prominence in the political world was attracting considerable attention in the social, and we were bombarded with invitations of every kind."[2] Soon her drawing room had morphed into an adroitly choreographed salon where artists and editors mingled with senior politicians of all parties.

A guest might find himself seated next to one of Randolph's political opponents, and it might be an establishment figure like the Liberal prime minister himself, or a "dangerous radical" such as Sir Charles Dilke or Joseph Chamberlain, who were both pushing to widen the franchise. Jennie, witty and well informed, played to her guests' egos while keeping a watchful eye on her mercurial husband. The excellence of her dinners (interesting French entrées rather than boarding school starch) and the hostess's lively conversation, along with murmured male intrigues over port and cigars, made Churchill invitations highly prized.

One of the first signs of Randolph's growing political ambition was the "Fourth Party," a subversive little cadre he founded within Conservative ranks that lobbied for "Tory democracy." He wanted to challenge the Liberal Party's claim to be the champion of the masses, and he was hell-bent on bringing down Gladstone's government. Jennie adored the intrigue, especially when her husband and his allies, the portly Sir Henry Drummond Wolff, the monocled John Gorst, and (occasionally) the patrician Arthur Balfour, a future prime minister, assembled at her dining table. The St. James's Place house became "a hornets' nest," Jennie would recall. "Many were the plots and plans that were hatched in my presence by the Fourth Party, who, notwithstanding the seriousness of their endeavours, found time to laugh heartily and often at their own frustrated machinations."[3]

In one parliamentary session, the Fourth Party was particularly mischievous. A fellow Tory reproached its members for being obstructive in the chamber. During four months, Gorst had spoken one hundred five times and asked eighteen questions; Sir Henry Wolff had spoken sixty-eight times and asked thirty-four questions; Lord Randolph Churchill had delivered seventy-four speeches and asked twenty-one questions.[4]

Jennie was a keen observer. Later in life she would write a light-hearted political comedy in which the wife of a prominent politician tells her husband's colleague, "If it were not for women like Corisande and myself, who supply the frivolous element in your lives, you politicians would become unendurable."[5] But the frivolity was a facade. She made things happen. Her encouragement and support had helped Randolph acquire the supreme self-confidence that made him such a powerful orator. Equally significant were her personal magnetism and piano skills, which reinforced the group's glue. She shared musical tastes with Sir Henry Wolff and Arthur Balfour; they attended concerts together as a threesome. Arthur Balfour, who was the nephew of Lord Salisbury, Conservative leader after 1881, might not have been such a regular visitor to St. James's Place if he hadn't so enjoyed playing Schumann duets with his hostess.

Lord Randolph was in demand as a speaker all over the country, and Jennie eagerly accompanied him. She charmed the local organizers, soaked up local gossip, attended prize-givings, visited schools and factories. Her soft New York accent intrigued working-class

118   Passionate Mothers, Powerful Sons

voters who might have bristled at too aristocratic a drawl. She still deferred to her husband's needs, and her focus was his issues rather than the causes championed by activist women of the day—child welfare, education for women, and female suffrage. Soon, Lord Randolph Churchill had a national reputation and was being mentioned as a potential Conservative leader. The former Tory leader Disraeli, who now sat in the House of Lords as Lord Beaconsfield, told a friend that when the Conservatives replaced the Liberals in government, the Conservatives "will have to give him anything he chooses to ask for, and in a very short time they will have to take anything he chooses to give them."[6]

In *Reminiscences*, Jennie makes it clear that she was particularly proud of the role she played in election campaigns, often during her husband's absences. "Revelling in the hustle and bustle of the committee-rooms, marshaling our forces, and hearing the hourly reports of how the campaign was progressing, I felt like a general holding a council-of-war with his staff in the heat of a battle."[7]

As a leading political hostess, Jennie was a celebrity. This was the era of "Professional Beauties"—stylish society women whose photographs were exhibited in the windows of Fleet Street. In her memoirs, Jennie downplayed the hype: "Privacy seems a luxury no one is allowed to indulge in."[8] But as an extrovert who relished fashion, she was one of the most popular "P.B.s," as the celebrities were nicknamed. Mass-circulation photographs of her dramatic good looks— the diamond star in her thick dark hair, sultry eyes peeping through thick lashes—were sold in tobacconists for a few shillings. Artists vied to sketch her, along with P.B. rivals such as the actor Lillie Langtry and several languid duchesses, many of whom were, like Langtry, mistresses of the Prince of Wales.

P.B. status guaranteed Jennie glamorous dinner invitations plus advantageous terms at milliners or couturiers who were eager to advertise their wares. Invitations poured into the Churchills' town house: in the first seven months of 1882, Jennie's diary is filled with engagements as well as painting sessions and piano practice. As

Churchill biographer Andrew Roberts calculated, "She shopped eleven times, painted twenty-five times, had lunch or tea with her friend Lady Blanche Hozier twenty-six times and had tea with Conservative MP Arthur Balfour ten times . . . she hunted, spent weekends in house parties in the country . . . played the piano, dined at the Café Royal, played billiards . . ."[9] Roberts dismissed such activities as evidence of Jennie's "socially accomplished if somewhat vacuous life," with little acknowledgment that the gregarious young wife of a Victorian aristocrat and politician had few alternatives, or that Jennie was building up a network of powerful friends.

Weekdays in London were a great deal more congenial than the weekends that she and Randolph spent with her in-laws. A letter to her mother during a long stay in Blenheim Palace in the winter of 1881 reflects the frustration of a warm extrovert within a frosty family.

> I quite forget what it is like to be with people who love me. I do
> so long to have someone to whom I could go and talk. Of course,
> Randolph is awfully good to me and always takes my part in
> everything, but how can I always be abusing his mother to him,
> when she is devoted to him and would do anything for him . . .
> The fact is I loathe living here. It is not on account of its dull-
> ness, that I don't mind, but it is the gall and wormwood to me
> to accept anything or to be living [off] anyone I hate. It is no
> use disguising it, the Duchess hates me simply for what I am –
> perhaps a little prettier and more attractive than her daughters.
> Everything I do or say or wear is found fault with. We are always
> scrupulously polite to each other, but it is rather like a volcano,
> ready to burst out at any moment.[10]

However, Jennie's and Randolph's two sons spent extended periods of their childhoods with their grandparents at Blenheim Palace, in the care of the devoted Mrs. Everest. Mrs. Everest also took the two little boys to visit her family in the Isle of Wight village of Ventnor. One of the earliest surviving letters from Winston to his mother was written from there. "My dear Mamma," wrote the six-year-old. "I am so glad you are coming to see us. I had such a nice bathe in the sea to day. Love to papa, your loving son, Winston."[11]

Randolph ignored his sons, but Jennie loved the two boys; she cuddled them when they were babies and read to them when they were toddlers. She would take Winston to the Horse Guards Parade in nearby St. James's Park to watch the soldiers. When they were all under the same roof, she might spend an hour or two with them before bedtime, before handing them back to Mrs. Everest. Jack was always an easygoing child, but Winston, red-haired and boisterous, was a handful. She reported to her mother that he was "a very nice boy . . . [but] a most difficult child to manage."[12] On one of Mrs. Everest's rare nights off, Winston insisted that his mother should play endless games of Pirates and Indians with him. It was intoxicating for him to spend energetic hours with the "fairy princess," and he repeatedly begged for just one more game. For Jennie, who was incapable of saying no, the evening was exhausting. She was happy to follow British aristocratic custom and leave child-rearing to a professional nanny. It allowed her to focus her energies on her husband's career and stay on top of salon chatter and political plotting in London.

In early 1882, the family moved into a new house on Connaught Place, less fashionable but larger than the Mayfair residence, which Jennie filled with beautiful antiques purchased in Ireland. Her first exciting dinner party there was thrilling. With a spendthrift's glee and an American embrace of the new, she had installed a dynamo in the basement, so that this was "the first private house in London to have electric lighting," she claimed.[13] The blazing white light was a sensation, and so was the total darkness into which her dinner guests were plunged when the dynamo overheated.

III

Randolph's dizzying rise was always fragile, periodically interrupted by savage bouts of ill-health. Debilitating headaches, aching joints, exhaustion, and mood swings dogged him. He was out of action for much of 1882, too sick to go to the House of Commons. Leonie Je-rome had arrived in London, hoping her popular sister would take her to smart parties, but found a disagreeable Lord Randolph fulminating on a sofa and a fretful Jennie dealing with a mountain of bills. The Churchills still had no income other than their marital settlements, which were far outstripped by their spending. Neither partner was capable of reining in the extravagance. Lord Randolph continued to travel and gamble; the price tag on one of Jennie's gowns was more than a teacher's annual income. Regular explosions about each other's debts, alongside Randolph's health issues, ate away at their relation-ship.

Once the 1882 bout of ill-health passed, Randolph launched him-self in a new direction: promoting the Conservative Party to Britain's rapidly growing working classes. He and his Fourth Party allies had come up with the idea of a new kind of political club, which would be called the Primrose League. (Primroses were the favorite flower of their former leader, Lord Beaconsfield.) Rather like a service club, the league appealed to "all classes and all creeds except atheists and enemies of the British Empire." It developed an elaborate structure of local branches (called Habitations), ceremonies, grand titles, and membership diplomas, and the Duchess of Marlborough was made president of the Ladies' Grand Council.

For Jennie, the Primrose League offered an opportunity to partici-pate in a national campaign. "For many years I worked strenuously on behalf of the league," she later wrote. "I became the 'Dame President' of many Habitations, and used to go all over the country inaugurating them . . . A strange medley, the labourer and the local magnate, the county lady and the grocer's wife, would troop up and sign the roll."[14] She honed her own speaking skills as she addressed cheering crowds about the need to defeat Gladstone's Liberals (and further her own husband's career in the process). The Primrose League, which put Lord Randolph Churchill as well as the Conservative Party in the news, grew rapidly. By 1891 it had over a million members and would prove to be a formidable canvassing machine.

Lord Randolph took further initiatives to cement his appeal beyond the Conservative Party's traditional squirearchy supporters. He campaigned for "Tory democracy," a creed that sought through paternalism and established institutions, rather than by radical change, to improve the lot of the growing and increasingly militant working class. Old-fashioned Tories—the landowning elite who still took for granted their right to run the country—thought Tory democracy was an oxymoron and Randolph Churchill a nuisance. But they didn't object when he went on the attack against Joseph Chamberlain, the self-made Birmingham businessman and leading Liberal, who condemned hereditary power, and demanded that power and wealth should be shared more widely. Chamberlain repeatedly pointed out that in America and France, one in four men had the vote, and in Germany one in five, but in Britain only one in eleven.[15]

In 1885, another opportunity arose for Jennie to use her by now formidable campaigning skills. The Liberal government fell, and Randolph once again ran in the constituency of Woodstock. But he was scarcely there. Instead, his wife and his sister Lady Georgiana careered through the Oxfordshire villages in a dashing horse-drawn tandem. With her enormous hats and thoughtful questions about farm life, Jennie captivated voters, and her candidate won by 532 votes to 405. Randolph was not present to celebrate his victory; instead, he sent his wife a grateful telegram: "Brilliant success almost entirely due to you and Georgie." Despite her indifference to women's emancipation, she reveled in the vicarious thrill of victory. "I surpassed the fondest hopes of the Suffragettes, and thought I was duly elected, and I certainly experienced all the pleasure and gratification of being a successful candidate." She later told the crowd at a Primrose League event that she had no doubt that ladies could have great influence in politics if only they chose to exert it.[16]

The Conservative Party scraped to electoral success, but without a clear majority in the House of Commons. The next few months were a political roundabout dominated by the politics of Irish Home Rule. Randolph Churchill finally achieved front bench status, as secretary of state for India, and Jennie immediately set about learning everything she could about the country.[17] But the Conservative government was short-lived, and soon Randolph was back on the hustings, focusing his energy and fierce rhetoric on the election scheduled for the following year. Surprisingly, the recently enfranchised working classes embraced this sporting aristocrat who championed Tory democracy without ever defining it, and Lord Randolph became the campaign's star. Lord Salisbury, the Conservative prime minister, confided to Queen Victoria that he couldn't keep Randolph away from a senior cabinet post after such an effort. The Queen was unimpressed: "He is so mad and odd and has also bad health."[18]

All Jennie's hopes were realized in the 1886 general election, when the Conservatives won a majority. The prime minister invited Lord Randolph Churchill to become chancellor of the exchequer and leader of the House of Commons, which brought the Churchills a much-needed annual income of £5,000. (The modern equivalent of this sum is £500,000. Today's chancellor is paid about half this amount.) These were the two most senior cabinet positions, after the prime ministership. Jennie heard the gossip: her husband could be a future leader of his party.

Yet Jennie's joy at Randolph's success was dampened by the deterioration in their marriage. Randolph ricocheted from being charming and lively one day to abusive the next. When he was with Jennie, he often treated her with appalling rudeness, and his contemporaries noted that he spent more and more time at his club and seemed happy to be away from his wife.[19] Women in particular found the rising political star not to their taste. The prolific diarist Lady Paget, wife of the British ambassador to Austria, noted that "the worn, middle-aged man with the heavy tawny mustache hardly recalled to me the smooth-faced, dark-haired stripling I remembered. Only the rolling eyes, set in orbits like saucers, and the turned-up nose remained." She found his manner disagreeable. "The shyness and the silence was gone. But the insistence and at times impertinence of manner were still there."[20]

IV

Jennie rarely let her pressing debts and her husband's erratic behavior depress her, and she continued to be widely popular with her fellow Professional Beauties as well as her husband's colleagues. According to one contemporary, "One never thought of giving a party without her. She was as delightful to women as to men . . . Lady Randolph was like a marvelous diamond—a host of facets seemed to sparkle at once."[21] The passing years had only enhanced her sensuous appeal: in a sparkling evening gown, her creamy-white shoulders, tightly cinched waist, and luscious décolletage continued to draw men's eyes, while her carefully polished wit and warmth ensured a crowd of admirers.

With the Churchills as *the* power couple within the London elites, the Prince of Wales deigned to rekindle his friendship with them after a decade of froideur. Jennie was now welcome at social events to which the heir to the throne was invited. As she wrote in her memoir, "The fashionable world, which had held aloof, now began to smile upon us once more."[22] Bertie remembered how much he had enjoyed Jennie's repartee. Soon Jennie, occasionally accompanied by her husband, was a regular guest at the prince's newly renovated Norfolk country house, Sandringham.

The seal of royal acceptance came in November 1885 with a summons from Queen Victoria to Windsor Castle to receive the badge of the Imperial Order of the Crown of India. Attired in "bonnet and morning dress; grey gloves,"[23] as instructed by a lady-in-waiting, Jennie took the train from Paddington Station to Windsor, where she was picked up by a royal carriage. At the castle, a footman ushered her down lengthy, drafty corridors and into the presence of a dumpy figure shrouded in a long white veil. Jennie sank into a deep curtsy; the sixty-four-year-old widow said a few inaudible words.

Jennie loved every minute of the ceremony, and even managed to suppress a cry of pain when the queen stuck the pin holding the pearl and turquoise decoration straight into her shoulder, through the thick jet embroidery of her black velvet dress. She treasured the note she received the following day from the lady-in-waiting, which included the sentence: "The Queen told me she thought you so handsome."[24] The royal recognition was important for Jennie; it signaled her respectability.

However, friendship between Victoria's dissolute son and a beautiful woman was always complicated. It was widely assumed that Jennie Churchill, for whom the prince had always had a soft spot, was one of his numerous sexual conquests. The prince liked to drop into the Churchills' house for lunch when Randolph was out of town, and he was a regular dinner guest. (Jennie was not the only attraction. Her cook Rosa Ovenden usually prepared one of the prince's favorite dishes: plain boiled truffles "served like little ebony apples on a silver dish wrapped around with a white linen napkin.")[25] Ralph Martin, one of Jennie's first biographers, implied in the first volume of *Jennie: The Life of Lady Randolph Churchill* (published in the U.S. in 1969) that the relationship was sexual. He wrote that Prince Edward often gave her expensive jewelry, and "It was well known that he seldom gave such gifts to a woman with whom he was not having an affair."[26]

Martin's biography irritated the Churchill family. In the same year that it was published, Jennie's great-niece Anita Leslie would explore the relationship further in her book, which had the same title as Ralph Martin's. She compared correspondence between the prince and Jennie with the prince's letters to "Darling Daisy," the ravishing Countess of Warwick, who was firmly ensconced as Edward's principal mistress. Leslie argued that Jennie adroitly established herself as "the Prince's buddy rather than his lady love . . . His Royal Highness certainly loved Jennie's company by day (and may have sought it at night) but the hundred-odd [surviving] notes which he wrote to her give no inkling of the ultimate relationship." The friendship between them lasted until Edward's death in 1910.

As the Churchill marriage crumbled, Jennie looked elsewhere for the emotional and sexual fulfillment for which she yearned, and which would distract her from Randolph's bad temper. There were several rumored lovers in addition to the heir to the throne, but her most significant relationship began around 1883, as her thirtieth birthday approached. The object of her passion was Count Charles Kinsky, an Austrian diplomat who shared her equestrian skills, love of music, and zest for life. Slender, debonair, and the heir to the Kinsky Palace in Vienna, he was also a welcome contrast to Randolph because he was kind, wealthy, and adored Jennie. Every hostess in London wanted him at her dinner table, but nobody wanted him more than Lady Randolph Churchill.

Kinsky's diplomatic duties required him to travel extensively, but even when transferred to Paris, then Brussels, he kept a string of hunters at a stable in Leicestershire, and a flat in London with an English butler. This allowed plenty of opportunities for assignations at home and abroad for the two lovers. Within Jennie's circles, her romance with the suave Austrian was an open secret, but she never flaunted it. She was a married woman, and her husband was a leading political figure in the British Isles; they kept up appearances.

Randolph also enjoyed Kinsky's company and does not appear to have resented his friendship with Jennie. But the Churchill marriage was soon in serious trouble. At one point Jennie was convinced that Randolph was involved with another woman, and she had heard whispers that he had male lovers.[27] Her mother and sisters were out of reach, so she confided her misery to her mother-in-law. Her letters have not survived, but the duchess's replies have. At first, she was sympathetic: "Oh dear Jennie you are going through a great *crise* in your life & on yourself will depend whether your hold & influence becomes greater than ever or not . . . I know in his Heart he is truly fond of you."[28] But soon her tone changed. "If you wish to regain your influence over him & make him fonder of you, you *must* sacrifice yourself and lead a different life . . . Oh dearest Jennie before it is too late I do pray you to . . . give up that fast lot you live with racing flirting and gossiping."[29]

Jennie's sisters, who often stayed at Connaught Place, watched Lord Randolph's periodic rudeness and cruelty to his wife, and knew

he was frequently absent. Throughout Jennie's life, her greatest con-
fidantes would always be her sisters, who divided their time between
her house and their mother in Paris. Clara and Leonie both hoped that
their glamorous, in-demand sister would secure suitors for them, but
by now resentment had built against the surge of American beauties
into London social life. One day Leonie met Sir William Gordon-
Cumming, a supercilious bachelor, while walking in Hyde Park and
he sneered at her, "Over here husband-hunting?"[30] Despite their
mother's hopes of a wealthy suitor for each of them, all three Jeromes
married for love, then struggled to stay afloat financially.

In June 1881, Clara, now twenty-eight, insisted on marrying a
good-looking, penniless Englishman named Moreton Frewen, whose
skill at persuading people to invest in various doomed enterprises
would earn him the nickname "Mortal Ruin." Clara Frewen embarked
on a lifetime of scrambling to keep ahead of her household expenses
and husband's debts. Leonie, the youngest Jerome sister, began her
married life in equally tough circumstances. Four years after Clara's
marriage, twenty-five-year-old Leonie married Jack Leslie, an Anglo-
Irish Grenadier Guardsman. Jack's mother and father, who owned
considerable estates and a crumbling castle in Ireland, were appalled
that their only son was marrying the daughter of an American speculator and sister of the well-known socialite Lady Jennie Churchill.
Eventually, Sir John and Lady Leslie would come around to Leonie,
but at the time of the wedding, Sir John had threatened to cut Jack
off and told him that he and his new wife were not welcome at the
Leslies' London mansion.

The three sisters turned to each other for support and companionship whenever they needed it, scraping together a few pounds when
one or the other was fending off debt collectors. Appeals to Leonard
Jerome from his daughters for financial help were constant.

V

During these years of intense political activity and passionate love affairs, Randolph continued to ignore his children, but Jennie kept her

eye on her sons' upbringing. However, she left much of the responsibility to Mrs. Everest. To the despair of a string of governesses, Jennie's elder son had already learned to attract attention and get his own
way by misbehaving. As an adult, he would enjoy recalling how he
had hidden from his first governess, and subsequently found master-
ing elementary mathematics cast "a steadily gathering shadow over
my daily life. They took one away from all the interesting things one
wanted to do."[31] He far preferred to spend his time with his miniature
steam engine, magic lantern, and nearly a thousand toy soldiers. Only
Mrs. Everest could control him.

When Winston turned eight, he had reached the age when
upper-class British children were sent away to boarding schools.
Like many other members of the peerage, Lord and Lady Randolph
Churchill elected to send him to an expensive preparatory school
with an impressive reputation. Unfortunately, the school they chose
was St. George's School at Ascot, which was run by an insensitive
headmaster who was particularly sadistic toward unruly students
like Winston Churchill.

The most influential version of Winston's childhood story has
come from Winston himself. His entertaining and breezy *My Early
Life* is a vivid account of a brave, vulnerable little boy who survived a
wretched childhood to become an important statesman. The tone of
the memoir is a mix of pathos and irony.

It fell to Jennie to take her son to Ascot. "The fateful day arrived,"
Winston would write. "My mother took me to the station in a hansom
cab. She gave me three half-crowns, which I dropped onto the floor
of the cab, and we had to scramble around in the straw to find them
again. We only just caught the train. If we had missed it, it would
have been the end of the world. However we didn't, and the world
went on." Winston pulled no punches about his experiences. "How
I hated this school, and what a life of anxiety I lived there for more
than two years." The headmaster regularly administered "cruel floggings . . . on the little boys who were in his care and power." When
Winston was caught taking sugar from the pantry he received one

of those floggings, which he later wrote "exceeded in severity any-thing that would be tolerated in any of the Reformatories under the Home Office." His unhappiness, combined with his habitual defi-ance, earned him a school report in March 1884 that described his general conduct as "very bad—is a constant trouble to everybody and is always in some scrape or another. He cannot be trusted to behave himself anywhere."[32]

Surviving letters from Winston to his mother reveal nothing of the torments. Instead, they are the formulaic missives encouraged by such schools. "My dear mamma," he wrote a month after his arrival. "I hope you are quite well. I am very happy at school. You will be glad to hear I spent a very happy birthday. I must now thank you for your lovely presents you sent me. Do not forget to come down on 9th December. With love and kisses I remain your loveing [sic] son, Winston kisses xxxxx."[33]

Perhaps she can be forgiven for taking at face value these letters, written under the close supervision of school staff. Perhaps Randolph's mood swings and ill-health were all that Jennie could handle. Perhaps there were simply too many demands on her time in London—dinner parties, debates in the House of Commons, Primrose League meet-ings, assignations with Count Kinsky. However, she does seem to have ignored Winton's more direct appeals. "It is very unkind of you not to write to me before this," he wrote. "I have had only one letter from you this term."[34]

Mrs. Everest knew something was wrong. On Winston's visits home, she took note of the vivid scars from the floggings, and re-marked on his decline in health, his constant infections, and his general dejection. She finally persuaded Jennie to remove him from the school. Years later, Winston would tell his cousin Anita Leslie, "If my mother hadn't listened to Mrs. Everest and taken me away I would have bro-ken down completely. Can you imagine a child being *broken down?*"[35]

The Churchills then packed Winston off to a far less prestigious school in Brighton that had been recommended by their doctor, Robson Roose. The eleven-year-old was happier there, enjoying "an

element of kindness and of sympathy which I had found conspicuously lacking in my first experiences."[36] Instead of the Latin that had
stumped him at St. George's, he learned "things that interested me:
French, History, lots of Poetry by heart and above all Riding and
Swimming."[37] Those of his letters home that have survived are filled
with spontaneous affection. "My dear Mama" or "My dear darling
Mummy" are the standard openings to the scrawled epistles, and they
end with such phrases as "With love and kisses I remain your loving
son." He often signed them "Winny." Cheerful accounts of his activities are interspersed with requests for visits and money.

Lord Randolph frequently promised and almost always failed to
visit his son. But Winston followed his father's political career avidly,
and wrote to him: "Every body wants to get your signature will you
send me a few to give away?" Winston realized that Jennie also had
star power, and wrote: "[Papa] sent me half a dozen autographs I
have been busy distributing them today everybody wanted one, but
I should like you to send me a few of yours too."[38] Selling his parents' autographs to school friends was one of Winston's few sources
of pocket money.[39]

Early in 1886, Winston had managed to capture both his parents'
attention when he fell dangerously ill with pneumonia. Jennie and
Randolph rushed down to Brighton (this was Randolph's first visit to
the school), where their son was struggling for life. They brought him
back to London for a month of convalescence under Mrs. Everest's
care, and the Duchess of Marlborough sent Jennie a note of sympathy. "I am so thankful for God's goodness for preserving your dear
child . . . Poor, dear Winnie, and I hope it will leave no troublesome
after-effects, but even if it leaves him delicate for a long time to come,
you will make the more of him after being given back to you on the
very threshold of the unknown . . ."[40]

VI

In 1886, Jennie's dreams about her husband's brilliant future, to
which her campaigning and networking had contributed so much,

came to a crashing end. Once again, Lord Randolph Churchill allowed his impulsive arrogance to distort his political judgment. Ten years earlier, in the Aylesford affair, he had provoked the wrath of the Prince of Wales. This had led to the Churchills' humiliating fall from social grace and exile to Ireland. Now, after only six months in office and with party leadership within his reach, Randolph again overplayed his hand.

Lord Randolph had never allowed party discipline to cramp his defiant style, and although he was now number two in his party, he showed little interest in being a team player. He was becoming manic, erratic, and often disagreeable, too impatient to study lengthy budgetary files or be civil to colleagues. His success as the champion of Tory democracy—a shrewd appeal to the newly enfranchised urban voters—had persuaded him that, as chancellor of the exchequer, he should slash the budgets of the Admiralty and the War Office. He wanted, according to his nephew, a budget that would "be felt by the Classes and appreciated by the Masses."[41] This flew in the face of Conservative Party orthodoxy that a well-funded navy and army were essential for the defense of the British Empire. From the House of Lords, Prime Minister Lord Salisbury remarked that he felt as though he was "leading an orchestra in which the first fiddle plays one tune and everyone else including myself wishes to play another."[42]

The crunch came in mid-December. Confident in his national popularity, and assuming that Lord Salisbury would not dare to lose him from cabinet, Randolph sent the prime minister a letter offering his resignation.

Why did Lord Randolph take this gamble? It was a blatant power play: he calculated that with this tactic he might get his way with the budget. (There is no evidence that he particularly cared about the cuts he demanded; he just wanted to flex his muscles.) He may have felt his health failing again, or he may simply have been tired of fighting with colleagues who found him insufferable.

But he had miscalculated. Cool and sure-footed, the prime minister accepted his offer with no suggestion that there was anything more to say. He would later observe, "Did you ever hear of a man who, having got rid of a boil on the back of his neck, ever wants it back again?"[43] The cuts were not made.

It was a dreadful shock to Jennie. Randolph and she had grown so far apart that he hadn't bothered to discuss his decision with her, although it would have a dramatic impact on their lives. When the letter of resignation was already in the prime minister's hands, she was planning a lavish reception at the Foreign Office. The evening before the news broke, she and Randolph had gone to the theater to see Sheridan's *The School for Scandal*. While there, she asked her husband about the guest list; he shrugged her off with the comment "Oh! I shouldn't worry about it if I were you; it [the reception] probably will never take place."[44] Randolph left the theater after the first act and delivered a copy of his resignation letter to the *Times*, hoping to provoke an editorial supporting him. The editor refused, but news of the resignation was in the paper the following morning.

"When I came down to breakfast," Jennie recalled in her memoir, "the fatal paper in my hand, I found him calm and smiling. 'Quite a surprise for you,' he said. He went into no explanation, and I felt too utterly crushed and miserable to ask for any, or even to remonstrate." As a shocked Jennie sat at the breakfast table, speechlessly staring at the newspaper, a pale, anxious man was shown into the room, clutching the newspaper. This was the permanent undersecretary at the Treasury, appalled by developments. Randolph had likely already shut himself into his private study, so the undersecretary poured out his anguish to Jennie. She described how "with a faltering voice [he] said to me, 'He has thrown himself from the top of the ladder, and will never reach it again!'"

Jennie would learn the truth of this prophecy. "If he had but known it," she wrote, he had "signed his political death warrant."[45] He had also killed her dream of being the woman at his side while he, as prime minister, ran the vast British Empire. "When I looked back at the few preceding months, which seemed so triumphant and full of promise, the *debacle* appeared all the greater."[46]

The incessant drama was not yet over. Within days, rumors were flying that the Churchills were heading for a divorce. Count Kinsky was hurriedly recalled to Vienna. In early January, Jennie received a letter from Arthur Brisbane, London correspondent of the *New York Sun*, asking for confirmation of her pending separation from Lord Randolph. "Unwilling to publish so grave a statement without [verification]," he had already called twice at Connaught Place and also tried to contact Leonard Jerome, but no one would speak to him. The Churchills were barely speaking to each other—Jennie wrote wretched letters to her sisters from her Connaught Place sitting room, while Randolph lay moodily on his study couch, chain-smoking and nursing his grievances. However, Jennie bridged the silence by handing the letter over to her husband. Randolph wrote Brisbane a blistering reply, but the speculation continued.[47]

In February, Lord Randolph took off for an Italian adventure with a male friend for two months, leaving his wife to face his critics and manage their domestic affairs without the ministerial income they had both depended on.

The Churchill marriage did not fall apart. Both partners knew that divorce would trigger a scandal that would kill Lord Randolph's hopes of political rehabilitation and turn Jennie's affair into salacious public gossip. Besides, Jennie did not want to lose her husband; even though he rarely showed her much affection, she had been raised to view divorce as unacceptable. She continued to offer Randolph comfort and tenderness. He would draw on those reserves ever more greedily in the next decade.

The first twelve years of Jennie Jerome Churchill's marriage had been stormy and stressful, as she steered her way through British society, royal favor and disfavor, constant financial challenges, and the delicate management of extramarital affairs. Always high-spirited, she undoubtedly enjoyed herself, but letters to her sisters and mother-in-law reveal that beneath her gorgeous, glittering exterior was often anguish.

Jennie's political acumen has rarely been recognized, but, while

Randolph's absentee behavior as a father has seldom drawn reproach, his wife has been criticized for neglecting their sons when they were young. However, even though she was not responsible for their day-to-day care, they were never far from her mind, and she was certainly concerned for their future. When a representative from Parliament came to collect the official robes Randolph had worn as chancellor of the exchequer, she refused to surrender them. "I am saving them for my son," she announced.[48]

Perhaps unconsciously, she assumed that, if she could not be the wife of a political star, she could be the mother of one. She certainly didn't want to think of a future where she would not be engaged with politics. Unlike Sara Roosevelt, she thought a man who entered politics was embarking on a glorious career. As a woman, she was excluded from that world. But she had already tasted the delicious excitement of helping to promote such a career.

CHAPTER 9

Churchills: Love and Death
1887–1895

F ew people feel the humiliation of an individual's ruin more than their partner, and this was particularly true for women in an age when a wife's status was defined by her husband's reputation. Because Sara Roosevelt lived her life so carefully within the guardrails of conventional behavior, she would never know such mortification, but for Jennie, who had always lived on the edge, Lord Randolph's political crash was painful.

Jennie's first concern was to put on a good show. While her husband disappeared on a lengthy trip to Italy, she was left to face alone gossip-addicted Mayfair and her own dashed hopes. "How well I remember my bitter feelings in those days!" she would write later, as former allies defected and rivals gloated. "How dark those days seemed! In vain I tried to console myself with the thought that happiness does not depend so much on circumstances as on one's inner self. But I have always found in practice that theories are of little comfort. The vicissitudes of life resemble one of those gilded balls seen in a fountain. Thrown up by the force of the water, it flies up and down—now at the top, catching the rays of the sun, now cast into the depths, then shooting up again . . ."[1]

Only her sisters heard about her unhappiness; in public Lady Randolph glided serenely through ballrooms in satin and long white gloves, a Professional Beauty to her fingertips. Although that eighteen-inch waist was a distant memory, in many eyes she became more beautiful as she moved into her mid-thirties, with deeper dimples in her cheeks and an even more voluptuous body. She was a welcome guest at Sandringham shooting parties, where the Princess of Wales might invite her to play duets in the evening, or to slip into her room after dinner "to offer her sympathy if she thought you needed any."[2] Danish-born Princess Alexandra had much in common with Jennie, including a passion for fashion, hunting, and ice-skating. Neither woman had been born into the viciously snobbish British aristocracy, which strengthened their bond. The princess evidently felt that Jennie, quick-witted and warm, was a "safe" companion for her philandering husband.

Extended visits to friends allowed Jennie to save money and keep out of her mother-in-law's way. She traveled from one country house to another, applauding in the most gratifying way the men's hunting skills. ("I remember . . . seeing Lord de Grey shoot in one stand fifty-two birds out of fifty-four, and for a bet this was done with one hand.")[3] She continued to give lively dinner parties on Connaught Place, where Rosa Ovenden, her cook, always knew which butcher had fresh game and which guest was allergic to shellfish. Laura Lady Troubridge, author of a definitive guide to etiquette, recalled how, after dinner, Jennie could often be persuaded to play the piano. But instead of Schubert Lieder, she might surprise her audience with an African American folk song such as "Razors a-flying in the air." Recalled the admiring Lady Troubridge, "The white dress, the Castilian darkness of her colouring, the dim background, all made up a vision to me."[4]

Head held high, Lady Jennie Churchill refused to crumple under the social ignominy of her husband's flameout. And her sense of mischief was irresistible. Queen Victoria celebrated her golden jubilee—fifty years on the throne—in 1887, and "everything that year was dubbed 'Jubilee,'" according to Jennie. One evening, she told her guests that she had acquired a "Jubilee bustle" that played "God Save the Queen" when she sat down. She then installed a young servant with a music box under a chair, so that when she solemnly lowered herself onto the chair the national anthem tinkled forth. "Every time I rose, it stopped; every time I sat, it began again. I still laugh when I think of it and of the astonished faces about me." Her friends adored the musical bustle—especially the Prince of Wales, who spent much of the year enduring long-winded tributes to his mother during the official celebrations.

Admirers swarmed around her, and there was always tittle-tattle. Columnists noted that she was often seen with men other than her husband, including, but not exclusively, Count Kinsky. She was sighted in Dublin at a party given by the viceroy. According to *Town Topics*, she danced the cancan. "She suddenly touched the mantelpiece with her foot, making a dreadful exposé," the magazine reported. "This is only one of her many freaks which have caused much scandal."[5] Snide comments like this on both sides of the Atlantic dogged her.

Misogyny was rampant: a man who had many affairs was regarded as more of a man; a woman claiming similar freedom was regarded as immoral. Toward the end of her life, the Irish novelist George Moore asserted that Jennie Jerome Churchill had slept with two hundred men.[6] The assertion has been endlessly repeated, although it is an absurd claim by a man whom she had likely spurned. She led an active romantic life, but she was discreet and fastidious. When Sir Charles Dilke, a radical politician and well-known womanizer, attempted to seduce her by kneeling before her, she remarked, "I never saw anything so ridiculous in my life."[7] She never boasted about her affairs or divulged secrets, so she was the only one who knew the figure. Somehow, she survived the gossip, partly because she was well liked by women as well as men. Her laughter, wit, and bravura piano playing added buzz to social occasions.

In biographer Ralph Martin's words, "She had as many friends as her husband had enemies; London society was full of people who would say: hate him, love her."[8] But Jennie wanted more from life than social success. Still deeply tied to her husband, she hoped for a turnaround in her husband's political career that would allow them both to resume their political activities. Instead, she faced what was probably the worst period of her life. She had all the constraints of being a wife, with none of the benefits. Sara Roosevelt was less ambitious than Jennie, and her world was much smaller than Jennie's, but Sara had the satisfaction of a firm grip on her environment. Jennie's position was more precarious.

II

On his return to London from Italy, Lord Randolph was in better health and began to plot a political comeback. "What a fool Lord S. was to let me go so lightly," he told Jennie.[9] Only months earlier his prospects had seemed so glittering, and when he strolled back into the House of Commons, once again his fellow MPs crowded onto the benches, eagerly anticipating his verbal firecrackers. He still didn't disappoint. But he made little effort to cultivate allies, and, except for a few old friends, his party had written him off.

So he turned to another pursuit—racing—that the Churchills could ill afford. Jennie and he moved into a handsome old house, Banstead Manor, that Randolph's mother had rented close to the famous Newmarket Racecourse, and found tenants for their Connaught Place house in order to raise some money. Jennie embraced the chance to be back on horseback, regardless of the expense.[10] "We would ride out in the early morning from six to seven to see the horses do their gallops. It was a most healthy and invigorating life."[11] Their shared delight in horses bound the Churchills together.

In late 1887, they embarked on a six-week pleasure trip to Russia and Germany, where they delighted in being treated, as she wrote to her mother, "like royalty."[12] Jennie captivated the Russian elite with her exquisite gowns and her figure-skating skills. Years later, Anita Leslie met elderly Russian princes who had survived the Russian Revolution and still recalled "Dark Jennie . . . no other woman could so deliberately impose her beauty. When she entered a ballroom, there was always a moment's hush."[13] The trip raised the morale (and fed the egos) of both Jennie and her husband.

Yet there was no real improvement in Randolph's health, temper, or political prospects. Jennie often found herself alone while her husband, on his doctor's orders, went south each winter to protect his delicate lungs. In the fall of 1890, he and a friend leased a houseboat on the Nile for several months, where he lived a life, he wrote to a friend, of "good food, hock, champagne, Pilsener beer, Marquis chocolate, ripe bananas, fresh dates, and literally hundreds of French novels."[14] Back in London, Jennie juggled bills, managed their household and family, and kept up her brave front.

Randolph did make one successful move to secure his family's future. While in Egypt, he announced that he had decided "to have done with politics and try to make a little money for the boys and for ourselves . . . More than two-thirds, in all probability, of my life is over, and I will not spend the remainder of my years in beating my head against a stone wall."[15] On his return, he immediately departed for a nine-month trip to South Africa sponsored by his schoolfriend Lord Rothschild, to explore the gold mining industry there. His investment in a new mine in the Witwatersrand district proved to be a godsend; it funded the Churchill family for the rest of his life.[16]

Despite the Witwatersrand gold mine, the constant flow of invitations, and her high-kicking spirits, Jennie faced one crisis after another in the early nineties. In March 1891, Leonard Jerome died in Brighton, England. Exhausted and sick, he had finally agreed to leave New York the previous fall so his wife and daughters could look after him. He was seventy-three and weakened by tuberculosis. Jennie, Leonie, Clara, and their mother kept watch over their family linchpin as he coughed, spat blood, and finally expired. He had won and lost at least two fortunes and had always tried to help his daughters when their husbands could not provide. He left a mountain of debt. His wife, Clara, dedicated her remaining years to settling these debts and trying to instill some financial discipline into her children. She achieved the former, but the latter was a hopeless crusade.

Churchill finances were in a worse state than ever, and now there was no Leonard Jerome in the background, able to send a few dollars to his favorite daughter. Jennie was obliged to rent out Connaught Place and move into her in-laws' house, 50 Grosvenor Square. She wrote to her husband: "I feel rather 'mis' over it all—I know 'beggars cannot be choosers' but I feel *very* old for this sort of thing."[17] Randolph, holed up in the Carlton Club, fumed about her extravagances and affairs. From there he traveled to Scotland to stay with his sister, but he was then summoned back to London, because Jennie fell danger-ously ill with what was diagnosed as "pelvic peritonitis." Randolph alerted their sons to their mother's grave condition, but grumbled to his own mother, "There is a fate against me fishing this year."[18] In-credibly, Jennie recovered, thanks to her robust constitution.

Lord Randolph continued his attempts to reestablish himself in politics by speaking at Westminster. But his speech was growing slurred and his voice was often inaudible. The arrogant strut, glossy curls, and pink-cheeked good looks had been replaced by a stoop, a balding dome, and a mottled complexion half-hidden by a ratty beard. According to his nephew Shane Leslie, "Without Randolph the caricaturists would have gone out of business."[19] He insisted that he was on the verge of recovery, and in letters to him, Jennie continued loyally to shore up his spirits and to try and protect him.

One of Randolph's final speeches was on the complicated and controversial issue of Irish Home Rule. It was, as Jennie had dreaded, a disaster. Fellow MPs were appalled by his gaunt, trembling ap-pearance and struggled to hear what he was saying. He was "dying by inches in public," in the words of his friend Lord Rosebery.[20] His colleagues begged Jennie to keep him away from Westminster, but she refused to further demoralize her angry, sick husband. She knew that she had gained entrée to Britain's inner circles thanks to his name and title, and she continued to mourn the loss of his political career. "The cruelty of it!" she would later write to Leonie. "He was so nearly Prime Minister. There wasn't time."[21]

Lord Randolph doggedly insisted that his medical issues were temporary and that the only thing making him ill was "all this stupid gossip and fuss about my health."[22] However, Jennie decided she had to understand the cause of his steep decline, so without Randolph's permission she visited Dr. Roose, his physician. To Randolph's fury, the doctor explained the diagnosis that had first been made several years ago: "general paralysis," the euphemism for syphilis.[23]

Was Lord Randolph Churchill suffering from syphilis, a highly contagious and destructive sexual infection? This has been a widely held belief ever since the claim was published in 1924 by the famously unreliable Frank Harris, an Irish American journalist. Harris repeated secondhand gossip that while Randolph was at Oxford, he was infected by a prostitute. He was treated with mercury (the only treatment then available) and warned off alcohol. Despite being a poison itself, mercury was the standard medication for syphilis in the days before there were imaging techniques or a definitive blood test.

This would have meant that Randolph was already infected when he married Jennie Jerome. Other authors have suggested a later infection. His nephew Shane Leslie alleged that Randolph was infected by a chambermaid at Blenheim Palace soon after Winston's birth.[24] Shane Leslie's daughter speculates that Randolph may have had a French mistress who had syphilis.[25] Both authors suggest that Randolph was likely told by his physician that he had syphilis, and that this persuaded him to stop having sex with Jennie to protect her. There is no indication that Jennie or her sons were ever infected.

Modern authors have suggested alternative explanations, such as epilepsy, multiple sclerosis, chronic alcoholism, or a brain tumor. Those conditions all share with syphilis the symptoms that Randolph exhibited, including headaches, slurred speech, depression, exhaustion, and increasingly violent outbursts of temper. In the magazine of the International Churchill Society, the late Dr. John H. Mather, a gerontologist and medical biographer, has cast doubt on the syphilis diagnosis: "Lord Randolph Churchill's main symptoms are much more consistent with a less titillating but far more logical diagnosis." According to Dr. Mather, syphilis was overdiagnosed in the late nineteenth century and Lord Randolph's symptoms were most likely to have been caused by "a tumour deep in the left side of his brain."[26]

However, syphilis is what Lord Randolph himself thought he

had, and most members of his family believed it was what would kill him. After Jennie had finally heard the horrifying news, she decided that she had to remove him from London, to prevent their sons' witnessing their father's final stages of illness and to keep him out of the public eye. At one London dinner party, according to a fellow guest, Lord Randolph's conversation was "as mad a one as I ever listened to from mortal lips.[27]

III

Throughout Randolph's long and unpleasant decline, Jennie also had the pressure of being virtually a single parent to their two sons. Jack was sweet-natured and manageable, but his elder brother was endlessly demanding. From his Brighton school, Winston begged for visits and attention. "I suppose you are coming down for my birthday. I also suppose that we are going to have a party, are we not?!!!!" he wrote to "Dearest Mother" on October 22, 1887.[28] But neither of his parents visited him on his thirteenth birthday, and he was further disappointed when he learned that he would not be spending Christmas with them because they were off on their Russian trip. He and Jack were shuttled between relatives over the holidays and were particularly wretched when their beloved Mrs. Everest fell dangerously ill with diphtheria.

When he returned to his Brighton school, the Duchess of Marlborough told Randolph that she wasn't sorry "because he is certainly a handful. Not that he does anything seriously naughty except to use bad language which is bad for Jack."[29]

By early adolescence, Winston Spencer Churchill had grown into a good-looking boy, with thick reddish hair, an engaging smile, and a confident manner that bordered on aggression. On the brink of exchanging his cozy little school in Brighton for Harrow, one of Britain's oldest and best-known private schools, the thirteen-year-old was still chubby and clumsy, but he was now almost as tall as his mother. Both parents and grandmother looked forward to packing the youngster off to a large, well-run school with clear lines of authority. The duchess observed: "I am sure Harrow will do wonders for him for I fancy he was too clever and too much the boss at that Brighton School."[30]

Winston managed to scrape through the Harrow entrance examination in April 1888, but the school did not do wonders for him. In *My Early Life,* he enjoyed exaggerating his failures there, but the letters and reports that have survived from these years make mention of his "phenomenal" slovenliness, forgetfulness, carelessness, and unpunctuality. One teacher reported to Jennie that her son was "so regular in his irregularity that I really don't know what to do . . . As far as ability goes, he ought to be at the top of his form, whereas he is at the bottom."[31] Jennie found herself constantly remonstrating with Winston about his poor performance. When the headmaster urged him to spend a month in Paris to improve his French, he absolutely refused until Jennie finally put her foot down.

Winston Churchill spent four and a half years at Harrow. His closest link with home continued to be his mother, and his letters to her alternate between promises of better reports and anguished requests for visits and money. "My darling Mummy," he wrote in December 1891. "I am so wretched . . . Let me at least think that you love me—Darling Mummy I despair. I am so wretched. I don't know what to do. Don't be angry I am so miserable."[32] Jennie's surviving letters alternate between reproaches for her son's poor reports and assurances of her affection. "Dearest Winston you make me very unhappy," she wrote on June 12, 1890. She listed his shortcomings and mentioned that his father was particularly upset because he had sent Winston £5, which his son had belatedly acknowledged in a carelessly written note. "I had built up such hopes about you & felt so proud of you—and now all is gone . . . Your work is an insult to your intelligence." However, she ended the letter, "You know dearest boy that I will always help you all I can."[33]

But it was Randolph's attention that Winston wanted. Years later, in conversation with author Frank Harris, the adult Churchill said that his father "wouldn't listen to me or consider anything I said. There was no companionship with him possible to me and I tried so hard and so often. He was so self-centred no one else existed for him." He added quietly, "My mother was everything to me."[34] During these years, he learned to rely on Jennie to take his side, and to rescue him when he got into too much trouble.

Randolph Churchill did make one important decision for Winston: his choice of career. After seeing Winston's collection of toy soldiers, lined up in battle array, he announced that his son should go into the army. Winston's last two years at Harrow were then geared to the entrance examinations for the Royal Military College at Sandhurst. In September 1891, Jennie wrote to her husband, who was (as usual) traveling, "Honestly, he is getting a bit old for a woman to manage. After all, he will be 17 in 2 months and he really requires to be with a man . . . Winston will be alright the moment he gets into Sandhurst."[35]

It took Winston three attempts to pass the entrance examination for Sandhurst, but in the summer of 1893, he finally scraped through and sent his parents a letter full of boyish self-congratulation. Jennie, who had taken Randolph to a German spa, found herself torn between her unruly son and his irascible father. She scribbled a warning to Winston: "I am glad of course that you have got into Sandhurst but Papa is not very pleased at yr getting in by the skin of yr teeth & missing the Infantry by 18 marks."[36] Failing to get into the infantry division relegated Winston to the cavalry, which meant his parents had to provide horses, saddles, and other expensive equipment.

Two days later, Lord Randolph sent his son a withering message. "I am rather surprised at your tone of exultation over your inclusion in the Sandhurst list. There are two ways of winning an examination, one creditable the other the reverse. You have unfortunately chosen the latter method." After complaining about Winston's "slovenly, happy-go-lucky *harum-scarum* style of work," he reminded his son of the advantages he had been given. Despite "all the efforts that have been made to make your life easy and agreeable and your work neither oppressive nor distasteful, this is the grand result that you come up among the second or third rate who are only good for commissions in a cavalry regiment." He predicted that Winston might end up as a "mere social wastrel" living "a shabby, unhappy and futile existence," and ended the letter, "I no longer attach the slightest weight to anything you may say about your own achievements and exploits."[37]

Even the most happy-go-lucky eighteen-year-old boy would have been deeply wounded by such a contemptuous tone and cruel message.

Yet with his mother's help, Winston bounced back. In the end, he did receive an infantry cadetship, and he soon felt confident enough to beg Jennie to organize an allowance from Lord Randolph. Within a couple of weeks, he wrote to his mother, "I am going to buckle to at Sandhurst & to try and regain Papa's opinion of me. I will send you a Photograph of myself in my uniform—which I am longing to put on . . . Thanking you once more for your letter and sending you my very best love & many kisses."[38]

Winston enjoyed Sandhurst and was soon overspending his allowance and begging his mother for more funds. Jennie was now his only source of emotional as well as financial support, and he directed all his emotional neediness at "Dear darling Mummy."[39] Mrs. Everest was gone—sacked by the Duchess of Marlborough, who had never liked her. (Jennie did find Mrs. Everest a new job with a bishop in Essex.)

But Jennie was endlessly torn between a demanding Winston and an ailing, short-tempered Randolph. She found herself protecting the former from the latter's rages. "I am sending enclosed cheque for £2. I don't wish to be disagreeable but I wish to remind you that this makes £6 I have given you the last month . . . I really think that Papa gives you a very fair allowance . . . He wld be very X [cross] if he knew that I gave you money."[40]

IV

The ultimate test of Jennie's resilience came when she acceded to her husband's request that they embark on a world tour. The doctors were horrified by their plans, but Jennie decided her husband was best out of public sight. Randolph insisted on an extraordinarily ambitious itinerary that would take them from New York to Boston, Montreal, Vancouver, San Francisco, Yokohama, Shanghai, Hong Kong, Macao, Singapore, Rangoon, Mandalay, Calcutta, Bombay, and Cairo, finishing up in Monte Carlo in June 1885.

On June 29, 1884, they set off on SS *Majestic*, with Dr. George Elphinstone Keith, a young physician, plus Gentry, Jennie's lady's maid, and Walden, Randolph's valet, in their party. Winston and Jack waved from the dock.

The account of this "tour around the world" that Jennie wrote in *Reminiscences* is dappled with a hey-nonny-no cheerfulness and lists of charming new acquaintances and experiences. It concealed what was really going on. So did Jennie's letters to her sons, in which she insisted that Randolph's health was improving. She was more candid with her sister Leonie, to whom she wrote on August 7, from Banff Springs Hotel, Alberta, "As soon as [Randolph] gets a little better from having a rest . . . nothing will deter him from doing what he likes. He is very kind & considerate when he feels well—but absolutely *impossible* when he gets X [cross] and excited—and as he gets like that 20 times a day—you may imagine my life is not a very easy one."[41] Jennie later gave Leonie an even more brutal picture of Randolph's behavior, describing how at one point her husband had pointed a loaded revolver at her. Leonie told Frank Harris that her sister had "snatched it from him at once, pushed him back in his berth, and left the cabin, locking the door behind her. Jennie is the bravest woman I ever knew."[42]

Randolph's decline was precipitous; the numbness and irritability were increasing, and during their October stopover in Japan, Dr. Keith reported to Dr. Roose, "One hour he is quiet and good-tempered, the next hour violent and cross."[43] By the time the party had reached Singapore, Dr. Keith wrote, "This has been the worst week since leaving home by a great deal. Lord Randolph has been violent and apathetic by turn."

The heat was overpowering, and both Jennie and Dr. Keith tried to persuade Randolph that it was time to go home. But he was determined to visit Burma, because he had directed its annexation during his brief tenure as secretary of state for India in Lord Salisbury's 1885 cabinet. Dreading the consequences of this trip, Jennie added a lead-lined coffin to their baggage.[44]

Watching her husband slide into dementia was not the only strain on Jennie during this nightmare odyssey. In Hong Kong, she heard that Freddy Wolverton, a young admirer with whom she had cultivated a close relationship and toyed with the idea of marriage, was breaking off their relationship. In Rangoon, there was a further, harsher blow. She received a telegram from Count Kinsky telling her of his engagement to a young, Catholic Austro-Hungarian aristocrat. Kinsky had warned Jennie that he would not wait for her if she took the journey with her husband, and his father, eager for an heir to the extensive Kinsky estates, had seized the moment to pressure him into a far more suitable match. Jennie was devastated; as Randolph neared death, the dream of marrying her longtime lover had seemed within her grasp.

Her anguish exploded in her letters to her sister. "Oh Leonie, darling, do you think it is *too late* to stop it? Nothing is impossible, you know. Can't you help me? For heaven's sake, write to him." She was scared to face the future alone; she begged Leonie to "urge him to put off his marriage anyhow until I have seen him . . . Tell him I'm so suited to him, that my troubles have sobered me and that I could be all that he desired. Besides, I could help him in his career. The future looks too black and lonely without him."[45]

Still Randolph insisted on stumbling around Madras, insisting that he was not ill. But by the time the sad little party reached Bombay, it was obvious that they should get home as soon as possible. They reached 50 Grosvenor Square the day before Christmas.

Winston already knew his father was dying; he had insisted that Dr. Roose tell him the truth, and Dr. Roose gave him the diagnosis that he had shared with Jennie. Winston's self-absorption was shaken by the idea that his father had syphilis, and from now on, alongside the endless requests for money, there ran a greater concern for Jennie's well-being. "I had never realized how ill Papa had been and had never until now believed that there was anything serious the matter," he wrote. "Darling dearest Mummy keep your pluck & strength up. Don't allow yourself to think . . . God bless you and help us all."[46]

Lord Randolph Churchill died on January 24, 1895, at forty-five, a month after he had arrived home. In *Reminiscences*, Jennie does not mention her husband's demise (just as she had not mentioned Winston's birth). Nor does she mention that two weeks before she was finally widowed, Charles Kinsky had married Countess Elisabeth Wolff-Metternich zur Gracht.

Lord Randolph's funeral was held at Westminster Abbey, and his coffin was taken by train through the snowy countryside to Bladon churchyard, close to Blenheim. Almost numb with exhaustion and grief, Jennie retreated to her room in her mother-in-law's Grosvenor Square residence and wondered how to rebuild her life. Shane Leslie, her ten-year-old nephew, would never forget her lying in bed, "the most beautiful vision of woman I have ever seen: raven black hair caught with diamonds over her face whiter than death, and eyes that shone like wet ebony."[47]

V

"I shall return without a friend in the world & too old to make any more now," Jennie had written to her sister Clara during the journey home. She yearned for companionship, but she was now a widow with a too-colorful past and uncertain prospects. What would she do— what *could* she do with the rest of her life?

Part of the uncertainty was financial. From now on, Jennie's income derived from the annual income from Lord Randolph's estate (worth £54,237 then or £5,423,700 in today's values, including the South African windfall and after his debts were paid), with the capital bound up in a trust for her sons, plus the marriage settlements that Leonard Jerome and the Duke of Marlborough had created in 1874.[48] This amounted to an annual income of £5,000 a year (£500,000 today), which should have been more than enough for the forty-one-year-old widow to move in the well-heeled circles she enjoyed. But she had no home, no access to capital with which to buy one, and two sons—now twenty and fourteen—for whom she would have to provide allowances. Moreover, she had wildly expensive tastes and no experience of, or even interest in, living within her income. For the rest of her life, she would be dependent on moneylenders.

But Jennie took a deep breath and prepared herself to deal with those "vicissitudes of life" that she had faced nine years earlier, when her husband's political career had come to an abrupt end.

Her sons were never far from her thoughts, and after Randolph's death, she and they became a tight little threesome. Jack was safely lodged at Harrow, acquiring the study skills and self-discipline that had eluded his elder brother. Winston, who quickly recovered his ebullience after his father's death, demanded far more of Jennie's attention. He had decided he wanted to switch from the infantry to the cavalry, and relentlessly pressed his mother to pull strings to make this happen. She did, and Winston was soon sending a volley of requests for funds so he could establish himself in the style to which cavalry officers in the prestigious Fourth Hussars aspired. "I am at present very hard up. Would it be possible and convenient to you to pay at present so large a sum as £100–£120?" . . . "My darling Mamma – let me beg you to try and send me a little money."[49]

Yet somehow, mother and son—each as outrageously extravagant as the other—scraped through this latest installment of their insolvency crisis. And if Jennie could not send Winston the funds he demanded, she could supply two more precious gifts.

The first, now that her husband was gone, was undiluted emotional support. Jennie may have been heedless of Winston's needs while Randolph was still alive, but now she began to take some pride in this bumptious, clever young man. He had an energy and ambition that Randolph had never displayed at his age; perhaps she saw that he might fulfill the hopes she had once nursed for his father. She encouraged him in all his ventures, nurtured his talents, and was soon reassuring him that he had unusual gifts and would go far.

Winston's need for this kind of emotional buttress was stark after two more losses. In March 1895, his grandmother Clara Jerome passed away, having used most of her capital to pay off her husband's debts. Four months later Mrs. Everest died suddenly of peritonitis. For Winston, the loss of his beloved nanny was by far the greater shock. "I shall never know such a friend again," he wrote to his mother. "I feel very low—and find that I never realized how much poor old Woom was to me. I don't know what I should do without you."[50] At the moment that Winston had lost the most important woman of his childhood, Jennie was ready to step into the role. From now on, mother and son were in constant contact as they worked together to promote the young Winston Churchill's career.

Jennie's second gift to Winston was a network of government ministers, royalty, financiers, aristocrats, editors, and writers. She had easy access to them all, and she never hesitated to call in her contacts on Winston's behalf. Besides the courage and drive she exemplified to him, besides the self-confidence she instilled in him, she constantly exposed him to ideas and debates that would stretch his mind and she introduced him to people who might help determine his future. Soon after Lord Randolph's death, she would meet a formidable Irish American lawyer and orator who would become a major mentor and father figure to the ambitious young Winston Churchill.[51] But in early 1895, Jennie's own future looked bleak. She had her freedom from Lord Randolph, but nothing in her life so far had prepared her to deal with the new start that widowhood would require.

She began to tighten the ties that bound her elder son to her, not unlike Sara had done with Franklin.

CHAPTER 10

———◇———

Sara's "Dear, Dear Boy"
1890–1903

Sara Delano Roosevelt was more than happy to define herself as a wife and mother, and to stick to the same respectable routines, year after year. The carefully curated placidity of her existence could not have been a greater contrast to the turbulence in Jennie Churchill's life. During the winter months, the Roosevelts remained firmly within their privileged cocoon of wealthy Hudson Valley friends; each spring there would be a trip to Europe; summers were spent on Campobello Island.

Sara continued to note in detail, in her diary and letters, her son's development, including his Delano determination not to make a fuss. When the family was in Paris one winter, James Roosevelt hired a governess at great expense for their son. Fiercely protective of her own close relationship with Franklin, Sara found the young woman too intrusive—"we were never without her at all"—but eight-year-old Franklin did not grumble. Finally, Sara told her son that she didn't really like the governess and asked him, "Now tell me truthfully: are you really so dreadfully fond of her?"

Franklin promptly replied, "I think she's perfectly awful." Why had he not said so? Franklin explained to his mother that "I thought after father had gone to such trouble and spent so much money to get her, it wouldn't be right for me to complain."[1]

But from 1890, Sara found herself with divided loyalties. James Roosevelt's heart attack had depleted his stamina and his self-confidence, and the age difference between husband and wife seemed wider than ever. Sara turned her formidable energies to the challenge of restoring to health the man to whom she had promised total fidelity.

Like Jennie Churchill, Sara Roosevelt would spend several years nursing her ailing husband. Unlike Jennie, Sara quietly took control of the family finances and prepared for widowhood as her uncomplaining husband slowly declined. The two women's lives followed similar paths, but Sara had the means and temperament to develop an autonomy that would always elude Jennie. Sara understood that she was about to enter a new stage of life, in which she would make all the family decisions. As James's energies faded, Franklin became her emotional anchor.

II

While James was still well enough to travel, a London heart specialist named Dr. Weber recommended a new spa, at Bad Nauheim in Germany. Warm, salty, carbonated water bubbled up from ancient springs there, and in 1859 a local physician had published a pamphlet suggesting that it was an elixir for patients with heart problems. Soon, up to one thousand people a day were drinking the orange-tinted water and bathing in the spa's marble tubs. The Roosevelts tried the spa in 1891, and there were four subsequent visits, although no discernible improvement in James's health. However, Sara and James believed that the waters were doing James good, and Franklin absorbed the idea that immersion in restorative waters might have medical benefits.

However, there was little in this town of sulfur fumes and wheelchairs to amuse an active nine-year-old boy. So Sara enrolled her son in a local state school for six weeks. Despite his unfamiliarity with a classroom of exuberant schoolboys, Franklin apparently handled the challenge with Delano self-possession. "My dear Muriel and Warren," he wrote to two of his Delano cousins in May 1891. "It is lovely here and on this paper is a picture of the big lake on which we row and Papa got me a great big boat, and I sail it every day . . . I have a splendid bow and arrow and I shoot in the park . . . I go to the public school with a lot of little mickies and we have German reading, German dictation, the history of Siegfried, and arithmetic."[2]

With Franklin occupied, Sara was now free to attend to James's needs, and to meet other visitors to the spa. Together she and James would rise early each day and, cups in hand, make their way to the colonnaded Kurhaus, or Cure House, to join the slow-moving line shuffling toward the octagonal fountain in the center. There a white-aproned fräulein would fill their cups with the warm, salty water.

After breakfast, James went to one of three bathhouses, where he immersed himself in a tubful of the warm, murky water that emerged from the spring. He lay in it for fifteen minutes, feeling the water fizz gently against his skin. Nauheim promotional literature claimed that the bubbles formed in the bath would "dilate blood vessels, relieve the heart and circulatory system, improve blood system."[3] Sara spent the time strolling through the beautifully landscaped park or reading the British newspapers and magazines provided in the Kurhaus lounge. Tall and chic in a tightly waisted gown with the puffy leg-of-mutton sleeves that dominated women's fashions in the 1890s, she would pause to chat with "people one knows," as she described acquaintances who met her approval.

When James's course of treatment at Nauheim was complete that first year, the Roosevelts took a trip to the Black Forest. Now Sara, still in her thirties, could change gears, and take energetic hikes with her son. One day, she and Franklin scrambled up the Blauen, an Alpine mountain with a peak 3,820 feet above sea level. Such a feat was beyond sixty-three-year-old James. Mother and son spent the night in the rustic mountain lodge at the top, and Sara noted in her journal the "very strange effect" at three o'clock the next morning as the first rays of sunshine glimmered on the distant peaks.[4]

But for Sara, nowhere could compete with the Hudson Valley. After the lengthy European trip, she noted, "It is lovely to be at Hyde Park again. All the trees are turning and it is beautiful."

From now on, the Bad Nauheim visits were preceded by extended stays in London, where there were plenty of "people one knows." One of them was her younger sister Catherine, known as Cassie, now married to American author Price Collier. In the years ahead, Sara would come to rely more and more on her sisters, as Jennie Churchill did on Clara and Leonie Jerome, and their names recur frequently in her journals. Laura Delano, the youngest of the beautiful Delano sisters, had died in a tragic fire in 1884, but the remaining four were close. Sara's two older sisters, Dora and Annie, had both married men who worked for their father's former firm: Dora was the wife of Russell partner Will Forbes, while Annie's husband was Frederick Hitch, a young clerk who worked his way up the company. They would get together to share memories of their revered parents and their golden childhood at Algonac. Sara was still the bossy sister who made most of the arrangements, but Dora, Annie, and Cassie were her supporting cast.

In England, Sara sailed through society, heedless of the anti-American prejudices that had struck Jennie during her early married days. Perhaps she never encountered them because she rarely strayed outside the company of wealthy American friends and relatives—Cassie, Bamie Roosevelt (who had introduced Sara to James Roosevelt), Sara's stepson Rosy Roosevelt, his wife, Helen, and their two children, Taddy and Helen. The Rosy Roosevelts had moved to England after his father had helped him secure a diplomatic post there—first secretary at the embassy of the United States.

Sara filled her days in London with visits to James's physician, shopping expeditions to Regent Street department stores and Jermyn Street tailors, lunch parties, and visits to museums and galleries. In 1895 she noted that she had gone with "kind Bamie to the Grafton Gallery and lunched with her . . . went to dinner at Rosy's." Another day she recorded, "To Dr. Weber's. I had a little talk with him about my dear James. We lunched with the Cholmeleys. Took Helen [Rosy's daughter] and Franklin to the South Kensington Museum, and to Fuller's for ice-cream."[5]

She was also keen to pass on her love of opera to her son, and one year she took him to Bayreuth, the Bavarian home of Richard

Wagner's music. "We heard Rheingold, Die Walküre, Siegfried and Gotterdämmerung and all were most beautiful, the orchestra so full and yet soft and the scenery perfect, the singing very fine taken as a whole, tho' the singers were not all faultless, nor did the costumes satisfy my ideas."[6]

III

Sara was convinced that family travels, supervised reading, and well-qualified tutors provided an education superior to anything a regular school might offer. By the age of ten, Franklin had a firm grasp of French and German, an impressive knowledge of naval history, natural history (thanks to his bird-watching), and geography (thanks to his stamp collection). Sara would write, "It was hard for people to believe that he had never been to school, and they marveled at his grasp of subjects that did not ordinarily interest children as young as he."[7]

But as Franklin entered his teens, his mother (probably nudged by her husband) conceded that "the time had come when we could no longer allow our desire to keep him with us to limit his scope of experiences." He needed to move beyond the parental bubble and meet "boys of his own age, with whom he might exchange ideas and form friendships that would endure through time."[8]

When their son was only one year old, Sara and James Roosevelt had enrolled Franklin in an as-yet unbuilt school in Massachusetts, promoted by the Reverend Endicott Peabody. Peabody was a big, broad-shouldered Episcopal minister from a well-established banking family. Educated in posh British schools, he now wanted to instill in American boys the same heroic masculinity promoted by British public schools—"manly, Christian character, having regard to moral and physical as well as intellectual development."[9] Wealthy New England families found him irresistible, and he soon assembled a board of prestigious trustees, including the great financier J. Pierpont Morgan himself.

The first class arrived at Groton School's handsome red brick buildings thirty-five miles north of Boston in 1884 and were immediately subjected to a spartan existence (cold showers and little privacy), a rigid schedule punctuated by bells, and a curriculum heavy on classics and languages and light on sciences. The school motto for these offspring of the New England elite was a triumph of humblebrag: *Cui servire est regnare*, or "To serve is to rule." Groton, like Winston Churchill's school Harrow, was an expensive all-boys institution that groomed its pupils to support the class and power structures into which they were born.

If the Reverend Peabody had had his way, Franklin Roosevelt would have entered Groton in 1894, when he was twelve. But Sara could not bear to part with him then. A photo of mother and son taken in 1893 captures her protective instincts. Still a head taller than "my boy," as she referred to Franklin all her life, Sara stares almost defiantly at the camera while holding her son close with her right arm and catching his right hand in her left hand. Franklin, looking uncomfortable in a stiff white collar, tie, and check waistcoat, hair neatly parted in the center, has a far more wary expression.[10]

But Franklin's entry into Groton could not be postponed forever, and when the Roosevelts returned from Europe in 1896, Sara prepared for the parting. She began the packing, then spent the day with Franklin. "We dusted his birds, and he had a swim in the river. I looked on . . . with a heavy heart." The next day, September 15, the three Roosevelts boarded their private railroad car and headed north. Once they arrived at Groton, Sara "helped Franklin to unpack and get settled." Franklin was "dry-eyed and resolute," his mother noted, "though white-faced." His parents then retreated to their railroad car, and Franklin dropped in to say goodbye.

"It seems strange to have him come over to call on us from the school," Sara confided in her diary. "We left at 9.19. James and I feel this parting very much. It is hard to leave my darling boy." Within a couple of days, she was writing to him, "I shall be anxious to know how you get on with the boys. It is a great change to be with so many of all sorts."[11] His absence was keenly felt at Springwood; Sara continued to display almost religious attention to his stuffed bird collection.

Franklin must have felt homesick during his first days of boarding school, but his ability to hide his emotions is evident in his biweekly letters home, which were corrected and lovingly preserved by his mother. (If Franklin forgot to mail even one, Sara would telegraph Peabody to make sure he had not fallen ill.)[12] Only three days after Sara had parted from him, she received a note in her son's sloping, blotched script: "Dear Mommerr and Popperr, I am getting on finely both mentally and physically . . . We have just had Latin and Algebra, and we study French tonight. We went to Mrs. Peabody's Parlor last night for half an hour and played games." Three days later, he wrote, "Dear Mama . . . I am getting on very well and so far I have not had any warnings, latenesses or marks."[13]

Sara and James Roosevelt visited Groton in October and "found Franklin well and handsome." His first report recorded steady progress academically, and high marks for punctuality, neatness, and decorum. Sara noted, "We are so pleased. His father is so anxious for him to study well and he certainly does."[14] For the rest of his Groton schooldays, she proudly noted in her diary his triumphs — prizewinning Latin essays, punctuality awards, success on the debating team.

Sara assumed that winning friends should be effortless for her son. As FDR biographer Geoffrey Ward put it, "It probably never occurred to her that a Roosevelt and a Delano would ever find it hard to win acceptance. Roosevelts and Delanos accepted or rejected *others*."[15] But how genuine was his early cheeriness? A classmate who entered the school at the same time as Franklin would recall that "Franklin D. before he went to Groton had never been with other boys very much, had had tutors at home and besides had a father who was quite well on in years when he went to school. He therefore found it difficult at first with these handicaps to adjust himself to boarding school life."[16] Franklin had perfected his ability to please adults in his life so far, but his rowdy adolescent peers were less impressed by good manners, neatness, and an accent that they mimicked as affected and too "English."

Sara knew nothing of the schoolyard tortures Franklin underwent. Nor did she understand that her son was too slight and delicate to achieve what Groton staff and boys really valued—success in team sports. He was hopeless at football and baseball, and regularly wrote home about injuries in athletic endeavors—a dislocated finger, a cut on his eyelid, a "whack" on the nose. Sara wrote that she hoped he hadn't inadvertently hurt anybody, and she sent bottles of castor oil to build up his stamina. Like Winston Churchill at Harrow, Franklin Roosevelt did not shine as an intellectual, athlete, or leader at Groton.

IV

James Roosevelt was so exhausted by the trip to Groton in September 1896 that he retreated to bed for several days after he got home. He had caught a cold; "I was terribly frightened, it has almost made me ill," Sara noted.[17] His increased dependence on his wife left Sara little time to worry about Franklin. Soon she was planning the next trip to Bad Nauheim—the first that she and James would do without their son. "Nothing but James' health would induce me to cross the ocean without Franklin."[18]

In mid-April 1897, the Roosevelts sailed to Europe on the SS *Teutonic*, after Sara had arranged to have a cedar strip canoe delivered to Groton for her son. Franklin wrote wistfully, "I am thinking of you as sitting in your chairs on deck enjoying this lovely weather."[19] As usual, they knew several of their fellow passengers, so every evening was a dinner party. Once they arrived in Germany, they once again settled into the Villa Britannia. Sara slipped into the familiar routine: tea with friends from previous years, visits with the Episcopal minister with whom they were planning an American church for the spa, leisurely strolls in the park.

Franklin got most of his mother's attention during school holidays, but for the rest of the year, Sara's priority was caring for James. But even her willpower couldn't keep her husband alive forever.

The following year, while they were at Bad Nauheim, a telegram from Groton shook them: Franklin had a mild case of scarlet fever—a dangerous infection in the days before penicillin. "James is so upset that I dare not show how I feel. I am so anxious for James to take his cure that I encourage him to stay and *not* go home."

Sara's iron self-control collapsed when a further cable arrived: "Franklin developed inflamed kidneys. Doctors do not consider very serious."[20] Within twenty-four hours she had organized their rapid departure from Germany and a berth on the *Teutonic,* heading west. During the eight-day voyage home, they had no news. Only the cheerful expressions of Fred Hitch and her sister Annie, along with her old friend Nellie Blodgett, who greeted them at the Manhattan docks, relieved their fears.

Franklin was still in the Groton sickroom, where he was quarantined with two other boys. Sara was told that she had to stay in isolation with him if she wanted to see him. "I have to choose between going into him and staying in and deserting James or merely seeing F. thru the window and being with James," she agonized in her diary.[21] But she refused to be blocked. She commandeered a ladder from Groton's maintenance staff and leaned it against the wall of the school's infirmary. Then, carefully lifting the front of her skirt, she climbed up until she could look inside the second-floor window.

She must have made an extraordinary figure—an elegant woman in the wide-brimmed hat and full skirts of the 1890s, precariously perched on top of a workman's ladder several times each day. But from this vantage point, she could see into the room and beckon Franklin over to her. "He loved to see me appear over the window ledge, and, at first sight of me his pale, little face would break into a happy, albeit pathetic smile."[22]

James Roosevelt's need for his wife's attention, along with Franklin's own growing maturity, had allowed the boy to assert his independence. Although James's family visited his Oyster Bay relatives infrequently, Franklin regarded these distant cousins with some envy; the contrast between his own uptight little family and Teddy Roosevelt's energetic, gregarious gang, which was always hiking through woods and swimming across bays, was striking. One year, a

note addressed to him arrived at Springwood, inviting him to join the
Oyster Bay Roosevelts for their Fourth of July celebrations. Without
consulting her son, Sara politely declined. This triggered a surprisingly testy response from the usually agreeable Franklin.

He immediately told his cousins that he would, after all, be joining
them, and wrote to his mother, "Please don't make any more arrangements for my future happiness."[23] He also insisted on spending part
of his summer at a New Hampshire camp that Groton sponsored.
There he taught poor boys from New York and Boston tenements
how to swim, sail, and paddle. Sara concealed her irritation at his absence from Hyde Park with loftier sentiments. "It will interest you
in doing for others," she wrote to him. "Nothing is so helpful to ourselves as doing for others and trying to sink all selfishness."

Sara continued to spend a few nights each month in Manhattan,
and her diary is a catalogue of plays starring famous actors, including
Johnston Forbes-Robertson and Edwin Thomas Booth (brother of
President Lincoln's assassin), opera performances, and dinners with
relatives. But many of these outings were with sisters or friends. There
was more sadness in her life, besides James's decline. Her intimate
circle was shrinking. Her seventy-four-year-old mother had died in
1896, and two years later, at the age of eighty-nine, the redoubtable
Warren Delano passed away, with Sara at his bedside. He had been the
most important man in her life for her first twenty-eight years, until
James Roosevelt joined him in Sara's pantheon. But now James was
too frail to attend Warren Delano's funeral. It was Franklin, already
taller than Sara, who stood alongside her at the grave.

She and James were at Campobello in June 1898 when they heard
the news that the irrepressible Teddy Roosevelt was on his way to
Cuba, with his own cavalry unit nicknamed the Rough Riders. Teddy
had resigned from his post as assistant secretary of the navy, in the
Republican administration of President William McKinley, in order
to fight in the Spanish-American War. This was the bold, not to say
grandstanding, move of an impulsive and ambitious Republican,
keen to expand American influence within its hemisphere. His pluck

galvanized the nation, including the Democratic Roosevelts of Hyde Park. Sara immediately organized a group of women to come to her Campobello cottage to sew for members of Teddy's regiment who had been wounded. "Today sent off a large box to Leiter Hospital, Chickamauga, 4 doz. Sheets, 4 doz. Pillowcases, 43 sets of pajamas and a few odds and ends."[24]

Family trumped politics. When Theodore Roosevelt, or "the Colonel," as he was now known, returned to New York a hero and ran for the governorship of New York State, Sara recorded in her diary, "Went to a Republican meeting to hear Theodore speak."

"We were all wild with delight when we heard of Teddy's election," Franklin wrote from Groton. The following January, Sara and James went to Albany to see Franklin's fifth cousin inaugurated as governor of New York.[25]

But James had become Sara's main priority. She was determined to push her husband into as much activity as possible. She presented him with a handsome new saddle horse, Bobby, for his seventy-first birthday: "a beauty, only five years old and kind and gentle . . . Kentucky-bred."[26] In a photograph of him on Bobby, a dapper James, crop in hand, looks sturdy and pleased. By the following spring, however, his tweeds hung loose on his shoulders and Bad Nauheim was out of the question.

James Roosevelt was also increasingly tetchy. He had not been happy when the railroad baron Frederick Vanderbilt and his wife moved into a fifty-four-room mansion they had built close to Springwood. When the Roosevelts were invited to dine there, James overruled Sara's enthusiasm, insisting they decline the invitation because he considered them nouveau riche. "If we accept we shall have to have them at our house."[27] He quarreled with neighbors, scolded servants, and harrumphed when village boys played baseball games on Sundays.

In the summer of 1899, there was a new Roosevelt yacht at Campobello, *Half Moon II*. Sara, along with James, Franklin, and a school friend of Franklin's, set off for a two-day sail up the Bay of Fundy, along the New Brunswick coast. But the trip proved too much for James. Sara noted, "I was so afraid he [would] be really ill that I slept not at all."[28] They quickly returned to shore, and James spent most of the rest of the summer reclining on the veranda, watching his son sailing in the bay as Sara danced attendance on him.

V

On the family's return from Campobello in the fall, Franklin moved further out of the parental orbit. In September, following the pattern set by his father, he started at Harvard.

Sara's diary entries in the days before Franklin's departure are as poignant as those before his departure for Groton. At her forty-sixth birthday party: "My dear James surprised me with a cake and candles and sapphire sleeve links." Three days later, her son took her for a long, quiet canoe paddle on the Hudson. The following day, he headed for Boston. Sara wrote, "Our dear Franklin left us for *college*, a great step."[29]

Franklin's first weeks at Harvard were disrupted by a family scandal. James—Taddy—son of Franklin's half-brother Rosy, had started at Harvard the previous year, but he was now discovered to have dropped out and disappeared into the sleazy dancehalls and bars of New York's Tenderloin district. Taddy had never been particularly bright, and after his mother Helen's death in 1893 he had become wayward, and an embarrassment to Franklin when both attended Groton. But now he had gone too far. Sara was appalled; Taddy's behavior broke all the rules of Knickerbocker society, and it threatened his grandfather's health.

"I am sorry Taddy has Papa's name if he is not going to grace it," she wrote Franklin. Then she heard that Taddy had married a Hungarian-born prostitute named Sadie Messinger, who was brown-eyed, "short and plump," but "accounted a beauty of her type," according to one scandal sheet.[30] This was catnip for New York's newspapers, given that Taddy's Uncle Teddy was now the vice presidential nominee of his party. "Boy Millionaire Weds; Astor

Scion's Bride Won in Dance Hall," read one lip-licking headline in Manhattan's press.[31]

James Roosevelt was horrified. He had dragged himself into Manhattan to attend to business in the Delaware and Hudson Railway office, where reporters cornered him with the story. He managed to maintain his dignity as he protested that his grandson was "a good boy on the whole, though notoriously weak." But two nights later, when he was safely back at Springwood, he had a serious heart attack. "The dreadful and disgraceful business about Taddy was the last straw," Sara wrote to Franklin. "Your father cannot get . . . out of his mind the thought that his grandson has been leading a wicked life for months . . . Poor Papa has suffered so much in the night for breath that he thought he could not live. He talked of you and said, 'Tell Franklin to be good and never be like Taddy.' Then he said, 'I *know* he is good and will be good.' He says he never remembers a disgrace coming to his family before, and it is dreadful to him."[32]

Sara poured out her own fury and concern in letters to Franklin. Her husband "thinks of it when awake and dreams of it when he is asleep. It is *too* bad." She warned Franklin to avoid the kind of friends that Taddy had made. "It is difficult to touch mud and not get soiled." In his responses, an adolescent and unforgiving Franklin mirrored his mother's shock at the family humiliation. "I do not wonder that it has upset Papa, but although the disgrace to the name has been the worst part of the affair, one can never again consider him a true Roosevelt."[33]

Sara's concern, mixed with dread about James's imminent death, was justified. There was another heart attack in late November and a nurse moved in. Franklin came home for a day, and Rosy arrived for lunch. "James is happy to have his two sons . . . he and Franklin and I sat together in the south parlor all afternoon . . . James very delicate and tired-looking in a velvet coat, but it was sweet just to be together."[34]

Desperate to keep James alive, Sara took him by train to New York so he was closer to his doctor. But his breath became more labored, and Sara realized the end was close. She sent for Franklin, who came immediately and for the next three days alternated between sitting with his father and trying to comfort his mother. Early in the morning of December 8, 1900, with his wife and two sons at his bedside, seventy-two-year-old James Roosevelt died. "All is over," Sara noted in her diary.[35]

Three days later, he was buried in the cemetery behind St. James Episcopal Church in Hyde Park, then Sara returned to Hyde Park for the first time without him. For the next few nights, she filled her diary with her sorrow. "The days drag on," she wrote. "We have to bear them." Franklin tried to console her, and they shared a desultory Christmas together. Knowing that Franklin had to return to Harvard in the new year, she noted, "I dread his leaving."[36]

Yet Sara Roosevelt did not allow her intense grief to immobilize her. Soon she had adopted James's routine of riding Bobby around the estate, seeing to it that snow was cleared and the estate's two icehouses filled with ice cut from the Hudson River. In mid-January she wrote to her son that she had lain awake "and lived over in my thoughts that night four weeks ago and thought of the help it was to me when you, my dear, dear boy, came to me and I realized how much I still had to live for, even with your darling father's spirit flown . . . You need not worry about me for I am all right."[37] She called on the Vanderbilts; she spent more time with her siblings. There were no more restful sojourns at German spas; instead, Sara began to make annual trips to London and Paris to visit her sisters.

In words that echoed Sara's own fortitude (and which she almost certainly dictated herself), biographer Rita Halle Kleeman wrote, "Many women, bereft, spend the rest of their lives mourning the dead and leaning on the living. Not so Mrs. Roosevelt . . . Life had to go on and she did not whine." (A powerful model for Franklin, when he was felled by polio.) Until this moment, insisted Kleeman, Sara had "subordinated her own views always, first to those of her father, then to those of her husband, for both of whom she had profound respect as well as deep affection." After James's death, she might easily have switched her dependence to her stepson, son, or one of her brothers, "clinging to them and making them pay constant tribute to her helplessness and her grief. But the rest of her life was to give abundant proof of her strength and her capabilities."[38] Sara's exemplary stoicism and courage were behaviors that Franklin, consciously or subconsciously, absorbed.

James's death allowed Sara to start living; as her spirits slowly lifted, her outlook expanded. James had left her everything—investments plus both Springwood and the Campobello property—except for trust funds of $120,000 (around $4 million today)[39] for each of his sons. This was a sizable estate, but it was still smaller than her share of her father's estate, which had been at least $1,300,000 (about $44 million today) and which she had already received. There must have been suitors for this wealthy widow—regal in bearing, always exquisitely dressed, well-connected, and immensely rich—but none got beyond her imperious manner. She had no interest in divided loyalties. Her adored Franklin, still legally a minor, was now the man in her life.

Jennie Churchill's bereavement five years earlier, when she was forty, had forced her to reassess how to live her life. Sara, now forty-six, faced the same challenge. Their lives had been vastly different until each was widowed—Jennie's husband had catapulted her into the British aristocracy and the seductive fishbowl of imperial politics, while Sara's married life had followed the quiet rhythms of Hudson Valley, familiar from her own childhood and preferred by her husband. Now each woman was on her own, with no obligation to cater to her husband's wishes. Each now could shape her own future.

PART 4 · MAKING HER OWN CHOICES

CHAPTER 11

――――◇――――

Jennie: "No Wire Unpulled"
1895–1899

As young widows, Jennie Jerome Churchill and Sara Delano Roosevelt had little in common beyond their immense social privilege, and their responsibility for sons on the cusp of adulthood. With the loss of Lord Randolph in 1895, five years before James Roosevelt's death, Jennie had found herself left with no home and no fortune, and Winston and Jack, aged twenty and fourteen, each looking to her for guidance and support. Her husband's lineage had been her passport into the British aristocracy; her marriage had given her the respectability required to shield her from malicious chatter. Now she was on her own in a way that Sara Roosevelt, with her wealth and cozy network of Roosevelts and Hudson Valley neighbors, could not begin to imagine. Sara could sail through life; Jennie had to paddle furiously, reliant on her wit, charisma, and innate optimism.

And yet both women demonstrated resilience as they adapted to their new status. Each came to revel in her newfound sense of agency—the chance to make her own choices rather than defer to a man's, as she had been raised to do.

II

Jennie soon rallied from her husband's death. "You are the only person who lives on the crest of a wave," her friend Lady Curzon wrote to her, "and is always full of vitality and success."[1] Had Jennie stayed in London, convention would have obliged her to emulate the aging

Queen Victoria and wear widow's weeds—head-to-toe black crepe for one year. The monarch had stuck to this macabre outfit ever since her husband's death thirty-four years earlier. For other widows, a few pallid colors trimmed with black might be worn during the second year, and social invitations finally considered after that. However, the French had little time for oppressive conventions and dowdy outfits; nor did Jennie. Within weeks of Randolph's death, Jennie resorted to a time-honored Jerome strategy to escape the muck and gas lamps of sooty London and her pressing debts. By late February 1895, accompanied by Gentry, her maid, and Walden, Randolph's valet, she had left Winston to Sandhurst's challenges and Jack to Harrow's routines and had crossed the channel and installed herself in Paris.

There she could welcome her sisters, her two closest friends in the world—the threesome shared their secrets, their limited funds, and their maternal responsibilities. Paris of La Belle Époque was celebrated for its glamor, scientific discoveries, and artistic vitality, despite nasty undercurrents of decadence, anti-Semitism, and corruption. The Jerome sisters—raised in the French capital and fluent in the language— loved reacquainting themselves with its sophistication. It was still a city that appreciated wealthy Americans, dismissing most English-women as large, awkward outdoorswomen, manifestly inferior to Frenchwomen. The sisters strolled along the Champs-Élysées as horse-drawn omnibuses, barrel-laden wagons, and elegant carriages rumbled past.

Jennie reconnected with admirers and lovers who would raise her spirits, reassure her that she was more beautiful than ever, and help her forget the dreadful last years with Lord Randolph. Soon her Avenue Kléber apartment was a magnet for expatriate Americans, suave French noblemen, artists, and musicians. Her large circle of friends ensured that the beautiful forty-one-year-old widow always had company. One of the first visitors was Edward, Prince of Wales, a loyal friend to Jennie throughout her long ordeal, who continued to write frequently to "Ma chère amie," signing his letters "Tout à vous."[2]

As the weather grew warmer, she joined in the enthusiasm for the newfound sport of bicycling through the Bois de Boulogne. A woman on a bicycle, displaying her bloomers and athleticism to passersby, was still considered a shocking sight, but it only hinted at more substantial changes during the decade that would come to be known in Britain as the Naughty Nineties.

The slow erosion of Britain's global preeminence had begun. As Queen Victoria's reign drew to its end, the vibrant economies of the United States and Germany were challenging the empire's industrial supremacy. Despite infusions of dollars from American heiresses who had married into the British aristocracy, many of the ducal families' estates were crumbling and their grip on political power was weakening. More men in the rising middle class had the vote, thanks to successive Reform Acts, and they represented a formidable threat to the ruling class's assumption of its right to govern. And within the moneyed middle class, the 1890s was the decade of the New Woman, pressing for more rights, including marriage reform, better employment conditions, educational opportunities, and the vote.

Jennie Churchill and her sisters were largely indifferent to this feminist ferment. Trapped in their class cocoon, they were also insensible to the dire conditions in which Britain's working class continued to live: overworked, underpaid, and crowded into slum properties. A manservant earned about £25 a year (£2,500 today); a kitchen maid could expect about £15 a year (£1,500).[3] The average woman could expect six to ten pregnancies; she would also likely face the death of at least one or two infants. Most blue-collar households lived with hunger; state pensions and health care were still years in the future. But the world that the Jerome sisters knew was captured in the complacent hymn sung in Anglican churches on Easter Sunday throughout the empire: "The rich man in his castle, the poor man at his gate."

Jennie was deeply in debt, but she and Leonie, who arrived with her two young sons, still managed to rent an apartment in a seven-story gray stone mansion. A large staff overseen by the indispensable Walden and Gentry kept 34 Avenue Kléber humming. "I fancy

Walden and Gentry will become quite French scholars with so many French servants around," Jennie wrote Jack, who arrived from Harrow for the Easter holiday.[4] Leonie's son Shane, who was ten at the time, would remember the Jerome sisters' homes as "full of servants who all looked as though they needed a holiday by the seaside. Footmen seemed constantly harassed, cooks in a suicidal state tho cheering up when royalty consented to praise the soufflé . . . The successive ladies' maids were as ambitious as their mistresses, but usually reached [a] tearful state before the 'Miss Jeromes' [were ready for] an important dinner."[5]

With her gift for stylish interiors, Jennie transformed her new high-ceilinged, gloomy apartment into a warm and welcoming salon, with brightly colored curtains, huge bouquets of fresh flowers, and sofas that guests could sink into. At the same time, she somehow found the capital (likely from moneylenders) to purchase and renovate a large town house in London, at 35a Great Cumberland Place, close to Marble Arch—an area significantly cheaper than Mayfair, but not beyond the pale. Her favorite couturier remained the revered and ludicrously expensive Charles Worth, on the rue de la Paix. Years later, a friend of her son's would quip, "Winston is a man of simple tastes. He is always prepared to put up with the best of everything." It was a lesson that he had absorbed from his mother.

As the sisters sauntered along spacious tree-lined sidewalks, twirling their lace parasols and eyeing the delicious little desserts in patisserie windows, they could recall their childhood years spent here. Back then, the path ahead had appeared clear—engagement, marriage, motherhood. The lives of both Jennie's sisters had adhered to that script, although money continued to be a problem for both Clara Frewen and Leonie Leslie. But against the backdrop of endless balls and weekend house parties, Jennie's life had deviated from convention. During the past decade, her ambitious, sick husband and her several affairs had consumed her attention, and she had largely ignored her sons. Now there was a large hole in her glittering existence.

Winston rushed to fill it. And his mother was happy to let him.

The Sandhurst cadet was a high-spirited, ambitious young man, hungry to launch himself into the world. But first, there were all those pesky bills he kept accumulating. He was constantly overdrawn at the bank. He needed horses, uniforms, funds to pay off his debts and his mess bills. "I have got a lot of tiresome financial details to write to you about . . . I am at present very hard up . . . Would it be possible and convenient to you to pay at present so large a sum as £100–£120?" he wrote in April 1895.[6] Jennie, as hard up as her son, failed to meet Winston's endless demands and scolded him for extravagance—even as she was unable to curtail her own.

However, Winston's letters also reflect his adoration of and dependence on his "darling Mama." He longed "for the day when you will be able to have a little house of your own and when I can really feel that there is such a place as home." Four months later, still grieving for his father and his nanny, he wrote, "How I wish I could secrete myself in a corner of the envelope and embrace you as soon as you tear it open!"[7]

Soon after Jennie arrived in Paris, she made a new friend. Among the visitors to the Avenue Kléber salon was Bourke Cockran, a wealthy Irish American lawyer and Democratic congressman from New York who was a friend of her sister Clara's husband, Moreton Frewen. Recently widowed, Cockran was a powerful bull of a man: wide-shouldered, with deep-set blue eyes and a huge head. Even more imposing than his size was his seductive voice. In conversation, his low baritone with its Irish lilt was musical; at a political meeting, it was spellbinding as he spoke for one or two hours on such tricky subjects as his support for the gold standard. Jennie found this erudite and charming politician irresistible. Fluent in French, he was a tremendous addition to her dinner parties, with his wit, warmth, and fund of anecdotes. He drove Jennie around Paris in his open landau and lavished on her all the treats she loved and he could easily afford: the best seats at smart restaurants, the theater, and the opera.

Was this another love affair? Probably—both Jennie and Cockran were recently widowed, and both were sensualists eager for diversion. But according to Anita Leslie, they were "two beings of violently tempestuous nature . . . their duet was that of two pairs of cymbals."[8] Each complained that they found the other exhausting; they wore each other out. Although a wealthy husband would dig Jennie out of all her debts, perhaps she was enjoying the novelty of control of her own life too much to enter into partnership with such a forceful character. She and Cockran remained friends and he probably helped her from time to time, when she was in a financial jam. But he returned to America alone, where he would be elected twice more as a Democratic congressman for New York and would become a significant influence on Jennie's elder son.

III

During the next five years, Jennie's relations with her sons evolved significantly. Winston and Jack were a study in contrasts. Winston was an energetic, arrogant extrovert who disregarded rules; Jack was quieter, less challenging, and now thriving at Harrow. The boys had been allies through their turbulent childhood, with Winston looking out for Jack, and now Jennie herself drew closer to them both. She was gentler with Jack, urging him to look after his health and assuring him, "I miss you very much. I love you more!"[9] But her elder son monopolized her maternal attention. After Randolph's death, Jennie and Winston's relationship often verged on that of co-conspirators as they plotted his advance. She was as convinced of her son's potential as Sara Roosevelt was of Franklin's, but the Jennie-Winston relationship developed along different lines.

Winston was beginning to question whether soldiering was his métier: "I find I am getting into a state of mental stagnation."[10] The ignominious end to Lord Randolph's political career and his cruelty to his son had never dented Winston's starry-eyed admiration for his father. He was now rereading Randolph's parliamentary addresses, and in a letter to his mother, he mused about a career in politics: "It is a fine game to play."[11] He knew his intellectual deficiencies. The army had not prepared him for debates on economics or politics or history, and he began casting around for some "mental medicine."[12] In late August 1895, while Jennie was traveling in Switzerland with Jack, Winston announced an ambitious reading program for himself, including Edward Gibbon's six-volume *History of the Decline and Fall of the Roman Empire.*

If Jennie responded to Winston's literary objectives, the letter has not survived. Anyway, now that Winston seemed more settled in his regiment, she was indulging her own interests. After the Swiss trip, she left Paris and moved on to the Isle of Wight for one of her favorite events: the Cowes regatta. Princess Alexandra had made white sailor outfits particularly popular this year, and Jennie loved strolling over the lawn of the Royal Yacht Squadron in her jaunty sailor cap and full-sleeved serge naval jacket. As she greeted old friends, she was often in the company of a new admirer, a twenty-seven-year-old guards officer named Hugh Warrender, who was more pliable than Bourke Cockran.

After Cowes, Jennie spun out visits to country houses, relying on friends' hospitality until her new London house was ready. She hoped to move there in November, but as she told Clara, "You know how long it takes to do anything & I am going to have it all painted from top to toe, electric light, hot water etc."[13] (The renovations included an elevator to enable the corpulent Prince of Wales to ascend from street level to her boudoir.)[14]

As if the renovations weren't enough to drain Jennie's purse, she now faced new requests from her son. Winston was already bored with soldiering and wanted an adventure. He had conceived an ambitious plan to cross the Atlantic—but he needed his mother's help.

"My dearest Mama," he wrote in October. "I daresay you will find the content of this letter somewhat startling. The fact is that I have decided to go with a great friend of mine . . . to America and the West Indies." He was anxious to travel to New York and then on to Cuba, where a revolt was simmering. "The cost of the [first-class] ticket is £37 a head return . . . I do not think the whole thing should cost £90

[£9,000 today]—which would be within a good margin [of] what I can afford to spend in 2 months."[15]

Jennie was exasperated that Winston had simply announced he was going; "It may have been nicer & perhaps wiser to have begun by consulting me." She predicted that the trip would be much more expensive and that he would find New York boring. She told Jack that she thought the Cuban trip was "a foolish business."[16] But Winston forged ahead, so Jennie went to work. Soon the twenty-year-old redhead had permission from his commanding officer (a friend of Jennie's), a request for military information from the director of Military Intelligence (another acquaintance), and an arrangement with the *Daily Graphic* (owned by family friends) to publish his dispatches from the front. Jennie offered to pay his ticket, then alerted Bourke Cockran to her son's imminent arrival in his country.

In early November 1895, Winston first set foot in New York, the city of his mother's birth. Bourke Cockran welcomed him and his friend Reggie Barnes to his sprawling apartment at 763 Fifth Avenue, which dazzled Winston. He wrote to his mother that it was "beautifully furnished and fitted with every convenience," that "everybody is very civil and we have engagements for every meal for the next few days about three deep . . . Mr. Cockran is one of the most charming hosts and interesting men I have met."[17] Cockran invited twelve judges, including a Supreme Court justice, to dine with his guests on their first evening; he also arranged for the young men to dine at the Waldorf, tour the cruiser *New York,* observe five fires with the fire commissioners, meet the railroad mogul Cornelius Vanderbilt (with whom Leonard Jerome, Winston's grandfather, had done business), and visit West Point.

Cockran would be a formidable influence on Jennie's son. At the candlelit dinner table and over brandy next to the fire, Winston was captivated, as Jennie herself had been, by a conversationalist and orator with an unequaled command of language. Cockran introduced him to the works of Edmund Burke, and to Burke's success as a speaker. He told him, "Burke . . . was simple, direct, eloquent, yet there is a splendor in his phrases that even in cold type reveals how forcibly he must have enthralled his visitors." Winston never forgot Cockran's own titanic vigor and the poetry of his words. He studied his speeches and stored key phrases in his memory. Years later, he would write of him, "I have never seen his like or, in some respects, his equal. His conversation, on point, in pith, in rotundity, in antithesis and in comprehension, exceeded everything I have ever heard."[18] Their New York encounter was the start of a lifelong correspondence.

Winston's feelings about his beloved mother's homeland could not have been more positive. "A great, crude, strong young people are the Americans—like a boisterous healthy boy among enervated but well-bred ladies and gentlemen," he wrote to his brother Jack. "Their hospitality is a revelation to me and they make you feel at home and at ease in a way that I have never before experienced."[19]

On November 17, Winston and Barnes took the train from Manhattan to Tampa, Florida, and the following day made their way by boat to Havana. Within the next few years, he would put himself in harm's way all over the globe—in Cuba, on India's North-West Frontier, on the Nile, and in South Africa. He would display extraordinary courage during these years, but also the recklessness that was in the Jerome genes.

After a skirmish against the rebels in the Cuban countryside, he wrote to Jennie, "I heard enough bullets whistle and hum past to satisfy me for some time to come . . . if . . . I had not changed my position one yard to the right I should infallibly have been shot."[20] He spared no gory details when he described subsequent exploits to Jennie as he ricocheted around the British Empire. Later, in northern India, he would describe how he rode his gray pony "all along the skirmish line where everyone else was lying down in cover. Foolish perhaps but I play for high stakes and given an audience there is no act too daring or too noble."[21] He admitted, "These sorts of things make life worth living."[22]

How did Jennie react to her son's determination to be at the center of the action? Alongside maternal anxiety, she displayed surprising equanimity, because she knew why he was doing it. He was convinced that daring exploits would win medals and publicity and give him political momentum. "I feel sure that if you live you will make a name for yrself," she reassured him in March 1897. "I believe in your lucky star as I do in mine."[23] She had transmitted her own sense of destiny to her son; he replied, "I have faith in my star – that is that I am intended to do something in the world."[24] His glorious optimism was a continual theme in the correspondence: "I am so conceited I do not believe the Gods would create so potent a being as myself for so prosaic an end."[25] A little while later, he bragged that he had now "been 10 complete times under fire. Quite a foundation for a political life."[26]

Winston demanded his mother dip into her address book to lubricate both his army career and his political ambitions. Besides her own friends and lovers and Randolph's family and former colleagues, Jennie Churchill's network encompassed a semihidden mafia of other expatriate Americans. Lady Curzon, who had described Jennie as living on the crest of a wave, was the Chicago-born wife of George Curzon, the undersecretary of state for foreign affairs who would soon be governor-general of India. Joseph Chamberlain, secretary of state for the colonies, had recently married Mary Endicott, born in Salem, Massachusetts. In 1895, Randolph's nephew Charles Spencer-Churchill, 11th Duke of Marlborough, had made a spectacularly advantageous but loveless marriage to Consuelo Vanderbilt from the Manhattan society that Sara Roosevelt knew so well.

A letter that Jennie wrote to Winston from Sandringham, the royal estate in Norfolk, gives a glimpse of her powerful contacts: "I came here Monday . . . a very pleasant party although not wildly exciting . . . the Pembrokes, Marlboroughs, Cadogans, Cooch Behars, etc. I am going to stay over Sunday when the Salisburys, Arthur Balfour and the new Bishop of London are coming."[27] The names she had just dropped included a former prime minister, a future prime minister, a duke, two earls, a maharaja, and of course the Prince and Princess of Wales.

In August 1896, Winston leaned heavily on his mother when he was trying to wriggle out of a routine three-year posting to India so he could travel to a threatened Boer revolt in South Africa: "I cannot believe that with all the influential friends you possess and all those who would do something for me for my father's sake – that I could not be allowed to go—were those influences properly exerted."[28] Such requests would intensify throughout his twenties. In 1897, he implored Jennie to help him leave India and join Sir Herbert Kitchener's campaign to reconquer the Sudan, despite Kitchener's hostility toward such a brash youngster. "You should endeavour to stimulate the Prince into writing to Kitchener on the subject . . . Indeed my life here is not big enough to hold me. I want to be up and doing and cannot bear inaction or routine."[29] Two months later he wrote: "Oh how I wish I could work you up over Egypt! I know you could do it with all your influence—and all the people you know. It is a pushing age and we must shove with the best."[30]

Jennie shoved, and by August 1898 Winston was back in khaki and on parade in Cairo as a supernumerary lieutenant attached to the 21st Lancers, with a commission from the *Morning Post* at the rate of £15 per column. On September 2, he would participate in the last significant cavalry charge in British history, at the Battle of Omdurman. His accounts of the battle, in both his *Morning Post* columns and the subsequent two-volume book, *The River War*, were triumphalist. Although British victory was inevitable thanks to superior training and technology—the latest European armaments annihilated the entire Sudanese army before it even had the enemy within range of its older guns—Winston crowed with delight.

Through her extensive web of carefully massaged contacts, Jennie was happy to give Winston's career far more momentum than Sara Roosevelt's network, fenced in by prejudice and protocol, bestowed on Franklin. Part of Jennie's motivation was the need for her extravagant son to earn his living as well as raise his profile, but she also yearned for Winston to enjoy the prominence that her husband had once enjoyed. Many years later, Winston would acknowledge how much energy his mother had exerted on his behalf. "She left no wire unpulled, no stone unturned, no cutlet uncooked."[31]

IV

This period of Jennie Churchill's life has usually been seen through the lens of her efforts on Winston's behalf. Her son's biographers (all men) have disparaged Jennie's flamboyance, as though her eagerness to reinvent herself and have fun was a shameful distraction from her maternal role. Robert Rhodes James wrote, "Behind Lady Randolph's vivid beauty and warm vivacity there lay an essentially selfish and frivolous character"—a judgment repeated by William Manchester.[32] These writers paid little attention to the constraints within which a woman had to operate back then, or the ways in which Jennie challenged those restrictions.

But Jennie's biographer Ralph Martin struck a different note, suggesting simply that "Jennie always reserved a large part of her life for herself."[33] In the late 1890s, she made it obvious to her contemporaries that she was not going to dwindle into a sad widowhood. Instead, now that she was single again, she would continue to move in the circles where she might help her son's ambitions. And she would also explore her own cultural interests and indulge her sense of theatrics.

"Rarely had the London social world been so stirred as by the fancy-dress ball given at Devonshire House on the 2nd of July, 1897," begins a chapter of Jennie's *Reminiscences*. "For weeks, not to say months, beforehand it seemed the principal topic of conversation. The absorbing question was what characters our friends and ourselves were going to represent. Great were the confabulations and mysteries." Jennie's mischievous humor shines through her description of the excitement. "Historical books were ransacked for inspiration, old pictures and engravings were studied, and people became quite learned in respect to past celebrities of whom they had never before heard."[34]

In the late nineteenth century, fancy dress balls were all the rage among the elites of both New York and London. These were lavish and enormously expensive events. The Duke and Duchess of

Devonshire issued more than seven hundred invitations to the extravaganza at their London residence. In theory, they were celebrating Queen Victoria's Diamond Jubilee that year; in practice, such balls—on either side of the Atlantic—were exercises in conspicuous consumption, at which aristocrats and plutocrats competed for attention. An invitation to the ball confirmed a guest's status as part of the cream of society. Not only was Lady Randolph Churchill invited to the 1897 Devonshire House ball; at the dinner, she was seated at the top table, with the Prince of Wales and other royal guests.

Devonshire House was a massive three-story, many-chimneyed brick mansion situated on Piccadilly, with a view across Green Park to Buckingham Palace. It was shielded from pedestrians by a high brick wall, but its plain exterior hid some of the most imposing interiors and artworks in the capital. On that warm July night, it was still light when carriages started rolling toward the mansion. Just as, a century later, hundreds of fans would converge in Hollywood to watch movie stars walk the red carpet into the Academy Awards ceremony, the London crowds craned their necks for a glimpse of the heavily bejeweled and fantastically costumed occupants of the carriages before they vanished through the wooden gates. Once the illustrious guests had disembarked at the front door and entered the entrance hall, with its marble floors and pillars, they were ushered up the grand staircase to the ballroom. There, under an elaborately coffered ceiling and huge chandelier with flickering wax candles, they were welcomed from a raised dais by the Emperor Charles V (in reality, the host, the Duke of Devonshire), with Zenobia, Queen of Palmyra (his wife Louisa, Duchess of Devonshire) at his side. When guests tired of dancing, they could stroll in the large garden behind the mansion, where Japanese lanterns were strung in the trees and the flower beds were outlined in red, white, and blue fairy lamps.[35]

As Jennie would write, "Everyone of note and interest was there, representing the intellect, beauty, and fashion of the day." A bulky figure disguised as the grand master of the Knights Hospitaler of Malta (clearly recognizable as the Prince of Wales) held court in the

Devonshire picture gallery, while Marie Antoinette (his mistress, Daisy, Countess of Warwick) fluttered nearby. A Napoleon was appalled to discover that he had a double on the dance floor, and a duchess known to be on the brink of bankruptcy was swathed in priceless jewels. The costumes were so elaborate that the host invited the London photographic firm of James Lafayette to set up a tent in the garden to record his guests in all their splendor. However, the cumbersome glass plate photographic process (then the most up-to-date available) meant that the photographer only had time to capture about two hundred guests on his glass plates.

It was the kind of occasion made for Jennie Churchill. She chose to represent the famously beautiful Theodora, who had risen from being an erotic courtesan to a Byzantine empress. (Gibbon's *Decline and Fall* quotes Procopius in describing one of her lewd practices, involving barley grains, servants, and geese.) Sarah Bernhardt had recently played the title role in a Paris production of a play based on Theodora's story. Despite all her debts, Jennie had commissioned a magnificent costume from Worth that was inspired by a mosaic at San Vitale in Ravenna.

The effect was stunning. Over a silky underdress she wore a tunic richly embroidered with golden Byzantine patterns and studded with gems. On her head was a heavy golden crown and a jewel-encrusted headband; lengthy strings of glistening pearls, borrowed from the Marlborough family, were wound around her neck. In her right hand she carried the Imperial Orb of the Eastern (Byzantine) Empire, borrowed from the British Museum; as she did not dare put it down, she could not dance. Instead of sweeping her hair up into the elaborate chignon that was the convention of the time, she had let it tumble loose over her shoulders, something which in Victorian England could indicate either an unmarried state or licentiousness. Needless to say, she was one of Lafayette's chosen subjects, and appears in the commemorative album sitting on a carved throne, radiant and imperious.[36]

Gossip about such an audacious woman was inevitable, particularly because she remained close to the Prince of Wales while attracting the admiration of younger men. A much-repeated anecdote concerned Major Caryl Ramsden, an officer of the Seaforth Highlanders fourteen years her junior, whose looks had earned him the nickname "Beauty Ramsden." In early 1898, Jennie had stayed with him in Cairo's Continental Hotel while she bombarded General Kitchener with requests that he take Winston onto his staff. Jennie and Ramsden then took a cruise up the Nile together, before Ramsden was transferred elsewhere. But the affair went sour when Jennie unexpectedly returned to the Continental Hotel and found her lover in bed with his commanding officer's wife. News of the incident, and of Jennie's sharp rebukes to her duplicitous lover, reached the ears of London's chattering class.[37] Her reputation suffered; Beauty Ramsden's was enhanced.

There was more to Jennie than love affairs; she was impatient for issues more challenging than costume balls. Lord Randolph Churchill's political career had once fed that appetite, and she was eager to play a similar role for Winston. But he was often out of the country, and Jennie felt a lack of purpose.

She was not alone. A few other women of her class were starting to question the assumptions instilled during their privileged childhoods. Daisy, Countess of Warwick, had given a fancy dress ball earlier in the year at Warwick Castle, a hundred miles outside London, at a time when she was aware of "great distress among the poor." Working-class wages on the Warwick estates had been cut, and many agricultural laborers were in dire need of food, fuel, and clothing. As she would write in her memoir, at the time "I felt happy in the belief that our ball was giving work to so many people who would otherwise have been idle. The festivities of the Lords and Ladies Bountiful were being translated into terms of meat and bread for the workers."

Then she read an attack on her in a left-wing London newspaper, the *Clarion*, "for holding idle junketing in a time of general misery." Her ball was described as "a sham benevolence, a frivolous ignoring of real social conditions."[38]

Furious, Lady Warwick confronted the editor of the *Clarion*, who listened to her rationalization for her ball and then quietly explained that Lady Bountiful gestures glossed over much larger problems of systemic inequality. Lady Warwick left his office a convert to socialism, and though she never lost her taste for the high life (and indeed continued to occupy Bertie's bed), she threw herself into more sustainable philanthropy. She established a home for the disabled, a needlework school for rural girls with a Bond Street outlet to sell their products, and a women's training college. She loudly endorsed the 1917 Russian Revolution, fearlessly appointed left-wing clergy to the churches on her estate, and campaigned for women's suffrage. By the end of her life she had run for Parliament as a Labour Party candidate and acquired the nickname "the Socialist Countess."

Her reputation as the royal mistress and her lifelong penchant for ropes of pearls and elaborate hats would mean that she was rarely taken seriously. But her socialist epiphany suggests another woman eager for more than fancy dress. Nor was she alone, even within circles where women were raised to be social ornaments and usually accepted the role without question. Some plunged into the suffrage movement. Lady Constance Lytton, sister of the second Earl of Lytton and daughter of Robert Bulwer-Lytton, a viceroy of India, would be imprisoned for taking part in a suffragist demonstration in 1909. To protest the way that she was given better treatment in jail than her fellow marchers, she carved the words VOTES FOR WOMEN across her chest with a hairpin.[39]

Jennie Churchill chafed at the limitations of her own life. She lacked the deep pockets for philanthropy that Daisy Warwick enjoyed, and she still resisted the argument that women should have the vote so that they might influence the government. And carving up her décolletage was not her style. What to do? In her memoir, she describes a visit to the Duke of Portland at Welbeck Abbey, his vast stone mansion in Nottinghamshire, which boasted an underground ballroom and a tunnel to the stables. The occasion was a farewell house party for George Curzon, husband of her friend Mary, who had recently been ennobled as Lord Curzon of Kedleston and appointed viceroy of India. Sitting next to Lord Curzon at dinner, "I bemoaned the empty life I was leading at the moment. Lord Curzon tried to console me by saying that a woman alone was a godsend in any society, and that I might look forward to a long vista of country-house parties, dinners and balls. Thinking over our conversation later, I found myself wondering if this indeed was all that the remainder of my life held for me. I determined to do something, and cogitating for some time over what it should be, decided finally to start a review."[40]

The result was an arts and culture "quarterly miscellany." Although she knew nothing about publishing, printing, or budgets, she knew a lot about music, theater, and literature. "My ideas were of the vaguest, but they soon shaped themselves,"[41] largely because she was smart enough to recruit colleagues who knew more than she did. Chief among her helpers was the American-born writer Pearl Craigie, a shy but clever woman who had already published several books and a successful play under her pen name, John Oliver Hobbes. Craigie helped Jennie find an assistant editor and a publisher. Despite objections from Winston, it would be called the *Anglo-Saxon Review*, and the first issue would appear in June 1899.

Jennie loved her new project, which was a bold initiative for a woman of her class. "A most delightful and enthralling period began, which absorbed me from morning till night in the most interesting of occupations," she wrote later.[42] She enjoyed commissioning articles from her friends; even Lord Salisbury, the prime minister, was invited to be a contributor. He thanked her for her "flattering invitation" but declined on the grounds that he was busy. The first issue included a column by novelist Henry James and an article on wireless telegraphy by Professor Oliver Lodge. The Duchess of Devonshire contributed some unpublished letters written by her famous eighteenth-century predecessor, Georgiana, Duchess of Devonshire.

When Jennie arrived at smart weekend gatherings now, her basket was crammed with papers—manuscripts, page proofs, and correspondence with authors. She was determined that "Maggie," as she nicknamed her creation, should feature the best writers on both sides of the Atlantic. She reached out to literary lions; George Bernard Shaw produced an article called "A Word More about Verdi." However, when Jennie invited Shaw, a strict vegetarian, to lunch, he replied, "Certainly not! What have I done to provoke such an attack on my well-known habits?" Jennie responded, "Know nothing of your habits; hope they are not as bad as your manners."[43]

Other friends were waspish. Daisy Warwick would write in her memoirs, "It was at one time one of Lady Randolph's amusing foibles to be regarded as literary."[44]

The *Review* attracted extensive coverage from cartoonists, columnists, and satirists. One wag wrote a lengthy poem that began:

Have you heard of the wonderful Magazine
Lady Randolph's to edit, with help from the Queen?
It's a guinea a number, too little by half,
For the Crowned Heads of Europe are all on the staff;
And everyone writing verse, fiction or views –
The best blue-blood ink must exclusively use . . .[45]

Jennie's purpose was more complicated than a simple urge to fill her life constructively, as is clear in her weekly correspondence with Winston, now unhappily stationed with his regiment in India. She was desperate to make some money. When she discovered in early 1897 that Winston was badly overdrawn at the bank and had spent his allowance before it was even due, she explained her situation in a letter of reproof. "I do wish you wld try & reform – if you only realized how little I have, & how impossible it is for me to get any more. I have raised all I can, & I can assure you unless something extraordinary turns up I see ruin staring me in the face. Out of £2,700 [£270,000 today] a year £800 of it goes to you 2 boys, £410 for house rent and stables, which leaves me £1,500 for everything – taxes, servants, stables, food, dress, travelling—and now I have to pay interest on money borrowed. I really fear for the future."[46]

Her fraught finances had been further damaged by a swindler named James Cruikshank, who had persuaded the Jerome sisters to invest in a get-rich-quick scheme that left them poorer by £4,000 (£400,000 today). Jennie constantly juggled bank loans, insurance guarantees, and unpaid bills—yet her Theodora outfit would have cost between £200 and £400 (£20,000–£40,000). One can only assume that the generosity of friends kept her afloat. She continued to resist the notion that she might marry for money, despite public speculation. When an engagement to the millionaire William Waldorf Astor was rumored, she wrote to the Countess of Warwick: "Dearest Daisy, I am *not* going to marry anyone. If a perfect darling with at least £40,000 a year wants me *very much* I might consider it . . ."[47]

Winston was now doing well with his pen. Each time he took leave of his regiment to sprint off to another military engagement, he pushed his mother to sell his articles to one of the London newspapers. She was a formidable agent. The *Daily Graphic* had paid him a guinea for every dispatch he sent from Cuba in 1895. The *Daily Chronicle* offered him ten guineas an article if he covered a conflict in Crete (it was settled before he could get there). When he rushed off to help suppress a Pathan uprising on the North-West Frontier in 1897, he took with him a commission that Jennie had negotiated with the *Daily Telegraph* for £5 a column, plus a further paying commission from the *Allahabad Pioneer* for daily telegrams. (He was furious that Jennie had agreed with an editor that his byline should not appear on the *Daily Telegraph* columns, on the grounds that it would be inappropriate for a junior officer to be writing about his seniors. He wrote to his mother that the fact that his letters were published unsigned meant that "an excellent opportunity of bringing my name before the country in a correct and attractive light – by means of graphic & forcible letters, [has been] lost."[48] As Jennie had warned him, his senior officers were angry when they learned who had written the columns.) When he turned his *Daily Telegraph* articles into his first book, *The Story of the Malakand Field Force* (1898), he received £382 (£38,200 today) in royalties from his publishers, Longmans—more than he could earn in four years as a subaltern.[49] He next embarked on a novel, for which he received a substantial advance plus £100 from *Macmillan's* magazine for serial rights.

Taking note of her son's success, Jennie hoped that her *Anglo-Saxon Review* might similarly replenish her bank account. For Winston, the intellectual gloss it might give his volatile mother was more important than the possible financial boost. On January 1, 1899, he wrote a letter from India that captures the changing dynamics of their relationship, with Winston sounding more like a patronizing older brother than her harum-scarum son, to use his father's phrase. He suggested that the *Review* might give her "an occupation and an interest in life which will make up for all the silly social amusements you will cease to shine in as time goes on and which will give you in the latter part of your life as fine a position in the world of taste & thought as formerly & now in that of elegance and beauty . . . It may also be profitable. If you could make . . . £1,000 a year out of it, I think that would be a little lift in the dark clouds."[50]

The *Anglo-Saxon Review* was an imaginative initiative, but it was also a costly failure—too expensive, too muddled in its editorial priorities. There were plenty of cheaper publications available. The last of ten issues appeared in September 1901.

Jennie's finances were in a worse state than ever. She had already mortgaged her sons' inheritances to save herself from bankruptcy. Winston acknowledged that they were both "spendthrift and extravagant . . . but it seems . . . suicidal to me when you spend £200 on a ball dress . . . The pinch of the whole matter is we are damned poor."[51] He continued to assure his mother of his love for her, but the tone of his letters from India became more reproachful: "In three years from my father's death you have spent a quarter of our entire fortune in the world. I have also been extravagant: but my extravagances are a very small matter besides yours . . ."[52] Despite the ongoing argument between them about who was the bigger spendthrift, neither mother nor son allowed the state of their finances to constrain them from spending more.

During the years of financial insecurity, the *Anglo-Saxon Review* gave Jennie Churchill confidence in her creative instincts. Suddenly she was invested in something more permanent than fancy dress. Now she was about to embark on an ambitious new project that would give her an even greater sense of purpose and reinforce her celebrity. It was an initiative that Sara Roosevelt would probably have admired, although she herself would never take such a leadership role.

CHAPTER 12

◇

Jennie Goes to War

1899–1901

In October 1899, hostilities erupted in two Boer states that bordered the British colonies on the southern tip of Africa. The Boer War was one of the last great imperial adventures, and it dominated debate in Parliament and discussion at Mayfair dinner parties. Although still preoccupied by the *Anglo-Saxon Review*, Lady Randolph Churchill craved the chance to join the imperial war effort.

In these circumstances, Sara Roosevelt would have minded the home front while applauding the fighting troops, but Jennie wanted to go beyond the traditional role for women during wartime—a Greek chorus of wailing wives and mothers. It was particularly galling to her to watch her son enjoying opportunities that would never have been offered to a woman—a commission to be a foreign correspondent, the chance to be at the center of military action. She wrote in *Reminiscences*, "The people who were the most to be pitied during the war were those . . . who had to remain at home," adding with blithe insensitivity that it was almost as depressing as seeing fellow guests at a country house party going out to hunt and not being allowed to join them.[1]

Then a chance to go out hunting came her way. She was asked to preside over a committee of twenty prominent American women in London who would organize an American hospital ship to go to Cape Town. This would be an extraordinary venture, which only someone with Lady Randolph Churchill's connections and drive might pull together. She threw herself into the task.

II

The conflict in South Africa was a naked grab by Britain for wealth. Recent discoveries of vast diamond resources in the Orange Free State and gold in the Transvaal had attracted swarms of English-speaking immigrants into the two small Afrikaans-speaking independent republics. "Uitlanders," as the immigrants were known, now outnumbered the original settlers, but they had not been given the right to vote. The Conservative government led by Lord Salisbury decided it was a great excuse to go to war. The government proposed to annex the Boer Republics unilaterally, claiming that this was the only way to defend the rights of the English-speaking Uitlanders.

Although the tide was ebbing on the British Empire, it remained a vast colonial sphere. Queen Victoria reigned over half of North America, much of Africa, both ends of the Mediterranean, the whole Indian subcontinent, Malaya, Singapore, Australia, several Caribbean islands, New Zealand, and islands scattered across the Atlantic and Pacific Oceans. Britain's maritime strength had allowed it first to colonize distant lands that might yield valuable resources, and then to defend the lucrative transcontinental trade in enslaved peoples and raw materials that sustained British wealth (and frequently impoverished Britain's overseas possessions). London, the largest metropolis history had ever known, was still one of the world's greatest ports and the largest exporter.

The empire was built on trade, but it was sustained by a deeply embedded belief in white supremacy. The miners, millworkers, and domestic servants of Britain enjoyed little benefit from all the foreign conquests and imperial wealth. While their employers were growing rich and building large country houses through the Midlands and the north of England, they themselves lived in squalid red brick terraces.

But as yet, few blue-collar workers questioned the racism that, in British eyes, entitled a handful of representatives from the upper class to rule over millions of people thousands of miles from the imperial center. This was in part why the queen's subjects within Britain were fiercely loyal to the empire, belting out the words to patriotic songs and hymns like "Rule, Britannia!" and "Land of Hope and Glory." And if trouble flared up in an imperial outpost, the writer Hilaire Belloc had the answer:

> Whatever happens, we have got
> The Maxim gun, and they have not.

However, there was a powerful anti–Boer War sentiment in Britain, especially among supporters of the Liberal and fledgling Labour Parties. And observers outside Britain were unimpressed with the all-powerful British Empire's aggression against a beleaguered minority of Boers. Mark Twain, one of Winston's boyhood heroes, was explicit about his disapproval of the British treatment of the Boers. Although he pronounced the young Churchill "the perfect man" because he had an English father and an American mother, he also announced in public, "I think England sinned when she got herself into a war in South Africa which she could have avoided."[2] Jennie's good friend Bourke Cockran told his protégé that he disliked Britain's bullying conduct.

But for twenty-five-year-old Winston, there were no existential doubts about the need to go to war. Two years earlier, he had written, "For the sake of our Empire, for the sake of our honour, for the sake of the race, we must fight the Boers."[3] He had recently resigned his army commission to focus on his political career. Now, bristling with jingoism, he wanted to be in the thick of the excitement, so he snatched the chance to be a war correspondent. The *Morning Post* offered him £1,000 (£100,000 today) for the first four months, followed by £200 a month (£20,000), plus all expenses. This was a tremendous sum; a rising young professional man would have thought he was doing well if he earned £500 a year (£50,000).

Winston had no intention of stinting on supplies. He had inherited the loyal Walden as his personal valet, and Walden was soon packing into one of his young master's black tin steamer trunks "Six bottles of vin d'Ay sec, eighteen bottles of St.-Émilion, six bottles of 'light port,' six bottles of French vermouth, eighteen bottles of Scotch whiskey ('10 years old'), six bottles of 'Very Old *Eau de Vie* 1866,' and twelve bottles of Rose's cordial lime juice."[4] Sporting a smart yachting cap, Churchill left Southampton on October 14, with Walden and several steamer trunks, on a Royal Mail steamer bound for Cape Town.

Within days of his departure, Jennie had accepted the invitation to acquire, refurbish, and staff a hospital ship to provide medical care during the war. From late October, she chaired daily meetings in her house on Great Cumberland Place. Most of her fellow expatriates on the committee were dear friends: they included her two sisters as well as Mary Chamberlain (wife of colonial secretary Joseph Chamberlain), Consuela Vanderbilt (who had recently married Lord Randolph's nephew Sunny, the 9th Duke of Marlborough), and her father's old friend Fanny Ronalds. They organized glamorous fundraisers in Manhattan, attended by Vanderbilts and Astors, and in London, where Jennie's piano recitals attracted members of the royal family.

These female-run events were extremely successful. Within two months, Jennie and her friends had raised £41,597; their goal had been £30,000 (£3,000,000 today). Jennie had also spearheaded the acquisition of a ship, the *Maine*, hired a crew, and begun to recruit medical and nursing staff. In her view, she told committee members, the project would do "more to cement that friendship [between England and America] than years of flag-waving and pleasant amenities."[5]

Soon, the converted Atlantic cattle boat boasted electric lighting, a state-of-the-art operating theater, and five wards comprising 218 beds. The British army's commander in chief appointed a principal medical officer for the *Maine*, while Jennie recruited nurses from America. So many medical stores were donated that there was a storage problem. "The War Office and the Admiralty were badgered and heckled [for advice and help]," wrote Jennie. "We would not take No for an answer." It helped that she was already on first name terms with the ministers involved, and that Queen Victoria took a personal interest in the project. The monarch twice invited Jennie to Windsor Castle for updates and gave a reception there for the American nurses.

A series of defeats in South Africa punctured British confidence that Boer resistance would collapse. But Jennie was on a roll. She decided to sail on the *Maine* herself, she told the *New York Times* in an appeal for funds. "I think I may prevent any kind of friction between the American nurses . . . and the British officials."[6] She designed a special costume for herself: a starched white nurse's uniform with lace frills at the wrist and a red cross on the arm, and a fashionable high-crowned white cap that perched on her glossy black curls. On the eve of the *Maine*'s departure, the Prince of Wales sent a note she would always treasure. "I admire your courage, but you were always the most plucky as you were one of the most charming of women."[7]

For Jennie, the excitement of outfitting the *Maine* had been a welcome distraction from "some terribly anxious moments."[8] On November 17, she had received a telegram from the editor of the *Morning Post*. "I regret to inform you that Mr. Winston Churchill has been captured by the Boers. He fought gallantly after an armoured train in which he was traveling was trapped."[9] In theory, as a press correspondent Winston should have been considered a non-combatant and released immediately. In practice, his position was more questionable, as he had been so keen to see action that he had persuaded Captain Aylmer Haldane, an old friend from the Malakand Field Force who was now running a reconnaissance mission, to draft him into service. Winston had been wearing an army jacket and brandishing a pistol when he was captured.

From the Boer jail in Pretoria, Winston wrote a letter to his mother that was designed for his captors' eyes. He reassured "Dearest Mamma" that he had been "quite unarmed" so that "you need not be anxious in any way but I trust you will do all in your power to procure my release." Jennie received telegrams of support from, among others, the Prince of Wales, Charles Kinsky (now in St. Petersburg), and Empress Eugénie. From South Africa, the trusty Walden described in a letter Winston's bravery during the ambush on the train.

"The driver [of the train] was one of the first wounded, and he said to Mr. Winston, 'I am finished.' So Mr. Winston said to him, 'Buck up a bit, I will stick to you' and . . . he helped the driver pick 20 wounded up . . . He [the driver] says there is not a braver gentleman in the Army."[10]

Jennie was proud of Winston's courage, and also concerned that he had obviously been more than a noncombatant. "Had it not been for the absorbing occupation of the *Maine*, I cannot think how I could have got through that time of suspense."[11] But her faith in her son's invincibility proved justified. The day before the *Maine* sailed, the headline in the *Post* read, "CHURCHILL ESCAPED." Winston had broken out of jail and was stealthily making his way into Portuguese East Africa. His hair-raising escape helped to make him a household name back home, which did wonders for sales of the newspapers that carried his articles about his dramatic adventures, and the even more heroic version he would tell later in *My Early Life*.

In late December 1899, dressed in her sparkling white uniform, Jennie stood on the deck of the *Maine* as it steamed out of Southampton harbor in a thick fog. By the first day of the new century, it was sailing through a six-day gale in the Bay of Biscay. "No fiddles can restrain your soup from being shot into your lap, or the contents of your glass into your face," she would recall later. "The green of my attractive little cabin, which I had thought so reposeful, became a source of acute suffering . . . I remember thinking, as I rolled in sleepless wretchedness, that if we went to the bottom, at least we should be counted as victims of the war."[12]

A tailored uniform, a suite of cabins specially furnished for her by a London department store, and the companionship of Miss Warrender, her assistant—sister of Jennie's admirer Hugh—were not enough to keep Jennie's spirits up. As she hung on to her skirts with one hand and the deck rail with the other during inspections of the vessel, she realized that there was a lot to do. Decks and gangways were piled high with excessive goods and supplies that had not been properly stowed. The wards were still littered with wood shavings and debris.

Moreover, her dimpled smile and aristocratic manner did not soothe professional rivalry among her fellow passengers. The British medical staff clashed with the American nurses. The ship's officers insisted on dining in their cabins rather than with the American nurses' snippy superintending sister. There were complaints about the size and luxury of Jennie's quarters—a large reception room, a bathroom, and a bedroom on the promenade deck, plus the inevitable lady's maid—and grumbles about the piano recitals she organized to amuse herself, the medical and nursing staff, and crew. One nurse suggested that she played "the great lady philanthropist with much fuss and feathers." On January 9, her birthday, the lady philanthropist glumly stared into the night sky, picking out the Southern Cross. "I confess I felt no keenness, having seen it often before [during the round-the-world trip with Lord Randolph], and I thought its beauty a delusion."[13]

Once the *Maine* was in the warm sunshine of the southern hemisphere, sailing into Cape Town's harbor at dawn on January 23, Jennie's spirits were raised by the sight of troops disembarking from transport ships and feverish activity on the docks, against the extraordinary backdrop of Table Mountain. Awaiting her arrival was a letter from Winston, now in a British camp in Natal, in which he praised her with almost parental pride: "I am so glad & proud to think of your enterprise & energy in coming out to manage the *Maine*. Your name will be long remembered with affection by many poor broken creatures. Besides it is the right thing to do, which is the great point."[14]

But Jennie was dismayed by another sentence in the letter, telling her that, thanks to a few strings pulled by Winston, Jack was on his way from England to join the fight. "I hope you don't mind," Winston wrote. Jennie did mind. Jack was only nineteen and had none of Winston's ambition or bravado. He had recently started a job in the City, and Jennie was relying on him for financial support. Instead she now had two sons in harm's way. (Jack was shot in the calf during his first military engagement and was nursed on the *Maine*.)

Jennie's work in South Africa was that of a forceful woman confined to the sidelines. Informed that the army wanted to load the *Maine* with casualties, then send it straight back to England, she fought like a tigress to ensure that it fulfilled its function as a proper hospital ship, supplying on-deck surgical and medical care, rather than serving merely as a floating ambulance. She won. At the same time, the Jennie who wanted adventures was busy. She enjoyed several receptions on shore, reunited with both Jack and Winston, and went military sightseeing. She twisted enough arms among the generals to receive passes to reach the war zone, found a handsome young man to escort her there, and saw the wrecked train where Winston had been captured. She immersed herself in the logistics and strategies of the various battles, and ate breakfast served in tin mugs and pewter plates with the 7th Fusiliers, despite the "terrible plague" of flies. "I longed to be a man and take some part in the fighting, but then I remembered my red cross."[15]

The *Maine* was soon filled with casualties. At the same time, "interested visitors . . . flocked on board" to see the celebrated Lady Randolph Churchill in action. Her contribution to the nursing care was to write letters. "One very gallant Tommy, who lay with a patch over his eye, and inflamed cheek and broken arm, asked me to add to his letter, 'The sister who is a-writing of this is very nice.' "[16]

In late March, she decided it was time for the *Maine* to go home, although the military authorities now wanted the ship to stay. Imperiously overruling the chief medical officer in Cape Town, she cabled her friend the minister of war in London to back her up. Soon the ship was en route to Southampton. Over 354 men had been treated onboard, and 12 officers and 151 men were brought home.

When Jennie wrote her account of the hospital ship in *Reminiscences,* she described it as "a very successful enterprise . . . [and] one of the most thrilling experiences of my life, certainly the most important public work I have ever tried to do." As the *Maine* docked at Southampton on April 23, 1900, she stood triumphant on deck, wearing a white straw hat with a blue ribbon decorated with the British and American flags.

III

Not everybody saw Lady Randolph Churchill's hospital ship as pure altruism. Consuelo Vanderbilt Marlborough, who was on Jennie's committee, wrote in her memoirs that "Lady Randolph was going out on the ship to join her son Winston. We knew that she was equally anxious to see young George Cornwallis-West."[17]

The Hon. George Frederick Myddleton Cornwallis-West had been in Jennie's life since 1898. He was her type—a tall, slim Old Etonian, often described as the best-looking man in England. He cut a dashing figure in the tight pants of his Scots Guards dress uniform. Only sixteen days older than Winston, he certainly was not sufficiently wealthy to dig Jennie out of debt. But such considerations did not deter her. As George would write in *Edwardian Hey-Days*, his memoir, Jennie was "then a woman of forty-three; still beautiful, she did not look a day more than thirty, and her charm and vivacity were on a par with her youthful appearance."

Their relationship had begun during a summer weekend party at Warwick Castle, a stunning medieval stone building with landscaped gardens overlooking the meandering River Avon. It was the perfect stage for the start of a love affair, and when George took Jennie rowing on the river, a romance seemed inevitable. According to George's memoir, Jennie spoke about her pride in Winston and her ambitions for him. He did not describe her behavior, which likely included a delicate hand trailing in the water, a radiant smile as she looked admiringly at her muscular oarsman, and a flattering interest in him. But he didn't need to; Jennie knew how to make a conquest, and George was instantly besotted. Within a few weeks, he had embarked on a passionate correspondence, decorated with loving hearts, that Jennie would keep all her life.

"Jennie Dearest," he wrote on July 3, 1898, in the first of hundreds of letters. "I do so miss you, & long for you to be with me here. I wonder now what you are doing & who you are on the river with, I am sure Sweetie you are behaving yourself well . . . Good night you dear angel, *à bientôt*, yours always, G."[18] Three weeks later, he wrote, "I thought about you all yesterday & built castles in the air about you & I living together . . ."[19]

Jennie loved it. She encouraged her friends to include George in country weekends, and she arranged to be at home, on Great Cumberland Place, whenever his Scots Guards battalion was in London barracks. Judging by George's enthusiasm for the loose silk kimonos that Jennie wore for their private meetings, a departure from the whale-boned gowns worn by women in public, it was an ardently physical relationship.

Of course it was a scandal. At first, most of her friends (including the Prince of Wales) did not take it too seriously. There was a silent consensus that Jennie was just toying with the rather dim George. As Anita Leslie points out, "Many of [his] letters read like pages from a game book: 'We had a very good day—about 1100 head all told, 700 pheasants & the rest rabbits & hares.' " Bulletins describing how "I was shooting extraordinarily well" were closely followed by accounts of deer-stalking and salmon-fishing expeditions."[20] How could an intellectual lightweight keep the attention of a woman accustomed to mingling with powerful politicians—a woman who had founded the *Anglo-Saxon Review*?

In the early days, Jennie made casual mention of George in letters to her sons, but they probably considered their mother's latest beau little more than evidence of her continuing magnetism. She herself suggested she was just having fun. She wrote to her friend the composer Ethel Smyth, "Of course, the glamor won't last forever, but why not take what you can, and not make yourself or anyone else unhappy when the next stage arrives?"[21]

However, she was making the Cornwallis-Wests very unhappy. Although George's family had extensive land holdings—five thousand acres in North Wales and two thousand in Hampshire, around their country mansion called Newlands Manor—the agricultural recession had forced them to into debt. George's mother, Patsy, was a formidable woman who had managed to marry George's sister Daisy off to Hans Heinrich, Prince of Plessy, heir to a Prussian fortune. But the prince had no interest in bailing out his British in-laws. In time, Patsy would marry off George's younger sister Constance Edwina, known as Shelagh, to the Duke of Westminster, one of Britain's wealthiest peers. But that was an unhappy marriage, and none of the Westminster millions flowed toward the Cornwallis-Wests.

Patsy West wanted George to marry an heiress and produce an heir to the family name. Her worst nightmare must have been to discover that Jennie Churchill, her own contemporary with a louche reputation, might become her daughter-in-law. Jennie was too cash-strapped to pay off the Cornwallis-West debts, and probably too old to produce any offspring.

As George's letters to Jennie became steadily more adoring, Jennie's friends started to tut-tut. The Prince of Wales was not impressed with her affair with his godson, and wrote to her, "It is a pity that you have got yourself so talked about – & remember you are not 25!" Jennie began to make some effort to disentangle herself. When her friend George Curzon was busy assembling the staff who would accompany him to the viceregal palace in Delhi, Jennie recommended he take George with him. Curzon politely declined.

George's devotion to Jennie intensified. "I dreamt about you last night, only too vividly, some-one tried to take you away from me, I can never allow that, the mental pain was awful even in my dream, Heaven knows what it would be if it actually happened . . ."[22] The letters kept coming, addressed to "My dearest Jennie," "You sweetie," and "My darling little Missus." At Cowes in 1899, the Prince of Wales took George aside and pointed out the inadvisability of marrying a woman so much older than he was. The same month, Winston wrote to Jennie, "I have seen several very spiteful cuttings about your projected alliance."[23] But by now, Jennie was in love with George. She was flattered by his devotion and animated by his passion. So what if, out of bed, he was a bit dull? They spoke of marriage, but then Jennie had second thoughts . . .

The imperial adventure in South Africa interrupted the romance.

JENNIE JEROME CHURCHILL

Clara Jerome, Jennie's mother, raised her daughters to be genteel and accomplished.

Leonard Jerome, Jennie's reckless father, was known as "The King of Wall Street."

The Jerome Mansion on Madison Avenue boasted internal fountains, a three-story stable, and a private theater.

From an early age, Jennie knew how to play to the camera.

Jerome Park Racetrack attracted both Leonard's friends and Rosy Roosevelt.

Mrs. Jerome and her three adult daughters (*right to left*): Vivacious Jennie overshadowed shy Leonie and dreamy Clara.

Edward, Prince of Wales: The heir to the throne welcomed American women to his "Marlborough House set."

Lord Randolph Churchill, second son of the Duke of Marlborough: "instant chemistry."

Lord Randolph and Jennie: "a very dangerous affair."

Jennie, with two-year-old
Winston, before the Irish exile.

Blenheim Palace: Magnificent and forbidding.

Jennie with her sons Jack (*left*) and Winston, 1889.

The devoted Mrs. Everest.

Jennie as Professional Beauty, with her diamond star.

Jennie, in riding outfit: "radiant . . . intense."

Lord and Lady Randolph Churchill in Japan, on
the wretched round-the-world trip in 1895.

Jennie between Count Charles Kinsky (*left*) and Lord Dudley, two of her lovers.

Jennie as Empress Theodora at the Devonshire House Ball, 1897.

Jennie's quarters on the *Maine*, 1899.

The Hon. George
Cornwallis-West, "the
best-looking man
in England."

Winston recruited his glamorous mother to help in
the Oldham election campaign in October 1900.

Jennie, at fifty-six, could still dominate a party.

Churchill, First Lord of the Admiralty, 1914, with inset of Clementine.

Jennie with grandson Peregrine.

At Bladon churchyard on July 2, 1921, Winston (*left*) and Jack lead the mourners.

In October 1899, George's battalion set off for Cape Town. Unlike Jennie, Winston, and even Jack, George did not have a glorious war. As a result of his own carelessness (he had lost his pony and failed to fill his water flask,) he contracted sunstroke during the Battle of Modder River, and was rushed unconscious to hospital. After four days he walked out of the hospital, feeling sorry for himself. "I am sick of this war," he wrote Jennie. "Three big battles in six days is enough for any man, and I think most of us think the same."[24] Within days, he was invalided back to Britain, just as Jennie was on the point of sailing out of Southampton. The sunstroke had done lasting damage to his heart.

For the next four months, Jennie was besieged by notes from George bewailing her absence. "Missie I am so miserable & want you with me so much. You do love me as much as you used to, don't you darling?" he wrote on December 23, 1899. "Oh little Missie mine don't stay long out at the Cape I implore you," he wrote a month later.[25] The longer Jennie remained in South Africa, the more reproachful George's tone became.

Meanwhile, George's father was furiously writing letters to Winston and to Jennie's sister Leonie about Jennie's "insane infatuation for my son." In his note to Leonie, Colonel Cornwallis-West wrote, "The life of a couple so ill-assorted is doomed, is painful to think of."[26] He threatened to cut off his son's inheritance if he married Jennie. The Prince of Wales advised her not to proceed. George's commander warned him that he could not remain in the regiment if he married Lady Randolph Churchill.

Winston's loyalty to his mother was unswerving. He reassured her, "Whatever you may do or wish to do, I shall support you in every way." However, in a clear reference to money, he added, "Reflect most seriously on all aspects of the question . . . Fine sentiments & empty stomachs do not accord."[27]

Once back from South Africa, Jennie told Winston in late May 1900 that "all my plans are vague. Sometimes I think I may marry G. W." But she reassured her elder son, who was still in South Africa, "You know what you are to me and how you can now and always count on me—I am intensely proud of you and apart from this my heart goes out to you and I understand you as no woman ever will . . . your political career will lead you to big things."[28] Her younger son received a similar missive. "My darling Jack . . . I pray from the bottom of my heart that it won't make you unhappy—you know how dearly I love you both and the thought that it may hurt you—is the one cloud in my happiness—You won't grudge me the latter?"[29]

The emotional turmoil intensified as Jennie struggled to make a success of both the *Anglo-Saxon Review* and Winston's political liftoff. George and Winston were both demanding young men who wanted her full attention, but perhaps George's boyish adoration was a welcome contrast to Winston's intense pressure on her to help his career. Now back from her South African adventure, and with rising concern about the *Anglo-Saxon Review*'s costs, Jennie's future was more insecure than ever. Her beauty was her currency, but it was a dwindling asset. And she hated being alone. Even though George had no money, he was a man—and all her life, Jennie had assumed that men would handle debts.

Jennie finally made up her mind. "I won't do it in a 'hole & corner' fashion as tho' I was shamed of it," she told Jack.[30] On July 28, 1900, when Winston was back in England (but before Jack was safely home), she married George Cornwallis-West at St. Paul's Church in Knightsbridge. Anything involving Lady Randolph Churchill was a newsworthy event in London, and hours before the church doors were opened, an eager crowd of several hundred spectators began to gather. "It was only with the aid of policemen that they were in any way controlled," according to the *New York Times*. The bride was "wonderfully handsome and young-looking . . . [and] looked as if just from Paris, instead of the South African veldt." Winston's cousin, the 9th Duke of Marlborough, walked Jennie, magnificent in a pale blue chiffon gown and enormous hat decorated with osprey feathers and a diamond ornament, up the aisle. Most of Lord Randolph's siblings were there; "their approval ratified the business," Winston told his brother.[31] George's family was conspicuously absent.

What did her sons feel about their mother's remarriage? The only remark recorded in their correspondence is in a letter that Winston wrote to Jack: "As we already know each other's views on this subject, I need not pursue it."[32] In public, they were as fiercely loyal to her as always. Perhaps in private they shared hopes that this would satisfy her need for excitement and reduce her dependence on them, and that George might help with the bills.

The newlyweds departed for a honeymoon in France and Belgium, before going to Scotland to stay in a friend's castle. However, within three weeks of her marriage, Jennie had taken temporary leave of George to be at her son's side. "All my political ambitions shall be centred on you," she had promised Winston in December 1896.[33] Winston had summoned her to support him in his second run for a parliamentary seat. His needs would always trump her husband's now.

IV

Ever since leaving Sandhurst, Winston Churchill had been sharpening his political skills, and Jennie had been instrumental in his belated education. She supplied the reading material that her son consumed when he had been stuck in India with his regiment between 1896 and 1897: Gibbon's *Decline and Fall*; Thomas Macaulay's five-volume *History of England from the Accession of James the Second*; Plato's *Republic*. Jennie wrote encouraging notes with the flow of parcels: Adam Smith, Schopenhauer, Malthus, Darwin, the memoirs of the Duc de Saint-Simon, and *Bartlett's Familiar Quotations*. In March 1897, Jennie sent him the twenty-five most recent volumes of *The Annual Register*, a compilation of each year's most significant events. He slogged his way through them with more effort than he had ever put into his Harrow courses, and he tried to express his blossoming political philosophy to his mother in his letters: "Extension of the Franchise to every male. Universal Education. Equal Establishment of all religions. Eight hours . . ."[34]

On leave in England, Winston divided his time between his short-term eagerness to get published and see military action and his long-term goal of climbing the political ladder. He always made a point of lunching with several up-and-coming Tories, and by 1898 he was nudging Conservative Party managers to find him a constituency. And throughout these years, by letter and in person, he nagged his mother to help him find patrons and supporters. Jennie knew that the most important boost for a political career was money, which she couldn't supply. Instead, she worked her connections while Winston strove to supplement his income with earnings from books and newspapers. In June 1898, he urged his mother to arrange some political meetings at which he could speak. "I want a really big meeting [in Bradford] at least two thousand men. Compel them to come in. I'm sure I can hold them." After the meeting, he sent a triumphant account. "The meeting was a complete success . . . with practice I shall obtain great power on a public platform."[35]

Winston's first attempt to be elected came in June 1899, at a by-election in Oldham, a working-class Lancashire constituency on the edges of Manchester that was the center of the British textile industry. He immediately wrote to his famous mother to tell her that "everything is going capitally" and to invite her to come and campaign for him. He added, "Send me a box of good cigarettes—Jack knows the sort—and let me have all my letters to this address, Write every day . . ."[36] The local newspaper was equally eager for a visit. "Tonight's Meeting – Lady Randolph Churchill expected," read the headline in the *Oldham Daily Standard*, over an article that described her as the "talented mother of a talented son." The piece promised that "there are thousands of true hearts in this constituency which have a warm corner for Lady Randolph Churchill."

Oldham, with its dozens of towering red brick mills and chimneys belching coal smoke, was a far cry from rural Woodstock, where Jennie had campaigned for Randolph in the 1880s. But a campaign is a campaign. Soon Jennie, in white gloves, picture hat, and full-skirted silk gown, was going door-to-door along the town's narrow streets, encouraging residents to vote for her son as she had once done for her husband. On polling day itself, the crowds cheered lustily as she arrived at election headquarters in a magnificent carriage, elegantly dressed in Tory blue. To nobody's surprise, Winston was not elected, but the *Manchester Courier* declared that he "had not been disgraced," and Jennie rushed back to London to tell her powerful Conservative friends how well her son had done. It was a promising start.

Winston's lively *Morning Post* dispatches from South Africa and his dramatic escape boosted his profile immeasurably. Speeches on South Africa became a lucrative sideline. But his focus was back on Oldham. Immediately after his mother's wedding, he prepared to stand as the Conservative candidate in the general election expected for October 1900. "I must concentrate all my efforts [and will be] speaking at 2 or 3 meetings every night upon the African question, and trotting through Cotton Mills and Iron works by day," he wrote Jennie.[37]

As the election approached, Winston urged Jennie to break her honeymoon and join him again in Oldham. "I write again to impress upon you how very useful your presence will be down here . . . I think it will be worth your while to see the close of the contest."[38] His election committee had requested her presence. The wife of his rival was there all the time.

Jennie answered the summons while George remained in Scotland, salmon fishing and hunting game. She also asked Joseph Chamberlain, now the powerful colonial secretary, to visit Oldham and speak on behalf of her son. Afterward, Chamberlain wrote to her, "He has so much ability that he must succeed – & he is so young that he can afford not to hurry too much."[39] Winston would relish Chamberlain's praise and ignore his note of caution.

On October 1, twenty-six-year-old Winston Churchill was elected to Parliament as the Conservative member for Oldham. Jennie was at her son's side as he finally got his foot on the first step of the political ladder.

No mother could have been prouder. She was soon inviting political leaders to lunch or dine at Great Cumberland Place with Winston. She also helped him organize profitable lecture tours, first in Britain and then in North America, that might earn him some much-needed cash. He continued to depend on his mother to pull strings for him and to keep his name in front of senior cabinet ministers such as Chamberlain and Arthur Balfour. He relied on her for all kinds of practical help too—to order his clothing ("I send you a specimen sock for a pattern,")[40] to find him a secretary, to help her furnish the Mayfair apartment lent to him by his cousin Sunny. "Please try to find me a . . . large compendious cabinet, with all kinds of drawers and holes of every kind that I can put papers in."[41]

However, now that he was launched, he rarely asked her advice or consulted her on his career decisions. Busy with speeches, lectures, lunches, and dinners, his letters were less frequent. He had even achieved some measure of financial stability; he managed to save £10,000, and though backbench MPs were unpaid, his lectures and journalism yielded a steady cash flow. On February 14, 1901, the day he took his seat in the new House of Commons, he sent a check for £300 to his "dearest Mama," who was, as usual, floundering in debt. "In a certain sense it belongs to you; for I could never have earned it had not you transmitted to me the wit and energy that are necessary . . ."[42]

The mother-son bond was finally starting to loosen. But Jennie was still the most important woman in her son's life. She was in the gallery of the House of Commons to hear Winston make his maiden speech, as she had so frequently been when Lord Randolph Churchill rose to speak in the early 1880s. Alongside her were four of Winston's aunts—Lord Randolph's sisters—plus Consuelo, Duchess of Marlborough. Jennie had been careful to burnish her gold-plated ducal connections despite her second marriage.

Unusually for a maiden speech, the House was full. On the front bench sat many who had served alongside Lord Randolph and who thought of Winston as "Randy's boy." Lord Salisbury, the rock-solid Conservative who (in Jennie's eyes) had destroyed Randolph's career, was again prime minister. Others in the House were anxious to see how this controversial journalist and hero of the South African war fared in the nation's toughest debating chamber. Observed the *York-shire Post*, "In that packed assembly, everybody a critic, watching to see what sort of start he made in politics, Winston Churchill made his debut."[43]

Jennie's twenty-six-year-old son had the same nervousness and slight lisp as his father, and he deliberately adopted Lord Randolph's characteristic hand-on-hip stance. But he spoke with less affectation, more confidence, and more humor than Randolph had ever managed. Jennie and her son had both known the importance of the inaugural speech. She had once coached her husband on his early speeches in the House of Commons. Now she helped her son rehearse an address that he had carefully prepared and learned by heart.

Winston did not stumble as he spoke about the war in South Africa and his respect for the Boer settlers and farmers there. He made a plea that it should be made "easy and honourable for the Boers to surrender, and painful and perilous for them to continue in the fields." According to Roy Jenkins, "the welter of comment, largely favorable, aroused by Churchill was exceptional."[44] Many of the comments in the nineteen newspaper cuttings that Churchill kept among his papers were "adulatory without qualification." Jennie's elder son had established himself as a rising political star. Jennie's high hopes for him, nurtured ever since Lord Randolph's death, finally seemed justified.

CHAPTER 13

—◇—

Sara Acquires a "Daughter"

1901–1904

Jennie's early widowhood was packed with unconventional escapades—literary, medical, marital, and political. No such adventures intruded on the first years of Sara's widowhood, according to the limited sources available: pocket diaries, a handful of letters, her careful memoir. Sara, who had never shared Jennie's restless appetite for excitement and love affairs, kept to the ordered pattern of her life. Unlike Jennie, she enjoyed the rituals of widowhood, and adopted the floor-length black veil that Queen Victoria had worn.

None of this is surprising—no two women could have been a greater contrast in personality. Yet in her own way Sara, a regal figure in her elegant black silk mourning attire, was just as imposing as Jennie as she supervised her large household and estate, dispensed largesse to neighbors less fortunate than herself, and took no nonsense from her employees.

The two women's lifestyles might have differed, but their attitudes converged when it came to their concerns for their sons' careers and marital prospects. Their contemporaries would all have approved their shared assumption of a widowed mother's role, given that it put a man's interests first. In fact, neither woman was as selfless as the role assumed—each had a strong personal investment in her son's choice of career and wife. Jennie wanted Winston to succeed so she could stay in the thick of political action, and to find a partner who would relieve Jennie herself of Winston's often overbearing emotional and practical demands. Sara wanted Franklin to flourish in a prestigious profession in keeping with Roosevelt tradition, and to find a congenial partner who would allow Sara herself to continue her central role in Franklin's life.

Franklin Roosevelt, like Winston Churchill, was more than happy to take all the help he could get from his mother. Yet while Jennie's relationship with Winston had already matured beyond the mother-son bond, Sara continued to treat Franklin as a child—especially where money was concerned. But she would soon discover that, behind her son's facade of cheery devotion, he was more elusive than she had quite grasped.

II

After James Roosevelt's death, Sara's siblings closed ranks around the widow just as Jennie's sisters had rushed to her side in Paris. Sara's stepson Rosy, now a widower himself, spent much of the spring at his Hudson Valley property, next to Springhill. Sara's diary lists visits from neighbors, philanthropic activities, the comings and goings of servants. She treasured the letters of condolence that came flooding in, along with newspaper tributes to her husband as "a gentleman of the old school." In her letters to Franklin, she celebrated James's vigor in the early years of their marriage. "I remember what a delight all the beauty of nature was to him, and how he could enjoy it even when he fell ill . . . In all my journals I read how indefatigable he was and how it was never too cold or stormy for him to go out to walk, drive and ride. I was the one who often stayed indoors on account of the weather when you were small."[1]

But her son was now her focus. "Remember," she admonished him, "it takes only 10 or 15 minutes to write a nice letter to your ever-loving Mother."[2]

Franklin dutifully wrote from Harvard every four or five days, describing the crew he rowed on, his articles for the *Crimson*, the celebrated campus newspaper (he would eventually become editor-in-chief), and the clubs he joined. His steady drumbeat of good news assuaged Sara's anxieties about him. "His father and I always expected a great deal of Franklin," she once remarked. "We thought he ought to take prizes, and we were pleased but not surprised when he did."[3] Franklin kept from his mother his bitter disappointment when he was rejected by the Porcellian, the exclusive club to which his father had belonged. He knew that the slightest hint of illness or distress would bring his formidable mother straight to his door. He was protecting himself from her intrusion into his Harvard life as much as he was shielding her from bad news.

The highlight of 1901 for her was the summer cruise to Norway that she took with Franklin and some family friends. On their return to New York, they were met with the news that President McKinley had died after being shot at the Pan-American Exposition in Buffalo. Franklin's distant cousin Theodore Roosevelt was now president of the United States. The shock of a political assassination was soon supplanted by family pride in Teddy's new eminence.

Sara was too energetic to allow herself to sink into grief, and like Jennie she carved out a new life, its events not contingent on her son's. She ramped up family visits and charitable activities, and instituted a cooking class for twelve girls held in the St. James rectory. At home, there was a substantial household staff to manage—cook, butler, caretaker, kitchen maid, parlor maid, personal maid, chambermaid, laundress, and of course the indispensable but now elderly Elespie. She issued each of her employees a notebook of instructions and list of duties and a receipt book in which they could record their monthly wages.[4] There was also the Hyde Park estate to oversee—the gardens, greenhouse, woodlot, farm, and cow barn. Sara was efficient and busy.

But as winter drew near, boredom set in. The Hyde Park routines may have become monotonous, and the reassuringly familiar landscape of the Hudson Valley could also feel like a monochrome desert. Deep snowdrifts curtailed socializing, and even her love for books dwindled when she had neither James nor Franklin to read aloud to. (Edith Wharton's novels were favorites—somewhat surprising, given the steely eye that the author cast on Sara's class.) With no one else in the house, she started taking her breakfast in bed so she didn't have to face an empty table. There were frequent servant problems—a new cook, "fat and ugly," whom she dismissed because she was "too cross and careless"; a caretaker who was "a disgusting old creature"; Simms, the coachman, who "has been drinking and is most unpleasant . . . I tried to get Simms to sign the pledge [to abstain from alcohol] but he refuses."[5]

Like Jennie, Sara was not going to let herself wither away. In the spring of 1902, she took a furnished apartment in Boston with her sister Dora. She was, as she put it in *My Boy Franklin*, "near enough to the University to be on hand should he want me and far enough removed not to interfere with his college life."[6] She would do the same the following year.

Did Franklin, now twenty-one and a head taller than Sara, welcome his mother's initiative? Hard to know, although he assured her that he was happy to have her nearby. And Sara saw little of him during the week, when he was busy with his studies and clubs. She and Dora, both energetic and intellectually curious, attended all the cultural events on offer. "Doe and I have paid a long visit to the Museum of Art. Saw Copley Hall's picture exhibition, fine portraits by Sargent . . . We have been to a French lecture in Cambridge . . . Went to hear Mr. Lang play at King's Chapel . . . To hear Sarah Morton play with the orchestra at the Conservatory of Music . . ." She organized lunch and tea parties with relatives and friends she had made in Bad Nauheim, Campobello, and elsewhere. She made new friends—the art collector Isabella Stewart Gardner; the activist Julia Ward Howe, author of "Battle Hymn of the Republic," whom she described as "a dear old thing . . . always dressed in a soft white woolen dress, as plain as a little night-dress."[7]

Weekends, however, were dedicated to Franklin. There were dinners with Harvard friends and their sisters. "At tea time we had Franklin, Paul, Teddy, Grant Forbes and Jefferson Newbold. F. went to church with us . . . Franklin was here all day. We went to the Water

Color Exhibit and I bought for him a little portrait of Theodore Roosevelt by Charles Hudson . . . A young dinner, 12 in all, very pleasant and jolly." She encouraged her son's interest in collecting books about the American navy, facilitating his purchase of several treasures. (Eventually his library, with a strong naval focus, would include almost seven thousand books and ten thousand pamphlets. He also had numerous model ships and about six hundred paintings, lithographs, and etchings.) She had more fun in Boston than at Hyde Park, where she was treated as a decrepit widow.

Franklin developed strategies to deal with Sara that would last him a lifetime. One common excuse, a way to lessen the time spent with her, was to say that he was kept late at the *Crimson*. Other times, he simply didn't appear. "I was *very* sorry Franklin did not dine at home," Sara scribbled in her diary when he did not make the trip from Cambridge to help her entertain his godmother, Nelly Blodgett.[8]

Franklin also concealed his growing interest in young women. In his letters home, "my boy" was always careful to suggest that time spent with any girl was either an easy friendship or a passing "flirtation." While he was at Groton, Sara had suggested the name of girls who might join parties at Springwood. Franklin often dismissed as "pills" or "ice-carts" or "elephantine" young women not endorsed by Sara. His mother had no rivals, he implied, for his affection. "He seems to have known that any sign of romantic interest on his part would be seen by Sara as betrayal of their exclusive devotion to each other," writes his biographer Geoffrey C. Ward.[9]

But the appointment book he occasionally kept told a different story. A handful of girls' names crop up in several entries, and one in particular—that of the beautiful Boston debutante Alice Sohier—featured over several months. Some of these entries were in code, in order to shield them from prying eyes, and in later years Alice recalled that they had discussed marriage. Sara remained ignorant of the relationship.[10]

Sara was aghast when Franklin, now twenty-one, gently raised the possibility that he might take a four-week trip to Europe with a classmate rather than her as companion in 1903. It was his first major gesture of independence—not part of his mother's plans. It would mean that she would spend the first few weeks of their Campobello summer without him. Franklin gently suggested that she was perhaps being a little overprotective. Sara took the hint. "I am perfectly willing for you to go as it is only for a month and with a nice fellow. I do not think I should feel the same if it were for longer, or if it were with several fellows. Of course, dearest Franklin, I shall miss you but I am not so silly and I have no intention of 'tying you to my apron strings' . . . You are a dear boy to insist on leaving it entirely to me."

But she could be as manipulative as Franklin, and their correspondence reflected the way each neatly guilted the other. Franklin maneuvered his mother into thinking that she was the major influence on decisions he made; Sara maneuvered Franklin into bearing responsibility for her emotions. Sara's relationship with her son was much more complicated than Jennie's relationship with Winston, with its outbursts and reproaches.

Sara didn't hesitate to let Franklin know how sad his decision to undertake his transatlantic voyage to England had made her. Her resolve to allow him some freedom, she wrote to him, crumbled when she waved goodbye to him as he sailed away on the White Star liner *Celtic*. She had begun to weep quietly, she explained. "I *meant* to be very brave, but after all I played baby at the last . . . It is . . . the thought of the ocean between me and my *all* that rather appalls me . . . I watched your great steamer going further and further from me with such a sinking of my heart."[11]

Although she was far from alone at Campobello, Sara insisted to Franklin in her letters that she was lonely and incapable of enjoying the usual pursuits—sailing was now "mere drifting." Franklin wrote constantly (in a single day six postcards arrived from him), and he finally reached Campobello on August 26. Sara exulted. "A perfect day . . . such happiness to be together again . . . Now that Franklin is back the Island is changed to me."

By the time Franklin returned to Harvard for his final year, most of which he spent editing the *Crimson*, his mother was planning his next move. She felt he should follow his father's footsteps into the law—suitable training for a country gentleman—but at Columbia Law School rather than at Harvard. A network would be invaluable for a young man on the verge of adulthood, and the best Delano and Roosevelt connections were all in New York City. "I still have a few friends of your dear father's who could take an interest." Besides, Manhattan was closer than Cambridge to Springwood. "I merely wish you would think seriously of it, and realize how much it will be for you and for me, for you to be near your own home, and not too much out of reach."[12]

For Sara, the mother-son bond was tighter than ever. She looked forward to doing exactly what Jennie Churchill would do for Winston—help him shape his career. However, Franklin had learned how to keep his imperious mother at arm's length, even as he let her think he had no secrets. Jennie was often drawn into her endlessly demanding elder son's life more than she really wanted, while Sara would now discover that her chatty son had been keeping secrets from her. She needed to find a way to manage this.

III

One of Sara's favorite events each year was the traditional Thanksgiving at Fairlawn, the old Delano homestead in New Bedford, Massachusetts, where her Delano grandparents had lived. In late November 1903, she took the train from New York City for the family Old Home Week. The trees were bare, but the sun shone brightly on the harbor, and the rendezvous with her sister Annie and brothers Warren and Fred, plus their families, was exuberant. Her siblings were gray-haired now, and so were the elderly servants who kept the large mansion going. It was often empty these days. On a bright, clear Sunday morning, the Delanos attended morning service at the local Unitarian church, then returned to Fairlawn for Thanksgiving dinner.

Warren took their father's place at the head of the long table to carve the turkey. Sara could look across the starched linen and sparkling silverware and see her handsome twenty-one-year-old son, with his thick brown hair and engaging smile, surrounded by elderly relatives. Franklin was always a great talker and loved amusing his listeners. She could think with pleasure of the months and years ahead, after his graduation from Harvard the following spring and his return to her household, as she helped him get established. When the Delanos gathered around the parlor piano to sing favorite songs and sea shanties, she smiled at the sound of his confident tenor.[13]

Within hours of their arrival, her composure was severely shaken. As she wrote in her diary that night, "Franklin gave me quite a startling announcement."[14] He had taken her aside after lunch and told her that he had asked nineteen-year-old Eleanor Roosevelt, niece of President Teddy Roosevelt, to marry him. She had accepted. And they would like to marry as soon as possible.

In *My Boy Franklin*, Sara skimmed over the announcement, merely noting that "Franklin, unknown to any of us, had become engaged to his distant cousin." She went on to write: "I suppose one should not have thought it unusual that Franklin, without so much as an intimation to any one, had fallen in love. It probably surprised us only because he had never been in any sense a ladies' man."[15]

In fact, Franklin's announcement came out of the blue; in the previous months, he had rarely mentioned Eleanor in his letters to Sara, although he had been quietly courting her for a year. Sara was also shocked because both Franklin and Eleanor were so young (she referred to Eleanor in her memoir as "a delightful child"). James Roosevelt had been twenty-five and established in a law practice when he first married, and fifty-two when Sara became his second wife. She herself was twenty-six when she got engaged, seven years older than Eleanor was now. Franklin's trust income was insufficient to support a wife and family while he studied for the bar and established a career.

Did Sara admit to herself a more fundamental objection—the fact that she now had a rival for Franklin's love and attention? That she would have to share "my boy" with a debutante who appeared to be as sweet and guileless as a newborn foal?

That Sunday, as the majestic middle-aged woman in black stared with shock at her gangly, breezy son, Franklin was as surprised by his mother's dismay as she was taken aback by his news. Her standard reaction to all the previous triumphs he had described to her (failures were largely concealed) had been a maternal gush of pride. Now there was a shocked silence. Sara finally drew breath. In Knickerbocker circles, marriage customarily came six months after the engagement. Sara could not countenance events moving so rapidly. She bluntly told Franklin that he was in no position to marry. Franklin might have been confident that in the end he would bring his mother around to the idea of his marriage, but he also came face-to-face with a reality that would shape the rest of his life. His mother controlled the purse strings, so her support was critical for almost anything he might want to do.

Sara extracted a promise from her son that he would keep the engagement secret for a year. Since he couldn't afford to marry without her approval, he agreed to her terms. Then mother and son returned to the family festivities; with typical Delano self-discipline, they didn't breathe a word to anybody of their conversation.

Within a week, Sara received anxious letters from both Franklin and Eleanor (who was staying with relatives in Manhattan, nervously awaiting news). Eleanor wrote, "I know . . . how hard it must be, but I do so want you to learn to love me a little. You must know that I will always try to do what you wish . . . It is impossible for me to tell you how I feel toward Franklin. I can only say that my one great wish is always to prove worthy of him."[16]

Two days later, Franklin wrote from the *Crimson* office: "Dearest Mama – I know what pain I have caused you and you know I wouldn't do it if I really could have helped it – mais tu sais, me voilà! That's all that could be said – I know my mind, have known it for a long time, and know that I could never think otherwise; Result: I am the happiest man just now in the world; likewise the luckiest – And for you, dear Mummy, you know that nothing can ever change what we have always been & always will be to each other – only now you have two children to love & to love you – and Eleanor as you know will always be a daughter to you in every true way."[17]

Sara had put them both on the defensive, as Eleanor's plea for love and Franklin's combination of lovestruck nonchalance and nervous reassurance suggest. Sara had bought herself a year to absorb the shock of her son's announcement, and to get to know her future daughter-in-law, Anna Eleanor Roosevelt.

Sara Delano Roosevelt had no objection to the match itself. Eleanor was Franklin's fifth cousin once removed. She was from the Oyster Bay side of the family, and niece of the president, so her social credentials were impeccable, and Roosevelts had frequently married cousins. Sara had known Eleanor since she was a baby—Eleanor's father, Elliott, had been Franklin's godfather, and Eleanor herself first visited Hyde Park when she was two years old. (She had no memories of four-year-old Franklin carrying her across the nursery floor on his back, but the game of "horsey" is enshrined in Roosevelt lore.) Sara's primary concern was the couple's youth, plus perhaps Franklin's duplicity.

But Sara soon discerned that there would be a role for her in the Franklin-Eleanor relationship. Eleanor was not simply young for her age; in 1903, she was also unworldly, impractical, and emotionally needy, and (in Sara's eyes) she cried out for guidance. Sara's relationship with her future daughter-in-law, which would evolve from one of bossy benevolence to uneasy forbearance and, at times, outright hostility, would be a dominant theme in her life from now on.

IV

The supremely self-assured Sara would never really understand her future daughter-in-law. She knew that Eleanor's upbringing had been miserable, but how could a Roosevelt—inheritor of one of the greatest names in American history and the niece of the president—not surmount childhood challenges? In the early 1880s, Eleanor's parents had been a golden couple; good-looking, well connected, wealthy, and welcome in the all-important old money circles. And now Eleanor herself was being courted by "my boy."

But Eleanor's childhood had been absolutely wretched, and in memoirs written after Sara's death, she would describe with almost gleeful masochism the endless abandonments and losses. Those early traumas, beyond the experience of either Sara or her son, scarred Eleanor for life and would warp the relationship between the two women.

Eleanor's mother, Anna Hall, was another product of Hudson Valley affluence. With her large, dark eyes and delicate coloring, she had been one of the most beautiful debutantes of the 1881 season, radiating languid charm. Eleanor's father, Elliott Roosevelt, was an exuberant, athletic sportsman, and the younger brother of the future president Teddy Roosevelt. The birth of their first child, Anna Eleanor, in 1884, was noted in society pages, and her uncle Teddy, then a rising Republican politician, agreed to be her godfather.

Social success hid growing tensions within Eleanor's parents' marriage. Elliott was a feckless playboy. Anna never bonded with her daughter because she found her solemn and graceless. On the famous visit to Hyde Park when two-year-old Eleanor first met Franklin, the little girl was too shy to venture into the parlor. Her mother noticed the woebegone figure sucking her finger in the doorway and called out to her, "Come in Granny." Anna cheerfully explained to Sara that she called her daughter Granny because Eleanor was "such a funny child, so old-fashioned."[18] In later years, Eleanor recalled how this explanation, frequently made by her mother, made her want to "sink through the floor in shame."

Eleanor's relationship with her father was equally unsatisfactory. Elliott Roosevelt was an alcoholic, increasingly dependent on narcotics to dull the pain of various injuries. While Anna tried to get his addictions under control, she farmed her little girl out to relatives. But to Eleanor, Elliott was a loving and romantic figure. At one point he disappeared to Europe, in search of a cure. Eleanor's aunt Tissie Hall reported: "Eleanor lunched with us yesterday . . . She rushes to the stairs every time the bell rang to see if it was her Papa. 'I shall be so glad to see my *dear* father,' she kept saying."[19]

By the time that Eleanor had two little brothers, her mother had decided that her husband should not live with them again. Instead, he was banished to a small town called Abington, in Virginia, and given the job of managing extensive properties there owned by a relative. Back in New York, Eleanor would eavesdrop on her aunts discussing the situation. "Something was wrong with my father," she decided, "but from my point of view nothing could be wrong with him."[20]

Eleanor was already an anxious, insecure child by the time she was eight, but worse was to come. In late 1892, her twenty-nine-year-old mother died of diphtheria. Her father reappeared, and lavished affection on his daughter, but then returned to Virginia, and rarely kept his promise to visit. On one occasion when he did come to New York, he set off for a walk with Eleanor and his three terriers. In front of the exclusive Knickerbocker Club, then located on Fifth Avenue and Thirty-Second Street, he handed the dogs' leashes over to Eleanor and told her to wait on a bench while he popped in to see a friend. Six hours later, the doorman sent Eleanor home in a cab. Elliott, blind drunk, had been dispatched home a couple of hours earlier.

A few months after the death of her mother, Eleanor's brother Elliott Jr. died of scarlet fever. Her father followed him to the grave on August 13, 1894, his death ascribed to alcoholism and a catastrophic carriage accident (he drove into a lamppost while drunk). Ten-year-old Eleanor refused to accept his disappearance from her life. After crying herself to sleep, she would later recall, she woke up the next day "living in my dream world . . . From that time on I . . . lived with him more closely, probably, than I had when he was alive."[21]

Eleanor and her brother Hall spent the next five years at yet another secluded Hudson Valley mansion: Oak Terrace (sometimes known as Oak Lawn), at Tivoli, twenty-two miles north of Hyde Park. This was the large, cheerless mansion in which their mother had been raised, and where their maternal grandmother, Mary Livingston Ludlow Hall, "was incapable of giving them anything but a meagre, weary, left-over love,"[22] according to Corinne Robinson

Alsop, Eleanor's cousin. By the time Eleanor was in her early teens she had become a fearful bookworm. "Looking back I see that I was always afraid of something: of the dark, of displeasing people, of fail-ure."[23] Elliott's sister-in-law Edith wrote to Bamie, his sister: "Poor little soul, she is very plain. Her mouth and teeth seem to have no future. But the ugly duckling may turn out to be a swan."[24]

Eleanor's life improved briefly when she was fifteen and was sent to England to attend Allenswood, a girls' boarding school in London. The school was run by Mademoiselle Marie Souvestre, a fierce blue-stocking who took the gawky young American in hand, replacing her outdated dresses with elegant French gowns and showing more inter-est and tenderness toward her than Eleanor had ever experienced be-fore. At Allenswood, Eleanor learned that there was more to life than good looks, feminine charms, and a habit of subservience. Under the benevolent guidance of Mademoiselle Souvestre, she traveled, read widely, learned to think for herself, and began to shake off her feelings of inferiority.

But three years later, Eleanor was pulled back to New York so she could do what young women of her class did: go through the rituals of attending receptions, at homes, teas, and balls in order to find a wealthy, reliable suitor. While she had been in London, her family had become even more dysfunctional. At Oak Lawn, her grandmother was almost a recluse, her little brother Hall was a lonely eleven-year-old with only a tutor for company, and her uncle Valentine Hall was now a drunk who took pot shots out of his bedroom window at visitors. There was little family money left with which to launch her as a debutante.

In the fall of 1902, a year before the fateful Thanksgiving dinner, Sara Roosevelt was sitting in the parlor car of the train from Manhat-tan, wondering where her son had disappeared to. He had announced that he was going to stretch his legs, but he had been gone nearly thirty minutes. Then she saw coming toward her, accompanied by Franklin, a tall, elegant young woman, gripping the seat backs as the car rattled along the curving rails alongside the Hudson River. She recognized Eleanor, cousin Teddy's niece.

On his stroll through the carriages, Franklin had spotted his distant cousin quietly reading. They had not seen each other since a family Christmas party four years earlier, before Eleanor went to Allenswood. They chatted so easily to each other now that Franklin almost forgot he was escorting his mother. With a start, he rose from his seat, then urged Eleanor to come and say hello. Eleanor, clad in a smart traveling outfit, deferentially greeted "Cousin Sally" when Franklin introduced her to the distinguished middle-aged woman who remained seated as she looked up through her thick black veil.

Sara knew nothing of Franklin and Eleanor's frequent meetings in the months following—at parties, country houses, family gatherings. Both were present at a sumptuous New Year's Eve dinner at the newly renovated White House as guests of ebullient Uncle Teddy. Eleanor came to rely on her good-looking cousin, whose height matched her own, to fill her dance card at formals. Franklin was still busy at Harvard, while Eleanor had become involved in social work at a settlement house on Manhattan's Lower East Side. Twice a week, she rode the Second Avenue Elevated train into the bedlam of pushcarts, market stalls, and crowded tenements in order to teach dance to the daughters of Italian immigrants.

Franklin never mentioned to his mother that one day he went down to the Lower East Side to meet Eleanor after a class and helped her bring home a child who had fallen ill. Struggling up three narrow flights of stairs to a tenement flat with the little girl in his arms, he was overwhelmed by the filth, malnutrition, and overcrowding he saw. He kept repeating that he "simply could not believe human beings lived that way."[25] By now he had learned that there were depths to Eleanor he rarely saw in other debutantes. Her determination, nurtured by Mademoiselle Souvestre, to improve the lives of those ground down by crushing poverty went far beyond his mother's genteel food baskets and sewing classes. "E is an Angel," wrote Franklin in his journal, encoding her name as he had when noting his passion for the Boston debutante Alice Sohier.[26]

Sara assumed that Franklin was simply showing good manners

when he included Eleanor in a weekend party with friends at Spring-wood. The engagement announcement at the Delano Thanksgiving dinner a year after the train encounter was a shock. Although she did not reveal her feelings in public, Sara must have been suffused with intense emotions—incomprehension, that this had been sprung on her; dismay, that she was losing her precious son; outrage, that Franklin was capable of such deceit; confusion, that her maternal antennae had not picked up what was happening. Franklin had staked out his independence as an adult. He had not consulted her. He had turned her world upside down.

IV

Immediately after Franklin's surprise announcement, Sara made it her business to meet Eleanor alone for lunch in New York.

Sara assumed that Franklin's promise to her to keep the engagement secret meant that Franklin and Eleanor would simply put their plans on hold until the year was up. She told her future daughter-in-law that Franklin should not plan on spending too many weekends with her in New York because people would begin (horror of horrors) to "talk." She also informed Eleanor that she planned to rent a house in Boston for the coming months to be close to Harvard, as she had in recent years, and expected Franklin to spend time with her there. She would invite Eleanor to visit her there as well, but only "once or twice."

The atmosphere at lunch was friendly, but it soon emerged that the young couple had ideas that were not in line with Sara's wishes. "Boy darling," Eleanor wrote to Franklin after the encounter, "I have rather a hard letter to write to you tonight and I don't quite know how to say what I must say and I am afraid I am going to give you some trouble." Eleanor tried to see Sara's point of view: "You see it is hard for her to realize that any one can want you or need you more than she does. So I suppose I ought not to mind, only I do mind terribly, as you can understand dear, however I mustn't complain, must I?"[27]

Franklin responded by sidestepping the conflict entirely. While he knew enough to reassure Sara that she was still a vital part of his life, he was not about to let his mother keep him and Eleanor apart. He persuaded Sara not to rent the house in Boston, as she had done the previous two winters; this freed him up to spend winter weekends with Eleanor in New York. He also suggested to Sara that he and she and his schoolfriend Lathrop Brown might take a six-week Caribbean cruise without Eleanor. Although taking the trip meant that he would miss several classes and graduate from Harvard with mediocre grades, he had always been an indifferent student and now considered his relationship with his mother to be more important.

Sara thoroughly enjoyed the cruise on the luxurious Hamburg-American excursion ship the *Prinzessin Victoria Luise* with two handsome young men. She would catalogue for Rita Halle Kleeman the exotic locales that the threesome visited—the Danish West Indies, Puerto Rico, Barbados, the Bahamas, Venezuela, Jamaica, Cuba. By the time the ship docked in Washington, on the way back to New York, she had almost accepted Franklin's plans. She even arranged for Franklin and Eleanor to meet at the Georgetown house of Aunt Bamie, who had moved to the capital when her brother Teddy became president. She herself enjoyed a dinner at the White House. ("The President was very delightful," she wrote to her sister Dora. "I wonder how *small* men . . . can criticize and belittle him.")[28] Back in New York, Sara made frequent visits to Manhattan to visit, lunch, and shop with Eleanor. Eleanor wrote Franklin that, in future, the three of them should take vacations together. "I know three will never be the same to her [as just two, on mother-son trips], still someday I hope she will really love me and I would be very glad if I thought she was even the least bit reconciled to me now."

However, Sara was not completely reconciled to the idea of a quick marriage, and she put out a feeler to an old friend of hers, Joseph Choate, the American ambassador to Britain. Was there a diplomatic post in London for Franklin? Such a posting could delay any wedding plans. Unfortunately, replied the ambassador, he had no post available.[29]

Meanwhile, Franklin agreed with his mother that he should study law at Columbia. President Roosevelt, now a national hero, was a Columbia Law School graduate, and Franklin was already taking boisterous Uncle Ted rather than his own restrained father as his role model. He aped his speaking style and his body language; he had taken to wearing pince-nez like Teddy. Sara, who would be paying the fees, liked the choice because he would be closer to home. Franklin knew that attending Columbia would allow him to be in the same city as Eleanor.

Sara rented a brownstone at 200 Madison Avenue to provide a home for Franklin that would also be a residence for her. She ensured his comfort by bringing Elespie from Hyde Park to run things and by hiring several servants. These were the kind of responsibilities that Winston Churchill regularly asked Jennie to assume. Franklin Roosevelt did not need to ask Sara for help but rather took it for granted that his mother would attend to such details.

With Franklin back at school, Sara was lonely again, and a familiar note of self-pity emerged in letters. "I am feeling pretty blue. You are gone. The journey is over & I feel as if the time were not likely to come again when I shall take a trip with my dear boy." But she promised that she would "love Eleanor & adopt her *fully* when the right time comes." She assured him that she would "try to be unselfish & of course dear child I *do* rejoice in your happiness & shall not put any stones or straws even in the way of it."[30]

What she did not say in the letter was that the "right time" would be at her choosing, not Franklin's.

CHAPTER 14

—◇—

The Ups and Downs of
Churchill Marriages

1901–1912

While Sara Roosevelt was reluctantly preparing herself to be mother of the groom at Franklin's wedding—a time-honored role, though new to her—Jennie Churchill was reprising a previous role. She was once again a new bride, but this time in an unconventional relationship. Her new husband was the same age as her son.

Although she never shared Sara Roosevelt's regard for conventional expectations, Jennie appears to have taken her marital vow of fidelity more seriously the second time around. Sara was learning to enjoy the independence that her widowhood dictated, but Jennie was happy to be back under the legal protection of a man who, in theory, would handle all their financial affairs. After the ordeal of Lord Randolph Churchill's protracted decline, and the insecurity of early widowhood, she enjoyed being squired around town by the best-looking man in London, who at first was as devoted as a lapdog. In her magnificent velvet hats and huge skirts, she was as gregarious and eye-catchingly vivacious as ever. George's sister Daisy, Princess of Pless, met Jennie at Cannes in 1903 and confided to her diary that she was "as charming as usual and looking very well . . . gambling and wearing lovely clothes."[1]

Had Jennie stayed single, her flirtatious manner and network of former lovers might have compromised her respectability. But as a wife, she was "safe," even if the age difference between her and her second husband caused comment. Jennie wrote *Reminiscences* after she had married George in June 1900. The frontispiece was one of her Professional Beauty photos from the 1880s; she sports a diamond star (long since sold) in her hair and a come-hither expression. But the name "Mrs. George Cornwallis-West" is on the title page, and the volume ends with the coy sentence "I bade farewell . . . to Lady Randolph Churchill, who then took the name of the chronicler of these reminiscences." For the fourteen years of this marriage, Jennie styled herself Mrs. George Cornwallis-West.

Glimpses of the Cornwallis-Wests' married life would come from George in 1930, in *Edwardian Hey-Days*, which he subtitled, with characteristic levity, *Or, a Little about a Lot of Things*. Years before he wrote it, he had left Jennie for another woman (also glamorous, also several years his senior), yet his description of his first wife shimmers with affection and admiration.

> Jennie was a very remarkable woman. She dressed beautifully, and her taste, not only in clothes, but in everything, was of the best. She had a marvelous *flair* for decorating a house, and there are many houses in London which, thanks to her, have a *cachet* of their own and which bear to this day the unmistakable proofs of her artistic talent. Like many well-bred American woman, she had the will and power to adapt herself to her immediate surroundings. She was equally at home having a serious conversation with a distinguished statesman, or playing on a golf-course. A great reader, she remembered much of what she had read, and that made her a brilliant conversationalist . . . Possessed of great driving force in matters which interested her, she was a good organizer, as was proved by the success she made of the *Maine* hospital ship in the South African War.[2]

II

In January 1901, six months after Jennie's wedding in Knightsbridge, Queen Victoria died, after a reign of sixty-four years. The British

Empire wallowed in mourning for a monarch that few of her subjects ever saw, and who had largely withdrawn from public life since the death of her spouse, Prince Albert, four decades earlier. When the news broke, Winston was in North America on a speaking tour. In Winnipeg, where he had just given a lecture and where flags now hung at half-mast, he tried to grasp how the crown would change their good friend Bertie. "I am curious to know about the King. Will it entirely revolutionise his way of life?" he asked his mother in a letter. "Will he sell his horses . . . ? Will he become desperately serious? Will he continue to be friendly to you? . . . I am glad he has got his innings at last."[3]

Jennie and her son did not need to worry; they would not lose the valuable friendship of the monarch. Stout and sensual—a "corpulent voluptuary," as Rudyard Kipling described him—Edward VII had waited half a century to wear the crown, and he was too old to change his ways. At his coronation in Westminster Abbey, Jennie was one of the king's favorites, all wearing diamond tiaras, who watched the proceedings from his box. Mrs. Alice Keppel had replaced Daisy, Countess of Warwick, as Edward's chief amour, but clever Jennie continued her role as confidante. For Edward's pals within Britain's upper class, his ascension to the throne just made their social life even more exclusive. The wider British public embraced their new king regardless of his appetite for twelve-course dinners, fast horses, and beautiful women.

"Those were wonderful days," George Cornwallis-West later wrote. "Taxation and the cost of living were low; money was freely spent and wealth was everywhere in evidence. Moreover it was possessed largely by the nicest people, who entertained both in London and in the country." Few of "the nicest people" had to earn a living; instead, Jennie's friends spent their days hunting, shopping, attending race meets, and entertaining each other with an ostentation that would have shocked Sara Roosevelt. George recalled dinners that were "gargantuan affairs, far too long . . . Champagne, port and old brandy were the order of the day, or rather, night." No wonder that

Daisy of Pless had also sniped that Jennie was now "SO fat." Jennie also kept up the spending to retain her title as a leading fashionista: as George noted, "women's dresses at dinner parties were very elaborate, and quantities of jewelry were worn."[4]

Immune to irony, George reveled in the opulence. "I doubt whether in any period of history of the modern world, except perhaps that immediately preceding the French Revolution, has there been such a display of wealth and luxury as during King Edward's reign." He didn't make any connection between the French aristocracy's revolutionary fate in eighteenth-century France and the changes he would see in his own lifetime in England. Jennie probably didn't either. But others—including the eager young politician Winston Churchill—did, thanks to the pioneering research of social reformers such as Charles Booth and Seebohm Rowntree. Their studies showed the dreadful impact in Britain of steadily declining wages and lack of adequate public and welfare services. One in three families in London lived in abject poverty; one infant in four died because their malnourished mothers could not produce milk; diseases like rickets were widespread among the children of the industrialized north. Jennie's elder son was taking note of Rowntree's research and showing signs of a twentieth-century social conscience, to the exasperation of some of his more traditional Conservative colleagues within Parliament.

Jennie would have been aware of the conditions in which the poor lived, even if she never went anywhere near the East End of London, with its open sewers and soot-darkened, disease-ridden slums, where only a few years earlier Jack the Ripper had murdered five women. The privileged enclaves of Mayfair and Knightsbridge, where she lunched and dined in five-story mansions, were close to rough Dickensian neighborhoods like Paddington. A huge amount of manufacturing took place in the imperial capital, and the smoky factories and cramped workshops of Lambeth were visible across the Thames from one of Jennie's favorite haunts, Westminster's splendid neo-Gothic Houses of Parliament. When Jennie and George strolled along Pall Mall or spent an evening in a West End theater, they would have seen brightly painted prostitutes loitering on street corners and children in rags begging for pennies.

But the Cornwallis-Wests averted their gaze from deprivation and enjoyed the lavish hospitality of others, although they could never reciprocate. By now George's senior officers had decided his marriage was too scandalous for the regiment to swallow, and he had reluctantly agreed to resign. As the man of the household, he had a vague intention of taking control, but he quickly discovered what he was up against. A hamper of unpaid bills had accompanied them on the honeymoon, and he would later confide to Shane Leslie, Jennie's nephew, "Of course I was eager to put her affairs in order, but I found it a bit thick when expected to pay for Lord Randolph Churchill's barouche purchased in the 'eighties.'"[5]

George and Jennie might have been able to live on George's meager allowance from his father, and Jennie's income from her 1874 marriage settlement, had it not been for Jennie's extravagance and the debts she and Lord Randolph had accumulated. George now grasped that his wife's lifestyle floated on a cloud of financial blindness.

> In money matters she was without any sense of proportion. The value of money meant nothing to her: what counted with her were the things she got for money not the amount she had to pay for them. If something of beauty attracted her, she just had to have it; it never entered her head to stop and think how she was going to pay for it. During all the years we lived together the only serious misunderstandings which ever took place between us were over money matters. Her extravagance was her only fault, and, with her nature, the most understandable and therefore the most forgivable.[6]

Before the honeymoon was over, George had realized that taking control of his wife's financial affairs was an impossible challenge. Within a year of his marriage, he had followed her example and resorted to moneylenders.[7]

III

Since both the Cornwallis-Wests acknowledged that living within their means was impossible, they looked around for other sources of income. George needed a job, but his childhood and education had prepared him for little more than crashing through undergrowth with a gun or waltzing around dance floors with debutantes.

Jennie had always relied on wealthy, influential friends to help her out of jams, and one of the most important was Sir Ernest Cassel. Sir Ernest, who had been a good friend of Lord Randolph, was already lending Jennie money, advising her older son on his finances, and assisting her younger son to make a career in the City. A German-born Jewish banker who was penniless when he arrived in Britain in 1879, Cassel had become one of the world's wealthiest men, thanks to astute investments in railways, mining, government loans, and megaprojects such as Egypt's Aswan Dam. His wealth ensured him access to aristocratic circles, and he had even acquired the nickname "Windsor Cassel" because he was so close to the Prince of Wales.[8] In 1899, after helping establish the National Bank of Egypt, he was knighted.

The same year, when Winston Churchill needed funds to buy kit and provisions for his adventures in South Africa as a war correspondent, Cassel gave him £100 (£10,000 today). Lord Rothschild, another friend of both Lord Randolph and the Prince of Wales, had given him £150. Now Jennie ensured that Sir Ernest Cassel was a fellow guest at a Mayfair dinner party, and she asked that the financier be seated next to her husband. In the flickering light of candelabra and amid the guffaws of London gossip, the stocky, bewhiskered Cassel sized up the young Adonis next to him. George confided to Jennie's good friend that he wasn't interested in becoming a stockbroker and "touting for orders from my friends," but that running an engineering company appealed to him.

Cassel must have been surprised by this admission; Britain's landed class tended to sneer at businessmen as much as at Jews, and he knew that George's intellect was rated far below his looks. However, he agreed that a career in the City was not for everybody, and made the shrewd suggestion that George might benefit from training. Then he leaned on a Glasgow industrialist with whom he had dealings to employ this Old Etonian in an engineering firm that was building a power station. George became an apprentice, living near Glasgow during the weeks, "putting on overalls and acting as a sort of unpaid plumber's mate to the highly-paid experts." Other than his experience during the Boer War, this was likely George's first glimpse of life beyond that of "the nicest people."

After a few months, George went for an interview with the company's managing director—an impatient, hardworking industrialist with penetrating steel-gray eyes under fierce bushy eyebrows who was "prepared to find in me a useless sprig of aristocracy, out of a job and not particularly wanting one." But George protested that he was not interested in a seat on the board; he wanted real responsibility. He was slotted into the executive ranks of the Potteries Electric Traction Company, which was building tramways in Staffordshire.

For the first few years of the Cornwallis-West marriage, George's job and income, plus various loans, kept them afloat. Weeks were spent apart; while George worked in his office in the Midlands, Jennie lived her life of friends, music, and parties in London. At the end of each week, George would take the train back to London and join Jennie for weekend visits to various friends' country houses. They spent many days at two of the greatest ducal homes in Britain—Blenheim Palace, as guests of Jennie's nephew the Duke of Marlborough, and Chatsworth, as guests of the Duke and Duchess of Devonshire—and as household guests of Alfred Rothschild, at Halton House, where a private orchestra and a small circus entertained gatherings. Their fellow guest King Edward had made it clear that he liked Jennie to be part of any party he attended.

If a party veered toward mischief, Jennie would be in the thick of it. One weekend, she and George were guests of Lady Georgiana Howe (one of Randolph's sisters) and her husband, Earl Howe, at Gopsall Hall, in the Midlands. During an elaborate game of charades, the women dressed as men. The acknowledged star of the risqué cross-dressers was Jennie, who appeared as "a roistering Spanish cavalier. She wore black silk tights, a doublet and hose, a dark crimson velvet cloak . . . diamond buckles on her pretty shoe and a black moustache waxed and ferociously curled like the Kaiser's."[9]

It may have been at the same party that Jennie entertained the party with a music hall song:

Ruby lips, ruby lips,
Oh who will kiss these ruby lips
When I am far away far away?

The chorus ran:
Some other man,
I don't give a damn
Some other man.[10]

One can imagine Edward VII's chuckle. But not everyone was amused. A fellow guest was General Sir Ian Hamilton, whose wife, Jean, kept a diary in which she scribbled candid impressions. After the weekend, she described Jennie as "an interesting, dominating, vulgar woman," though she then crossed out "vulgar." She also recorded a conversation that reflects Jennie's hunger for something more than small talk. "When she and I walked back together from skating, she told me that the other day she had said something about Fiscal Policy, and that Lady Howe and Co. had seemed so bored that she, Mrs. West, had flown into a rage and said, 'Oh, I forgot, nothing must be mentioned in this house but golf and bridge,' and flounced out of the room . . ."[11]

George was happy with intellectually undemanding pursuits. His salary allowed him to indulge a new craze—motoring. "Darling Old Puss Cat," reads a typical letter to his wife in April 1906. "Had a lovely run yesterday. I averaged 31 miles an hour the whole way. It was a glorious day and the roads were lovely . . ."[12] Marital stability encouraged

Jennie to indulge her love of beautiful houses. In 1904, partly to reduce expenses, she had let her London house and rented a charming manor house near St. Albans. Salisbury Hall had everything she wanted: an enormous dining room with a stone fireplace, oak paneling, eight bedrooms, a pheasant shoot for George, and a garden in which she could cultivate the blossoms required for the enormous floral arrangements that she was helping to popularize. It even had its own ghost.

Meanwhile, to his mother's discomfort, Winston was becoming a political gadfly. In 1904, he shocked his Tory colleagues by abandoning the governing Conservative Party, the only political home his father had ever known, and joining the Liberals on the other side of the House of Commons. The ostensible reason was his support for free trade—a policy that was anathema to a growing majority of the Conservative Party, which was deeply invested in the empire and preferred "imperial preference" to protect its trading block. But he was also ambitious for office and knew that he had voted against his own government too often to be promoted.

Winston's former colleagues erupted with fury at his desertion. The prime minister, an ally of Lord Randolph's in the 1880s and a frequent guest at Jennie's dining table, walked out of the House while Winston was speaking. Jennie reacted with her usual passionate defense of her son: "That *detestable* Arthur Balfour—I'll *never* speak to him again."[13] To escape the party acrimony, Winston visited his mother's new home in early August and built a platform in an old lime tree where he could draft his caustic speeches. According to Anita Leslie, "Jennie complained that if he dropped his notes the grass around that tree would be scorched."[14] For Jennie, who had watched Lord Randolph sharpen his speeches until they cut deep, Winston's growing fame as an orator must have inspired both pride and apprehension.

Salisbury Hall was too small for large house parties. However, it could accommodate fifteen servants—Cornwallis-West economy campaigns did not include cutting staff. ("The servant problem was never acute," George Cornwallis-West noted. "A first-rate cook could be got for fifty pounds a year and a butler for eighty."[15]) The faithful Walden remained with Jennie, and his wife now took charge of the large kitchen. As usual, Jennie had a full-time lady's maid, who managed her wardrobe, packed and unpacked when Jennie traveled, and accompanied her on weekend visits that usually required at least three elaborate changes of clothes each day. There was also a gaggle of parlor maids and gardeners.

Jennie was happy to have a home where her sons could regularly join her. She told Winston, "Salisbury Hall is at your disposal if you want to come."[16] Jack, now taller than his older brother but still in awe of him, regularly escaped his City grind to help her in the garden. Jennie's greatest social coup were private visits by the king himself, often but not always accompanied by Mrs. Keppel. For occasions when Edward spent the night at Salisbury Hall, Jennie reorganized the whole house to give him a ground-floor bedroom suite because he was too portly to climb stairs. The royal friendship guaranteed Jennie's continuing social eminence—and powerful guests for the lunch parties designed to promote Winston's career.

IV

Life in those Edwardian years may have been peaceful and pastoral, but it lacked the adrenaline on which Jennie thrived, and the rented Salisbury Hall never had the emotional resonance that Springwood had for Sara Roosevelt. She hungered for more involvement with the world, and despite the failure of the *Anglo-Saxon Review* she continued to nurse literary ambitions, particularly if they paid. She turned to her elder son for help.

Now in his early thirties, Winston churned out articles and books when he wasn't making speeches in the House of Commons and the country. He strode along the marble-floored corridors of Westminster, grinning at allies and impatiently brushing his floppy ginger hair out of his eyes. He also found time for dinners, weekend parties (the king invited him to Windsor Castle in 1902), polo, holidays abroad, and attendance at the races. His brash overconfidence, which irritated some observers, was blamed on his mixed parentage (although it was most reminiscent of his father). After sitting next to him at a dinner in 1903, Beatrice Webb, the economist and social reformer, described him as "egotistical, shallow-minded and reactionary . . . More of the American speculator than the English aristocrat."[17]

Jennie was seeing less and less of her elder son. As early as 1901, obviously in response to a reproach, he wrote to her, "No my dear, I do not forget you. But we are both of us busy people, absorbed in our own affairs . . . Naturally we see little of each other. Naturally that makes no difference to our feelings."[18]

Jennie asked Winston for help with her writings. In early 1902, she sent a draft of a newspaper article to him for comment. This was a reversal of roles from the days when he relied on his mother to clean up his prose and get his war reportage published, and he was a harsher editor than she had been. "I have read through the article. There is a great deal of interesting matter in it; and I have nothing to say to the style; but I think there is a great lack of arrangement which makes it hard to follow and would militate against its success . . . [Make] up your mind exactly what is the intention of each particular paragraph . . . I enclose you a suggested skeleton which I have sketched out for you."[19]

Winston's own prose, although verbose, was sharp and well structured, and his advice would benefit any rookie writer ("group your ideas"), and especially Jennie, whose writing tended to be formless. By now, Winston was the bestselling author of five books, and, even as he pushed his way into frontline politics, he had embarked on his next ambitious project. He was working on a two-volume biography of his father, whose reputation he was determined to salvage despite Lord Randolph's political recklessness and cruel treatment of his sons. The publisher Macmillan gave him an extraordinarily generous advance of £8,000 (£800,000 today), and when it was published in 1906, it sold well.[20] Seeing Winston's success and undeterred by his bluntness, Jennie conceived the idea of writing a memoir.

Writing projects drew mother and son together. The tone of their correspondence became once again collegial, with each relying on the other's skills. In 1902, Winston asked Jennie to send him "the scrap-book you have of my Father's newspaper cuttings."[21] Three years later he wrote, "Dearest Mamma, Will you write me three or four sheets of recollections about your life in London and Ireland with my father from 1874 to 1880? You will remember how you first began in Charles Street I think – entertaining Mr. Disraeli, hunting at Oakham, then the row [with the Prince of Wales]."[22] For her part, Jennie repeatedly asked Winston to read draft chapters of her memoir and to add mate-rial to strengthen her prose. As a rising politician, Winston urged his mother to be discreet. "You have a great chance of making a charming woman's book about the last 30 years, & I do beg you . . . [to] ban-ish ruthlessly anything that will hurt other people's feelings. It is well worth while."[23]

Jennie was confident that her book would sell well, given the fame of the Churchill name, and it did. It was published in the U.S. in 1907 and a year later in England and went through several editions. While she had taken her son's advice and spilled no secrets, the book was riddled with inaccuracies. She claimed that she spoke Italian as a toddler (she did not), and she padded the text with lengthy extracts from irrelevant letters. There was no mention of marital separations, passionate extramarital affairs, or political rows; the discretion that served her well in her private life was dull on the page. She wrote in the preface that "there may be some to whom these *Reminiscences* will be interesting chiefly in virtue of what is left unsaid." It was politely reviewed, perhaps because, in the adulatory words of the New York monthly *Current Literature*, Jennie was "The Most Anglo-Saxon Woman in the World."[24] Her own husband noted that it was so "cau-tiously written, there was not a line in it to which any of her many friends could take exception." The *Spectator* considered that the book showed her "in her true character of a frank, indefatigable, and gener-ous woman."[25] Generous words, but the review was no franker than Jennie's memoir.

There was one way that she might have improved her sales and filled her purse: a lecture tour in America. Writers as diverse as

Charles Dickens, Oscar Wilde, and her own son had done well with such marketing trips, and Americans liked that one of their own was prominent within the British elite. The novelist Henry James encouraged her to go as long as she was paid adequately: "*you* can't possibly fail, I am sure, to have a huge success & vulgarly speaking, a big harvest." He warned her that she would need stamina and a thick skin, because audiences would want far more personal details. "That is really all they want and to look at you for all they are worth."[26] Jennie had stamina to burn and proven skill to rise above malicious gossip. But she did not go. She had concerns closer to home.

Once again, her finances were a mess; the bank refused to honor several checks she had written, and the Wests had to move out of Salisbury Hall. There was an additional problem: George's career had taken a nosedive. Drawn back to the glittering lights of the metropolis, he had left his post in the Potteries after only a couple of years and had gone into partnership with a glib North Countryman named Wheater, who regarded George's posh friends as ripe for the picking.[27] George had not bothered to consult Cassel or any other City advisers on his new venture. The investment firm Wheater, Cornwallis-West & Co. started well, but George was soon out of his depth. Only a surreptitious check from his brother-in-law the Duke of Westminster saved him from bankruptcy. Jennie treated the money troubles with her usual shrug and went to Paris. But she told Winston that their financial situation "preys dreadfully on poor George, who is getting quite ill over it all." And, as his friends had noticed, George had begun to stray from Jennie's side.

V

Although Winston resisted many of Jennie's attempts to share his life, he recognized that his glamorous mother could still be of value to his political campaigns. In January 1906, Jennie wore her most exotic hat and charming smile as she helped him campaign for a Liberal seat in Manchester. She found it as exhilarating as Lord Randolph's campaigns, although all her assumptions about feminine behavior were offended by disruptive suffrage activists who noisily demanded that women be given the vote. She rarely questioned those pre-feminist assumptions, although her own behavior frequently challenged convention and she was judged for it. Nevertheless, she clung to the patrician belief that women could have more impact backstage than in the spotlight. In a letter to her sister Leonie, she expressed her disapproval of feminism in words that might have been uttered the same year by Sara Roosevelt. "The female suffrage women are too odious. Every night they make a disturbance and shriek and rant. They damage their own cause hopelessly."[28]

Winston won the seat of Manchester North West for the new Liberal government. Jennie reported to Leonie, "Manchester was wonderful! I have been to lots of elections but I never saw such excitement." Her son was immediately appointed to the non-cabinet position of undersecretary of state for the Colonial Office.

There were other ways in which Winston relied on Jennie for assistance. In 1900 he had turned to her for help with furnishing and staffing the bachelor flat, 105 Mount Street, near the eastern edge of Hyde Park, that his cousin Sunny—the Duke of Marlborough—had passed on to him. Five years later he moved to 12 Bolton Street, a Regency town house near the Ritz Hotel, that could house all his books (many of them purchased for him by Sir Ernest Cassel). Jennie again provided the kind of domestic advice for which most of his contemporaries turned to wives. Now in his thirties, Winston was already a decade older than Franklin Roosevelt had been when the latter became engaged to Eleanor Roosevelt. As we have seen, Franklin's engagement had *not* been welcomed by Sara, who had enjoyed making plans with her bachelor son and was shocked to learn she would have a rival for his affections. Jennie's situation was the reverse. Still clinging to her youth, she was likely in no rush to have grandchildren. But she must have wondered if Winston's ambition was too all-consuming to allow for the kinds of romances on which she herself thrived.

Winston's self-regard and social awkwardness had not impressed the handful of women he had courted. Sitting next to Violet Asquith at one dinner, he abruptly asked her how old she was. Hearing that she was nineteen, he glumly replied that he was already thirty-two: "Younger than anyone else who *counts* though." Then he uttered one of his most-repeated lines: "We are all worms, but I do believe I am a glow-worm."[29] He was equally uncouth when he met Clementine Hozier, the beautiful daughter of Jennie's old friend Lady Blanche Hozier. At a ball one evening in 1904, he asked to be introduced to her and then, according to Clementine, "Winston just stared. He never uttered one word, and was very gauche. He never asked me for a dance, he never asked me to have supper with him."[30] A more adroit suitor elbowed Winston aside and escorted Clemmie (as she was always known) onto the dance floor.

But the circumstances of both Winston and Jack were about to change dramatically. In April 1908, Herbert Asquith became the leader of the Liberal Party and prime minister, and immediately invited Winston to join the cabinet as president of the Board of Trade. This was a meteoric start to his political career. The thirty-three-year-old was now more than "Randy's boy" within the political sphere, and his celebrity began to equal his mother's.

Next, to Jennie's delight, Jack Churchill got married. For over a year, he had been courting Lady Gwendeline Bertie, the artistic, dark-haired daughter of the 7th Earl of Abingdon. There were obstacles: "Goonie," as Gwendeline was known, was a Roman Catholic, and Jack had no money. But in August, they were quietly married in the Church of St. Aloysius, in Oxford. The press notices included such headlines as "Marriage of a Cabinet Minister's Brother."[31]

And finally, after reconnecting with Clementine Hozier at a London dinner party, Winston decided he needed a partner. He asked his mother to invite Clemmie and Lady Blanche Hozier to Salisbury Hall the following weekend, a couple of days after he had joined the cabinet.

Despite her titled relatives, Clemmie's immediate family was scandal-ridden. Her mother's marital exploits made Jennie's look tame: Clementine's natural father was almost certainly not Sir Henry

Hozier, and she had spent several years of her childhood in France because her mother could not afford to live in England. Her mother then settled in Berkhamsted, and Clementine was sent to the Girls' Grammar School, where she received an excellent education. However, her classmates were decidedly middle-class rather than the daughters of peers or baronets. Lady Blanche had no money to send her anywhere posher.

Clementine shared with Eleanor Roosevelt the scars of an erratic upbringing, but she was a far sturdier character and had been less damaged by scandal and loneliness. She had watched her own mother challenge convention and stand up to a volatile and violent husband, and she worked as a French teacher and occasional seamstress to make ends meet. She had none of Eleanor Roosevelt's insecurities and no fears about developing and expressing her own views. A committed Liberal, she liked Winston's politics and admired his success.

After the weekend at Salisbury Hall with the Cornwallis-Wests, Clemmie wrote a note to Jennie: "At this moment your whole mind must be filled with joy & triumph for Mr Churchill, but you were so kind to me that you made me feel as if I had known you always. I feel no one can know him, even as little as I do, without being dominated by his charm and brilliancy."[32] Jennie decided that Clementine was absolutely the right wife for a son who, she acknowledged to a friend, could be "difficult."

Jennie's enthusiasm for her son's pursuit of Clementine could not have differed more sharply from Sara's shock at Franklin's romance. Eager to see Winston married, Jennie agreed to chaperone her future daughter-in-law during a weekend stay at Blenheim Palace because Clementine's own mother was unavailable. Winston wanted to propose to Clemmie in the magnificent ducal setting where he was born; Clementine accepted the invitation, although she dreaded the Edwardian house party rituals where ladies were expected to wear at least three exquisite outfits during a single day. She had neither a maid nor a suitable array of gowns. But Jennie wanted to ensure her son's success in this as in other initiatives. As soon as she heard that

Clementine had arrived at Blenheim, she sent her maid to her room to help her dress.[33]

Despite his mother's efforts, Winston nearly missed his chance to propose. He had promised to take Clemmie for a morning walk through the park, but then he overslept, and Clemmie nearly caught an early train back to London. The promised stroll finally happened that afternoon. In the ornamental Temple of Diana where they had sheltered from a shower, Winston asked Clementine to marry him and she accepted. However, she asked her impatient suitor to keep their engagement a secret until she had told her own family. The rain stopped, and the two of them left the little stone temple.

Jennie had emerged onto the Blenheim terrace in the watery sunshine and was anxiously scanning the manicured grounds for a glimpse of her son. As the couple strolled back to the palace, Winston caught sight of her and broke into a run through the wet grass. Forgetting, for the moment, his promise to Clementine, he jubilantly announced his engagement to his mother.

A mere three weeks after the Blenheim proposal, Winston and Clementine were married in St. Margaret's Westminster, the parish church of the House of Commons. A wedding gift of £500 (£50,000 today) from Sir Ernest Cassel helped finance the society wedding, attended by thirteen hundred guests. The marriage of a political celebrity to a society beauty drew crowds.

Jennie, who was escorted down the aisle by Jack, wore a gold satin gown and stole the show with an enormous hat decorated with velvet and satin lilies. The American press still loved Jennie, and some reporters suggested that the plump fifty-four-year-old woman outshone her elegant twenty-three-year-old daughter-in-law, who glowed with youth and happiness. *Current Literature* reported that "As the widow of 'Randy' and the mother of 'Winny' swept up the aisle on the arm of her strapping son John there was a murmur of admiration among the crowded pews which the appearance of the bride herself quite failed to evoke . . . It seems too cruel to say, [but she] seemed the junior of the bride by at least two years."[34]

The newlyweds spent their first night together at Blenheim Palace. The letter that Winston wrote to Jennie that night was deeply touching. "Best of love my dearest Mamma," he wrote. "You were a great comfort & support to me at a critical time in my emotional development. We have never been so near together so often in a short time. God bless you . . . Your loving son."[35]

Both Jennie's sons had married for love, and each had chosen a partner who would be supportive and loyal. Jennie was delighted with her daughters-in-law, although neither could help shore up the family's finances. But her sons now had their own lives, and her role as "Mommer," as she sometimes styled herself, dwindled. In particular, Winston's neediness was now directed at his wife rather than his mother, and marriage supplied the comfort and protection he craved. He and Clemmie drew close, and used baby talk with each other. "There was much mention of lapping cream and stroking warm, furry coats" in their correspondence, writes Clementine's biographer.[36]

The Winston-Clementine correspondence is voluminous—it includes over two thousand lengthy epistles, love notes, telegrams, and memoranda. This "lifelong dialogue" convinced their daughter Mary Soames to publish a selected volume, bound together by "the golden thread of love."[37] Clementine's importance to Winston's ego is glimpsed in hundreds of the missives. In a rare admission of self-doubt, he wrote in one letter, "At times, I think I cd conquer everything – & then again I know I am only a weak vain fool. But your love for me is the greatest glory & recognition that has or will ever befall me: & the attachment wh I feel towards you is not capable of being altered by the worst of things that happen in this world."[38]

How could Jennie compete with this? She had always identified with her elder son, seeing in Winston both Randolph's brilliance and her own dynamism as he burned with red-hot ambition, reckless courage, a thirst for fame, and insatiable energy. She wanted her own life, but she also wanted to accompany him on his giddy upward path. But with Clementine now enveloping Winston with reassurance, there was less room for her.

VI

The final drama of 1908 was the collapse of Jennie's own marriage. There had been tensions for some time. Jennie could handle the constant financial crises, but George was not so carefree, and he began to resent playing second fiddle to a wife whose reaction to angry letters from the bank was to go shopping. He often didn't come home at night, and Jennie was growing lonely. She had turned to Jack rather than George to walk her down the aisle at Winston's wedding. She was less of a "royal pet" these days, as she admitted in a letter to Winston. In a 1907 letter to her sister Leonie, who had a livelier social life than she did, Jennie wrote, "I like to think that you are enjoying yrself & making up for all those dull years when as you say yrself – your greatest excitement was to see me dress for a ball – Make the most of it all while it amuses you."[39]

The ultimate rupture with George was occasioned, indirectly, by a new venture of Jennie's that, like her literary magazine and her hospital ship, demonstrated her impressive creativity and her desire to be more than a society beauty. The stage was thriving in Edwardian England; a whole generation of playwrights, including George Bernard Shaw and Sir Arthur Wing Pinero, were producing their best work. As usual, Jennie had seen a wave and wanted to surf it. Once she had finished *Reminiscences*, she plunged into the professional theater with a play, *His Borrowed Plumes*, that she had been working on for some time.

Initially, Jennie's foray into drama went well. Her dialogue, written with the dry wit that made her such a good conversationalist, reflected her own views. In an early draft, the heroine explains to an MP why she doesn't want the vote. "It would never do for us to appear to have got what we wanted, you must be allowed to think yourselves the masters of the situation . . . How could we otherwise really rule the roost, and make you do exactly as we like? All you ask is the appearance of power, all we want is Power!"[40] Sara Roosevelt might easily have agreed with this subversive suggestion, given the manipulative tactics she often employed with Franklin.

Jennie persuaded Mrs. Patrick Campbell, an immensely successful actress since she'd first stepped on stage in 1888, to produce and
appear in her play. Dark-haired, velvet-voiced, and deliberately out-
rageous (she smoked cigars in public and enjoyed gambling), she and
Jennie worked hard to make Jennie's drawing room comedy come to
life. "Mrs. Pat has really been an angel," Jennie reported to Leonie.
"The play would not exist without her."[41]

When the play opened at the Hicks Theatre in London's West
End on July 6, 1909, it was initially well received. The distinguished
critic and writer Max Beerbohm described it as "a very good entertainment." Another critic praised "the unburdened brightness of its
dialogue and the undercurrent of cheery satire upon the foibles of
either sex . . ."[42] The critics shared his view. Celebrities and peers
packed the opening audience, and there was talk of a Broadway production.

But *His Borrowed Plumes* ran for only two weeks and, as usual, Jennie lost money. She also lost her husband—the charismatic Mrs. Pat
had begun to entice George over to her charming little house in Kensington Square. Soon he was spending most nights away from the marital
home. In her memoirs, Mrs. Pat airily wrote that she believed George's
life "was unhappy, and [I] warmly gave him my friendship and affection," although this "caused gossip, mis-judgement and pain."[43]

Jennie still loved George, and she did not want to lose him. She
and Sara Roosevelt had been raised in a world where divorce was unacceptable, and although the rules were slowly changing, a divorced
man or woman was still a pariah. In August 1910, Jennie wrote a letter
to George's mother, of which a draft has survived. "I have loved him
more than anyone on earth & have *always* been true & loyal . . . He can
have his freedom if he wants it – free to marry Mrs Patrick Campbell
or anyone else he thinks would make him happy – I have done my best
& have failed . . . In respect to money & extravagance with which he
has reproached me there is absolutely nothing to choose between us."[44]

George dithered—a weak man torn between two strong-willed
women. There were attempts at reconciliation, and Jennie's sons

came to their mother's rescue both emotionally and financially. But George was now brazenly squiring Mrs. Pat around town and refusing to help Jennie with her bills (he had little money and besides, most of the disputed expenses were Jennie's). Jack deplored George's behavior and wrote, "Dear Mama, Don't be too depressed – when all this is over – you will find yourself more settled & happier than you have been for some time, and you will come back again nearer to W & me whose love is always just the same . . . I have sent £100 to Smith Bank—from both of us "[45]

Recognizing that Mrs. Campbell had the momentum, Jennie was as magnanimous as her own mother had been with Leonard Jerome's mistresses. George wrote to his wife in anguish in late 1912: "Dearest Jennie, I was glad to get your kind generous letter . . . I can honestly say I have never done anything in my life that I so hated doing . . . Dearest Jennie that we could be true friends after it is all over . . . you are a splendid woman."[46]

The Cornwallis-West divorce catapulted Jennie's name into the headlines when the case arrived in the courts in July 1913, with Jennie's petition based on the claim that George had withheld her conjugal rights. But the press treated her kindly, fawning over her good looks, her eyes that were "still sparkling with fire," and her lips that were "full of character." The following year, George was declared bankrupt, with liabilities of £15,000 and assets of £900. The divorce decree was made absolute a month later. Two days before the final rupture, Jennie returned her engagement and wedding ring to George, with a note that read, "I say Goodbye – a long long Goodbye."[47]

George married Mrs. Pat a few hours after the divorce was finalized, then got into an uncharacteristic brawl with newspaper photographers outside the Kensington Registry Office.[48] His new wife pronounced crisply, "Wedlock is the deep peace of the double bed after the hurly-burly of the chaise lounge."[49] This marriage lasted less than five years, but Mrs. Pat refused to divorce him. After Jennie's death, the hapless George, who by now had acquired the nickname "Old Wives' Tale,"[50] would confide to Winston that "the greatest mistake I ever made in my life was in allowing myself to be persuaded into a separation from [your mother.] I can assure you that I have lived & am living to bitterly regret it."[51]

Even before the divorce was finalized, Jennie was alone again. It was perhaps one of the lowest points in her life. Her sixtieth birthday approached; could she recover the vitality for which she had always been admired? Was she now destined to dwindle into the invisibility of widowhood that afflicted most women in her circumstances? Given Jennie's personality, this was unlikely. Mrs. George Cornwallis-West was not going to slip into the shadows or allow herself to be erased by scandal. She continued to demonstrate control of her story. One of the first things she did was to reclaim her title; she announced in the Court Circular that she would in future be known once again as Lady Randolph Churchill.

CHAPTER 15

—◇—

Sara Stays Close

1904–1913

The role of mother-in-law was one that, in the long term, neither Jennie Churchill nor Sara Roosevelt would find altogether easy, as they watched their sons each make another woman central to his life. But for Sara, everything began almost too well.

In accordance with his mother's wishes, Franklin kept his engagement secret for a year. When he told Sara, at the 1903 Thanksgiving dinner at Fairlawn, of his commitment to Eleanor, he promised her that Eleanor would "be a daughter to you in every true way." During that year, Sara got to know her future daughter-in-law, and, since Eleanor's own mother was dead, helped her with many of the decisions that confronted a bride and her family in early twentieth-century Manhattan. Sara took on these duties with gusto; it placed her in a role with which she was entirely comfortable.

In early December 1904, a couple of days after the engagement was finally announced in the *New York Times,* Sara watched Eleanor being welcomed by the Delanos at Algonac. Eleanor would write later, "The Delanos were the first people I met who were able to do what they wanted to do without wondering where to obtain the money." Still a timid orphan with a very small trust fund, Eleanor realized that Sara's and Franklin's self-assurance came from immense stability and wealth. No Delano had drunk or gambled the family wealth away, as her own mother's family the Halls had done. Sara and her siblings also demonstrated to Franklin's fiancée the unquestioning family

cohesiveness that would be expected of her. "The Delanos might dis-
approve of one another, and if so, they were not slow to express their
disapproval, but let someone outside so much as hint at criticism, and
the clan was ready to tear him limb from limb."[1]

Once the news was out, Sara found "sublimination for her sorrow in the joy of her children," according to her biographer Kleeman.[2] She took charge of wedding arrangements and the bride-to-be,
proudly noting in her diary, "Eleanor dined with us alone and spent
the night with me . . . Today I had a dinner of 12 for Eleanor . . .
Eleanor lunched and we went over lists and F. took her out to pay
visits . . . I took Eleanor to Pach. She looked charming as she posed
for her photos."[3] Newspapers covered the engagement of the two
Roosevelts, with more attention paid to the president's niece than to
Franklin. Good wishes poured in from Delanos, Halls, Groton staff
and classmates, and from the White House. "I am as fond of Eleanor
as if she were my own daughter," wrote President Roosevelt.

Later Eleanor's cousin Corinne Robinson Alsop would recall her
doubts about the match. Eleanor had "lived through so much unhappiness, and then to [plan to marry] a man with a mother like Cousin
Sally . . . A more determined and possessive woman than I have ever
known."[4] Nevertheless, in the short term Eleanor was almost patheti-
cally grateful for the firm but generous guidance that her own family
had never offered.

II

On the evening of March 16, 1905, Sara wrote in her journal, "This
is Franklin's last night at home as a boy." The date had been set to accommodate the president's schedule, as he was going to walk the bride
up the aisle. The following morning, Teddy Roosevelt blew into Sara's
Madison Avenue house to pay his respects to her and greet the groom
before he rushed off, top hat in hand, to head Manhattan's St. Patrick's
Day parade. At a more leisurely pace, Sara and Franklin made their
way to the home on East Seventh-Sixth Street of Eleanor's cousin and
godmother, Mrs. Henry Parish, where the wedding was to take place.

Sara had given Eleanor a pearl choker with diamond bars, a style popularized by England's Queen Alexandra, as a wedding present. Now the bride wore it along with a stiff satin dress covered with a family heirloom—rose point Brussels lace, worn by her mother and grandmother at their weddings, that was so valuable it was stored in a bank vault. Eleanor looked magnificent but privately felt "decked out beyond description." In a portrait photograph of her in the outfit, her expression is one of uncertainty, almost misery.

The two-hundred-strong guest list was made up of heavy hitters from Manhattan's old guard—Vanderbilts, Van Rensselaers, Winthrops—and large numbers of Roosevelts, Delanos, and Halls. Sara cut her usual regal figure, in white silk with black lace that had belonged to her own mother. The president managed to make it to the ceremony at 3:30 p.m., a wilted shamrock in his buttonhole, while the St. Patrick Day's parade continued up Fifth Avenue. Sara watched the president walk her future daughter-in-law toward the temporary altar that had been set up in the Parishes' parlor. The cacophony of Irish songs and brass bands outside made it difficult for guests to hear Franklin and Eleanor exchange their vows. More audible was President Roosevelt's comment as he reached up to kiss the bride: "Well, Franklin, there's nothing like keeping the name in the family."[5]

Minutes later, bride and groom found themselves standing alone. Teddy Roosevelt had made his way into the library, followed by all the guests, who were more interested in talking to the president than to the newlyweds. He held forth for the next hour and a half, a performance (among others) that prompted his daughter Alice's famous remark: "Father always wanted to be the bride at every wedding and the corpse at every funeral." There were complaints about the shortage of champagne and the overcrowding.

But Sara was satisfied: "my boy" had received his bride from the president of the United States, and she cherished the many compliments she received "on the charm and distinction of the tall bridal pair." She wrote to Franklin, "*Everyone* says it was the most perfect wedding, so simple & yet so 'elegant & refined,' etc . . . I was very proud of both my dear children." She was not going to cede an inch of territory to critics, and she certainly wouldn't allow any daylight between the happy couple and herself. But even if ulterior motives underlay her enthusiasm, the young, hesitant Eleanor must have welcomed Sara's reassurance that she had been a beautiful bride.

After the wedding, while Franklin and Eleanor spent a week at Hyde Park, Sara remained in Manhattan, where she prepared a suite for them at the Hotel Webster. On the day of their return to the city, she noted in her diary, "Arranged flowers and went to my French lecture. Returned to find my children and brought them home to lunch with me."

When Franklin had finished his year at Columbia Law School, Sara said goodbye to them again as they boarded the RMS *Oceanic* in New York Harbor and disappeared to Europe for a three-month honeymoon. The newlyweds took turns writing to her. Franklin's letters were bouncy travelogues: "We are having a scrumptious time."[6] Eleanor's were barely veiled pleas for Sara's love and approval. "Dearest Mama," read an early letter. "You are always just the sweetest, dearest Mama to your children and I shall look forward to our next long evening together, when I shall want to be kissed all the time . . . Ever and ever so much love my dearest Mummy from your devoted Eleanor."[7]

Sara continued to choreograph the newlyweds' lives during their absence. She rented a house for them on East Thirty-Sixth Street, within three blocks of her house at 200 Madison Avenue, furnished it, and engaged a butler, housemaid, and cook for them. Eleanor welcomed these efforts and underlined her own domestic incompetence, in a letter from Strasbourg: "You have done wonders for us, in the way of a good bargain . . . I am looking forward so much to getting it in order with you to help us. I am afraid my unaided efforts would not be very successful!"[8] From now on, Sara expected "to be there always, in the background, to share their responsibilities and worries, to help when she was needed . . . part of her unconscious picture of her future."[9] When she was in Manhattan in the months ahead, "she kept a maternal eye on the Franklin Roosevelt household," frequently dining with them and expecting Franklin to escort her home afterward. When she was back in the country, she encouraged Franklin and Eleanor to spend frequent weekends at Springwood.

On those weekends, Franklin loved driving through the stone gateposts of his childhood home. There he could sink into the luxury he had always known, enjoy the undivided attention of his mother and Elespie, and lose himself in his collections of stamps, stuffed birds, and books. Sara continued to preside at the candlelit dining table, with Franklin opposite her and Eleanor on the side. After dinner, the threesome went to Sara's "snuggery," a cozy reading room with a couple of wingback chairs drawn up to a crackling fire. Sara took one and Franklin the other, leaving Eleanor to sit on the floor or at a distance on the sofa. "All her life an outsider in the homes of others, Eleanor was once again on the periphery," Eleanor's biographer Blanche Wiesen Cook wrote.[10]

Did Eleanor resent the sense that there were three people in her marriage, as Cook strenuously argues? Cook suggests that "for over a decade, she submerged and distorted her own needs and convictions" as she strove to be a pleasing daughter-in-law, a dutiful wife, and a mother.[11] It is true that, when Eleanor came to write her first memoir thirty years later, there was no Delano restraint about her criticisms of Sara. She deplored her lack of autonomy. "I was beginning to be an entirely dependent person—no tickets to buy, no plans to make, someone always to decide everything for me."[12] But at the time, she was still enjoying the novelty of marriage, financial security, and the presence in her life of a mother figure who had welcomed her into such a secure family and was now guiding her behavior as a new wife.

At a time when a laborer's wages ran around $700 a year, Franklin and Eleanor had a substantial income from their trust funds. Eleanor's was more than $7,000, Franklin's about $5,000, and their combined income of $12,000 would be worth over $384,000 today.[13] However, Sara's generosity allowed them to live better than they might have otherwise.

Franklin was happy to rely on his mother's munificence, but he would have liked to take over some of the management of the Spring-wood estate. On a visit to English friends during his honeymoon, he had decided that the farm operation should be modernized. However, Sara said no; this was a gentleman's estate rather than a business. Her son had to content himself with buying a small section of land from her to try out his ideas, and following family tradition by shouldering such community responsibilities as church warden, school trustee, and member of the volunteer fire brigade.

Sara remained firmly in control of the large fortune left to her by her father and her husband; Franklin would inherit it only after her death. Perhaps she thought that "the children" were not yet to be trusted with too much money; perhaps it was a way to remain needed. Her tight hold of the financial reins kept Franklin and Eleanor firmly in her debt. Franklin never objected.

III

The first grandchild arrived in 1906, giving Sara extensive opportunities to stay close to Franklin and Eleanor. She was a far more attentive grandparent than Jennie Churchill ever wanted to be.

Sara knew that Eleanor had returned from her honeymoon feeling queasy after a rough voyage. Noticing that her daughter-in-law was still wilting several days later, Sara summoned the doctor. Eleanor was just twenty-one years old when she learned that she was pregnant.

After her own childbirth traumas, Sara was determined to be with her son's wife when she gave birth, and as Eleanor's due date approached, she told her maid to prepare her clothes each night so she could be ready for a call at any time. When word came, at nine in the morning of May 3, that Eleanor was in labor, Sara hurried to her side. "At 1:15 a beautiful little girl was born, 10 lbs and 1 oz," Sara recorded. A well-trained pediatric nurse, Blanche Spring, had coached Eleanor through the birth and would teach Eleanor to care for the newborn, christened Anna Eleanor Roosevelt. This left Sara to keep Franklin company. "Dear Eleanor and Baby doing well. Franklin dines every evening with me," Sara noted in her journal.[14] When Miss Spring left the household a month after Anna's birth, Sara noted, "Poor little Eleanor is upset by it though she is brave."

Eleanor had as little confidence in her aptitude for motherhood as she had in her housekeeping skills, and Sara stepped into the breach. "For the first year of my married life, I was completely taken care of," Eleanor would later write. "My mother-in-law did everything for me." Sara advised her when the baby was ready for solid food, which physician should be called if the child fell ill. She selected a nurse for the baby and told Eleanor that, if the baby cried at night, the nurse should attend and should not let her cry. This instruction flew in the face of contemporary baby manuals, which advised that babies should be left to cry themselves to sleep. On occasion, Eleanor pushed back, but she could never rely on her husband to back her up. He preferred to sidestep such power struggles. "It was not in Sara's style to make an issue [of Eleanor's dependence on her]; it *was* in her style to make decisions," Sara's grandson Curtis Roosevelt told American author Jan Pottker.[15] So Sara extended her household sway while Eleanor, ill at ease as a mother, gratefully adopted a more passive role.

Sara continued with the velvet routines of a Knickerbocker grande dame—French lessons and trips to theaters and concert halls in Manhattan; visits to the local schools and hospitals during her weeks in Hyde Park. But her son's household was her first priority. Franklin, Eleanor, and the baby spent two weekends a month and all the holidays at Hyde Park, and Anna, with her nurse in tow, was regularly left with her grandmother for days at a time. "I held Baby from 6.00-7.00 and she was so lovely," Sara wrote in her journal.[16]

Sara never voiced any criticism of her daughter-in-law's maternal behavior, although she did comment in her journal on "the interesting modern ideas" of young mothers. Eleanor certainly had bizarre notions. One was that, because babies needed fresh air, Anna should be tucked into a box, constructed by the butler from chicken wire and wooden batons, which was then suspended outside from a sunless windowsill for a set period each day. She was persuaded to cease this practice only when screams alerted a neighbor to the child's chilly misery and the neighbor threatened to call the New York branch of the Society for the Prevention of Cruelty to Children.[17]

Occasionally Sara showed exasperation with "my boy" for ignoring his wife. At Christmas 1906, the Roosevelts joined their Hudson Valley neighbors the Rogerses and fifty other guests for an evening dinner and dance. Eleanor was not well, so Sara took her home early, leaving Franklin to party. It was almost dawn before Franklin arrived home. Eleanor's cousin Corinne met Franklin the following morning. He was "pale as a sheet and furious. His mother had upbraided him for staying out so late, especially with his wife unwell, and had forced him to come down for breakfast at 8 a.m." Meanwhile Sara had thoughtfully arranged for Eleanor to be served breakfast in bed.[18]

Having graduated from Columbia, Franklin started an unpaid clerkship at Carter, Ledyard and Milburn, executors of the Astor estate. The prestigious firm specialized in corporate law. It was exactly the kind of setting that Sara had hoped for—in fact, she had asked senior partner Lewis Cass Ledyard, an old business ally of her husband's, to find a place for her boy.[19] Franklin told his mother that he was merely a "full-fledged office boy," but the tall young man in elegantly tailored suits was popular among his fellow clerks, one of whom recalled his "sanguine temperament, almost adolescent in its buoyancy."[20] Before long, his affability was as much a hallmark as his long lunches and lazy habits.

The economy was in overdrive in the early twentieth century, growing at more than 4 percent a year as the United States leaped ahead of Britain in manufacturing output. Factories were churning out sewing machines, typewriters, telephones, and lightbulbs, while rail networks forged their way across the continent. Franklin made his way each morning to his Wall Street office past rag trade emporiums and machine shops. Bicycles and motorized buggies powered variously by steam, electricity, and gas crowded the streets, causing horses to rear and pedestrians to flinch. Farther uptown, department stores such as Macy's, Bloomingdale's, and Lord & Taylor helped

spawn a new class of consumers. Unbridled growth came at a price—
yawning inequality. Wages were low, working conditions dangerous,
and labor unrest was on the rise.

Under President Teddy Roosevelt, Washington tried to throttle
back the power of major corporations, with regulatory reforms and anti-
trust prosecutions. Franklin Roosevelt's employer, Carter, Ledyard
and Milburn, often provided the stiff-collared lawyers who represented such corporations as Standard Oil of New Jersey and the American Tobacco Company in their squabbles with Washington. At this
stage Franklin showed no particular interest in the principles at stake;
he remained politically agnostic. He did not display the raw hunger
for political success that Winston Churchill had demonstrated at the
same age.

Yet a fellow clerk would comment years later that the young lawyer
already harbored political ambitions. "I remember him saying with
engaging frankness that he wasn't going to practice law forever, that he
intended to run for office at the first opportunity, and that he wanted
to be and thought he had a real chance to be President." Franklin had
even mapped out the route—a route already followed by Teddy Roosevelt: "first, a seat in the State Assembly, then an appointment as
Assistant Secretary of the Navy . . . and finally the governorship of
New York." The governorship was the crucial launching pad for a run
at the top office. The cocky young lawyer, still only twenty-five years
old, convinced his colleagues that his ambition "seemed proper and
sincere and moreover, as he put it, entirely reasonable."[21] The fact
that his last name was Roosevelt, and his wife was the niece of the
sitting president, cut a lot of ice. But he would wait for opportunities
to come to him.

Sara remained ignorant of her son's White House dreams, and
there is no record that he discussed them with Eleanor. Neither
woman would have encouraged him—Sara because she continued
to find politics distasteful, and Eleanor because she was in a blur of
motherhood.

In the first ten years of her marriage Eleanor would have six children, one of whom died in infancy. Nineteen months after Anna arrived, James was born (December 23, 1907), followed by Franklin Delano Jr. (March 18, 1909–November 8, 1909), then Elliott (September 23, 1910), Franklin Delano Jr. (August 7, 1914), and John Aspinwall (March 13, 1916). As Eleanor would write, "For ten years I was always just getting over having a baby or about to have one, and so my occupations were considerably restricted."[22] Hovering in the background of all this procreation was Sara, always ready to step in and dispense child-rearing wisdom, summon a doctor, or whisk some of the brood off to Hyde Park or Campobello Island.

One after another, the babies would be christened. Each new baby was usually squeezed into Franklin's christening gown, and after the ceremony at Hyde Park's St. James Church, Sara would serve tea to the guests at Springwood. When her first grandson arrived, and was named James after her late husband, she distributed gifts to her servants. If it was a summer christening, she might then organize a game of croquet on the lawn. As the old maple trees cast long shadows in the rays of the setting sun, the air would fill with the thwack of wooden mallets on wooden balls and the laughter of spectators—men in summer flannels and straw boaters, women in long flounced dresses and big hats. It was a timeless picture.

Franklin was an enthusiastic father, roughhousing with his children and feeding them treats. But he left child-rearing to his wife and was frequently absent—there were sports events, club evenings, and sailing trips with Harvard classmates. Sara was a godsend for Eleanor, who was as diffident with servants as she was uncertain about motherhood. As Sara's biographer and friend Kleeman wrote, "she took many burdens off the shoulders of her young daughter-in-law."[23]

Did she notice her daughter-in-law's growing unhappiness? Eleanor had always been moody and was now depleted, physically and mentally. Sara was deeply sympathetic to her plight, noting in her diary in 1909, after the death of seven-month-old Franklin Delano Jr., that "poor Eleanor's mother's heart is well nigh broken. She . . . cannot believe her baby is gone from here."[24] Eleanor withdrew into her grief while Sara kept vigil, staying beside her grandson's still body for an agonizing twenty-four hours. After the funeral at St. James Church, Franklin and Eleanor returned to Manhattan, leaving their two older children at Springwood with their grandmother. Removed from their mother's paralyzing grief, the two children enjoyed the same kinds of activities—country walks and farm visits—that their father had relished at the same age.

IV

Before her first grandchild had even been born, Sara found a way to knit herself more tightly into the fabric of her son's marriage. Her Christmas gift to Franklin and Eleanor in 1905 was a little drawing of a tall town house with smoke curling from its chimney. She captioned it "A Christmas present to Franklin and Eleanor from Maman, number and street not yet decided." By the following Christmas the plot had been purchased, on East Sixty-Fifth Street just off Park Avenue, and construction began in the spring. The thirty-five-foot-wide building, with its buff brick and limestone facade, was a double, not a single, house. Sara would live on one side, Franklin and Eleanor and their children on the other, and, besides a common entrance, there would be connecting doors on the first and fourth of its eight floors. There were fifteen rooms and four bathrooms on each side of the house.

The family moved into 47–49 East Sixty-Fifth Street at the end of 1908. Sara chose the architect for the houses (Charles A. Platt, who also designed several buildings for the University of Illinois) and paid for the construction and furnishings. Eleanor had been excited about the building project, although she left most of the planning to Sara and Franklin. But she was not completely detached; she checked the plans for lighting, bells, and telephones, and wrote to Sara that "all the arrangements seem very good except in one or two bedrooms where I think . . . one would want lights over dressing tables."[25]

Sara was unaware that her daughter-in-law found the new house oppressive. She was not in Eleanor's bedroom when, on Franklin's return from work one day, Eleanor had a meltdown. Eleanor wrote years later, "When my bewildered young husband asked me what on earth was the matter with me, I said I did not like to live in a house which was not in any way mine, one that I had done nothing about, and which did not represent the way I wanted to live." Franklin was aghast; as far as he was concerned, Eleanor had shown little interest in the house. He could not deal with her tears and incoherence, so he walked out of the room after telling her that she was "quite mad." Eleanor began to understand that "it became part of his nature not to talk to anyone of interior things."[26]

Sara may have purposely ignored such problems. She continued to enjoy lunches with Eleanor and evening events with both Franklin and Eleanor and was an active grandparent. Upholding the Delano creed of not whining or making a fuss, she rarely spoke of "interior things." Besides, she had so many other activities; she was a member of several philanthropic boards and Red Cross committees, and she helped organize cultural events and public lectures. She enjoyed taking friends to lunch at the Colony, a new and exclusive women-only club on Madison Avenue whose members ate Waldorf salad off Crown Derby china.

The same year that the move to East Sixty-Fifth Street was effected, Franklin and his family took possession of their own cottage on Campobello Island. The spacious Dutch colonial house on Friars Bay, with thirty-four rooms and five acres of land, had belonged to Sara's friend Mrs. Hartman Kuhn of Boston, who at her death had particularly wanted Eleanor to have the property. Now Eleanor had the freedom of her own place each summer. She wrote cheerfully to Franklin, "I have moved every room in the house around and I hope you will like the change."[27] Sara paid for the property—$5,000, or about $1,250,000 to $1,500,000 today—and thereafter paid the taxes on it.[28]

V

The Roosevelts' life changed dramatically in 1910. This was the year that Franklin launched himself into what his mother still called the "messy business of politics."

Franklin admired Teddy Roosevelt enormously, especially his appeal to a new generation to devote themselves to the public good. Franklin regarded cousin Teddy's route to the White House, via the New York state legislature in Albany, as a logical path for himself, too, even though his own loyalties remained with his father's party, the Democrats. So when he was approached to run for office in Albany, he listened carefully. FDR biographer Jean Smith, among others, enjoys the story (perhaps apocryphal) that when Franklin was invited to become the candidate, he said, "I'd like to talk to my mother first." The Democratic backroom operator was taken aback and told the young lawyer that party members eager to support him "won't like to hear that you had to ask your mother." Franklin got the point. "I'll take it," he replied.[29]

Sara was initially unenthusiastic about her son's change of career. As her biographer Kleeman put it, "She did not see why she should receive all these people whom she had never called on and whose families she did not know."[30] She had looked forward to Franklin replicating his father's life. But she adjusted fast, knowing that if she wanted to stay close to him, she must swallow her snobbery and accept her son's decision.

"Many of our friends said it was a shame for so fine a young man to associate himself with 'dirty' politicians . . . But by this time I knew Franklin's ideas and ideals in going into politics. I knew not only that I would be proud of him, but I predicted the time when their ideas too would change, and when the younger members of other old families would enter politics and take their places in the government."[31] She began to talk about Franklin's commitment to public duty; politics became "statesmanship." And there was an upside. As Sara noted in her journal, "Franklin will be here now a great deal." The state capital was only sixty-five miles north of Hyde Park, with a direct rail line between them, and Franklin would frequently need to visit his voters.

The odds of success for Franklin were low; his district, which included the counties of Putnam, Dutchess, and Columbia, had elected only one Democratic state senator in over fifty years. But the good-looking, well-connected candidate with an oversupply of patrician confidence ran an aggressive campaign, traveling throughout the senate district in a snappy red roadster at a time when cars were an expensive novelty. He out-organized and outspent his opponent—helped by Sara's donation of $1,700 to his $2,500 campaign budget—and he won.

On November 10, 1910, the day after Election Day, Sara had the satisfaction of hearing the doorbell at Springwood ring repeatedly as she sat in the snuggery, just to the left of the front door. The Democrats had swept the state, winning the governorship as well as both houses of the legislature, and Franklin had won by a majority of 1,140 in the former Republican stronghold. "Telegrams coming all day for Franklin," she recorded. Within days, she was referring to the surrounding countryside as "Franklin's district."[32] From now on, "my boy" would launch all his political campaigns from his mother's porch.

Franklin's victory marked a new chapter in his career and his marriage, and Sara adapted with Delano stoicism. Her son announced that, as a state senator, he would live in the state capital, and within days of the election he and Eleanor, without Sara, went to Albany to find a house. A few days later Sara herself inspected their choice, a big three-story brownstone in the shadow of the Capitol, and pronounced it "a fine house that could be made comfortable." The annual rent was $4,800 (about $120,000 today), more than three times Franklin's senatorial salary, and Sara paid it.[33] Sara helped Eleanor settle her three small children, two maids, a wet nurse, and household staff into their new home.

Sara's first letters to Albany were wistful. "It seems like a very strange dream to be here & to think of you dear things all settled in that big Albany house and my boy sitting in the state Senate, a really fine and dignified position, if only lived up to as it should be and I know it *will* be by my dear one."[34] She continued to hover in the background. There was a regular exchange of letters with Eleanor, and Sara made frequent trips to Albany in her newly acquired car, for which she hired a driver. From now on, she sent large amounts of fresh milk, produce, and eggs to the State Street household. And her grandchildren, accompanied by nannies and governesses, spent weeks at a time at Springwood.

The well-heeled Roosevelt family caused quite a stir in Albany, still an undistinguished small town where most legislators spent only a few weeks a year in dingy rooming houses before hurrying home. Thanks to his own wealth and Sara's largesse, Franklin could afford to make Albany his full time occupation. Both still in their twenties, Franklin and Eleanor opened their home to Franklin's voters and political allies. Without her mother-in-law on the other side of a wall, Eleanor began to enjoy herself and to participate in her husband's activities. Within days of his arrival in Albany, Franklin had become spokesperson for a Democratic ginger group that challenged graft and corruption within the party, and its control by the New York City–based Irish mafia known as Tammany Hall.

"There is nothing I love as much as a good fight," he told the *New York Times* on January 22, 1911. "I never had as much fun in my life as I am having right now." Most of Franklin's colleagues found him insufferably arrogant, far more interested in making a name for himself than in improving the lives of voters. Frances Perkins, then secretary of the Committee on Safety for New York City and later FDR's labor secretary, recalled thinking that the affluent new senator from Dutchess County was oblivious to the concerns of social reformers. He "rarely talk[ed to] members, who more or less avoided him, not particularly charming (that came later), artificially serious face, rarely smiling, with an unfortunate habit . . . of throwing his head up. This, combined with his pince-nez and great height, gave him the appearance of looking down his nose at most people."[35]

But Franklin was making his mark. In February, the *New York Globe* commented approvingly, "Tall, with a well set up figure, he is physically fit to command. His face is a bit long but the features are well-modelled, the nose is Grecian and there is a glow of country health in his cheeks . . . His lips are firm and part often in a smile over even white teeth—the Roosevelt teeth." Sara could not have been prouder. Her only quibble with the *Globe*'s gush would have been that her son's good looks came from the Delano rather than the Roosevelt side of the family. It was a comment she often made. She liked to position Franklin firmly within his family tree and suggest that his character and looks owed to his pedigree. This was an approach to heredity that Jennie rarely took with Winston. Jennie—an expert in reinvention for herself—delighted in watching her son discover his own strengths.

On Franklin's thirtieth birthday, in January 1912, Eleanor organized a small gathering in Albany that included her brother Hall and his fiancée. Sara wrote from Hyde Park, "I planned to go up and surprise you today and spend one night but as Hall and Margaret get there today I think it would be foolish and also I should have to sleep with you and Eleanor!" As a birthday gift, she added, "I enclose a little motor car for the winter."[36] Even when absent, she had a way of making her presence felt.

VI

In the next couple of years, Franklin Roosevelt slowly became interested in progressive policies that would protect the interests of farmers, women, and children. Sara expressed approval of all his actions and presided at the head of the Springwood dining table whenever he brought guests to a meal, however rough their manners. She even became accustomed to seeing her son's name in the newspapers, and got over "the shock of hearing him called 'Frank' by the butcher, the baker, and the candlestick maker," according to Kleeman.[37]

However, there was one issue on which she initially did not support Franklin: women's suffrage. Like Jennie Churchill, she did not think women needed the vote; she considered that they could exert more influence behind the scenes. Brought up to believe that their first loyalty was to their class rather than their gender, both women particularly disliked disruptive suffragist tactics.

However, Franklin had been persuaded that women should be

given the vote, despite opposition from his rural supporters, his wife, and his mother. He claimed that he was persuaded by the glamorous lobbyist Inez Milholland, a Vassar-educated lawyer who perched on his desk in the Senate and told him that giving women the vote was "the only chivalric position for a decent man to hold."[38] Eleanor reluctantly followed suit. Her reasons differed from Sara's; she still didn't trust her own judgment and would later write, "I took it for granted that men were superior creatures and knew more about politics than women did. I realized that if my husband was a suffragist I probably must be too . . . I cannot claim to have been a feminist in those early years."[39] She did not support the Woman Suffrage Party or subscribe to *The Woman Voter*.

Sara would have agreed that men probably knew more about politics—hardly a surprise, since women had neither the vote nor the opportunity to become elected officials. But she was far too self-assured to give anything more than lip service to the idea of men as "superior creatures." However, like Jennie Churchill, once her son threw his support behind the suffrage campaign, Sara followed suit. Family loyalty was more important to her than political differences. American women finally got the vote in 1920 (two years after some British women), and Sara was more than happy to cast her vote for her son in all subsequent elections.

SARA DELANO ROOSEVELT

Ten-year-old Sara in China:
Conventional upbringing in
an exotic location.

A formal portrait of nineteen-year-old
Sara captures her self-possession.

The five beautiful Delano sisters in 1883: (*standing, left to right*) Laura, Sara, Cassie, (*sitting*) Annie, and Dora.

Warren Delano, seen here with Sara and Annie, demanded
unquestioning obedience. Sara idolized him.

From the moment of Franklin's birth in 1882, he had Sara's undivided attention.

Eleven-year-old Franklin was educated by private tutors, closely supervised by Sara.

As Franklin matured, his father James's health began to fail.

Forty-five-year-old Sara was a good-looking, very wealthy widow.

Sara Roosevelt realized that her son's fiancée, Eleanor, required a lot of guidance.

Sara stayed close to Franklin and his family during summers at
Campobello. Anna (six) and James (five) grew to depend on her.

With Franklin at the helm, Sara pours tea for
Eleanor and granddaughter Anna off Campobello.

As assistant secretary to the Navy during World War I, Franklin retreated
to his childhood home frequently, despite Eleanor's discomfort there.

Franklin's affair with Lucy Mercer
nearly destroyed the Roosevelt marriage
in 1918.

By the time Franklin entered politics, he and his mother
had remodeled Springwood into an impressive residence.

Sara with her son, granddaughter Anna, five grandsons, and
two great-grandchildren on the porch of Springwood in 1931. Eleanor,
standing behind Franklin, was a reluctant participant in family occasions.

On Franklin's victorious return to Springwood in 1932 as president-elect,
Sara was beside him as he waved to neighbors.

Franklin's fiftieth birthday party, in 1932, was
organized by his mother at Springwood.

Anna, Eleanor, and Sara listen to Franklin's speech
in 1936 at the Democratic nomination convention
as he accepts to run for a second term.

Sara and her son read the congratulatory
messages sent after his 1936 victory.

Sara Roosevelt and Mary McLeod Bethune, president of the National Association
of Colored Women, at a luncheon at Sara's East 65th Street house.

In June 1939, Sara hosted King George VI and Queen Elizabeth at Hyde Park.

Springwood, which evolved from a comfortable country house
to a presidential mansion during FDR's lifetime, remained
Franklin's beloved home and a monument to his mother.

Powerful Sons: Franklin D. Roosevelt and Winston S. Churchill
at the Casablanca Conference in 1943.

PART 5 · THE FINAL YEARS

Jennie: "On the Wrong Side of the Ladder"

1912–1918

Widowhood had given both Jennie and Sara control over their own lives, and both enjoyed their freedom. Sara's fulfillment came with her conviction that she was an indispensable component in Franklin's and Eleanor's family life, and with her growing pride in Franklin's political success. Jennie Churchill too had found fulfillment, both inside and outside the family circle; her sons' happy marriages plus her own adventures with her literary quarterly and hospital ship had kept her spirits as buoyant as ever.

But the split with her second husband, George Cornwallis-West, was a blow for Jennie. Like Sara, she clung to the Victorian insistence that a marriage should last until death parted a couple, and she knew that a stigma was attached to divorce. In the drawn-out years before the divorce was finalized in 1913, those who had predicted marital disaster and those who had never liked Jennie had a field day. Diarist Jean Hamilton, who had described her as "dominating" after watching her recite a music hall verse at Gopsall Hall, met her at another house party. "Mrs. George West . . . looks a terrible wreck of her former brilliant self—Lady Londonderry looked at her scornfully as we stood together before dinner for a moment and said 'How can [she] allow itself to get like *that*?' . . . Mrs. West was certainly very unsuitably dressed."[1]

The incessant house parties and libertine excesses of Edwardian society had subsided after the death of Edward VII in 1910. George V, Edward's son and successor, was a modest introvert whose chief hobby was stamp collecting. At Royal Ascot that year, Jennie, Alice Keppel, Lillie Langtry, and Edward's other favorites appeared at the famous race meeting with black feathers and ribbons in their hats— "wrinkled, graying women in their late fifties, but still slender, still pert, still flirtatious."[2] Jennie was not invited to the coronation of the new king, and she never visited Sandringham again. On her sixtieth birthday, she confided to her sister Leonie, "I shall never get used to not being the most beautiful woman in the room. It was an intoxication to sweep in and know every man had turned his head."[3] Yet the same refusal to be defeated by setbacks—the resilience that had kept her going after Lord Randolph's death—resurfaced.

On her own again, Jennie returned to the life she had lived in the years immediately after Lord Randolph's death. Back to being Lady Randolph Churchill, she traveled incessantly between friends. Letters to her family would arrive from Scottish estates during grouse season, English country houses on spring racing weekends, villas in the south of France, or German palaces when she was on the Continent.

II

Jennie's finances were in a particularly bad state, as she was now losing even the meager support that George had been able to offer. She continued to look for projects that would use her skills and bring in some much-needed cash. In 1910, she had purchased and renovated a run-down house on her street, Great Cumberland Place, then resold it for a handsome profit of about £5,000 (£500,000 today). Winston was admiring. "My dear Mamma, I am so glad to hear of your excellent stroke of business. The utility of most things can be measured in terms of money. I do not believe in writing books which do not sell, or plays which do not pay . . . I think it is very creditable indeed that you should be able after two or three months work, which you greatly enjoyed, to turn so large a sum of money as a Cabinet Minister can earn in a year."[4] He assured his mother that her "knowledge and taste are so good and your eye for elegance so well trained, that with a little capital you ought to be able to make a lot of money."[5] Jennie took his encouragement to heart and would make more successful forays into the real estate market.

However, not everybody shared Winston's opinion of his mother's skills. When he and Clementine returned from their honeymoon in Venice, Clemmie was upset to discover that her bedroom in Winston's flat had been renovated by her mother-in-law. According to Mary Soames, her daughter, Clemmie pronounced Jennie's passion for covering everything in sateen and bows "vulgar."[6] Was it aesthetic disagreement or irritation at her mother-in-law's interference that annoyed her?

In time, Clemmie would grow to admire Jennie's spirit, but in the early years she described her as "a trial" and thought her vain, frivolous, and somewhat ridiculous.[7] According to Clementine's biographer Sonia Purnell, Clementine was shocked by Jennie's extravagance, and exasperated that she had only "discovered" her older son when he started to establish a name for himself.[8] Jennie tried Clemmie's patience with her continual need for financial bailouts, particularly when Winston was so taken up with politics that he barely had time for his wife. It didn't help that Winston remained emotionally close to his mother. When the constant bedlam of his own household became too much for him, he decamped for the night to 72 Brook Street, his mother's graceful Georgian house in Mayfair.

Goonie was less critical by nature, but she too found "Belle Mère," as they called Jennie (shortened to B.M. in correspondence), trying. Both Clemmie and Goonie were pregnant soon after their weddings, and for the next few years were preoccupied with growing families. Jack and Goonie's son John arrived in 1909, closely followed by Winston and Clemmie's daughter Diana. Two years later, Clemmie gave birth to Randolph, who would be followed by Sarah (1914), Marigold (1918), and Mary (1922). Jack and Goonie's second son, Peregrine, was born in 1913 and their daughter Clarissa in 1920. Even though there were always nurses and nannies around, these were not years when Jennie's daughters-in-law had energy for much else.

How did Jennie feel about her sons' wives? "Of course she adored Clemmie and Goonie," her great niece Anita Leslie would write. "But she did not treat them as grown-up women as important as herself."[9] Jennie would return from her frequent trips to Paris with rather ordinary hats from Bon Marché for her daughters-in-law, while her own bags were stuffed with exotic designer outfits. Just as Jennie had never enjoyed the role of mother as much as Sara Roosevelt did, now she found the role of mother-in-law of less interest than it was to Sara. Gregarious extraverts always need companionship and activity, and Jennie preferred a more public role.

Soon after Edward VII's death, Jennie found a new outlet for her energies. She put together an organizing committee for a campaign for a national theatre, then mounted a magnificent ball as a fundraiser in the Royal Albert Hall. Six hundred paying guests in Shakespearean costumes danced until 5:00 a.m. in an indoor garden designed by the celebrated architect Edwin Lutyens. She was particularly pleased that the new king and queen made a brief appearance.

Fired up by that success, Jennie decided on a more ambitious and imaginative project: an enormous pageant, which she called Shakespeare's England, and which would run from May to October in 1912 in the Earl's Court Exhibition Centre, then a large outdoor arena with sideshows and restaurants. Once again, she enlisted Lutyens's help; he transformed the arena into an Elizabethan town with replicas of Tudor houses, the Globe Theatre, and the Mermaid Tavern. Jennie managed to raise nearly £60,000 (over £6 million today) to finance the extravaganza. Everything would be authentic and top-quality; the costumes would be accurate re-creations of Elizabethan fashions, and the programs were printed on vellum. London's *Daily Mail* called her "the busiest woman in London," writing, "When she first came to England, as Lady Randolph Churchill, she gave London Society a fillip. Never has she been content to travel in a groove. But just now, she has in hand a scheme which is by far the biggest she has ever evolved."[10] She had high hopes of a profit, and perhaps even an American tour with a 10 percent management fee for herself.

The London newspapers gushed about her hands-on direction of the project. A reporter from the *Daily Express* watched her take command of the accommodations, the refreshments, and the entertainment: "As one talked with her and realized the enthusiasm with which she has approached her work and the complete grasp that she has of all the details, one begins to understand how very much Mr. Winston Churchill is the son of his mother. He may have inherited his political genius from his father, but he certainly owes to his American mother [his] superb energy and thoroughness."[11]

Alas, it was one of the wettest summers of the decade, and the show lacked popular appeal. Londoners preferred music halls and greasy-pole contests to watching Jennie's titled friends perform in a medieval jousting tournament or mince around in ruffles and farthingales. Shakespeare's England was a testament to the same formidable organizing skills that Jennie had displayed when she was putting together the Boer War hospital ship, but, as with the *Anglo-Saxon Review*, she had misjudged the size of the potential audience and let expenses veer out of control.

While Jennie watched her finances deteriorate still further, she could at least take comfort in her son's giddy rise. First as president of the Board of Trade, and from 1910 as home secretary, Winston had moved into his "radical" phase. Following the lead of David Lloyd George, the charismatic chancellor of the exchequer, he had become a passionate advocate of social reform, proposing legislation to establish minimum wages, insurance against sickness, and old-age pensions. His fellow MP Charles Masterman, a deeply committed reformer, wrote rather skeptically that his colleague was "full of the poor whom he has just discovered. He thinks he is called by Providence—to do something for them. 'Why have I always been kept safe within a hair's breadth,' he asked, 'except to do something like this?' "[12]

Winston seemed unstoppable. He saw "little glory," he wrote in the *Nation*, "in an Empire which can rule the waves and is unable to flush its sewers." Unlike Sara Roosevelt, Jennie relished her son's constant appearances in the popular press. However, Winston's recommendation that the House of Lords should be abolished must have given her pause. The Liberal argument was that this was the only way that the government could pass its 1909 People's Budget, which the Conservative-dominated House of Lords had vetoed because it proposed a tax on the lands and incomes of the wealthy. The money raised would then be used to fund new social welfare programs. Jennie's friends, a healthy percentage of whom sat in the House of Lords, were horrified. How could this member of a ducal family, born in Blenheim Palace, weaned on privilege and befriended by kings, turn on them? King George V denounced him as "irresponsible and unreliable."[13]

Why had Churchill become "a tribune of the oppressed"? Biographer William Manchester suggests several reasons. Winston resented the Tory hierarchy who, in his view, had ruined his father and forced Winston himself to cross the floor. But he was also genuinely appalled by the plight of the downtrodden, and he, along with his leader Asquith, recognized the need to preempt the growing Labour Party from winning the working-class vote. However, Manchester argues that Winston's radicalism was a version of noblesse oblige; he wanted to improve the conditions of the downtrodden, but he did not want to remake society. At heart, he was a traditionalist, and when his political priorities changed, his radicalism evaporated.[14] And for Jennie, her son's flirtation with progressive policies was of little consequence, as she had no family estate to defend.

The House of Lords relented, the People's Budget passed, and in 1911 Prime Minister Asquith promoted Winston to First Lord of the Admiralty, in charge of the largest and most powerful navy in the world. He now had a new focus: to increase naval expenditure on warships, submarines, and seaplanes so that Britain would be prepared in the event of war with a rapidly arming Germany. His name was regularly in the headlines, and the prime ministership seemed within his reach.

One benefit of Winston's new job was that he had access to HMS *Enchantress*, the Admiralty's sleek steam yacht, with a crew of 196, which he soon turned into his floating office. In May 1913, he invited Jennie to join him on a Mediterranean voyage, in a party that included his close friend Lady Violet Asquith and Violet's father, Prime Minister Asquith, and his second wife, Lady Margot Asquith. Violet, an acerbic diarist who frequently clashed with her stepmother, noted the vast difference between Winston's lively, gregarious mother, who enjoyed every minute of the trip, and the moody, snappish Margot, who complained about everything.[15]

III

There were two drags on Jennie's buoyancy during these years.

The first was that the flow of stiff white invitation cards, with gold engraved lettering requesting her company at various prestige occasions, had begun to dry up. When Jennie felt herself sidelined, she wallowed in self-pity. Anita Leslie related an incident described to her by her grandmother, Leonie. One afternoon Leonie was resting before a ball when Jennie appeared, very upset, and proceeded to bemoan everything that was going wrong in her life—"she had lost her husband, no one was paying her any attention, bills were accumulating, she didn't know where to turn. Friends had forgotten her, a lonely life in penury lay ahead." After smothering her sister in her own gloom, Jennie swept out, insisting that Leonie should continue with her nap.

"But my grandmother, the most compassionate of mortals, could not rest," Leslie wrote. "She wept for poor Jennie and, deciding it would be too heartless to attend a ball when her sister was in such straits, took to her bed and turned out the light."

The following day Leonie's friends called to ask why Leonie had missed such a glorious evening. They told her that "Jennie was there looking wonderful—the life and soul of the party—never seen her in better form."[16] Her sister's sympathy had revived her, and she was eager to face the world again. The way that Jennie had offloaded her troubles onto her sister rankled Leonie for years to come.

The second painful drag on Jennie's spirits was debt. The family solicitors had failed to police her spending or produce proper accounts for the family trusts, and in 1908 the Churchill brothers had taken over administering the trusts, supposedly in conjunction with their mother. With Jennie's divorce from George Cornwallis-West, her sons finally came to grips with the appalling state of her finances. They learned that her annual income since Lord Randolph's death had been well over £5,000 a year (more than £500,000 today). However, she had always told them that it was barely over four figures, suggesting it was little more than £1,000. The gaping discrepancy between her authorized annual income and the much lower figure that she quoted to her sons was thanks to her staggering debts to moneylenders— £2,000 of interest payments on more than £22,500 of "official loans" and another £1,000 toward loans from unofficial lenders.[17]

By 1914, she had accumulated further bills of £5,000, a sum that George had claimed at his bankruptcy proceedings she had spent each year on her wardrobe. Her extravagance remained unchecked; according to Winston's new secretary, Eddie Marsh, "Life didn't begin for her on a basis of less than forty pairs of shoes."[18] Now her litigious creditors were closing in.

The more that Winston and Jack examined their mother's haphazard accounts, the more their eyes must have rolled. An alert lawyer discovered a clause in Lord Randolph's will that specified that, if she remarried, her sons would have access to his estate. This meant that Winston and Jack could each have had a formal allowance for the past fourteen years, which might have made a significant difference to their careers. Winston could have used the money for his political campaigns. Jack might have gone to Oxford, or entered a regiment, instead of being pushed into his City job; he also could have married Goonie a year earlier.

He and Winston were outraged to discover that she had never told them the truth. Winston was too preoccupied with his new post as First Lord of the Admiralty to deal with his mother's finances, and, like his mother, he himself was deeply in debt, thanks to his expensive tastes. So Jack took over the challenge of "managing" their mother. Jennie wrote to Winston, "Poor Jack is kept busy with my rotten affairs—I wonder if they will ever be settled."[19]

Jack's tone with Jennie was far sterner than Winston's. He wrote to his mother, in February 1914, "You have over £2000 a year . . . We have begged you so often to live within your income—which is not a very severe demand. Your income is larger than mine in most years and you have nothing whatever to keep up . . . If you start running up bills again—there is nothing that can save you from a crash and bankruptcy."[20] He pointed out that he and Winston were legally entitled to an allowance of about £600 a year, and that they could (but wouldn't) sue her for it.

Why had Jennie deceived her sons? Probably because she was hopeless with money and desperate to keep creditors at bay. She likely justified her deception by convincing herself that her sons had more earning power than she did, and that if Winston was kept on a short leash, he would be less extravagant. Money is an effective route to exerting power over others, particularly for a mother who wants to maintain a bond with her son but has few other means to do so. Sara Roosevelt would also use money to exert control over Franklin Roosevelt.

Jennie seemed incapable of retrenchment, and her defense was a dose of self-pity. When Jack urged her to return to London to put her affairs in order, she replied from Monte Carlo, where she always enjoyed the gambling tables, "Who cares if I return or not? . . . Not that I do not know you and Winston love me, and are very good to me—but you lead busy lives, & have yr own families to be absorbed in. What am I? only an old 5th wheel – I am not complaining, only stating facts."[21]

An equally miserable letter arrived at Leonie's house. "I wish we could see more of each other. Life is so short and we are both so down the wrong side of the ladder! . . . We pander to the world which is callous, and it only wants you if you can smile and be hypocritical . . . My sons love me from afar and give me no companionship even when it comes their way."[22] This was not true, but sixty-year-old Jennie could not adapt to the invisibility of single older women. And the verbal swipe at her sons probably indicates a measure of guilt at the way she had eaten into their inheritances.

Then the tempo of life changed abruptly. Germany invaded Belgium, and on the following day, August 4, 1914, Britain declared war on Germany. Jack was called up almost immediately. Before he left, Winston organized a family photo. Jennie is seated in the center of the group, between her daughters-in-law, with three-year-old Randolph at her right knee. Winston, balding and disheveled, stands next to Clemmie (then seven months pregnant), with five-year-old Diana between them. On Jennie's left are Jack, his mustache as neat as his Queen's Own Oxfordshire Hussars uniform, alongside Goonie and their two sons, five-year-old John and one-year-old Peregrine.

Jennie's hair is dark, her high-necked blouse elegant, and even though she is not looking directly at the camera, her presence dominates the group.

IV

"I dined with B.M. last night at 72 Brook Street," Goonie wrote to Jack, now training with his regiment, on September 1, 1914.

> Needless to say we had a seven course dinner beautifully
> served, Platters of luscious fruits etc. all in a lovely dining-room
> the walls of which were decorated with lovely pictures—We
> afterwards sat in a 'pickled' oak room, beautifully lighted in
> the cornices by invisible electric Lights, & filled with lovely
> bibelots, furniture, rugs, flowers, in fact it looked very rich &
> opulent, comfortable and luxurious—I did not go up the thick
> pile carpeted staircase to the drawing [room] but I hear its quite
> beautiful, green painted & tapestries & wonderful lighting . . .
> Downstairs alone I espied several new pieces of furniture—
> writing tables, chairs, tables, etc.[23]

Neither debts nor warfare would cramp Jennie's style; indeed, she seemed to be galvanized by the national crisis. The war gave her opportunities to take initiatives and, with imagination and humor, make a difference. Her butler, loyal Walden, had insisted on enlisting on the day that war was declared, despite being older than most volunteers. Now Jennie tossed aside the convention that only men waited at table by replacing him with two parlor maids who wore cut-down footmen's livery. Their photo appeared in the press. She wrote upbeat magazine essays, on subjects such "The Girl of Today," "Personality," "Benevolence," and "Friendships"; they would be published in a book called *Small Talks on Big Subjects*.

There were more substantial projects too. She edited a volume of reports on women's war work. She chaired the executive committee of the American Women's War Relief Fund, visited American military hospitals, and organized concerts and matinees for military charities. She helped with her grandchildren. When she wrote in one of her essays that the rapid onset of war had triggered "a general stiffening of shoulders and squaring of jaws," she was writing about herself.[24]

She even stopped trying to look younger than she was, noting in another essay that "to be dressed in the latest fashion is not to be in the right note."[25] Eddie Marsh noticed. He would recall after her death how her incandescent beauty had already faded by the time he met her, "but years afterwards she opened a second [chapter] when she suddenly decided to let hair, waist, complexion and everything go, and became, in a day, one of the most beautiful human beings I have seen."[26]

Once again she and Winston had to reduce expenditures. Under pressure from Jack, she reluctantly agreed to move out of her expensive house on Brook Street. Jack had bought a house on the distinctly unfashionable Cromwell Road, and Winston and Clementine had moved in to share expenses. Soon Jennie too had joined the household, which already included two young mothers, five children, and nine servants. Jennie contributed £40 toward the monthly bills, which, given Churchill spending habits, were considerable. Winston estimated that £140 a month should cover expenses; in practice, they amounted to over £220 a month. Nevertheless, he instructed Clemmie that she and Goonie should "keep a good table: keep sufficient servants & yr maid: entertain with discrimination, have a little amusement from time to time. I don't see any reason for undue skimping." Winston himself was already juggling an overdraft of £9,000 at his bank, plus overdue bills at his wine merchant, tailor, and several other merchants.[27]

As summer slid into autumn, there were few "little amusements" for anybody in the family. The German army had swept across Belgium and into France, shocking the Allies with its success but failing to take Paris. Casualties were appalling as the war settled into a grinding and murderous series of conflicts along the Western Front. British soldiers faced relentless shelling. Dreams of an early victory for the Allies faded. By the end of 1914, losses on all fronts had topped five million, with a million men killed—a scale of violence unknown in any previous war. By the end of the war, there would be between nine and eleven million military deaths, including those of nearly nine hundred thousand British soldiers.

Back in London, families clung together as they anxiously perused the casualty lists for friends and relatives. Jennie and her sisters scanned the names that occupied too many columns in the *Times* each morning. The first hideous blow came when Norman Leslie, Leonie's son, was shot dead in France by a sniper in October 1914. The following year, Wilfred Sheridan, who had married Clara's daughter Clare, was killed in the trenches.

Jennie consumed war news from and about Winston. At first he was applauded, because as First Lord of the Admiralty he had ensured that the Royal Navy was ready for war. As the trench warfare in France slowed to a stalemate, he became increasingly bellicose, demanding quick, decisive action. He and others lobbied for the Allies to open a new front in the eastern Mediterranean by launching a naval attack on Constantinople via the Dardanelles. In theory, such an attack on an already wobbly Ottoman Empire would knock it out of the war.

However, the Gallipoli operation of March 1915 went horribly wrong, because Allied plans were based on the mistaken belief that the Turks could be easily overcome. Allied troops were forced to retreat after sustaining a quarter of a million casualties, including close to fifty thousand deaths.

Winston Churchill was blamed for the disaster. The price of Prime Minister Asquith's survival was Churchill's demotion. Asquith held on to office by agreeing to head an all-party government, but the Conservatives only agreed to the deal on condition that Churchill was not in the cabinet. They had never forgiven him for deserting them eight years earlier. His luster dimmed; he was fobbed off with the minor position of chancellor of the Duchy of Lancaster.

Jennie's visits to friends were particularly frequent when she didn't have her own house in London. She was staying in Sussex when she heard the news of Winston's humiliating demotion. She immediately wrote to her son. "Darling old boy I am thinking of you so much & this is only to tell you so."[28] She hoped that he had seen an article in the *Observer* by their friend J. L. Garvin, the paper's editor, in which Garvin had written, "[Churchill] is young. He has lion-hearted courage. No number of enemies can fight down his ability and force. His hour of triumph will come."[29] Jennie was outraged by Asquith's behavior and his "slow and supine government." She could not believe that the prime minister was prepared to abandon a man as brilliant as her son. "It makes my blood boil," she wrote to her sister Clara.[30]

While Jennie's unquestioning belief in her son's genius remained undented, Winston was helpless with frustration. Clemmie admitted later, "I thought he would die of grief." Determined to play some role in the war, he resigned from the government (but not from his parliamentary seat, for which he received £400 a year). He shocked friends and family by donning the uniform of the Oxfordshire Yeomanry and sailing for France to find his regiment. Both Jennie's sons were now in theaters of war. Jack was behind the lines, as a staff officer, but Winston was headed for the trenches.

Jennie now resumed the habit of weekly letters to Winston that she had first developed when he was in India in the 1890s. In her mind, it was as though the old partnership had been reestablished. "We shall all of us 'hot up' your friends & keep the ball rolling."[31]

Her letters were a mix of reassurance, family news, and political gossip. "Please be sensible," she wrote. "I think you ought to take the trenches in small doses after ten years of more or less sedentary life—but I'm sure you won't 'play the fool'. Remember you are destined for greater things . . . I am a great believer in your star."[32] At the same time, she also resumed her practice of promoting Winston to anybody who she thought might help get him away from the front and back into government. "I mean now & then to have a dinner party," she told her elder son in November 1915. "Garvin is coming on Thursday & I have asked Bonar Law [secretary of state for the colonies] & George Curzon [Richard George Penn Curzon, 4th Earl Howe, who had been married to one of Lord Randolph's sisters and was well connected at court]. I wish you were going to be here—it is like *Hamlet* without Hamlet." Winston urged her to "keep in touch with people who can be useful and friendly."

These were harsh years for both Jennie and her son. Those political observers who had always found Winston too arrogant and pushy took delight in predicting that he had, like his father, irretrievably sabotaged his own career. Jennie tried to keep her son's spirits up, but her network was no longer as powerful as it had once been. When Winston decided in 1916 to return to political life in London, there was no promise of a return to ministerial office. Despite her total faith that Winston's star would rise again, Jennie had to acknowledge that this could be a repeat of history. Winston, like Randolph, might be locked out of office for ever.

CHAPTER 17

◇

Sara's Old-Fashioned Values

1913–1919

The extreme delight in new friends and ventures—and the emotional and financial turmoil that might follow in their wake—was part of Jennie Churchill's joie de vivre, but Sara Roosevelt rarely experienced such highs. Both women were now well into middle age, but while Jennie embraced twentieth-century challenges and continued to take new initiatives, Sara remained firmly embedded in nineteenth-century patterns of privilege and family stability.

Sara's days consisted of long stretches at Hyde Park supervising her estate and seeing relatives, frequent trips to Manhattan for concerts and plays, summers on Campobello Island, and regular transatlantic voyages to visit her sister Dora Forbes in Paris. She appears to have paid little attention to the growing instability beyond North American borders; only the naval arms race caught her notice, because it affected Franklin. Her tranquil routines were always fitted around opportunities to play a role in the lives of her son and his family. She was delighted that Eleanor continued to turn to her for emotional support and practical help. And now that Franklin's political ambitions were blossoming, Sara had convinced herself that perhaps politics could be an honorable profession after all if a gentleman like her son was drawn to it.

Yet Sara's composure would be shaken in the years ahead, and her reserves of Delano self-discipline tested by both her son and her daughter-in-law.

II

By 1913, there was one major change in Sara Roosevelt's life; the physical distance between her and her son had lengthened. Gone were the days when they were close neighbors on Manhattan's East Sixty-Fifth Street, or when his house in Albany was only a morning's drive north. In 1912, FDR had thrown his support behind Democratic presidential candidate Woodrow Wilson, the southern lawyer who was then the president of Princeton University. When Wilson defeated President William Taft, Franklin was rewarded by appointment to the post of assistant secretary of the navy in the Wilson administration. He, Eleanor, Anna (now seven), James (six), and Elliott (three) moved from Albany to Washington. Sara had a much longer journey from Hyde Park, involving an overnight stop in Manhattan, to see the family in the nation's capital.

Her journey often began at the little Hyde Park train station, on the bank of the Hudson River, where she would catch the New York Central Railroad train to New York City. She had put on weight; her face was rounder, with more prominent jowls, and her thick, upswept hair was gray. Still the tall, gracious woman she had always been, with a proud smile and an elegant presence, she always boarded first, fellow travelers courteously stepping aside. She would establish herself in a first-class carriage, while the chauffeur who had driven her to the station ensured that her luggage—numerous hatboxes, plus valises large enough to accommodate voluminous, long-skirted formal and informal gowns—was safely stowed in the baggage car and the maid seated in a second-class carriage.

In New York she would spend the night at her home on East Sixty-Fifth Street, and the following day she would travel on to Washington, most likely on the Baltimore and Ohio Railroad, which boasted private drawing rooms and deluxe lounge cars on its express trains. When she arrived, Franklin's chauffeur would meet her at the recently completed Union Station, the largest train station in the country. Washington had none of the boisterous energy of New York City, which, at nearly five million, was more than twelve times its size in population and growing rapidly. But in the previous two decades, successive presidents had encouraged efforts to transform it from a sleepy southern town of badly constructed buildings to a sophisticated capital of which Americans might be proud. The National Mall and several new parks had been established; President Teddy Roosevelt had presided over the groundbreaking for the National Cathedral; thousands of cherry trees, the gift of Japan, had been planted in the Tidal Basin.

The turmoil of regime change in 1912 had made Washington an exciting place to be. Franklin was part of the surge of triumphant Democrats from all over the country who replaced sixteen years' worth of Republican appointees to federal jobs. But he was in a particularly favorable position. His successes in Albany gave him status among his new colleagues, his family connections with the outgoing Republicans made him acceptable to the Georgetown elite that choreographed the city's social hierarchy. Like Winston Churchill in his first big political job, he was an insider from the start. Sara remarked with satisfaction that her son and his wife were immediately invited to all the smartest occasions, but that the instant acceptance "meant little to these two earnest young people who had had entrée there all their lives."[1]

"Dearest Mama," Franklin wrote to his mother on March 17, 1913, "I am baptized, confirmed, sworn in, vaccinated—and somewhere at sea! For over an hour I have been signing papers which had to be accepted on faith—but I hope luck will keep me out of jail . . . Your affect. son, Franklin D. Roosevelt."[2] It was a dream job for the passionate sailor, now thirty-one, who collected naval histories and whose hero, Teddy Roosevelt, had briefly held the same post in the 1890s on his march to the White House.

Sara replied by return of post. "You can't imagine the happiness you gave to me by writing yesterday. I just *knew* it was a *very* big job, and everything so new it will take time to fit *into* it." But Sara was already anticipating a brilliant future, and what her son would require.

"Try not to write your signature too small . . . So many public men have such awful signatures, and so unreadable."[3]

Eleanor's Aunt Bamie Roosevelt, who had hosted the dinner at which Sara met James Roosevelt all those years ago, owned a home in a fashionable Washington district. Both Sara and Franklin had stayed there on several occasions, especially when Bamie's brother Teddy was president. Bamie (more often called "Auntie Bye" these days) was now married to retired rear admiral William Cowles, and the Cowleses spent most of their time in Connecticut. Bamie was happy to lend 1733 N Street, NW, to "dear, dear Eleanor" and her husband. The four-story brick house, with a small walled garden, was six blocks down Connecticut Avenue from Franklin's office, itself situated in an imposing building across the street from the White House. Auntie Bye also supplied a live-in couple, and Eleanor would bring her own four servants and two nurses to look after the children. The house had never been wired for electricity and was too small for the growing family and overshadowed by the street's massive shade trees. Once again Eleanor moved into another woman's space, with little opportunity to make it her own.

The Roosevelts paid the expenses on the house but lived rent-free. Franklin's salary as assistant secretary was $5,000 (about $150,000 today); rent on the Manhattan house yielded another $5,000; with his trust fund plus other annual payments, his gross income was about $20,000 (over $550,000 today).[4] But this didn't begin to cover the expenses of his growing household, let alone his acquisitive fervor for prints and books, or his club membership fees, and custom-made shoes and suits. Sara knew this all too well. "Please cash enclosed cheque to restore the necessities of life!" read a typical letter. However, she did not give him a regular monthly allowance from her considerable fortune.

Sara soon arrived, and Eleanor noted, "My mother-in-law, as usual, helped us to get settled." Sara took enormous pride in Franklin's new role. One evening while staying in Washington, she was seated at a dinner next to Josephus Daniels, secretary of the navy and

Franklin's boss. Daniels, a canny, rumpled newspaper editor from Raleigh, North Carolina, knew just how to please Sara. He told her that soon after his own appointment, he had asked President Wilson if he had anybody in mind for the assistant secretaryship, as otherwise he himself had a suggestion. The president replied that he did have somebody in mind but asked who it was that Daniels might suggest. When Daniels volunteered Franklin Roosevelt's name, he told Sara, the president replied, "That is the young man I had in mind."

How could Sara not beam to hear that her son's potential was obvious to others beside herself? She particularly enjoyed telling her friend Rita Kleeman that she had confirmed the story with President Wilson at a subsequent dinner. She noted another conversation at that dinner; Mrs. Wilson sought to amuse her guests with disparaging stories about Black people. Sara made no further remarks about the Wilsons' overt racism —which was harsher than anything she would have come in contact with in New York or the Hudson Valley, where slavery had been abolished in 1827 and there was already a small but thriving Black culture and middle class.

The Wilsons came from the South—the president had spent most of his boyhood in Georgia and South Carolina. He was a vocal supporter of Jim Crow laws. Soon after his arrival in Washington, he had approved the segregation of the federal workforce—harmoniously integrated for nearly half a century. Now separate workspaces, lunch tables, and restrooms divided Blacks from their colleagues, and any Black official who was more senior than white women under his supervision was fired.

Nearly a third of Washington residents were Black, and one in ten federal workers was African American. Segregation severely restricted opportunities for Black workers in the government. Meanwhile, the city's Black slums were ignored by Wilson's administration. If there was any doubt about the Democratic president's embrace of white supremacist theories, it was scotched when he organized a White House screening of D. W. Griffiths's racist propaganda film *Birth of a Nation*, which glorified the Ku Klux Klan.[5] This blatant racism was more virulent and cruel than anything any Roosevelt was likely to have encountered.

Racism was also rampant in the Navy Department; Daniels, Franklin's new boss, was an unabashed white supremacist and suspicious of East Coast intellectuals. Why were he and the president so keen on Franklin Roosevelt, with his Groton and Harvard education and glossy pedigree? Largely to achieve regional balance in the administration, where southerners predominated, and to acquire a little of the Roosevelt cachet. Yet the Daniels-Roosevelt partnership worked out surprisingly well for almost eight years.

Franklin thrived in Washington, where his good looks and easy charm, plus the energetic commitment he gave the navy, impressed observers. He immediately began pressing for an expansion of the navy far beyond anything that the more cautious Daniels envisaged. He foresaw war in Europe, and was determined that the force be battle-ready despite the president's insistence that America would remain neutral. Sara followed his activities keenly, clipping articles by and about him for a volume that she kept at Hyde Park.

Franklin admired the way that Winston Churchill had impatiently pushed for an expansion of the British navy as soon as he was appointed First Lord of the Admiralty in 1911. In 1915, Franklin decided he should see how the British Admiralty operated under Churchill. But Churchill, who was exasperated that the United States had not entered the war, had no time to receive a delegation of visiting Americans and gave the youthful U.S. assistant secretary the brush-off. The U.S. ambassador was informed that "the present pressure of work . . . would render it impossible to offer the assistance necessary for the accomplishment of the object of such a visit." This was an inauspicious start to what would eventually become such an important relationship.[6]

Franklin's Washington life was by no means all work. His tall, athletic figure was frequently seen on the Chevy Chase golf course. He was known for his exuberant energy: "He would leap over a rail rather than open a gate, run rather than walk," his son Elliott would recall.[7] Best of all, his position also gave him access to the *Sylph*, one of two yachts that the navy maintained for the president. There were regular cruises on the *Sylph* down the Potomac with Groton and Harvard friends, and Franklin relied on other naval vessels for travel between Washington and Campobello. He sent breezy accounts of his exploits to his mother.

III

Sara continued to relish her role as family manager, always ready to take charge, whether at Springwood or in Washington or on Campobello Island, where a well-trodden path connected her cottage to her son's. Eleanor and the "chicks" (as the young Roosevelts were called by their parents) fled to Campobello each summer to avoid Washington's long, sticky summers.

In Washington, Sara watched with approval as her daughter-in-law dutifully followed the routines expected of the wife of a political up-and-comer. Eleanor attended official dinners; she took official trips with Franklin on navy ships; she submitted to the grinding obligation of calling on other Washington wives—on Monday, the wives of Supreme Court justices; on Tuesday, the wives of congressmen; on Thursday, the wives of senators; on Friday, the wives of diplomats. On Wednesdays she stayed home to receive calls. She had long abandoned hope of getting back to the kind of settlement work she had enjoyed in New York before her marriage.

"My mother-in-law always had an eye to the children when we were away, so there was really no cause for anxiety," Eleanor later wrote. Sara enjoyed reading in Eleanor's letters about Franklin's successes—how, for example, on a 1915 trip to the Panama-Pacific Exposition in San Francisco, "F. doesn't have time to breathe, but he seems to thrive on it."[8]

During these early years, Eleanor often expressed a snobbery and obnoxious prejudices that she would outgrow as she gained in confidence and began to think for herself. After one White House dinner, she confided to Sara that the president's youngest daughter, Eleanor Wilson, was "nice, but dear me, breeding is somewhat lacking in this political flower of the land." Despite her apprenticeship with the progressive Mlle Souvestre, Eleanor Roosevelt also mindlessly repeated anti-Semitic sentiments that were then common among the American ruling class, and which in later years she would find reprehensible. After an evening with Bernard Baruch, she sneered at the chatter about money, jewels, and furs. For today's reader, it is a shock to read her words in print.

Did she make such comments simply to please her "caste-conscious mother-in-law," as one of her enthusiastic biographers has suggested?[9] There is no evidence that Sara shared such vicious anti-Semitism, and no record of her reactions to this letter. But Eleanor's admirers have consistently shown more sympathy for the woman who in later years would become a passionate advocate for social justice than for her mother-in-law.

In August 1914, Sara was at her cottage on Campobello, with Franklin, Eleanor, and their children installed in their own place next door. Early one morning, Sara heard her son calling for the captain of their yacht, the *Half Moon*, to sail to the mainland and pick up the local doctor. Realizing that Eleanor must have gone into labor earlier than expected, Sara hurriedly grabbed her robe and ran across the lawn separating the two cottages. She was at Franklin's side as her fourth grandson was born. The little boy would be called Franklin Junior, like his deceased brother. Only days after the child's birth, Franklin was recalled to Washington where decision-makers were anxiously watching the war unfold in Europe.

Franklin could leave so fast because he knew his mother would take the reins. When the baby was less than a month old, Sara helped her daughter-in-law and household move to Hyde Park. Sara wrote Franklin, "All going well, but I think in consequence of Eleanor . . . being up rather late, Baby is a little fussy and hungry. I'm sure all will be as well as ever tomorrow, and Eleanor is very cheerful this afternoon and will go to bed early." Eleanor and her four children remained under Sara's roof for a month before Eleanor was finally strong enough to return to Washington.

It was the same story two years later, when John Aspinwall, Franklin and Eleanor's last child, was born. This time, the birth was in Washington; Sara appeared hours after the baby arrived, then left a week
later with the two eldest children because they had caught whooping
cough. They stayed with her on East Sixty-Fifth Street, where she
read to them for hours to keep them from talking and irritating their
throats. Once they had recovered, Sara kept them with her to supervise their education.[10] Throughout their childhoods, the chicks spent
long periods with their grandmother in New York or at Springwood,
arriving with a retinue of governesses and nurses.

Another woman might have felt that her help was taken for granted;
Jennie certainly never made herself so available for Winston and Clementine's children. But Sara's love for her grandchildren was, according
to Geoffrey C. Ward, "unqualified, her fascination with them apparently unending."[11] Unlike Eleanor, who had little experience of mater
nal affection and too many competing distractions, Sara gave them her
full attention. Her granddaughter, Anna, would recall that her parents
offered a mere peck on the cheek over the breakfast table, but "when
I was sent . . . to say Good Morning to Granny as she finished her
breakfast in bed, her kiss and hug were indeed warm - almost suffocating." As she had done for Franklin, Sara provided for her grandchildren "consistent, warm, spontaneous love," and it was more indulgent
than the love Sara had shown Franklin. Anna knew that she could not
expect such emotional support from her own mother, who was never
comfortable with children. Anna described her grandmother as "the
most solidly important" adult in her childhood. "I was raised," she
once said, "more by Grandmother than by my parents."[12]

Sara always insisted on the standards of decorum that she had imparted to Franklin, reprimanding her grandchildren for being late or
inappropriately dressed for meals or not washing their hands. She also
carefully monitored their contacts outside the home, to ensure they
only made "suitable" friends. Five children proved more of a handful than one submissive small boy, but she rarely punished them. As
an adult, James would recall that "we . . . quickly learned that the

best way to circumvent 'Pa and Mummy' when we wanted something they wouldn't give us was to appeal to Granny." One spring, James decided he wanted his own garden at Hyde Park. "Granny's idea of teaching me self-sufficiency was to provide the land, the seeds (free) and lots of advice, then purchase my crop at 50 per cent above the market." Sara was hurt when Franklin objected to the price hike. Surely "dear James" should be encouraged in his commendable display of initiative.

The war had a dramatic impact on Eleanor's life. Once America joined the conflict, in 1917, she volunteered to work in the Red Cross canteen at Washington's Union Station. In a grimy tin-roofed shed in the rail yards, she made sandwiches and brewed coffee, then handed out food and drinks to the trainloads of uniformed men who were traveling east. Suddenly Eleanor was doing the kind of work she enjoyed, and because she was good at it, she was in constant demand. Her dependence on her mother-in-law intensified; if the children were at Hyde Park with Sara, Eleanor could don her crisp gray poplin uniform and spend twelve-hour days at the canteen. Soon she was also helping with shell-shocked men at St. Elizabeths Hospital. "How lucky we are to have you," Eleanor wrote to Sara. "I wish we could always be together. Very few mothers I know mean as much to their daughters as you do to me."[13]

As the number of grandchildren increased, Sara decided to enlarge Springwood to accommodate Franklin's family and all the nurses, governesses, and servants who regularly arrived with him and Eleanor. She and Franklin enjoyed poring over plans together to double the size of the house; once again, Eleanor showed little interest. Two wings were added plus a full third story, and seven bathrooms were installed (five more than in the original house). On the second floor, two large, sunny bedrooms occupied the north wing, with a small dressing room between them. One of the bedrooms was Sara's; the other, Franklin and Eleanor's. A lift was installed to transport luggage between the ground floor and the bedroom floor. The front entrance was remodeled with a graceful round portico, and while the central portion of the house was covered in gray stucco, the wings were covered in fieldstone. The comfortable clapboard-covered country home had been transformed into a far grander Colonial Revival mansion.

The most splendid new room was the large library, on the ground floor of the south wing, which boasted at each end a marble fireplace with the Roosevelt coat of arms carved above it. "Dearest Mama," Franklin wrote from Washington in September 1915. "What have H. & K. [the contractors] told you about the Library? Do please not let any contract till I have a chance to see the offer and to go into details of construction, as I have several 'thoughts' and there is much to be decided about shelves etc. A great deal of love. Your affec. Son F.D.R."[14]

The library was the room where Sara could enjoy watching Franklin work on his stamp collection and display his collections of leather-bound naval volumes, model ships, and marine prints. Her son also received official visitors here, and held informal meetings with supporters like Louis Howe, his invaluable adviser. Sara had her own, enlarged snuggery, crowded with china, vases, family photos, and comfortable chairs, where her grandchildren could always find her at her desk in the afternoons. A glass-fronted cabinet in the main hall held the collection of ornithological specimens that Franklin had shot and stuffed himself when he was young.

The remodeled Springwood was the perfect showcase for Franklin, and not just for all those collections. Americans would become familiar with photographs of the successful politician standing on the colonnaded portico, launching election campaigns or giving speeches, with his wife and his mother at his side. However, Springwood was always Sara's house. She paid for all the alterations.

Sara's single-minded pride in Franklin's successes swelled as she read his accounts of his activities. She confided to biographer Rita Halle Kleeman that a scheme he had developed to keep the German navy out of the North Sea "had a great part in bringing about the end of Germany's submarine warfare and her request for an Armistice."[15] Not quite true, but Franklin rarely contradicted his mother's assertions.

IV

During summers when Franklin and Eleanor were apart, they frequently wrote to each other. The surviving letters are lengthy and affectionate; Eleanor described the children's activities and Franklin recounted strenuous days in the Navy Department and a busy social calendar. "Dearest Babs," a typical letter from Franklin began, and ended, "Kiss the chicks and heaps for yourself. Your devoted, F."[16] Elsewhere, he assured his wife, "I long to be with you dearest these days and you are constantly in my thoughts" and he frequently added, "Give my love to Mama."[17]

In the Franklin-Eleanor correspondence, there are hints of an amused complicity over Sara's deeply conservative views on social propriety. Sara remained steeped in the values of her class and upbringing, and found her daughter-in-law's more broad-minded attitudes difficult. Sara was particularly shocked when Eleanor's aunt Maude Hall, who had recently divorced her husband, asked if she might bring a gentleman friend to Campobello Island. Maude, whose gambling polo-playing former husband had left her penniless, had already upset Sara by doing something almost unknown within her social class: taking a job as manager of a dress shop. Now, when Maude's inoffensive admirer (and future husband) appeared, Sara "fairly snorted," Eleanor wrote Franklin. Franklin replied a week later, asking, "Does she snort any more?"[18]

Sara also found herself out of step with the next generation on the issue of, in her words, noblesse oblige and the role of a nation's upper class. The evidence for this rift is in a letter that she sent "Dearest Franklin and Dearest Eleanor" on October 14, 1917, after a discussion while they were all in New York about the future of Springwood and the considerable Delano-Roosevelt fortune. Franklin, who was absorbing progressive notions in Washington (where both welfare programs and a wealth tax were under discussion), had challenged his mother's firm support for the status quo. Sara had defended "the old-fashioned traditions of family life, simple home pleasures and refinements, and the traditions some of us love best." She believed in private philanthropy rather than government intrusions; she wanted Springwood to remain in the Roosevelt family.

Sara rarely exhibited self-doubt, but on this occasion when she returned to Springwood, she sat alone in the library, with its portraits of illustrious Roosevelt forebears, pondering the conversation. As she wrote in her letter, she asked herself if it would make sense to simply "spend all one has at once in this time of suffering and need, and not think for the future. . . . With the *trend* to 'shirt-sleeves,' and the ideas of what men should do in always being all things to all men, . . . of what use is it to *keep up* things, to hold on to dignity."

Such second thoughts did not last long. "One can be as democratic as one likes, but if we love our own, and if we love our neighbor, we owe a great example." She took her responsibilities to those around her seriously. "The foolish old saying . . . 'honneur oblige' possibly expresses it better for most of us, and my constant feeling is that through neglect or laziness I am not doing my part towards those around me." However, she continued, she didn't really believe that "my precious Franklin" really disagreed with her, and she was certainly going to "keep my 'old-fashioned' theories." She said that "*at least* in my own family I may continue to feel that *home* is the best and happiest place and that my son and daughter and their children will live in peace."[19]

"Perhaps, dear Franklin you may on second thoughts or third thoughts see that I am not so far wrong." Even if her son and his wife found her views quaint, they were more than happy to allow Springwood, and the benevolent rule of its matriarch, to be the emotional anchor of their children's lives. According to Elliott Roosevelt, it was Hyde Park rather than successive houses in New York, Albany, or Washington that "everyone but Mother regarded as our real home."[20]

V

In 1918, Sara's unwavering belief in her son's sterling character was shaken to its roots, and Franklin Roosevelt felt the full force of his mother's old-fashioned values.

Despite the warmth of Franklin's letters to Eleanor when they were apart, Franklin had begun an affair in wartime Washington. The object of his attentions was a twenty-three-year-old woman who in 1914 had come to work part-time for Eleanor, as her social secretary, and to help her with the weekly flood of bills, letters, and invitations that threatened to overwhelm her.

Lucy Mercer was pretty and slender, with perfect manners, an exquisite dress sense, and an easy self-assurance. She had been educated in Europe while her well-born but high-living parents ran through the family fortune. Three mornings a week, Lucy settled down on the rug in Eleanor's sitting room, according to one observer, and briskly sorted the mail into neat piles, then dealt with it. Lucy also helped Eleanor navigate the shoals of Washington society, which she had known since childhood. Elliott Roosevelt would recall later, "We children welcomed the days she came to work . . . She was femininely gentle where Mother had something of a schoolmarm's air about her, outgoing where Mother was an introvert."[21] Lucy's low, throaty voice was much easier on the ear than Eleanor's high, staccato one. Eleanor grew fond of her.

Sara approved of Lucy. During Franklin and Eleanor's trip to the San Francisco Exposition in 1915, Sara stayed in Washington to supervise the North Street household. "Miss Mercer is here," she wrote to her daughter-in-law. "She is *so* sweet and attractive and adores you Eleanor."[22]

The affair apparently started during the summer of 1916, while Eleanor and the children were with Sara at Campobello. The following summer, when his family once again disappeared to Campobello, Franklin insisted as usual to his wife that he missed her dreadfully. "I really can't stand that house all alone without you," he wrote on July 16. "You were a goosy girl to think or even pretend to think that I don't want you here *all* the summer, because you know I do! But honestly *you* ought to have six weeks straight at Campo."[23]

But this was Franklin at his personal worst. By now, he knew he was one of the best-looking and most debonair men in Washington, a popular party guest who flirted brazenly with admirers. And he was busy inviting "the lovely Lucy," as he called his wife's secretary, to join cruises aboard the navy's *Sylph*. There were other assignations. On sticky August afternoons, he would persuade Lucy to join him for a cooling drive in his Stutz automobile away from Washington's humidity and bustle and into the pastoral landscapes of Virginia. They made a handsome, happy pair—gallant Franklin in his linen suit and, smiling up at him, dark-haired Lucy, cool and classy in flowing summer garments that were nothing like Eleanor's severe gray uniform. One day, Franklin and Lucy were spotted twenty miles outside Washington by Eleanor's sharp-tongued cousin Alice Roosevelt, who was often scornful of Eleanor's lack of humor and her canteen work. Alice immediately drew her conclusions—but since she found Lucy "beautiful, charming and absolutely delightful," she allowed the couple to meet in her house. "Franklin deserved a good time," she wrote later. "He was married to Eleanor."[24]

Rumors may have reached Eleanor's ears; she was certainly feeling unsettled. In the absence of any close friends, she turned again to her mother-in-law for reassurance. On March 17, 1918, her thirteenth wedding anniversary, she wrote to Sara, "I often think of what an interesting, happy life Franklin has given me and how much you have done to make our life what it is. As I have grown older I have realized better all you do for us, and all you mean to me and the children especially and you will never know how grateful I am nor how much I love you dear."[25]

The secret came out shortly after Franklin returned from a whirlwind tour overseas. Franklin had long begged to get a glimpse of the war zone, and in the summer of 1918, with the war winding down, he achieved his ambition. In England, he met King George V and Prime Minister Lloyd George, and spent a weekend at Cliveden House with the immensely rich Americans Viscount Astor and his wife, Nancy, who were friends of Jennie Churchill and Winston. At a dinner at Gray's Inn, Franklin had his first face-to-face encounter with Winston Churchill himself, who was now back in cabinet as minister of munitions. As he had done in 1915, Churchill gave the eager young American the brush-off, barely deigning to shake his hand. Franklin was not impressed, and never forgot the older man's behavior. "I have always disliked [Churchill] since the time I went to England in 1918," he would tell Joseph Kennedy in 1939, when the latter was American ambassador in London. "He acted like a stinker at a dinner I attended, lording it over all of us . . ."[26]

From there Franklin went to France, where he telephoned Sara's sister, his aunt Dora Forbes, who had remained in her grand apartment on Avenue George V even when the Germans were at the city gates. Next, Franklin toured several battlefields, noting with horror the debris of war—rusty bayonets, broken guns, rain-stained love letters, men buried in shallow graves.

On the voyage back to America on the troopship USS *Leviathan*, Franklin came down with the savage Spanish flu that, in the next two years, would take more lives than the war. His condition was exacerbated by double pneumonia, and he lay in his bunk, fighting for breath as he listened to the burial services for sufferers who had succumbed. When Secretary Daniels heard how sick he was, he sent a telegram to Sara suggesting that she and Eleanor meet the *Leviathan* when it docked in New York. Franklin was so weak that he had to be carried off the ship to an ambulance. Sara supervised the four husky orderlies who carried the stretcher up the stairs of her house on East Sixty-Fifth Street. While he struggled to get comfortable, his wife started to unpack his suitcases.

And there Eleanor found it—a package of love letters from Lucy Mercer to her husband. Eleanor would later tell her daughter, Anna, "The bottom dropped out of my world."[27] Franklin had behaved like her father; he had made her promises that she believed, and then failed to keep them. Eleanor's insecurity once again exploded. Betrayed by both her husband and a young woman whom she had trusted, she was almost paralyzed with distress—but with little privacy to process the hurt.

Exactly how events unfolded in the next few weeks is not clear.

Sara's journals for 1918 and early 1919 are missing; documents referring to the turmoil were destroyed; the affair was never discussed in
print until after the principals' deaths; those who knew of it (and that
included much of Washington society) did not speak of it. Eleanor
never mentioned it in her memoirs, although she later discussed the
pain with Anna and a few friends. But the contrast between Sara's and
her daughter-in-law's behavior speaks volumes about each of them.

Sara must have learned about the letters immediately, while all
three of them were still in New York and she was already worried
sick about her son's dreadful case of influenza. Her distress about her
son's adultery must also have been intense, but she was certainly *not*
paralyzed; it wasn't in her nature to let events take their course. She
weighed in with the same take-charge attitude that she had displayed
on the transatlantic liner when Franklin was a child. While a pale and
wretched Eleanor confronted Franklin with the letters and told him
that she was prepared to let him go if that was what he wanted, an
incandescent Sara took a much tougher line.

Unlike her daughter-in-law, noble martyrdom was not in Sara's
emotional arsenal. Instead, she was angry—and there was disillusion
at a deeper level, too. With his deceitful behavior, her precious son
had betrayed the values of his family and his class, and everything
that his parents had stood for. Franklin had let her down by indulging
in the kind of dubious conduct that she had always felt characterized
politicians. The hurt done to her beloved daughter-in-law, and the
awful possibility that her grandchildren might grow up in a split family, horrified her. As Franklin languished in his sickbed, his mother
told him that if he left Eleanor, he could not expect another dollar
from her. In the words of historian Pottker, "Franklin might have
been able to leave Eleanor, but he knew he could never leave Sara."[28]

Franklin hesitated, wondering if he could pursue his political
dreams without his mother's support. But his political adviser Louis
Howe quickly squashed that hope; Americans would never vote for a
divorced man. Even Franklin's current job might be in jeopardy. Josephus Daniels was deeply traditional; he had fired his sister's husband

when the couple divorced, then run his former brother-in-law out of town. The coup de grâce to the dissolution of the affair was that Lucy drew back from the prospect of marriage to a divorced man with five children because she was a devout Catholic.

Sara got her way. Franklin and Lucy agreed to break off their relationship and promised never see each other again. From that moment, Sara regarded the matter as closed. Her capacity to move on from unpleasantness served her well. When a friend said to her, "You will never be disappointed in Franklin, he never will do anything you would not like, he is a splendid fellow," she passed the compliment on to her son, adding, "Was that not nice of him? I agreed."[29]

Franklin devoted more time to his children; Eleanor tried to be more sociable. But Sara could see that neither of them was happy; both missed the adrenaline of their wartime activities once the Armistice was signed on November 11, 1918. Franklin asked Secretary Daniels to let him go to Europe to oversee naval demobilization there, but his boss was reluctant.

Once again, Sara took charge. She called on the secretary in his office and persuaded him to grant Franklin permission and encouraged him to allow Eleanor to accompany him.[30] Next, she organized a little dinner at the Colony Club on New Year's Eve 1918. Guests included the skipper of the USS *George Washington*, on which Franklin and Eleanor would sail. The following day, the couple boarded the ship, leaving Sara to oversee the care of their children for six weeks until their return in mid-February. Sara sent the three older children and their governess back to Washington when their school term began but kept the two youngest with her in Manhattan. She ordered Hyde Park's first electric washing machine and mangle, and she continued her charity work. In the evenings, she sang hymns with Franklin Junior and John.

The *George Washington* was still mid-ocean when the newspapers announced the unexpected death of Teddy Roosevelt, Eleanor's uncle and Franklin's hero. Sara wrote to her son and daughter-in-law, "I am keeping some [newspaper] pictures and cuttings for you and only send the small ones, for I know you both want to read all you can of that splendid Uncle of Eleanor's."[31] There was a steady exchange of letters throughout her son and daughter-in-law's European trip. Sara enjoyed hearing Eleanor's impressions of Paris during the 1919 Peace Conference. "I can't tell you how happy I am that you are both doing all these interesting things and seeing these interesting people and it seems to me public life is so peculiarly what you are fitted for even tho' you are so extremely nice when leading the simple life at Hyde Park!"[32]

Eleanor's letters to Sara from Europe were equally affectionate. "I do hope we never have to separate again. As I grow older I miss you and the children more and more. I think instead of becoming more independent I am growing into a really clinging vine!"

The relationship between the two women remained intense, because Sara relinquished none of her financial power over Franklin's family; nor did she step back from her role as matriarch. Yet from now on, despite Eleanor's "clinging vine" remark, there was a subtle change. Sara may have implied that a more assertive wife would have kept her son from straying. Eleanor may have felt that the price she had paid to keep Sara's precious family united was too high. She began to develop a social life beyond her mother-in-law's social horizons and reject the Delano values that had once given her such a sense of security. She wrote to Franklin about Sara and her sisters, "In all their serene assurance and absolute judgements on people and affairs . . . [they] make me want to squirm and turn bolshevik."[33]

A cycle of reproach and regret began, with Eleanor snapping at Sara, then apologizing for losing her temper. Sara merely tightened her lips; within the family, her capacity to ignore emotional upheaval was legendary, and she never noted their clashes in her journal. But she kept Eleanor's letters. "I know, mummy dear," one reads, "I made you feel most unhappy the other day and I am so sorry I lost my temper and said such fool things for of course as you know I love Franklin and the children very dearly and I am deeply devoted to you . . . I had no right to hurt you as I know I did and am truly sorry."[34]

Sara could see that Eleanor was working hard to maintain an

amicable relationship with her husband, but also that she was finding it impossible to forgive him. After Franklin's death, Eleanor explicitly told her daughter, Anna, that she had never enjoyed sex, and most biographers agree that this was the point at which Eleanor moved out of the bedroom that she had shared with Franklin in her mother-in-law's house at Hyde Park. She established her new bedroom in the dressing room sandwiched between her husband's and her mother-in-law's rooms. Sara's reaction is unrecorded. The marriage had been saved.

Meanwhile, a few months later, twenty-nine-year-old Lucy Mercer announced her engagement to Winthrop Rutherfurd, a widower, aged fifty-seven. After the breakup with Franklin, she had joined the Rutherfurd household as governess to her employer's six children. Like the Roosevelt children a few years earlier, the Rutherfurd children quickly grew fond of her, and soon their father followed suit. It would be a happy marriage.

V

In June 1920, Sara welcomed her grandchildren and their mother to Hyde Park while Franklin traveled to the Democratic National Convention in San Francisco. He had already been identified as a young man to watch, and his name was being mentioned as a possible candidate for several offices. Sara wrote to him regularly, telling him how the children were riding, swimming, and running around barefoot. A letter of June 25 reflects both her continued distaste for politics and her pride in her son. "I can imagine that the time at San Francisco will be most interesting and I hope 'elevating' as the old letters would say, but I fancy the last epithet is not very likely in a crowd of every sort of politician." However, a friend had told her that if her son ran for vice president, "it will strengthen the ticket very much!"

It was a forgone conclusion that the Democrats would lose the upcoming presidential election, but it would be a big boost for Franklin, still only thirty-eight, to get a place on the ticket alongside Ohio governor James Cox, the presidential nominee. When Sara heard that Franklin was going to be Cox's running mate, she was elated. She immediately fired off a note—"I received your dear telegram"—and then instructed him that on his return journey he must stop the train at Hyde Park so that he could be given a rousing welcome from his local supporters. "If and when you are elected, you will belong to the nation, now you are 'our boy' of Hyde Park and Dutchess."

Eleanor and her children had moved to Campobello, and she learned about the nomination a day or two later, when a telegram from Sara arrived. Eleanor was less excited than Sara and wrote a cool note in reply to her mother-in-law: "Whatever Franklin achieves must be largely due to you."[35]

How could Sara Delano Roosevelt not enjoy this acknowledgment of her central role in her son's success? There would be even louder acknowledgments in the years ahead, but only after the Roosevelt family had dealt with a disaster far greater than the Churchills had ever faced.

Jennie's "Best Foot Forward"

1918–1921

U nlike Sara, who was more than happy to conform to sedate expectations of how a widow and grandmother might behave, Jennie Churchill still wanted to be a player. Well into her sixties, she continued to look and act as though she was at least a decade younger, and her appetite for life rarely faltered. She remained close to her sons—often too close for anybody's comfort, when they all shared Jack's house at 41 Cromwell Road in order to economize. Jennie had never enjoyed babies and small children in the way that Sara cherished her grandchildren from birth, and the Cromwell Road household was crowded.

Jennie followed Winston's career closely, and she continued to rage at the way he had been treated in 1915 after the Gallipoli disaster. "I grieve to have him out of office in these strenuous times," she wrote to her nephew Shane Leslie, who was in the United States. "He has been sacrificed to the jealousies and ineptitudes of the third-class intelligences which compose the majority of the coalition government."[1] She was convinced that his talents were being wasted, while the war in Europe was going badly for Britain and its allies.

Yet Jennie remained optimistic about Winston's future, and as usual she refused to be beaten down by her own circumstances. A new chapter was about to open in her life, and she would once again confound her critics.

II

Both Sara and Jennie had grown up in an era when, for women of their class, pleasing men was paramount. Sara had never felt an urgent need for male regard, and the need for male appreciation faded well before she turned fifty. But Jennie's striking beauty had allowed her to exert a powerful attraction since her adolescence in Paris, and she continued to draw strength from admirers' appreciative glances and playful remarks.

At a wedding in Rome in May 1914 she met a small, dapper, mild-mannered officer in the British Colonial Service named Montagu Phippen Porch. Porchy, as he was known to his family, came from the landed gentry in Somerset, and after graduating from Oxford University he had fought in the Boer War. Now he had a government job in Nigeria. In 1914 he was thirty-seven years old—twenty-three years younger than Jennie and three years younger than Winston—but his prematurely white hair made him look older. Like George Cornwallis-West before him, he was instantly smitten with this flirtatious woman. She had a magnetism and drive that he himself lacked. "I can remember still the first moment I saw her," he later told a reporter from the *Daily Express*. "She was sitting with some friends. She wore a green dress. Was it long or short? Don't remember."[2] When he asked her to dance, Jennie smiled and suggested he should find a younger partner. But Porch, sweet and unimaginative, persisted.

Over the next two weeks, Porch joined Jennie on sightseeing trips around Rome. When he left Europe to return to Nigeria, he wrote her a long letter telling her that he remembered "all the nice things you said of me & I would they were true . . . Goodbye dear Lady Randolph—I want your friendship & I mean to get it & keep it."[3]

Porch was not Jennie's only admirer, but she was busy with war work, including organizing buffets for thousands of soldiers at railway stations (as Eleanor Roosevelt would do in Washington) and visiting wounded soldiers in American military hospitals. In one of the

essays in her book *Small Talks on Big Subjects,* Jennie wrote of the
courage of some of these patients. "A man shot through the face will
smile crookedly and wink his one eye." She denounced society women
who, when volunteering to take wounded soldiers out for drives, requested "those with the most conspicuous bandages please. The last
lot of officers you gave us might not have been wounded at all, for all
anyone could see . . ."

As her grandchildren grew, those who shared her interests began
to catch Jennie's attention. She took them on visits and picnics, and
to concerts and the theater. When Jack's son Peregrine Churchill was
about five years old, he was picking out a tune from the opera *Siegfried* on a piano when Jennie was attending a lunch in the next-door
room. To his surprise, his grandmother abandoned the lunch table
and came to sit next to him on the piano stool. She told him the story
of the Wagner opera and played the main themes for him, including
the music that represented a bird's trill. She recalled for him a performance she had seen when the birdsong was sung by a very large
soprano who had to stand on a box behind the cardboard tree because
she was too fat to climb into the tree. None of it mattered, Jennie told
her grandson, because the singer's voice was extraordinary. "You
mustn't mind singers being fat," she told her grandson, "just listen
and use your imagination."[4]

House renovations helped keep some creditors at bay as Jennie's
reputation for creating modern interiors spread. Dark paneling and
thick curtains were giving way to brighter colors and better lighting,
and her interiors always included fresh flowers, table mats rather than
lace tablecloths, and yellow curtains. She made door handles out of
old silver watch cases and used tinted electric bulbs to provide more
flattering light. After she had made a handsome profit on 72 Brook
Street, she purchased 8 Westbourne Street in Bayswater, north of
Hyde Park, and worked her magic there.

But Jennie always needed people around her. She complained
to friends that her sons ignored her; often the only person available
to accompany her to the theater was her maid. (According to Anita

Leslie, the loyal Gentry had accompanied Jennie to the theater only twice in the previous ten years.)[5] Her health was no longer so robust: she had to have surgery on varicose veins and an inflamed toe. One day her nephew Seymour Leslie called on her and found her weeping over her piano as she played Debussy.[6] A burglary at her house further depressed her. "They carried off . . . all my most precious *objets d'art* including all my royal gifts," she told Winston.[7] Her sister Leonie advised her to see more friends her own age, but as Leonie confided to diarist Jean Hamilton, Jennie responded that her contemporaries "depressed her to the last degree, they were all blind or deaf or lame."[8] She acquired a little gray chow dog, but it wasn't enough to restore her spirits.

Throughout this period, Montagu Porch persisted. He wrote regularly to Jennie, and while he was on leave in 1916, he visited her in London. On his return to Africa, he wrote, "Do please send me a word to inspire me . . . I am so lonely."[9]

Two years later, in the final months of the war, he came home on leave again and Jennie invited him to accompany her on a visit to her sister Leonie at Castle Leslie in Ireland. "I don't think I remember proposing," Porch recalled years later. "By the time we got to the castle, there was an understanding." On their return to London, they quietly slipped into Harrow Road Registry Office on June 1. Jennie wore a gray coat and skirt and a light green toque. The devoted Porch recalled that "she looked very beautiful."

Winston was startled when his mother informed him, only days before the event, that she was taking the plunge for the third time. But his support for his mother was unfailing, and he signed the register as a witness along with his wife and sister-in-law. Then he told his new stepfather, "I know you'll never regret you married her." Jack, who was still in France at General Headquarters, was even more surprised. He wrote to his mother, "Whenever I go to war you do these things! . . . I know the last few years must have been lonely for you. With both of us married it was inevitable that you should be alone. I do not remember hearing you talk of him and I have never met him." But like Winston, his support was unconditional. "If he makes you happy we shall soon be friends."[10] Jennie had embraced her daughters-in-law, and trusted her sons' judgment; now they reciprocated with the same kind of unqualified love.

Montagu Porch's devotion would make Jennie happy—but not his means. His family had a small property in Glastonbury, and he had a modest salary as a colonial administrator. Nevertheless, astute observers understood exactly what was going on. Lady Cynthia Asquith, daughter-in-law of Herbert Asquith, the former Liberal prime minister, noted in her diary on June 2 that apparently Jennie was not in love with Montagu Porch "but suffers very much from loneliness and wishes for a companion"; "Porch has been madly in love with her for five years."[11] She had been amused to hear that Jennie had announced: "He has a future and I have a past so we should be all right."[12]

Jean Hamilton was equally sympathetic. She noted in her diary that Jennie was "at the top of her form . . . looking so handsome, quite twenty years younger."[13]

However, some of Jennie's male contemporaries sneered. They were offended by the idea of a sixty-seven-year-old woman having an active sex life with a man so much younger than herself, although they would have found an older man with a younger woman perfectly acceptable. Sunny Marlborough, Winston's cousin, wrote to his American fiancée, "How furious these old cats must be to find that the eldest of their gang can still get hold of a ring . . . Porch is physically in love with [Jennie] and she shows signs of his attention. Apparently . . . she can still create carnal desires among several men."[14] However, he had earlier noted rumors that Jennie "looked worn out after 3 days of Porch."

One new acquaintance found this aging Edwardian celebrity intriguing, if slightly bizarre. The notoriously catty author Lytton Strachey met her at the Theatre Royal, Drury Lane and described her as "an amazing character, tremendously big and square—a regular old war-horse sniffing the battle from afar." And the famous Churchill sense of style? Strachey told a friend that Jennie wore "a very shabby grey dress, which she from time to time rearranged with an odd air of detachment."[15]

Jennie shrugged off the inevitable chatter; she retorted, "They say. What *do* they say? *Let* them say!" Porch had done great things for her morale, and besides, he was smarter and more pliable than the thoughtless George had been, and much better-tempered than the irascible Lord Randolph. But she had no intention of losing control of her life. This time, she announced that she would remain Lady Randolph Churchill instead of taking her husband's name and that she would not accompany her new husband back to his government job in Nigeria. Instead, she remained in London and continued her house renovations and hospital work. One of her patients, the poet Siegfried Sassoon, described her as "a sort of Olympian head matron."[16]

Jennie threw a party to celebrate the Armistice. Unlike most of her Edwardian contemporaries, she welcomed the new postwar freedoms and pastimes. There were new adventures; she persuaded an RAF officer to take her up in his plane, and she took a small role in a film. She liked the wild new dances imported from America, and did the Boston trot for guests at one lunch party. She continued to attract headlines. This was the era of the flapper dress—short and revealing. A disapproving Philadelphia clergyman decreed that a gown was only "moral" if it did not display the chest or calves. Nonsense, Jennie told London's *Daily Chronicle.* "There is no such thing as a moral dress . . . It's people who are moral or immoral."[17]

Shrewd and witty one-liners had always characterized Jennie, and were part of the reason younger people were drawn to her. She was particularly close to her only niece, Clara Frewen's daughter, Clare, whom Jennie had helped make her society debut in 1903. "I grew to love Jennie as soon as I got over being intimidated by her. One had to admire her; she was resplendent." Clare always had a rebellious streak: "I was a wild animal being tamed." When Clare told her aunt that she'd had a tantrum at a ball because she had caught her beau dancing with another girl, Jennie gently chided her niece. "You must learn to hide things and to behave decorously. Never let a man see you care."[18]

Now Clare once again turned to her favorite aunt. She had married the man who had triggered the ballroom scene—Wilfred Sheridan, a London stockbroker who was a descendant of the playwright Richard Brinsley Sheridan—and they had three children, one of whom died in infancy. But Sheridan had been killed in 1915, leaving his widow with little support. Clare was having some success as a sculptor. Through family connections, she had received prestigious commissions, and the National Portrait Society had mounted an exhibition of her work. Tall and graceful, at thirty-five she sparked controversy with her bohemian parties and communist allegiance. She scandalized family and friends by slipping off to Moscow, where she sculpted busts of all the top Bolsheviks, including Trotsky and Lenin. Winston, who regarded all Bolsheviks as "crocodiles" and "vipers," was furious when she published glowing descriptions of her stay in Moscow in the *Times*. Although the two cousins had been close, he now refused to see her.

Jennie, who had become the family matriarch for Jerome descendants, was one of the few members of the family who had a lot of sympathy for the young rule-breaker who, like her, had been widowed so early. Early on an icy January morning in 1921, she made her way to Paddington Station to say farewell to her volatile, talented niece. Clare was off to America, where she had been offered a lucrative all-expenses-paid speaking tour after her descriptions of life in Moscow had been republished in the *New York Times*. Jennie could not help noticing how splendid Clare looked, in her Cossack hat and Siberian pony skin coat. "If you are not happy, come straight back," she told Clare as she hugged her goodbye. "You have a powerful family who love you and we are all here to open our arms to you."

However, Jennie later warned Clare, by letter, that she should not think only of herself. "Remember that you are the nearest thing to a sister that Winston ever had, and apart from the embarrassment you can cause him when your unusual doings are associated with his name – he can be deeply wounded. So don't do that again." Clare desperately wanted to mend fences with her cousin and sent Winston, via his mother, a long and affectionate letter from the United States, recounting her adventures. The always generous Jennie wrote her son, "It is rather pathetic how she hankers after your goodwill . . . don't be too hard on her."[19]

III

Winston Churchill's career had revived under Lloyd George, who had succeeded Asquith as prime minister in 1916. The following year, Winston reentered the cabinet as minister of munitions. He moved to the War Office in 1919 and reached the position of secretary of state for the colonies in early 1921. Once again, he was back in the center of events, with easy access to decision-makers in politics and the press. However, it was Clemmie, not Jennie, who gave the little dinners he wanted, and it was his wife, not his mother, to whom Winston turned for advice and emotional support. Yet Jennie—and the home comforts she offered—remained an important part of his life. They lived close to each other in Bayswater and met regularly for lunch or dinner; and when he found his own household too noisy and chaotic, he would slip along the road to hers for a few quiet hours so he could sleep or write in peace.

Yet Jennie still hankered after regular companionship. Perhaps recognizing her dislike of solitude, Montagu Porch resigned from the Colonial Service so he could stay in London with her. But as he trailed after his celebrity wife in Mayfair drawing rooms, the mocking glances and gossip made him uncomfortable. "I prefer the bullets of the Boer War or the flies of the Gold Coast to the stings of the snob in a London drawing room," he later told the *Daily Express*.

And then there was the perennial issue of Jennie's pressing debts. Like George Cornwallis-West, Porch grasped that he had to make some money to support Jennie. He returned to West Africa, confident that he would find business opportunities there. "My darling," Jennie wrote to him after he left, "Bless you and *au revoir* and I love you better than anything in the world . . . Your loving wife, J. P.S. Love me and think of me."[20]

In her husband's absence, Jennie resorted to her old habit of restless travel. In 1921 she had money burning a hole in her pocket: she had just sold a house in Berkeley Square, one of the grandest addresses in Mayfair, for a profit of £15,000, tax-free (£1.5 million in today's values). So she took off first for the Riviera, where she joined Winston and Clementine in the luxurious Grand Hotel at Cap d'Ail, and then traveled on to Rome to stay with an old friend, Vittoria, Duchess of Sermoneta.[21]

As the duchess would recall in her memoirs, "We ransacked all the old curiosity shops and Jennie bought profusely; her zest in spending was one of her charms. She was still a handsome woman, her dark eyes had lost none of their sparkle with the passing of years."[22] As Jennie impulse-shopped her way around Rome, she kept assuring her friend of her son's political resilience. And that "Winston's shoulders are broad enough to bear any burden." The duchess recalled how Jennie's faith in her son's capacities was "unswerving," and that she was absolutely certain that everything he did "was right."

The two women attended dances, went to the races, dined well— and shopped. Jennie bought a pair of elegant high-heeled evening slippers from one of Rome's best shoemakers. On her return to London, she resumed her hectic social activities of lunches and evening events, including a private view of paintings by Sir John Lavery, a well-known Belfast-born portraitist who was encouraging Winston's new enthusiasm for painting. In early June, she traveled down to Somerset for a weekend with friends. Hurrying down the stairs one evening in her glamorous Roman heels, she took a heavy fall and ended up helpless on the floor.

She had broken her left leg just above the ankle. Two days later, with her ankle and foot badly swollen, she was taken home by ambulance to 8 Westbourne Street. It all seemed straightforward—until within two weeks her calf turned black, and she developed a high fever. Gangrene had set in. Winston was called, took one look at the situation, and called a surgeon. Two hours later, Jennie's leg had been amputated above the knee.

She seemed to recover her spirits as the fever subsided. She joked that she would now put her "best foot forward." A flood of mail from sympathizers and admirers arrived. Porch, who was in Nigeria exploring investment opportunities, received a telegram from Winston: "Danger definitely over. Temperature going down."

And then abruptly, the life of Jennie Jerome Churchill was snuffed out.

On the morning of June 29, 1921, fourteen days after surgery, the main artery in her left thigh began to hemorrhage. Before a tourniquet could be applied, there was a rush of blood. She quickly slipped into a coma. Winston and Jack were summoned immediately and hurried over—Winston weeping and still in his pajamas—but their mother never recovered consciousness. Her sister Clara, rushing up from her Sussex home, learned the news when she saw headlines on the posters in Trafalgar Square announcing the "Death of Lady Randolph." Jennie was sixty-seven years old.

IV

A small funeral was held three days later, in Bladon Church on a stifling hot afternoon. Jennie Jerome Churchill's immediate family, along with close friends and the devoted Walden, traveled by train to Oxford and then by car to the country churchyard just outside Blenheim's gates. After a quiet service, she was buried next to her first husband, Lord Randolph. Her nephew Shane Leslie would recall that "her sons and sisters were affected almost beyond the grief that is claimed by ties of flesh and blood . . . Winston was bowed as under the greatest grief of his life."[23]

Montagu Porch made it back to London a month later, to a silent house and a mountain of debts. His marriage had lasted barely three years, and he and Jennie were apart more than they were together during their courtship and marriage. Jennie had died intestate, and it would take several years before her husband and her son Jack managed to close her accounts.

Winston Churchill kept copies of the more than two hundred

obituaries of his mother published in newspapers all over the world.
Her many achievements were catalogued; due recognition was given
to the vision and leadership she had displayed in such ventures as the
Primrose League, the *Anglo-Saxon Review*, the *Maine* hospital ship,
her Shakespearean pageant. The notice in the *Times* described her as
"a brilliant and high-stepping figure who flung herself ardently into
many occupations: literature, hunting, drama, politics, marriage . . .
To the last, no illness, no social change, could dim her courage and
kindliness."[24]

Letters of condolence poured in. Her old friend George Curzon
recalled in his letter his earliest memory of "the brilliant wife of a
brilliant statesman, then rising to fame . . . since then I have found
her—quite apart from the attraction of her radiant personality—to be
a true, constant and loyal friend, ever warm hearted and generous."
Winston replied, "I do not feel a sense of tragedy, but only of loss.
Her life was a full one. The wine of life was in her veins. Sorrow and
storms were conquered by her nature & on the whole it was a life of
sunshine."[25]

But his sense of loss was immense. Her unwavering support and
steadfast faith in him sustained him throughout his political life, before and after marriage. She had shared his sense of purpose. Four
years later, when Clementine's mother was dying, he wrote a letter
that captured his anguish. "My darling I grieve for you . . . the loss
of a mother severs a chord in the heart and makes life seem lonely &
its duration fleeting. I know the sense of amputation from my own
experience . . ."[26]

For the rest of his life, a bronze cast of his mother's sculpted hand
sat on his desk.

Jennie had lived almost her entire life in a period when women's
lives were shaped by men, and women could not vote, let alone hold
political office. She had spent ten years of her life expecting that her
husband would be prime minister, and twenty years convinced that
her son would lead his country, and she did not see either event happen.
In many respects she accepted patriarchal structures: she reluctantly

approved women's suffrage only when it was obvious that women would get the vote, and she never stopped fluttering her eyelashes at powerful men.

Yet she had found ways to demonstrate her own agency as an activist for causes she believed in—literary culture, Anglo-American friendship, a national theater—and she had never let Victorian conventions stifle her irresistible vivacity, whatever the consequences. She had drive, imagination, and intelligence; she used them all, and she passed them on to her elder son. She did not deserve the patronizing misogyny of her critics, most of them men who found her simply too challenging. In his letter of condolences to Winston, former prime minister Asquith wrote, "She lived every inch of her life up to the edge."[27]

Above all, she passed on to her elder son her conviction that a great destiny lay ahead of him. Nearly two decades later, he would prove her right. And he would credit her with much of his early success.

CHAPTER 19

———◇———

Sara: "Our Dear Invalid"

1921–1931

The decade of the 1920s was filled with giddy excitement in London and New York; the public in both Britain and America was keen to move past the horrors of the war to end all wars. It was as though the new century was finally launched, twenty years late, thanks to all the new inventions. Automobiles sped past the few remaining horse-drawn vehicles on the streets; electricity banished the Victorian gloom of unlit roads and homes. London's suburbs sprawled and Manhattan's skyscrapers soared as the two great metropolises of the English-speaking peoples swelled with commercial activity.

Lady Jennie Churchill missed it all. With her careless ebullience, it is easy to imagine how she would have enjoyed the gaiety of 1920s London, with its cocktails, flapper fashions, and jazz rhythms. She would have stayed closely in touch with Winston as he continued to make his strident mark on British politics, both inside and outside government, while continuing to pursue her dreams, however unconventional, in her own life.

Sara Roosevelt, who outlived Jennie by two decades, continued to weld herself to Franklin. Despite her ambivalence about both politics and Franklin's political beliefs, she would give rock-solid support to her son even as he pursued a political career. Her own deep-rooted conservatism meant she was not in tune with the new century or the ragtime energy of New York City in the 1920s. She never adapted to the postwar world of the American elite, and her son's progressive leanings often made her uncomfortable.

But first she faced another major family crisis, and this time she could not control it with either willpower or wealth. This crisis would remake the complicated triangle of emotions between her son, her daughter-in-law, and herself. Unlike Jennie, she would have the chance to discover how, as relationships fluctuate, life can shift gears even for a traditional woman in her seventies and eighties.

II

In 1921, Sara Roosevelt resumed her prewar habit of taking an annual trip to Europe. She delighted in telling Franklin, in a jaunty note, that she had taken a twin-engine airplane from London to Paris— a heady choice for a woman who had initially resisted the switch from a horse-drawn to an electric vehicle. The journey by air took five hours instead of the scheduled four, but she wrote Franklin that "I would not have missed it, and if I do it again I shall take an open plane as one sees more and it is more like flying."[1] The notion of his white-haired, sixty-seven-year-old mother clambering aboard a flimsy biplane horrified Franklin, who cabled her, "DON'T DO IT AGAIN."

In Paris, Sara settled into the luxurious apartment on Avenue George V that belonged to her older sister Dora Forbes. One of the tastes Sara had in common with Jennie Churchill was a love of Paris— the elegance of its boulevards, the sophistication of its cuisine, and, of course, the extraordinary workmanship of Monsieur Worth's salon. The French capital had been a haven for each of these privileged, fluently bilingual women since they had lived there in the 1860s, and for both it was a city that they enjoyed with their sisters. Now Sara and Dora sauntered around shops and art galleries together. In Dora's dining room, the sisters entertained friends with all the white-linen formality and silver candlesticks of an Algonac occasion. Back in America, prohibition was in full swing; Sara admitted, "I rather enjoy being where one has red and white wine on the table."

After several weeks in Europe, Sara boarded a luxury liner for the voyage home in late August. She was surprised to be met at the Port of New York not by Franklin, as had always happened before, but by her brother Fred Delano and her stepson Rosy Roosevelt. Fred solemnly handed her a letter from Eleanor, who was at Campobello.

"Dearest Mama, Franklin has been quite ill and so can't get down to meet you . . . to his great regret . . . We are all so happy to have you home again, dear, you don't know what it means to feel you near again . . . we are having such lovely weather, the island is really at its loveliest."[2]

Then Fred Delano broke some horrifying news: the diagnosis was "infantile paralysis," or poliomyelitis, a disease that was endemic among children during this prevaccination era but rarely affected adults. Barely stopping at her Manhattan residence, a troubled Sara set off on the long journey to Campobello, via Boston and Bangor, Maine, and finally by ferry from Eastport to the island. By the time she reached Franklin's cottage, she later told friends, she had realized "that I had to be courageous for Franklin's sake, and since he was probably pretending to be unworried for mine, the meeting was quite a cheerful one. I said, 'Well, son, this strikes me as a queer party to give me on my return.' And he replied, laughing, 'I'd rather have been at the steamer myself.'"[3] Roosevelt self-discipline was undented.

Sara successfully hid her shock at the spasms of pain that crossed Franklin's face and at her son's inability during these early days to lift even a hand. Until a nurse arrived, Eleanor and Louis Howe, her son's devoted political adviser, had to feed him, wash him, and attend to his bathroom needs. Eleanor and Franklin were determined to be cheerful and optimistic, partly to allay their children's fears, and Sara followed suit. Whenever Franklin had been sick—with childhood diseases such as measles or tonsillitis, or later afflictions such as typhoid or appendicitis—she had always been the first at his bedside. Now she felt obliged not only to suppress all signs of her desperate concern but also to yield her bedside seat to her son's wife and Howe. Playing second fiddle was a new experience for her.

But Sara was devastated. Her adored son, so full of life and vigor, had turned into a physical wreck. She wrote to her sister Dora, "Below his waist he cannot move at all. His legs (that I have always been proud of) have to be moved often as they ache when long in one position."[4]

Fearing that she was in Eleanor's way, after a few days Sara left to attend a family wedding. In an uncharacteristically shaky hand, she wrote to her daughter-in-law, "My thoughts are with you and our dear invalid all the time and I ever wake at night with a longing to know how Franklin is . . . It seems so dreadful I can do nothing to help you at this time when I know you are so full of grave anxiety."[5] Her one thought was that Franklin must focus exclusively on his recovery. His political career was over, she insisted; only the security and tranquility of Springwood would restore him to health.

In the short term, the immediate challenge was to get Franklin off remote Campobello Island to New York, where he could have specialized hospital care, without revealing to the press the full extent of his helplessness. Sara, Eleanor, and Howe worked together on a strategy. Franklin, who still had not recovered full use of his upper body, was loaded onto a stretcher, which was then maneuvered out of the cottage and onto a small boat for the two-mile crossing to Eastport. Franklin winced with pain as the boat rocked on the choppy waves. His stretcher was then carried up the wooden steps to the Eastport dock and finally over toward the rail lines and into a private railroad car, well away from eager reporters. Sara paid all the expenses of the private car for the five-hundred-mile journey to New York City, and she was at Grand Central to meet her son and his wife. She accompanied them to Presbyterian Hospital, where Franklin would spend the next six weeks. In late October, he left the hospital. Although Sara urged him to travel straight to Hyde Park, he insisted on being transferred to his Manhattan home on East Sixty-Fifth Street.

There was a painful irony to Sara Roosevelt's determination that her son should surrender all his political ambitions. The previous year, she had demonstrated to the family and the Democratic Party that she might be more of an asset to Franklin's blossoming career than her daughter-in-law, who shrank from the prospect of a life in politics. When Franklin was named Democratic vice presidential candidate by presidential candidate James Cox, Eleanor had been unenthusiastic, but Sara had organized a lavish reception for her son and his supporters at Hyde Park. "Franklin got to Hyde Park at 5," she entered in her diary. "Wonderful welcome at our own house, all the neighbors and about 900 people on the lawn."[6]

Two months later, at the official confirmation of her son's vice presidential nomination, Sara was even closer to center stage. As five thousand people congregated on Springwood's lawns and trampled her rose garden under a bright summer sun, she smiled approvingly up at her son as he gave his stump speech from the portico. She joined the applause as Franklin announced, "We oppose money in politics, we oppose the private control of national finances, we oppose the treatment of human beings as commodities."

The Cox-Roosevelt ticket was doomed from the start; by 1920, the country had had enough of Democrats. Franklin had returned to New York City and the practice of law, but he was already preparing for the next political campaign.

Now, polio had knocked those plans sideways. Sara switched gears and urged him to retreat into the same kind of gentleman's life his father had enjoyed in Hyde Park.

III

Life-changing events invariably shake up the kaleidoscope of family links. Franklin Roosevelt's illness triggered a major reset within the Roosevelt family, just as Winston Churchill's marriage had restructured Jennie's relationship with her elder son in 1908. In each case, the disruption weakened the bonds between mother and son.

For the next seven years, Franklin spent little time with his mother, wife, or children as he desperately explored ways to recover the use of his legs. During the winters, he could be found seeking renewed mobility in the warm waters first of Florida, where he had a houseboat, and then Georgia, where he discovered the mineral baths of Warm Springs. He also had a new gatekeeper, Missy LeHand, his secretary, who spent far more time with him than did either his wife or his mother.[7]

Sara did not appreciate the way that Missy guarded access to her boss zealously, and often seemed more offended than Eleanor at the amount of time the two spent together. Was Franklin having an affair with his petite, dark-haired secretary, who was clearly devoted to "FD," as she alone called him? Perhaps. But Eleanor chose to ignore the rumors. Sara must have realized that all she could do was look away.

At the same time, Eleanor Roosevelt was groping toward a more independent existence. Like Jennie Jerome Churchill, she yearned for a role that was outside patriarchal norms. Like Sara Delano Roosevelt, initially she found ways to assert herself that didn't rock the boat. At the outset of the 1920 vice presidential campaign, she had shown no enthusiasm for Franklin's candidacy and had kept her distance, while Sara shone at the Hyde Park events. But FDR adviser Louis Howe had grasped that the candidate's wife simply needed encouragement and sympathy—which her husband rarely gave her—and he had persuaded her to join the 1920 campaign train. Day by day, whistle-stop by whistle-stop, he coached her in public policy issues and reawakened the intellect that had lain dormant since she had left Mlle Souvestre's Allenswood in London.

Although Franklin was now disabled, Howe refused to acknowledge that polio might put him out of the political race forever, and he pushed Eleanor into frequent public appearances to keep Franklin's name in the news. And Eleanor came into her own. She got involved with the women's division of the New York State Democratic Party, and for the first time in years, she made new women friends among the political, unionist, and welfare activists she started to meet. She began to enjoy herself, partly because she was finally putting some distance between herself and her mother-in-law.

Where did this leave Sara Delano Roosevelt?

In the first half of the twentieth century, people with disabilities were dismissed as "cripples" and were rarely given the opportunity to play a useful public role. This bias shaped Sara's attitude to Franklin. Her eldest grandson, James, recalled that "Sara was bitterly opposed to her son's return to active public life after he was paralyzed, and she fought Louis Howe and Mother on this. Sara wanted her son to retire in his wheelchair to his Hyde Park estate, where the world could not hurt him."[8] There his mother would be able to look after him as she had protected her husband and tended to his needs thirty years earlier. She could not understand why Franklin was struggling with exercises in his third-floor bedroom, or why Eleanor and Louis Howe were encouraging visits by political associates.

However, Franklin refused to take sanctuary at Hyde Park. Instead, he worked to strengthen his upper body, and ordered crutches and braces to enable him to stand upright. Sara was exasperated by his attitude and by Eleanor's absences, and often appeared at the connecting doors that linked the two houses on East Sixty-Fifth Street to monitor the household. Elliott, then eleven years old, later recalled how "Mother in self-defense had a big breakfront moved against the [connecting door]. Granny's resentment of her daughter-in-law's newfound determination flared up over that. She saw it only as insulting ingratitude, coming from someone who had unfailingly needed and begged for her help in the past." There were acrimonious arguments "which left Mother fluttering with rage and Granny with her jaw outthrust in indignation."

Sara was further incensed that Louis Howe, whom she described as an "ugly, dirty little man," had now moved into the bedroom next to Franklin's, displacing fifteen-year-old Anna. She encouraged Anna to feel that she had been "banished," exacerbating the resentment felt by Anna against parents who now had little time for her.[9]

Anna was not alone in feeling this way. The five Roosevelt children, between five and fifteen when polio struck Franklin, were all deeply shaken by their father's collapse, and felt marginalized by their parents' obsession with his recovery and political network. Sara emerged as their most reliable caretaker. All five— plus their usual retinue of governesses—were packed off to Springwood in the spring of 1922, as soon as school was out. Anna developed both measles and mumps; Sara engaged a nurse to care for her. Franklin and Eleanor remained in Manhattan, with Eleanor busy sitting on committees and attending lunches. When she did arrive in Hyde Park, it was to host an outdoor luncheon for fifty mayors' wives for which Sara made all the arrangements. Still hoping that Franklin would spend more time at Hyde Park, Sara adapted her house to Franklin's needs, installing ramps and parallel bars. The luggage elevator was tested to ensure it could take Franklin's weight, and he could operate it by pulling on the ropes. But Franklin's visits were brief.

That summer, Sara swept the two eldest children, sixteen-year-old Anna and fifteen-year-old James, off on a European trip. While she was away, Eleanor (who had just learned to drive) knocked down one of Springhill's gateposts. When Sara heard the news, she was forgiving. "Your running into our gate post was all right, so long as you were not hurt. I am sure after this you are becoming an expert chauffeur. It is the only thing to do now, and if I were not 100 years old [she was sixty-eight] I would learn!" Meanwhile, Sara fell victim to an accident dangerously common among middle-aged and elderly women, then and now. In an ominous echo of Jennie Churchill's fate, Sara recorded in her diary that, on a visit to Versailles with her sister Dora and the two grandchildren, "I, like an idiot, caught my high heel on stone steps and had a bad fall."[10] The injury was sufficiently serious to keep Sara in bed; to the children's joy, they now went sightseeing by themselves, ignoring historic shrines in favor of street circuses.

The children learned to turn to Sara rather than Eleanor in a crisis. It was their grandmother, not their mother, who visited the boys at Groton, and during school holidays all five were frequently left in her care at Hyde Park. James recalled with gratitude how, when he first arrived at Groton, he was too shy to ask the location of the bathroom and ended up either soiling his underwear or going to the school sickroom with agonizing stomach pains. School officials suspected homesickness, and "asked my parents to take me home for a few days to ease my adjustment. It was my grandmother, not my mother or father, who came for me."[11]

Sara was generous to Eleanor, too, hosting luncheons and teas at both Springwood and East Sixty-Fifth Street for Eleanor's growing list of political and women's organizations. Sara still presided over each occasion, but as far as she was concerned, Eleanor's guests were her guests, too. Perhaps her only motivation was to stay close to Franklin and Eleanor by getting involved in their various activities. Or perhaps, as she met more and more people outside the Hudson Valley cocoon, her own views were shifting and she herself was becoming more open-minded. She had grown up within a society steeped in bigotry and sexism; now, as she saw how offensive and dehumanizing those assumptions could be, she herself was backing away from them.

Her guests noticed, and appreciated her gestures (although today they might smack of "white savior behavior"). Mary McLeod Bethune, president of the National Association of Colored Women and a friend of Eleanor's, attended a luncheon at Sara's house in New York. Bethune was an impressive figure: a dynamic teacher and civil rights activist from South Carolina who led voter registration drives for Black women, risking racist attacks. Bethune would recall with pleasure, "I can still see the twinkle in Mrs. James Roosevelt's eyes as she noted the apprehensive glances cast my way by the Southern women who had come to the affair. Then she did a remarkable thing. Very deliberately, she took my arm and seated me to the right of Eleanor Roosevelt, the guest of honor!"[12] Bethune recalled how the faces of Sara's Black servants lit up with pride. She and Sara would become friends.

Sara was able to secure a few precious visits with Franklin during these years of rehabilitation. In 1925, Franklin decided to spend time with Dr. William McDonald, a Massachusetts physician recommended by Sara's brother Fred Delano. McDonald had developed a particular treatment for polio patients. Sara was pleased when she heard of his decision. "I feel so hopeful and confident! Once able to move about with crutches and without braces, strength will come and now for the first time in more than a year I feel that *work* is to be done for *you*, my dearest."[13] She was even happier when Franklin suggested that she spend a couple of nights in his cottage there. She also spent a week with him at Warm Springs, although it was a little too rustic for her taste.

But the cracks in Sara's relationship with her daughter-in-law that had emerged after the Lucy Mercer affair now magnified as Eleanor gradually pulled herself out of Sara's powerful orbit. Resentment began to replace Eleanor's hapless dependence on Sara. She recognized her shortcomings as a mother, but she bristled when Sara told her grandchildren, "Your mother only bore you. I am more your mother than your mother is."[14] Eleanor's children might love Sara's house, where they always felt welcome, but Eleanor started to see Sara's devotion to them not as an excuse that enabled Eleanor to follow her own interests but as a strategy to retain her maternal hold on Franklin. Sara was irritated by Eleanor's new attitude and tried to rein her in. One visitor to Springwood heard her scold her daughter-in-law for not combing her hair before dinner.

As usual, Franklin avoided getting between the two women. Knowing that Eleanor never felt comfortable under her mother-in-law's roof, he masterminded a retreat for his wife—a stone cottage on a creek about a mile and a half east of Springwood with its own pool. There Eleanor could escape from both Sara and her own children and entertain the new friends she was making, particularly Nancy Cook and Marion Dickerman, two Democratic Party activists. She moved into Val-Kill, as the cottage was known, in 1926.

Sara found this new arrangement incomprehensible. She asked Eleanor's friends why Eleanor chose to have dinner in the Big House, as her own home was now tagged, then get into her car and drive to Val-Kill for the night. "She belongs here, and I don't know why she goes over there every night. If she wants to swim, she can go sometime in the day."[15]

The children were aware of tension among the three most important adults in their lives and sensed the basic incompatibility of their gregarious, sunny-tempered father and their anxious, insecure mother. Anna, James, and Elliott would all write about their upbringing and their parents in various memoirs, putting on paper or relating in interviews accounts that sometimes varied.

"Granny moved with unflagging firmness to fill the gap as it widened between our parents," Elliott Roosevelt recalled. "To her mind, her motives were unquestionable, like everything else she did. Her son was physically incapable of devoting all the time and attention that growing children need. Her daughter-in-law was obviously bent on building a career for herself at their expense."

Sara took care of her grandchildren when they were sick and always made them feel that they were her first priority. But her high-handed habits were not always helpful. She held the reins as well as the purse strings, and she continued to embrace and spoil Franklin and Eleanor's brood. "Where she had responded sympathetically in the past, she now chose to ignore her daughter-in-law's protests."[16] On one occasion, when the two youngest boys, Franklin Jr. and Johnny, had been especially naughty, their parents took away their pony. "Granny thwarted their efforts [at discipline] by buying each grandson a horse."[17]

Sara's generosity to her grandchildren grated on Eleanor. In June 1926, a month after her twentieth birthday, Anna married Curtis Dall, a New York stockbroker ten years older than her. Her brother Elliott later wrote that she was in a hurry "to escape the cold war which promised no armistice between Granny and Mother, Mother and Father." Without consulting Anna's parents, Sara gave her a luxurious apartment in Manhattan as a wedding present. Eleanor was furious; she suspected that the young couple would have to rely on Sara to staff their new abode and would become as financially dependent on Sara as she was. She wrote to Franklin that "It is all I can do to be decent."

Sara did manage a half-apologetic letter to her son. "I am sorry I could not consult with you and Eleanor, but as it is my wedding present, I felt I should do it alone, also two other people had options on it." Franklin resisted getting drawn into the argument. And Elliott recalled that "Granny had her way as usual, ignoring Mother's fears that misplaced generosity would trap the newly married Curtis Dalls into living beyond their means."[18]

However, all the children acknowledged Sara's central position within the family. They might laugh at her autocratic manner, but they loved her. She was the most reliable person in their universe, and Hyde Park was their safe harbor. When he was in his late sixties, James would write, "We were fortunate to have a grandmother who would do for us when we had a mother who could not and a father who would not . . . She was the last of a kind, a woman who considered herself a monarch. But she was a warm and loving mother and grandmother. She believed in decency and we received many good things from her besides material things."[19]

IV

The mid-1920s were perhaps the most difficult years of Sara's life, as her role within the family dwindled. She saw less of her beloved son, who was preoccupied with his attempts to walk and now spent winters in the South, usually in the company of Missy LeHand. When he came to East Sixty-Fifth Street or Hyde Park, he spent his time cultivating political contacts. Meanwhile, Eleanor kept Sara at arm's length and made it plain that she now had her own life, with interesting new friends. Although Sara welcomed those friends to her homes, she felt pushed aside by both her children and her grandchildren. As James would write, "What Sara thought became less and less important in our lives."[20]

Sara's routines continued. Every Sunday at Hyde Park, she attended St. James Church, sitting below the stained-glass window she had commissioned in "Beloved Memory of James Roosevelt." Most springs, she sailed for Europe, recording in her diary various purchases, including shoes and shirts for Franklin, from London's smartest tailors and bootmakers on Jermyn Street. In Manhattan, she dined regularly with relatives and went to meetings: "Mental Hygiene Committee, Babies' Ward, Nursing Committee, Plant and Flower Guild." There were plays and concerts, and frequent cultural events at the Colony Club.

In 1926, she decided that the village of Hyde Park needed a public library, and she proceeded to endow one on the main street in her husband's memory. Franklin was more reliant on his mother's checks than ever, since he had little income and was also about to purchase the Warm Springs resort in Georgia. He told her she was being too generous, and explained that she would now be responsible for the library's running costs. But Sara ignored her son's concerns and quietly funded its expenses for the rest of her life. She needed a purpose, and local philanthropy had always been a priority for the Delanos. It was all part of noblesse oblige.

There were also family events with her siblings, that loyal Delano clique who shared Sara's values and memories. But their numbers dwindled. By the end of 1926, of the eight who had reached adulthood, only three of Sara's siblings—her brother Fred and sisters Dora and Cassie—remained. From now on, Dora was Sara's chief confidante, but she lived in Paris.

Sara was still a handsome woman, in her pearls and furs and well-cut gowns, and one year she wrote Franklin from Paris, "I think Eleanor's judgment about me is correct—[I'm] so strong & tough that nothing tires me & I shall live for many, many years."[21] Nevertheless, age took its toll. She had ordered from France a motorized tricycle for Franklin which he refused to use. When Sara's arthritis was particularly bothersome, she used the discarded tricycle herself—but never in public. As the grooves of pain etched deeper onto her face, her habitual expression became one of grim determination.

However, this was not the final chapter in Sara's life. Franklin's political career began to pick up speed. In June 1924, Sara was in the audience at the Democratic Party's convention in New York's Madison Square Garden when her son made his first public appearance in three years, to nominate New York governor Al Smith as the party's presidential candidate.

Franklin Delano Roosevelt's entrance onto the stage that day would become a crucial event in the FDR legend. He was still unable to stand without braces or move without crutches, but he was determined not to use a wheelchair. Instead, he had enlisted his sixteen-year-old son James to take his left arm to help him maneuver forward, while putting most of his weight on the crutch below his right arm. The two of them had spent agonizing weeks in East Sixty-Fifth Street's library rehearsing his walk.

In Madison Square Garden, when the moment came for Franklin to "walk" up to the stage, James would later recall, "he leaned heavily on my arm, gripping me so hard it hurt. It was hot, but the heat in that building did not alone account for the perspiration which beaded on his brow. His hands were wet. His breathing was labored."[22] At the rear of the stage, James handed his father his second crutch, and Franklin lurched alone across the fifteen feet to the rostrum. Twelve thousand delegates first watched in silence, then erupted in a three-minute standing ovation when he arrived at the rostrum and threw his head back in a grin of triumph.

Twenty minutes later, when Franklin came to the end of his powerful speech, the crowd went crazy.

Sara confided to her biographer Kleeman an almost biblical moment. "As her son spoke, she saw a ray of light come through a crack in the roof of the old Garden and touch his head, giving the effect of a halo."[23] When she got home, she carefully glued into her scrapbook the United Press dispatch, headlined "Win or Lose, Roosevelt Stands Out as Real Hero of Convention."

Did Sara believe her lofty vision or the headline's implications? For the time being, the question was moot. To Sara's relief, Al Smith was not nominated at the convention, the Democrats under their candidate John W. Davis lost the election, and Franklin Roosevelt returned to Warm Springs. Al Smith resumed his duties as governor of New York. Tensions between the three adult Roosevelts continued to simmer. But it started to seem that, even if Franklin remained disabled (which he himself still refused to accept), there might be a future in politics.

Four years later, Sara was at Warm Springs when her son came under pressure to run for governor of New York, replacing Al Smith, who this time had won the Democratic Party nomination to be president. She knew that Franklin's doctor had advised against it, and she made it clear to Franklin that she agreed with the doctor. When Franklin finally consented to run, he told the visiting delegation,

"Don't let my mother know about this." She soon found out and told the delegates, "If this costs me my son, I shall never forgive you. I will hold you all responsible for the death of my son."[24]

Despite her doubts, Sara made it clear to friends that "I don't want my boy to run for office—but if he does, I hope he wins." She contributed generously to his campaign, and she installed a radio at Springwood so she could follow the election news. She also dropped him a confidential note. "Now what follows is *really private*. In case of your election, I know your salary is smaller than the one you get now. I am prepared to make the difference up to you."[25]

Franklin campaigned as energetically as he could on a platform of the social reforms and labor legislation that had already been initiated by Governor Al Smith. But, as in 1920, this was not a good year for Democrats, and despite Franklin's courage and growing charisma, his political ambitions seemed doomed. When the returns started arriving at New York's Biltmore Hotel, where the Roosevelts had taken a suite, both Smith and Franklin seemed headed for defeat. The first editions of the morning newspaper were already predicting their losses when he and Eleanor made their way back to East Sixty-Fifth Street.

However, his mother refused to abandon hope. So did Frances Perkins, a member of New York's State Industrial Commission, and the two women settled themselves on a sofa, close to the telephone operators and the tally men. Results kept dribbling in, and the gubernatorial tide slowly turned. Their eyelids drooped, but the two women maintained their vigil. At four o'clock in the morning, the tally men announced that, although Smith had no hope of the presidency, Roosevelt was elected governor of New York.

Perkins called room service and asked for two glasses of milk with which to toast the victory. "Mrs. Sara Roosevelt and I had a private if exhausted jubilation and I saw her home as dawn was breaking."[26] Sara almost ran up the front steps, eager to share her son's triumph with him. She and Springwood would be part of his political future.

Some years later, Sara blithely claimed that she had been perfectly

prepared for Franklin to resume his political career. She told her biographer that "she knew that he would never consent to remain quietly
at Warm Springs the year round."[27] Sara recognized that, though she
had never enjoyed politics, her son was fiercely ambitious. In Sara's
view, everything should be done to secure Delano success, and she
would do everything she could to help him.

V

Sara would now enjoy an experience that Jennie never knew: the satisfaction of seeing her son in a top job. She visited him frequently;
her chauffeur-driven Pierce-Arrow automobile, long and luxurious,
could cover the ground between Hyde Park and Albany in a morning. She delighted in playing the part of her son's First Lady of the
state while Eleanor spent weekdays in Manhattan, teaching at a small
progressive school called Todhunter School. Domestic routine in the
governor's mansion was left to the self-effacing Missy LeHand to
manage.

　　Franklin made extensive use of Hyde Park, which, according to
Frances Perkins, became "almost like a public recreation ground."
Perkins often arrived at Hyde Park to meet with him. She would recall
Sara "in a soft, light summery dress with ruffles, her hair charmingly
curled, sitting in a wicker chair [on the lawn] and reading," with her
son and his wife next to her.

　　Perkins admired the grace with which Sara greeted all callers. "Her
devotion to her son on his, to her, almost incomprehensible taste for
politics was sufficient to take her over the hurdles. She was on friendly
terms with people the like of whom she had never met. She asked these
political callers about their homes, families and journeyings with a
solicitude which endeared her to them. She . . . once told me, 'I have
always believed that a mother should be friends with her children's
friends.'"[28] Sara was polite even to those of whom she disapproved.
(Her grandson Elliott enjoyed describing how his grandmother veiled
her dislike of rough-hewn Al Smith by saying, in her "beautifully pre-
cise, clipped voice," that she knew he had relied on spittoons in the

governor's residence but "I am told that when he uses them, he *never* misses.")[29]

Meanwhile, Eleanor continued to be exasperated by Sara's gifts to her grandchildren—cars for both James and Franklin Jr.; a generous check for $3,000 to James when he got engaged. She demanded that Franklin tell his mother to send the car back. But he never did. His son Elliott would suggest that "he wanted no argument with the woman whose money made his career possible." The Roosevelts never discussed money, and Franklin knew only that his mother was very well heeled. In fact her wealth, invested conservatively, was probably larger than he realized, and it shielded her and Hyde Park from the 1929 stock market crash and the ensuing Great Depression. According to her grandson Elliott, in 1933 her estate was worth $3,500,000.[30] (In today's terms, the figure would probably be around $100,000,000.)

Franklin's political success had given Sara back what she most cherished—a pivotal place in the family. She was happy to watch him being reelected as governor in 1930 with a massive majority. Franklin Roosevelt proved an extraordinarily successful governor of New York State, introducing innovative government programs to shield needy citizens from the worst effects of the depression. But he and his adviser Louis Howe already had their eyes on the big prize. The muttered support for "Roosevelt for President" turned into a groundswell as the 1932 election approached. They began to plan their campaign.

Then, in 1931, a telegram arrived for Franklin from his Aunt Dora in Paris. In the middle of her annual trip to Europe, Sara Roosevelt had caught pneumonia and ended up in the American Hospital in Paris. Aged seventy-seven, she was seriously ill in the era before antibiotics. Franklin promptly canceled all his engagements and, accompanied by his son Elliott and McDuffie, his valet, boarded the Cunard liner *Aquitania* for Cherbourg. This was his first trip across the Atlantic since 1919. The *New York Times* made his journey a front-page story. "The Governor, an only son, and his mother are deeply attached and Mr. Roosevelt showed yesterday his distress at the news of her illness."

Sara was determined to be as cheerful when her son arrived at the hospital as she had been ten years earlier, when she had arrived at his bedside in Campobello. She sat upright, ensured her hair was brushed, then listened anxiously for the sound of his crutch signaling his approach to her room. "I shall never forget how they looked when they arrived at the hospital," she would recall. "My bed had been moved to the window so that I could look over the garden. But that one day I watched the door instead. When it opened and that handsome son of mine stood there with his arm around his own tall son, I am afraid I was very *émotionée*. I was still very weak."[31]

Thanks to "Granny's iron will," as Elliott put it, and her son's solicitude, Sara was soon restored to health, and sailed back to the United States in June.

Louis Howe had observed the public interest in Franklin's formidable mother and decided that she might help win the women's vote in the coming campaign. He persuaded Sara to be interviewed for a series of three articles in *Good Housekeeping* magazine, which Sara had never read but which had a circulation approaching two million. Two young women working at Democratic headquarters, Gabrielle Forbush and Isabel Leighton, interviewed Sara, and accumulated enough material for the first two articles in the series, which appeared under Sara's byline.

By then Franklin Roosevelt was the front-runner to not only win the Democratic Party presidential nomination, but also to defeat President Herbert Hoover, in the subsequent general election. For the magazine editor, a series on Sara was a major scoop; he couldn't wait to get them into print. Before the third article was even written, there were large advertisements on the side of the Hearst Corporation's delivery trucks announcing "My Boy Franklin By Sara Delano Roosevelt."

Sara was outraged: "My name is going all over town on *trucks*." She was particularly horrified that the first article mentioned that she had been given too much chloroform during childbirth; this was the kind of detail that would never have been discussed even within her own family. When Forbush and Leighton arrived for their final interview, she politely dismissed them with the explanation that she couldn't remember anything else. She had absolutely no desire to be a celebrity.

Franklin roared with laughter when he heard what had happened. "Mama is like that!" he told the two women. He then provided enough anecdotes to complete the magazine series and also *My Boy Franklin*, with Sara purportedly its author.[32] The book is a compilation of syrupy stories about Franklin's childhood, with little information about his parents or the larger context of events beyond Springwood. But it suited the times. A review in the *New York Times* began, "The boy is father to the man." The anonymous reviewer admitted that "one approaches with many misgivings a book by a mother about her son who is in the full flush of high success. But one does not read many pages in Mrs. Roosevelt's delightful little volume until all such doubts are cast away."[33]

CHAPTER 20

Sara: America's Matriarch

1931–1941

The last chapter in Sara's life was a startling contrast to Jennie Churchill's final days. Jennie had planned for and promoted her son's career from the moment that Winston's father, Lord Randolph Churchill, had resigned from cabinet in 1886. She had imbued him with the rock-solid confidence that he would walk with destiny. But she died twenty years before Winston became prime minister of Great Britain. Sara watched her son become president of the United States, in part because she gave him the personal and financial support that allowed him to succeed. And she did not simply enjoy his triumph; she shared it.

The arcs of the two women's lives differed dramatically. Jennie's finest hour came when she was in her late forties, and her major achievements—including her literary magazine and her hospital ship for the South African war—were not maternal. She acted alone when she took these initiatives—in a period when few women had either the agency or the ambition to jump-start such unconventional endeavors. Sara's finest hour came after her eightieth birthday, when she became a national figure in the completely traditional role of mother.

II

However, before Sara reached her apotheosis, "my boy" first had to win his party's nomination, and then the presidential election.

The early hours of July 1, 1932, found Sara in the sitting room of the governor's mansion in Albany, clustered around the radio with her son, who smoked furiously, and Eleanor, who soothed her jangling nerves with her usual distraction—knitting. They were listening to the nonstop news from Chicago Stadium, where the Democratic convention was electing the party's presidential nominee. Franklin was constantly on the phone to delegates and campaign workers on the convention floor. The first ballot began at 4:28 a.m., followed by two more. When the convention adjourned, at 9:15 a.m., Franklin topped the vote but was short of the required two-thirds majority.

The Roosevelt team of political operators in Chicago, led by Louis Howe and Jim Farley, a New York City businessman and former chairman of the Democratic National Committee, spent a day twisting arms and offering inducements to convention delegates. Sara looked at the drawn faces around her and decided to go home. She instructed her chauffeur to drive her back to Hyde Park, but as soon as they reached Springwood, she strode up the stone steps, through the colonnaded porch, and into the library to turn on her new radio there. The fourth ballot began in the evening, after a day of backroom deals. At 10:32 p.m., the final tally was announced. Sara beamed as she heard the party chairman announce that Franklin D. Roosevelt had secured his two-thirds majority. The convention hall organ struck up the tune that would become her son's theme song: "Happy Days Are Here Again."

In Albany, Franklin was already on the phone, telling his campaign team that he would fly to Chicago the following day to accept the nomination. Such a flight was unprecedented, but as his biographer Jean Edward Smith put it, "Roosevelt was demonstrating a spirit of urgency that a dispirited country could embrace."[1] An image of activism had replaced one of disability.

As the plane took off, the nominee-elect dictated a telegram to his mother: "All well. Much love. F.D.R." After a nerve-racking flight through headwinds and swirling gray clouds, Roosevelt and his entourage set down at Chicago airport. Franklin took a minute in the airport terminal to reassure his mother by phone that he had arrived

safely. Then he, Eleanor, and Louis Howe got into a big white lim-
ousine in the sixty-automobile motorcade to travel to the stadium.
When Franklin appeared onstage, thirty thousand delegates erupted
with noisy enthusiasm.

At Hyde Park, the phone rang repeatedly as reporters asked
for Sara's reaction to her son's nomination. Her reply reflected her
ironclad confidence in Franklin: "Of course, I am glad . . . he got it
by such a large majority. But I was not very much surprised." She
turned back to the radio to hear her son's reassuring voice propose
to his fellow Democrats an aggressive government platform of relief
to those who were suffering as the U.S. economy collapsed. He catalogued the planned programs: public works, securities regulations,
tariff reduction, farm relief, wages and hours regulation. "I pledge
you, I pledge myself, to a New Deal for the American people." These
were initiatives that would have horrified his mother's Delano relatives, whose Republican loyalties and suspicion of government over-
reach were bred in the bone. But Sara's views had evolved a long way,
in order to stay abreast of her son's.

Over the next four months, during the presidential race, Franklin
would cover thirteen thousand miles and Louis Howe would stage-
manage a huge direct mail operation, which carried campaign literature to every corner of the country. The outcome was never in doubt.
The voter turnout, almost forty million, was the greatest in American history, and the Republicans suffered a crushing defeat. Franklin
Roosevelt, newly elected president of the United States, returned to
his residence on East Sixty-Fifth Street to find Sara "waiting at the
door, weeping with pride and an overwhelming sense of fulfillment,"
according to Elliott Roosevelt. "This is the greatest night of my life,"
Franklin said, as he hugged his mother.[2] Aged fifty, he would remain
president for the rest of Sara's life—and his own.

Eleanor, however, was not happy about the election outcome. She
did not want to abandon all her friends and activities and, as First
Lady, become a prisoner in the White House, organizing formal receptions, "openings," dedications, teas, and official dinners. She was

already a national figure, with her own radio program and syndicated column. "As I saw it, this meant the end of any personal life of my own. I knew what traditionally should lie before me; I had watched Mrs. Theodore Roosevelt and had seen what it meant to be the wife of the president, and I cannot say that I was pleased at the prospect."[3] The following March, she initially refused to board the special train with the rest of the family that would take them from Hyde Park to Washington, preferring to drive herself down. In the face of her husband's dismay, she relented.

But formal receptions, dedications, and teas were exactly what Sara Roosevelt excelled at, and she glowed with pleasure as she did everything asked of her. Unlike Jennie Churchill, up to now she had always resisted being a public figure; in 1932, she did an about-face and outdid Jennie in smiling graciously for the press. (She did, however, object when asked to show too much emotion, or repeat a spontaneous peck on her son's cheek.) She had recently taken a quick trip to Paris to bring her sister Dora back for the inauguration on March 4, and both Delano sisters were on the special train to Washington.

Sara's neighbor on the journey south was Jim Farley, a key figure in Franklin's gubernatorial and presidential campaigns. As the train steamed through New Jersey and Delaware, passengers could see evidence of the nation's desperate economy—abandoned factories, foreclosed farms, For Sale signs in town and city. Farley described to Sara some of the challenges that would face Franklin. The country had just gone through a fourth bitter winter of depression. Bank failures had wiped out close to ten million savings accounts. One in three workers had lost their jobs. Farmers' incomes had collapsed and crops were rotting in the fields. States like Alabama and Georgia were closing their schools because they could not afford to pay their teachers. Children were starving, and there were few relief or welfare programs for the unemployed.

Sara thrust her chin forward and gave Farley a haughty look. "I am not in the least worried about Franklin. His disposition is such that he can accept responsibilities and not let them wear him down."[4] Over the course of his presidency, Franklin would prove his mother right.

III

By the time the train arrived in Washington, it was evident that the president-elect's mother had caught the public imagination. A week before the inauguration, her "memoir" had been published in New York.[5] Quotations from it appeared in *Time*, the most influential magazine in the country. A portrait of Sara, not Franklin, was on *Time's* cover during inaugural week. In the accompanying article, the writers predicted that, at Franklin's inauguration, "In all the crowd no heart will pound with such pride as that of an erect, white-haired, hazel-eyed old lady sitting close to the new President as he takes the oath before the Capitol . . . Few mothers have known the exaltation that Sara Delano Roosevelt will know as she watches her only son enter the White House."

The *Time* writer extolled Sara's strength while hinting at her controlling nature. "The Hyde Park estate is legally hers until her death but she has made it a home and a refuge for her boy. She still worries about his health, warns him to wrap up when going out in the cold, busies herself about his small comforts. When he returned to Manhattan from Miami a fortnight ago, it was his mother who first greeted him on the outside steps of his house. A great believer in heredity and 'good blood' Mother Roosevelt justly feels that she has contributed some of her son's best qualities."[6] Sara rarely failed to mention Delano genes in any interview about her son.

Saturday, March 4, 1933, was a scramble for the Roosevelts. The family had stayed the previous night at Washington's Mayflower Hotel, and Sara had had to rise early so that her maid could help her dress for the inauguration, then pack all her cases to be taken over to the White House. In her long dark coat and old-fashioned hat, with a glossy fox fur tippet draped round her neck, Sara radiated dignity as she sat near the podium in front of Congress, impervious to the cold wind and nervous anticipation, and watched Franklin take the oath of office. Back in the White House, her maid prepared Sara's room and laid out for her the silver gown she would wear for the inaugural ball. While Eleanor was downstairs, anxiously supervising tea and sandwiches to a mob of supporters in the unfamiliar State Dining Room, Sara withdrew to her room for a rest.

"Granny was jubilant," her grandson Elliott would later write. "She had anticipated this day, she convinced herself, for more than half a century, from the moment her incomparable son was born. If her daughter-in-law remained a trifle too *gauche* to carry off the occasion in the style it deserved, Sara Delano Roosevelt would set a model for her to copy."[7]

Sara had been largely responsible for the list of those invited to the pre-ball dinner, and that evening she was surrounded by seventy-two Roosevelts and Delanos. Seared in Elliott's memory was the impression she made. "Her spine was as straight, her jaw as strong, and her commanding hazel eyes as commanding as ever. She took special pains with her *toilette* this evening, with every gleaming hair arranged in place in her pompadour, resplendent in a long gown fitted snugly to her majestic frame, with her magnificent pearls looped on the pale skin of her imposing bosom."[8] As each family member crossed the room to pay court to her, she greeted them graciously, then let her eyes return to Franklin. The newly inaugurated president's smile was so magnetic, his face so handsome and his chest so powerful, that it was easy to forget that he could not walk unaided. Her fears that polio would destroy her son's health and hopes had proved groundless. The quiet life of an affluent country gentleman would never have suited him.

During Franklin Roosevelt's presidency, the White House resembled, in the words of historian Doris Kearns Goodwin, "a small, intimate hotel."[9] Besides the president's wife, family members, and personal staff, there was a constant flow of visitors—friends, royalty, political colleagues. If Franklin could not go out into the world, visitors would bring it to him. Both Franklin and Eleanor knew that White House expenses far outran the president's salary of $75,000 (between $1.5 and $1.7 million today) plus expense allowance of $25,000 (around $550,000 today). They kept their heads above water, according to Elliott, "only through Granny's largesse. She subsidized his Presidency to the extent of $100,000 (at least $2 million) every year, which she regarded as her duty to him and to her country."[10] She dug into her capital to do this. She had an extensive portfolio, but its value was squeezed by the depression and because, following her son's example, she had sold stocks in companies that competed for government contracts.

Between Inauguration Day and Christmas 1933, Sara would spend fifteen days in the White House, where her firm manner and imperious bearing earned her the nickname "the Duchess" among the staff. She liked to keep an eye on her son, and to ensure that space was found in his calendar for anybody she felt he should see. Within days of the inauguration, he agreed to receive two of her New York banking friends before he made any decision about the banking crisis.

With his bold new programs to protect the hungry, provide economic relief to the unemployed, and otherwise minimize the economic devastation still sweeping the country, Franklin Roosevelt was regarded as a traitor to his class, if not a detestable socialist, by his political opponents, Wall Street bankers, and family friends. Meanwhile, Eleanor Roosevelt shocked commentators by rejecting the title of "First Lady," working with civil rights groups, and giving speeches across the country about the need to help suffering Americans, particularly women, children, and Blacks. By and large, she had shaken off her early insecurity and neediness and become a powerful advocate for social justice.

In contrast, Sara became a reassuring symbol to older, wealthier Democrats who had their doubts about Franklin and Eleanor. Her popularity swelled as she continued to embody the traditional values into which she was born. Two months after "my boy" arrived in the White House, on Mother's Day, May 14, Sara Delano Roosevelt was named Mother of the Year. Mirroring Franklin's Fireside Chats, she began a tradition of giving a Mother's Day broadcast, in a voice that was slow, commanding, and unmistakably upper-class. This year's radio message reverberated with maternal pride, as well as benevolent concern for the underprivileged. "At last Mother's Day has a real significance for me since my son, the President, has issued a Proclamation which lifts this day somewhat above the largely sentimental expressions of other years. It suggests a 'new deal' for forgotten mothers and neglected children. Millions are unemployed and myriad of destitute mothers with dependent children are praying, not for flowers but for flour; not for candy but for bread; not for greeting cards and telegrams but for food, clothes, medicines, and the practical things of life."

Despite her devotion to Franklin, Sara Delano Roosevelt did not endorse policies simply because they were her son's policies. Exposure to new ideas and new people had continued to broaden her outlook, yet she was firm in her sense of right and wrong. One warm spring Sunday afternoon in 1934, she was sitting with Eleanor on the South Portico of the White House when they were joined by Walter White, a senior official with the National Association for the Advancement of Colored People. With Eleanor's encouragement, White was aggressively lobbying for passage of antilynching legislation.

The depression had triggered an ugly upsurge in lynching; in 1933, twenty-four Black people had been lynched in the South, where white supremacists relied on mob violence, terrorism, and murder to intimidate African Americans.[11] But when the president arrived on the White House portico, he laid out for White all the pragmatic reasons why he couldn't, at that moment, support the antilynching bill—he needed the votes of southern congressmen, the country wasn't yet ready to accept too much change, there were other priorities. . . . When White torpedoed every argument, Franklin was exasperated and turned to his mother. "At least I know you'll be on my side." Sara did not flinch. Political guile didn't outweigh principles for her. With a toss of her head, she told Franklin that she agreed with Mr. White.[12]

Despite Sara's stance and Eleanor's consistent and energetic endorsement of antilynching bills, Franklin kept his distance from the bills. So did several subsequent presidents. After two hundred failed attempts to muster enough votes in Congress to pass such legislation, lynching was finally outlawed in 2022.[13]

Throughout the 1930s, invitations poured in for the redoubtable dowager, with her gold lorgnette and the broad brow and smile so startlingly like her son's. She hired a secretary to help with correspondence and was feted wherever she went. An astonishing number of organizations requested her patronage. At the 1934 President's Birthday Ball in New York, the *Literary Digest* suggested that "America has never seen anything any more like a queen mother than the picture she made as she swept through the line of saluting soldiery." Later the same year, on a visit to England, she was invited to lunch with Britain's first Labour Party prime minister, Ramsay MacDonald, and tea at Buckingham Palace with King George V and Queen Mary. Soon after her return to New York, she was on the cover of *Newsweek* magazine; inside, an article entitled "Sara Roosevelt, Matriarch of an American Clan" extolled her breeding, intelligence, virtue, and wealth.

Sara Roosevelt stayed regularly at the White House, particularly for special events. She and her maid would usually take up residence in the Rose Suite, the principal guest quarters on the second floor.[14] However, as she moved into her eighties, she was seen less often in the bustling and overcrowded mansion, where strangers were constantly coming and going, and where the cuisine was notoriously indigestible. (She took her own tea, preferring the Delano private stock to what the famously grumpy White House housekeeper, Henrietta Nesbitt, provided.) Instead, she urged Franklin to come to Hyde Park. And he was happy to do so.

Over the course of his presidency, Franklin Roosevelt traveled to his childhood home every four to six weeks; it was soon known as the summer White House. A sentry box was built by the stone gate, and telephone wires were strung into the house. Sara would always greet her son on the portico, and fuss over him as she had when he returned from Groton for school holidays. When he was not receiving official delegations at Hyde Park, dictating to Missy LeHand, or reading official documents, pince-nez clipped to his nose, he would relax in the library with his stamp collection or sit on the south lawn, gazing down the slope at the peaceful, slow-moving Hudson River. Sara had successfully rooted him in the soil to which his parents and grandparents had held primal loyalty. Even in the toughest times, Franklin would emerge from a few days at Springwood relaxed and refreshed, confident that he was on the right course.

In her own home, Sara was a gracious hostess, putting visitors at ease even when she had never met them before. Social workers, archbishops, politicians, European aristocrats, and labor leaders signed her guest book. Only one man was ostentatiously treated to the withering scorn of which she was capable. The Louisiana politician Huey Long was notorious for corruption and vulgarity, but he was crucial to Franklin's nomination at the 1932 Democratic convention. One day, he arrived at Springwood in a loud blue suit and flamboyant tie, and at lunch harangued Franklin about election tactics. Sara watched with distaste from the other end of the table. During a lull in the conversation, she said in a stage whisper, "Who is that horrible man?"[15] Long's response was apparently that he felt sorry for Franklin. "He's got more sonofabitches in his family than I got in mine."

At a big party that Eleanor arranged at Springwood for her mother-in-law's eightieth birthday, Sara was radiant in a glimmering white crepe dress with a mauve corsage. Franklin proposed the toast: "To the best mother in the land." Sara's five grandchildren presented her with a scroll that read, in part, "Hyde Park has been, and always will be, our real home, and Hyde Park means you and all the fun you gave us there."[16]

Inevitably, Sara's son grew less available to her as he led the United States through the darkest economic times it had ever known, and kept his party sufficiently strong and united to win for him a second and then an unprecedented third term in office. Undeterred, she kept up a steady stream of notes to him, often offering advice that he quietly ignored; in return, he sent her brief missives reassuring her of his health and affection. One day, her eldest grandson, James, was with his father when Franklin was summoned to speak to his mother

on the telephone. James watched the president listen for some minutes in silence, then say: "Well, Mama, let me put it this way. Even
if I wanted to do that, I couldn't. It's against the law, and even the
president obeys the law."[17]

She also stayed in touch with her grandchildren, especially Anna.
She noted with regret the marital zigzags of her five grandchildren,
who between them would notch up fourteen divorces, quietly ascrib-
ing the instability to unreliable parenting.

IV

Sara Roosevelt's elevated status received the royal seal of approval in
June 1939.

That month, King George VI and Queen Elizabeth arrived in
Washington on a state visit intended to cement Anglo-American relations. FDR had invited the newly crowned king the previous year,
after the Munich Agreement had appeared to avert the possibility of
conflict in Europe. However, war against Nazi Germany now looked
inevitable. Aware of the strong isolationist sentiment in America,
Franklin Roosevelt had no wish to get ahead of public opinion (he
was still mulling whether to run for president again), but he was appalled by mounting Nazi brutality in Europe and the evidence of
Adolf Hitler's ambitions. He didn't trust the political leadership in
Westminster, and he foresaw a time when Britain would turn to the
United States for help. He was happy to establish an important new
relationship, and to stir American fascination with royalty.

The president's instincts were correct. A parade for the royal couple drew an estimated seven hundred and fifty thousand, the largest
ever assembled in the capital up to that time. A couple of days later,
the king and queen escaped the Washington humidity and headed
north for an informal weekend at Hyde Park, where the president had
promised them "a bit of rest and relaxation." Franklin and Eleanor
had raced ahead to be there when they arrived.

However, it was Sara, monumental in pearls and an ankle-length
dark silk floral tea gown, who welcomed the couple to her home on

that sunny afternoon. Her grandson Elliott would later write, "To her, reigning monarchs were among the few people in the world ranking in dignity with herself." She had covered the top of her grand piano with their autographed photographs in gilt frames, "like a pictorial *Almanach de Gotha*."[18] The president's mother was the first woman in American history to entertain a reigning British monarch in a private home.

Sara was not altogether happy with the arrangements for the royal visit, which had been planned in detail by her son. (Even the number of hot-water bottles deemed necessary was discussed.) She disapproved of the informal picnic lunch, including hot dogs and strawberry shortcake, which Franklin had organized to emphasize the informality of the occasion; it was, in her view, déclassé. Always abstemious herself, she deplored Franklin's plan to serve cocktails in the evening. When the king and queen entered the library before dinner, Franklin cheerfully announced, "My mother does not approve of cocktails and thinks you should have a cup of tea." The king responded, "My mother would have said the same thing," and the two men exchanged smiles as Franklin reached for the martini shaker.[19]

Sara's pièce de résistance was the Springwood dinner, for which all her finest crystal and china were deployed. To her discomfort, White House staff was brought in; Sara's elderly English butler was so taken aback that he offered to resign.[20] Sara was further mortified when a makeshift serving table laden with bone china collapsed, and the crash of broken plates resounded through the house. Nonetheless, the visit was a success. The king and the president chatted late into the night, covering the gamut of world affairs. Franklin's "charm, respect and paternal guidance won George's admiration. 'Why don't my Ministers talk to me as the President did tonight?' he asked Canadian prime minister Mackenzie King. 'I feel exactly as though a father was giving me his most careful and wise advice.' "[21] The smashed china had not derailed the warm impression that Sara and her son had conspired to create.

V

Sara was eighty-five at the time of the royal visit; her stamina was diminishing and her joints often ached. Her grandson James would later write, "Sara's love for her son was her reason for living." She wrote Franklin, "Perhaps I have lived too long, but when I think of you and hear your voice I do not ever want to leave you."[22]

Growing infirmity did not preclude her annual trip to Europe in the summer of 1939. When Nazi Germany and Soviet Russia signed a nonaggression pact and American citizens in Europe were advised to return to the United States, she cut short her visit: "I want to relieve my son of all unnecessary anxiety in this crisis," she told reporters as she boarded the *Washington* at Hamburg. But as war approached, she was often lonely at Hyde Park. "He could spare her fewer of the attentions which had been her principal source of joy for most of her life," her grandson Elliott would write. "Sometimes on the telephone he was brusque to her because he was so preoccupied." Eleanor was now in constant motion, making speeches, visiting army camps and housing projects, criss-crossing the country and writing My Day, the most widely syndicated newspaper column in the country. But to assuage her mother-in-law's sense of neglect, Eleanor made a point of visiting Sara often in the house where Eleanor herself had never felt at home. "She kept Granny up to date on events in the family and took her out in New York and Washington."[23]

The decline in Sara's health worried both Franklin and Eleanor. During 1940, the year of FDR's third run for the presidency, he increased his Hyde Park visits, spending fifty-six days there, more than in any previous White House year. He urged his mother to engage a companion, a suggestion that she indignantly rejected. She was at his side on the Hyde Park portico when his victory in the presidential race was announced, and neighbors staged a torchlight procession. She commented proudly that she was now "a mother of history. Few mothers of Presidents ever lived to see their sons elected even to a first term. Why, when you read history it seems as if most of the Presidents didn't have mothers, the way they fail to appear in the accounts."[24] Sara's longevity was one reason she is a large part of the FDR story. More important is the determination of both mother and son that they should stay tightly linked.

The following January, reporters marveled as Sara Delano Roosevelt walked slowly onto the inaugural platform, relying on a polished cane. Diplomats and cabinet members approached to pay their respects. "Perhaps she moved a bit more slowly than she did in 1933," reported the *Washington Star*. "However, she'd had a grand time throughout the inaugural weekend."[25]

In 1941, despite her advanced age, Sara once again made the arduous summer journey to Campobello that still involved changing trains at least twice, clambering in and out of boats, and climbing ladders onto the jetty. Eleanor accompanied her, to help her get settled, but she could see that Sara was struggling. By now, Sara had consented to have a companion, Kathleen Crawford, and in late July a nurse arrived from Boston. Franklin sent a handwritten note: "Dearest Mama, I'm so glad you really are feeling better, & that you like the nurse & that you do what she says!"[26] Sara dictated a letter to Kathleen Crawford in reply: "We have a lovely day & I am sitting in a sunny window . . . Here comes the doctor—I think laziness is *my* chief trouble—I think of *you* night and day." But she rarely ventured downstairs.

The end was near; her heart was failing and her memory came and went. It was time to leave Campobello. The journey home, which included a night's stopover in her Manhattan town house, drained her. When she arrived at her beloved Springwood in early September, Eleanor was there to greet her. Noticing Sara's labored breathing and pale face at breakfast the following day, Eleanor called Franklin in Washington. He immediately sent a telegram saying he would catch the overnight train. Sara brightened and announced that she would greet him on the portico. But the following morning she simply didn't have the strength, so instead lay in the chaise at the end of her bed, the same bed in which she had given birth to Franklin fifty-nine years earlier. Propped up on pillows, her long white hair wound into a braid with a bright blue ribbon, she waited impatiently for "my boy."

Tires crunched on the gravel outside, and soon there was the sound of the elevator being winched up to the second floor. Franklin wheeled himself into his mother's bedroom, beaming cheerfully. He spent the rest of the day with her, quietly chatting about old times and occasionally answering the most urgent messages brought in by his secretary.

One confidence he shared with her was that he had met the British prime minister, Winston Churchill, the previous month at a secret rendezvous in Argentia, on the shore of Placentia Bay, on the Newfoundland coast. It was the first formal meeting between the two men; Churchill did not recall their 1918 encounter in London, when his high-handed behavior had nettled the young American undersecretary of the navy.

Clad in a Royal Navy uniform, the British prime minister was now a baby-faced, paunchy war leader puffing away at a cigar and determined to make the best impression possible on Roosevelt. Britain had just lived through the horrors of the Blitz, during which over forty-three thousand Londoners had been killed and over a million homes damaged or destroyed by German bombs. The country and its distant colonies stood alone against the Nazi menace, its government in desperate need of American support and military supplies. Under the low clouds of a North Atlantic sky, Churchill employed all the tactics—ebullient charm, forceful reproaches, emotional appeals—on which, all those years ago, he had relied to catch the attention of his mother.

For his part, the American president wanted to avoid specific commitments, because he knew that if he made them, shrill isolationist factions would erupt back home. Wielding his cigarette holder with the ease of a magician, he had left the British prime minister reassured of the strength of their relationship but frustrated that the document they cosigned—the famous Atlantic Charter—had few specific commitments. Although Roosevelt believed that helping Britain was the right thing to do, he displayed the warm smile and evasive manner that he first mastered as a schoolboy to keep his imperious mother at arm's length.

Nevertheless, the two men forged a powerful personal link that bridged the Atlantic and would help them win the war. They had been raised so differently, yet each was infused with a self-confidence that carried him through extraordinary crises, and each had developed interpersonal skills that allowed the two of them to bond when they finally met.

Now that formidable matriarch who had wielded so much influence on Franklin was drifting away. But Sara had always loved listening to her son's voice, and he knew that she, too, was appalled at events in Europe. In recent months she had given generously to organizations helping the British war effort. And she would have enjoyed hearing his impressions of the British prime minister, now widely admired for his eloquence and his prescience about the Nazi threat. Did she remind her son that Churchill was half-American? That like Sara herself, his mother, Jennie Jerome, had been in Paris as a teenager, and that his grandfather was the flamboyant Leonard Jerome, well known in the wild, well-heeled Manhattan circles in which Franklin's half-brother Rosy Roosevelt had moved? Given the importance that Sara had always attached to family relationships, she would have been inclined to do so.

As the sun was setting over the Hudson's west bank and evening approached, Sara started to doze. Franklin kissed her cheek, then maneuvered himself downstairs for dinner. At the table, everyone agreed that his arrival had obviously lifted his mother's spirits; she just needed a good night's sleep.

Around 9:30 p.m., the nurse with Sara realized that her charge had slipped from sleep into a coma from which she could not be roused. Franklin immediately returned to her room, where he spent the night by her side. Meanwhile, Eleanor began calling close relatives and friends to say that Sara was not expected to live.

At noon the following day, Sunday, September 7, with her son still at her bedside, Sara Delano Roosevelt died.

VI

Sara's smooth exit from life was in keeping with the grace and dignity she had always valued highly—and quite different from Jennie's painful, bloody collapse twenty years earlier. But in both cases, their sons were overwhelmed with anguish.

Winston Churchill had run, weeping, through the streets of London in his pajamas, reaching his mother only after she had hemorrhaged to death. He had lost the parent who had pulled every string for him and whose resilience and joie de vivre became part of his inheritance. Franklin Delano Roosevelt had watched his strong-willed mother, the source of his own incredible self-assurance and equanimity, quietly withdraw, and felt the link to his perfect childhood snap. Rigid with Delano self-discipline, he kept his grief bottled inside him as he shut himself off from the world, canceling all his appointments and leaving Eleanor to call the undertaker, make the funeral arrangements at St. James Church, and begin to sort through Sara's clothes. The following Tuesday, after the funeral, he remained dry-eyed as he watched men from the Roosevelt estate lower his mother's coffin into the ground besides his father's grave.

A few days after the funeral, Franklin's secretary handed him a box in the newly completed building in which his archive would be stored. The president peered at its contents—small tissue-wrapped articles, neatly labeled in his mother's firm hand. The gloves she had worn at her wedding. Franklin's first baby shoes, and a lock of his brown hair. Bundles of his letters from Groton, Harvard, and elsewhere.

Tears filled the president's eyes. He murmured that he would like to be left alone. It was the first time any member of his staff had ever seen him weep.[27]

Eleanor paid public tribute to Sara in My Day. Her prose was far from generous. She described her mother-in-law as "a very vital person whose strongest trait was loyalty to her family . . . There was a streak of jealousy and possessiveness in her where her own were concerned." In a letter to a close friend, she was blunter. "I looked at my mother-in-law's face after she was dead & I understood so many things I had never seen before. It is dreadful to have lived so close to someone for 36 years & to feel no deep affection or sense of loss."[28] Until her own death twenty-one years later, she would struggle with contradictory emotions toward the woman who had saved her marriage and underwritten her domestic security, and whose love she had once craved. She never acknowledged that it was Sara's steady presence that had enabled her to escape the endless demands of motherhood, with which she was never comfortable, and plunge into the advocacy for international peace and social justice for which she remains so admired today.

Some weeks after the funeral, Eleanor suggested she make some changes to Springwood. Franklin immediately resisted. Throughout his life, Sara had given him unconditional love and nourished him emotionally in a way nobody else had. Springwood was and always would be her house, deeply imprinted with her personality, and he wanted to keep it that way. It remained a refuge for him until his own death less than four years later.

After Lives

Winston Churchill and Franklin Roosevelt would become states-men of global significance, figures so great that the extent to which their genius or characters were tied to the influence of their mothers is easily overlooked. But each of them clung to the memories of their mothers.

Winston wrote of Jennie, "The wine of life was in her veins." They remained close until her death, with Winston frequently escaping the domestic turmoil of his own household by disappearing to Jennie's house. His mad chase through London streets as she was dying and his subsequent anguish indicate the depth of his attachment. Jennie Jerome Churchill had instilled in her son a conviction that he had been singled out since birth to be a great leader, and this confidence enabled him to overcome mistakes and setbacks that would have destroyed most politicians. The sense of his destiny never deserted him, even during the "wilderness years" when he was out of power between 1929 and 1939. He knew how crucial she and her network had been as he began his career: as he put it, she had "left no wire unpulled, no stone unturned, no cutlet uncooked." A sculpted replica of her hand was one of his most precious possessions until his own death, forty-four years later.

Sara Roosevelt died less than four years before her son; she had been FDR's rock-solid source of support throughout his grueling journey to the White House. He kept a large photograph of her on his desk throughout his presidency. The only time that a member of FDR's staff ever saw tears in his eyes was after his mother's funeral, as he sorted through the box of Sara's memorabilia. He had a tighter emotional bond with his mother than with any other individual in his life, as his wife recognized and resented. Without the security and love Sara had given Franklin, he might never have got to the White House. He couldn't bear the idea that any trace of her might be erased from Springwood, the family home he had never left. It became his shrine to her.

Jennie's and Sara's reputations, intensely different in their own lifetimes, have undergone constant reevaluation since their deaths. The way that each is regarded today is a radical shift from the way that she was viewed immediately after her death, but both are still too often seen through a cruelly distorting lens.

When Jennie Churchill passed away so abruptly in 1921, she was mourned intensely by her family and old friends but soon faded from the popular imagination. Many in younger generations saw her as a pathetic reminder of Edwardian decadence. Her own son colluded in this disappearing act. In *My Early Life*, the future prime minister polished his self-image as a man destined for greatness who had thrived despite her neglect: "She shone for me like the evening star. I loved her dearly—but at a distance."[1]

After Winston Churchill's death in 1965, interest in Jennie was rekindled. Her great-niece Anita Leslie published an affectionate portrait, and the American author Ralph Martin produced a deeply researched two-volume biography. A lush television series, starring American actress Lee Remick as Jennie and partly filmed at Blenheim Palace, was broadcast in 1974. It was based on *Jennie—A Portrait with Letters*, by Jennie's grandson Peregrine Churchill (Jack's son) and playwright Julian Mitchell. However, Jennie might not have recognized herself in these portrayals. As her most recent and reliable biographer, Anna Sebba, points out, "Jennie had now morphed from an American adventuress and would-be editor into the Mother of the Great British Prime Minister, the man who, virtually single-handed, had stood up to Adolf Hitler. All subsequent works would have to look at her through the prism of world events and her son's role in shaping them."[2]

Anne Sebba has helped to rescue Jennie Churchill by focusing on her subject's ability to wield influence discreetly behind the scenes, her disdain for rules and taboos, her insistence on making her own choices despite Victorian values and the British class system. Thanks to Sebba's biography, Jennie's élan and disregard for convention have endeared her to a modern readership.

Yet Jennie Jerome Churchill continues to be shoehorned into the wicked seductress stereotype—too colorful, too promiscuous, and too spendthrift. In biographies of her son, she is often belittled as a shallow socialite. Winston Churchill's biographers (the majority of whom are men) have bought into her son's careless dismissal of her as a distant twinkling star, despite his later assertion, "My mother was everything to me." Reflecting a classic misogyny, they have suggested that Winston succeeded despite, rather than in part thanks to, his mother. Roy Jenkins wrote in his 2001 biography that "what emerges most clearly from photographs is that she . . . was hard, imperious and increasingly self-indulgent."[3] Andrew Roberts wrote in 2018 of Lord and Lady Randolph Churchill's "neglect and emotional cruelty" toward Winston, conflating Jennie's conduct with her husband's much nastier behavior.[4] Minimizing initiatives like her literary magazine and the hospital ship, several writers have dwelled on her extravagance and on the sensational but secondhand inventories of her lovers concocted by such unreliable and malicious commentators as George Moore and Frank Harris. She has become the subject of the snickering innuendo and slut-shaming that, when she was alive, she boldly faced down. Winston's status was burnished at the expense of his mother's.

Sara Delano Roosevelt has suffered a different reversal of reputation, but she too is now saddled with a misogynist trope. At her own death in 1941, she was the iconic mother figure who had upheld standards and values that were fast dissolving and had been a pillar of strength for him. At her death, newspapers across the Continent published tributes to her. King George VI sent a telegram of condolence from Buckingham Palace.[5]

But iconic mother figures have fallen from grace since then, and Sara has increasingly been depicted as smothering and manipulative. Franklin Roosevelt died less than four years after his mother, as World War II drew to a close. The national outpouring of grief for the president who had seen America through both depression and conflict eclipsed memories of his mother. Within months, the most frequently mentioned Roosevelt was Eleanor, Sara's daughter-in-law, already recognized as a champion of social justice, human rights, and peace. While Sara once caught attention as a symbol of stability and tradition, the spotlight now switched to Eleanor Roosevelt, a progressive and outspoken advocate for the causes she believed in, and for which she sought the world's attention.

Eleanor Roosevelt, who had never come to terms with her own complicated feelings about the mother-in-law on whom she had once been so dependent, was increasingly critical in remarks and writings. The girl who had been so tense and humorless when she married had overcome her personal insecurity to emerge as a powerful woman in her own right. But she directed her compassion to those she met as an adult, rather than to the woman who helped her mature. Her grievances accumulated as the years unrolled, and she portrayed Sara as snobbish, domineering, and unkind. She framed Sara's devotion to her grandchildren not as a protective urge toward children whose parents were frequently absent but as a strategy to retain her hold on Franklin. "As it turned out," Eleanor wrote bitterly, "Franklin's children were more my mother-in-law's children than they were mine." Often she directed at Sara the frustration that might more logically have been directed at her smiling, emotionally distant husband.

The stereotype of the malevolent mother-in-law was cemented once and for all by Dore Schary's 1956 Broadway hit *Sunrise at Campobello*, which was subsequently made into a movie. Ellie Roosevelt

Seagraves, daughter of Anna, Sara's eldest grandchild, was shocked by the portrayal of Sara. "She was a real harridan in that thing, an ogre, shrew! And that was not the way she was at all. I mean, she never raised her voice. That would be terribly out of character!"[6]

Sara's defenders struggled to protect her reputation. In 1952, *Time* published a feature on Eleanor Roosevelt that included a dismissive comment on Sara, and Sara's biographer Rita Kleeman wrote an indignant letter to the magazine. "The legend of her unkind treatment of her daughter-in-law grows and grows now that she is gone, and her son is no longer here to deny it." On the centennial of Sara's birth, in 1954, Kleeman submitted a profile of Sara to several publications, but none would use it. She later told an interviewer that the editor of *Ladies' Home Journal* told her that no magazine would publish a positive profile of Sara "in the face of the public idolatry of Eleanor."[7]

More recently, in her 2004 book *Sara and Eleanor*, Jan Pottker has tried to rescue Sara Roosevelt from Eleanor and her biographers who have "ignored, dismissed and criticized . . . this seminal figure."[8] Pottker suggests that the disdain heaped on Sara has been due to the bias against women of her time and class, and by the impulse to establish Sara as the antagonist in the story of how Eleanor "led the charge into the modern world."[9]

But the damage was done, and, as women's demands for less gendered roles exploded in the late twentieth century, the reputation of a woman who had devoted herself to her family had little chance of recovery. Public sympathy flowed toward Eleanor Roosevelt, justifiably admired for her tireless campaigns, rather than toward the old-fashioned matriarch who had enabled her and her husband to pursue their ambitions. Eleanor's progressive initiatives, and her ill-concealed condescension for her husband's mother, have left Sara looking stuffy and overbearing. Eleanor Roosevelt's biographers have often accepted only their subject's side of the story.

Maybe Sara was imperious. Perhaps Jennie was flirtatious. But is that the only way to remember two women who, despite the suffocating constraints of the time, took charge of their own lives and worked hard to help their sons? I don't think so. They were far more complicated and interesting than that. Imperious or promiscuous men would never be judged so harshly. I wrote this book because I wanted to reevaluate two remarkable characters on their own terms.

ACKNOWLEDGMENTS

I started thinking about this book in pre-pandemic days, but when Covid-19 surged into our lives I was thankful that I had chosen subjects for whom there was a superabundance of secondary sources. As archives and libraries closed, I could fall back on digitized sources plus the thousands of books on the Roosevelt and Churchill families available through online bookstores. When I finally reached the Churchill archive at Churchill College Cambridge, UK, and the Franklin D. Roosevelt Presidential Library and Museum in Hyde Park, New York, I found that the material on Jennie and Sara had been thoroughly mined by previous researchers, then quoted extensively in published materials.

I am therefore deeply grateful to biographers and historians who preceded me into the archives, and on whose work I drew. I have mentioned them in my Selected Bibliography.

Once I was in the various archives, it was wonderful to see my subjects' handwriting—Sara's firm, evenly spaced, sloping script; Jennie's more florid, rushed scrawl—and have tactile contact with their letters, appointment books, and personal photos.

I am grateful to Allen Packwood, director of the Churchill Archives Centre, for welcoming me warmly, suggesting sources, and answering queries. I'd also like to thank Nicole Allen, archives assistant in Cambridge, for her help. The Hon. Emma Soames graciously granted permission to reproduce the image of her great-grandmother campaigning with her grandfather in 1900.

After my first two attempts to visit the Franklin D. Roosevelt Library were foiled by Covid-19 lockdowns, archivists there—and especially Virginia Lewick—went out of their way to ensure I made the most of my time in the reading room. I'm also grateful to Matthew Hanson for his help with image research from the Franklin D. Roosevelt Library.

My good friend Ron Cohen has been an invaluable source of advice, introductions, and information throughout the process of putting this book together. The author of the definitive three-volume *Bibliography of the Writings of Sir Winston Churchill*, Ron persuaded me several years ago to join him on the board of the Sir Winston Churchill Society of Ottawa, which has allowed me to meet several preeminent Churchill experts. I am particularly grateful to Sonia Purnell, author of *Clementine*, for her insights into Jennie and her daughter-in-law, and David Lough, editor of *My Darling Winston: The Letters Between Winston Churchill and His Mother*, for his thoughts about the Churchill mother-son relationship and information about Churchill finances. I would also like to thank Dr. David Stafford, author of *Roosevelt and Churchill*, among other works of scholarship, for reading my manuscript and responding with enthusiasm just at the point when I wondered if I would reach the finish line.

As with my previous books, I depended heavily on informed and thoughtful feedback from Dr. Sandy Campbell and Dr. Duncan McDowall; Sandy read every word in draft and asked provocative questions. I'm also grateful to Bob and Arlene Perly Rae's hospitality in New York, and particularly to Arlene, who walked me around Sara's neighborhood and introduced me to the Colony Club. Dr. Margaret MacMillan was encouraging throughout, pointing me to invaluable resources. Other friends who offered their own insights into the changing status of women at different stages in life, as well as during the last two centuries, include Liz Hay, Barbara Uteck, Sandra Martin, Jane Urquhart, Susannah Dalfen, Wendy Bryans, Maureen Boyd, Judith Moses, and Cathy Beehan.

Once again, my experience with the editorial team at Simon & Schuster Canada has been wonderful. Phyllis Bruce, my longtime editor, first suggested to me that I look at these two women who were born in the same year and into the same New York moneyed elite but followed such different paths. Phyllis and editorial director Nita Pronovost did a great job critiquing drafts and helping me shape the story. (Nita, how did you manage to give these Passionate Mothers such thoughtful and thorough attention when you were handling your own brilliant bestseller?) Executive editor Janie Yoon gave me helpful and positive feedback. Thanks also to assistant editor Karen Silva and editorial assistant Kaitlyn Lonnee for their work and care, and to Janet Byrne for a rigorous copyedit. President and publisher Kevin Hanson is a force to be reckoned with, and I'm so happy to have him in my corner. The designers Paul Barker and Jessica Boudreau at Simon & Schuster Canada were sensitive to my determination to put Jennie Jerome Churchill and Sara Delano Roosevelt in a fresh light. Very special thanks to Adria Iwasutiak, vice president and director of publicity and Canadian sales, as well as Felicia Quon, vice president of marketing and communications. In New York, Emily Simonson was a rigorous editor. Wanda Taylor gave invaluable comments after a thorough sensitivity read.

As usual, my agent, Hilary McMahon, of WCA, worked hard on my behalf, safeguarding my interests at every stage in the process.

My most heartfelt thanks go to my husband, George Anderson, my Covid companion, literary critic, and constant supporter, who kept me well fed and confident about the project over the past few years. I'm also grateful to Alex, Nick, and Oliver, my sons, who consistently demonstrate that there is no cookie-cutter mother-son bond, and to Frances Middleton and Anna Kuntz, my daughters-in-law, who have enriched my life immeasurably with their affection and observations. Their assumptions and expectations about women's roles differ from those with which I grew up. The social rules that their own daughters, Jacqueline and Gwendolyn, will encounter as they mature will likely be different yet again.

NOTES

Chapter 1: Jerome Flings and Flash 1854–1867

1 Mrs. George Cornwallis-West, *The Reminiscences of Lady Randolph Churchill* (London: Edward Arnold, 1908), 3.
2 Quoted in Ralph G. Martin, *Jennie: The Life of Lady Randolph Churchill*, vol. 1, *The Romantic Years: 1854–1895* (Englewood Cliffs, NJ: Prentice-Hall, 1969), 4.
3 Anita Leslie, *Jennie: The Life of Lady Randolph Churchill* (London: Hutchinson, 1969), 21.
4 Leslie, *Jennie*, 5.
5 Anita Leslie, *The Remarkable Mr. Jerome* (New York: Henry Holt and Company, 1954), 35.
6 Leslie, *The Remarkable Mr. Jerome*, 44.
7 Leslie, *The Remarkable Mr. Jerome*, 29.
8 Leslie, *Jennie*, 3.
9 Cornwallis-West, *Reminiscences*, 3.
10 PCHL 1/9 Churchill Archives, Cambridge.
11 Martin, *Jennie*, vol. 1, 84–85.
12 Cornwallis-West, *Reminiscences*, 2.
13 www.measuringworth.com/dollarvaluetoday/?amount=35000&from=1861.
14 Quoted in Leslie, *The Remarkable Mr. Jerome*, 59.
15 Martin, *Jennie*, vol. 1, 18.
16 Quoted in Eric Homberger, *Mrs. Astor's New York: Money and Social Power in a Gilded Age* (New Haven and London: Yale University Press, 2002), 184.
17 Martin, *Jennie*, vol. 1, 8.
18 Quoted in Leslie, *The Remarkable Mr. Jerome*, 88–89.
19 Leslie, *The Remarkable Mr. Jerome*, 89.
20 Cornwallis-West, *Reminiscences*, 4.

Chapter 2: Delano Decorum and Discipline 1854–1870

1 Geoffrey C. Ward, *Before the Trumpet: Young Franklin Roosevelt, 1882–1905* (New York: Harper & Row, 1985), 86.

2 Ward, *Before the Trumpet*, 85.

3 Quoted in Ward, *Before the Trumpet*, 79.

4 Rita Halle Kleeman, *Gracious Lady: The Life of Sara Delano Roosevelt* (New York: D. Appleton-Century Company, 1935), 12.

5 Kleeman, *Gracious Lady*, 14.

6 By contrast, about 3 percent of Americans misused or were addicted to hard drugs such as prescription opioids, cocaine, and heroin in the 2010s. Robert Dallek, *Franklin D. Roosevelt: A Political Life* (New York: Viking, 2017), 19.

7 Kleeman, *Gracious Lady*, 15.

8 Kleeman, *Gracious Lady*, 21–22.

9 Quoted in Kleeman, *Gracious Lady*, 26–27.

10 Kleeman, *Gracious Lady*, 100.

11 Kleeman, *Gracious Lady*, 25.

12 Ward, *Before the Trumpet*, 85.

13 Kleeman, *Gracious Lady*, 25.

14 Kleeman, *Gracious Lady*, 34.

15 Ward, *Before the Trumpet*, 90.

16 Kleeman, *Gracious Lady*, 46.

17 Ward, *Before the Trumpet*, 92.

18 Kleeman, *Gracious Lady*, 58.

19 Dallek, *Franklin D. Roosevelt*, 19.

20 Kleeman, *Gracious Lady*, 59.

21 Quoted in Ward, *Before the Trumpet*, 71.

22 Kleeman, *Gracious Lady*, viii.

23 Kleeman, *Gracious Lady*, 65–66.

24 Kleeman, *Gracious Lady*, 68.

25 Ward, *Before the Trumpet*, 95.

Chapter 3: High-Spirited Jennie 1867–1873

1 Quoted in David McCullough, *The Greater Journey, Americans in Paris* (New York: Simon & Schuster, 2011), 248.

2 *Paris Guide, Par les Principaux Écrivans et Artistes de la France* (Paris: 1867), vol. 1, xliv.

3 Cornwallis-West, *Reminiscences*, 4–5.

4 Leslie, *The Remarkable Mr. Jerome*, 105–106.

5 Leslie, *The Remarkable Mr. Jerome*, 106.

6 Martin, *Jennie*, vol. 1, 23.

7 Cornwallis-West, *Reminiscences*, 5.

8 Leslie, *The Remarkable Mr. Jerome*, 114.

9 Quoted in Martin, *Jennie*, vol. 1, 28.

10 Cornwallis-West, *Reminiscences*, 21.

11 Michael Howard, *The Franco-Prussian War* (New York: Routledge, 2001), 327.

12 Anne Sebba, *Jennie Churchill: Winston's American Mother* (London: John Murray, 2007), 31.

13 Leslie, *Jennie,* 20.

14 Cornwallis-West, *Reminiscences,* 31.

15 McCullough, *The Greater Journey,* 260.

16 Anthony Camp, *Royal Mistresses and Bastards: Fact and Fiction* (London: Anthony Camp, 2007).

17 Frances, Countess of Warwick, *Discretions* (New York, C. Scribner's Sons, 1931), 12.

18 Cornwallis-West, *Reminiscences,* 30.

19 Gail McColl and Carol McD. Wallace, *To Marry an English Lord: Tales of Wealth and Marriage, Sex and Snobbery in the Gilded Age* (New York: Workman Publishing, 1989), 82.

20 Anne de Courcy, *The Husband Hunters: Social Climbing in London and New York* (London: Weidenfeld & Nicolson, 2017), 1.

21 Quoted in Leslie, *The Remarkable Mr. Jerome,* 166.

22 Quoted in Martin, *Jennie,* vol. 1, 49.

23 Martin, *Jennie,* vol. 1, 51.

24 Quoted in Homberger, *Mrs. Astor's New York,* 149.

Chapter 4: Self-Assured Sara 1870–1880

1 Ward MacAllister, *Society as I Have Found It* (New York: Cassell, 1890), 214.

2 Homberger, *Mrs. Astor's New York,* 155.

3 Homberger, *Mrs. Astor's New York,* 212.

4 Quoted in Homberger, *Mrs. Astor's New York,* 193.

5 MacAllister, *Society as I Have Found It,* 215.

6 Kleeman, *Gracious Lady,* 84.

7 Kleeman, *Gracious Lady,* 84–85.

8 Ward, *Before the Trumpet,* 87.

9 Ward, *Before the Trumpet,* 64.

10 https://www.newyorker.com/magazine/1996/07/08/stanford-whites-ruins?verso=true.

11 Kleeman, *Gracious Lady,* 83.

12 Kleeman, *Gracious Lady,* 92.

13 Homberger, *Mrs. Astor's New York,* 223–224.

14 Kleeman, *Gracious Lady,* 133.

15 Kleeman, *Gracious Lady,* 94.

16 Kleeman, *Gracious Lady,* 91–93.

17 Ward, *Before the Trumpet,* 99.

18 Elliott Roosevelt, ed., *The Roosevelt Letters* (London: George G. Harrap, 1950), vol. 2, 21.

19 Jean Edward Smith, *FDR* (New York: Random House, 2007), 4.
20 Ward, *Before the Trumpet*, 60.
21 Smith, *FDR*, 8.
22 Ward, *Before the Trumpet*, 59.
23 Kleeman, *Gracious Lady*, 101–102.
24 Ward, *Before the Trumpet*, 65.
25 Letter to FDR, May 8, 1932, Roosevelt Family Papers, FDRL.

Chapter 5: Jennie's "Very Dangerous Affair" 1873–1874

 1 Leslie, *The Remarkable Mr. Jerome*, 154.
 2 Winston S. Churchill, *Lord Randolph Churchill*, vol. 1 (London: Macmillan, 1906), 38.
 3 Primrose, Archibald Philip, Earl of Rosebery, *Lord Randolph Churchill* (London: Arthur J. Humphreys, 1906), 109, 32.
 4 Charles Higham, *Dark Lady: Winston Churchill's Mother and Her World* (London: Virgin Books, 2006), 51.
 5 Randolph S. Churchill, *Winston S. Churchill*, vol. 1: *Youth 1874–1900* (London: Heinemann, 1966), 467.
 6 Leslie, *Jennie*, 24.
 7 Martin, *Jennie*, vol. 1, 52.
 8 Peregrine Churchill and Julian Mitchell, *Jennie, Lady Randolph Churchill: A Portrait with Letters* (London: Collins, 1974), 20.
 9 Robert Rhodes James, *Rosebery: A Biography of Archibald Philip, Fifth Earl of Rosebery* (London: Weidenfeld & Nicolson, 1963), 25.
10 Leslie, *Jennie*, 26.
11 Martin, *Jennie*, vol. 1, 59.
12 Martin, *Jennie*, vol. 1, 64.
13 Letter, August 31, 1873, cited in Randolph S. Churchill, *Winston S. Churchill*, vol. 1, *Youth 1874–1900*, 12–13.
14 Martin, *Jennie*, vol. 1, 68.
15 Quoted in Churchill and Mitchell, *Jennie, Lady Randolph Churchill: A Portrait with Letters*, 44–55.
16 Quoted in Martin, *Jennie*, vol. 1, 71–72.
17 Martin, *Jennie*, vol. 1, 74.
18 Martin, *Jennie*, vol. 1, 87.
19 David Lough, "The Inheritance of Winston Churchill," in *The Cambridge Companion to Winston Churchill* (Cambridge Companions to History), ed. Allen Packwood (Cambridge: Cambridge University Press, 2023).
20 Quoted in Sebba, *Jennie Churchill*, 46.
21 Quoted in Sebba, *Jennie Churchill*, 51.
22 Quoted in Sebba, *Jennie Churchill*, 55.

23 Letter, April 9, 1874, cited in Randolph S. Churchill, *Winston S. Churchill,* vol. 1, *Youth 1874–1900; Companion Volume* 1, 20.
24 Quoted in Sebba, *Jennie Churchill,* 56.
25 Quoted in Martin, *Jennie,* vol. 1, 85.
26 Quoted in Martin, *Jennie,* vol. 1, 88.
27 Sebba, *Jennie Churchill,* 51.
28 Leslie, *The Remarkable Mr. Jerome,* 183.
29 Leslie, *The Remarkable Mr. Jerome,* 3.

Chapter 6: Toxic Churchill Dynamics 1874–1880

1 Cornwallis-West, *Reminiscences,* 57.
2 Cornwallis-West, *Reminiscences,* 57-58.
3 Cornwallis-West, *Reminiscences,* 61.
4 Cornwallis-West, *Reminiscences,* 59.
5 Cornwallis-West, *Reminiscences,* 60.
6 Cornwallis-West, *Reminiscences,* 61.
7 Consuelo Vanderbilt Balsan, *The Glitter and the Gold* (Maidstone, Kent, UK: George Mann Books, 1973), 69.
8 Cornwallis-West, *Reminiscences,* 37.
9 Quoted in Martin, *Jennie,* vol. 1, 98.
10 Cornwallis-West, *Reminiscences,* 47.
11 Cornwallis-West, *Reminiscences,* 47–48.
12 Quoted in Jock Colville, *The Churchillians* (London: Butler & Tanner, 1981), 85.
13 Quoted in Leslie, *Jennie,* 41.
14 Cornwallis-West, *Reminiscences,* 55.
15 Cornwallis-West, *Reminiscences,* 55.
16 Sebba, *Jennie Churchill,* 65.
17 Leslie, *Jennie,* 43; Martin, *Jennie,* vol. 1, 107; Churchill and Mitchell, *Jennie, Lady Randolph Churchill: A Portrait with Letters,* 75.
18 Winston S. Churchill, *My Early Life* (London: Macmillan, 1930), 5.
19 David Lough, ed., *My Darling Winston: The Letters between Winston Churchill and His Mother* (New York: Pegasus, 2018), xvii.
20 Daphne Fielding, *The Duchess of Jermyn Street: The Life and Good Times of Rosa Lewis of the Cavendish Hotel* (London: Eyre & Spottiswoode, 1964), 34.
21 Churchill and Mitchell, *Jennie, Lady Randolph Churchill: A Portrait with Letters,* 76–79.
22 Quoted in Sebba, *Jennie Churchill,* 75.
23 Quoted in Churchill and Mitchell, *Jennie, Lady Randolph Churchill: A Portrait with Letters,* 83.

24 This account of the affair is taken largely from Leslie, *Jennie*, because the author had the greatest access to family papers.

25 Churchill, *Lord Randolph Churchill*, vol. I, 74.

26 Churchill and Mitchell, *Jennie, Lady Randolph Churchill: A Portrait with Letters*, 92–93; in a note, Churchill and Mitchell translate Jennie's French: "And into the bargain! with a dreadful cold."

27 Churchill, *Lord Randolph Churchill*, vol. 1, 74.

28 Frances Evelyn Maynard Greville, Countess of Warwick, *Life's Ebb and Flow* (New York: William Morrow & Company, 1929), 175.

29 Cornwallis-West, *Reminiscences*, 69.

30 Cornwallis-West, *Reminiscences*, 70.

31 Cornwallis-West, *Reminiscences*, 72-73.

32 Leslie, *The Remarkable Mr. Jerome*, 187.

33 Churchill and Mitchell, *Jennie, Lady Randolph Churchill: A Portrait with Letters*, 103.

34 Quoted in Celia Sandys, *From Winston with Love and Kisses: The Young Churchill* (College Station: Texas A&M University Press, 2013), 31.

35 Cited in Sebba, *Jennie Churchill*, 86.

36 Leslie, *Jennie*, 69.

37 Leslie, *Jennie*, 5.

38 Quoted in Martin, *Jennie*, vol. 1, 126.

39 Quoted in Churchill and Mitchell, *Jennie, Lady Randolph Churchill: A Portrait with Letters*, 108.

40 Quoted in Sebba, *Jennie Churchill*, 102.

41 Churchill, *My Early Life*, 5.

Chapter 7: Roosevelt Harmony 1880–1890

1 Quoted in Ward, *Before the Trumpet*, 105.

2 Kleeman, *Gracious Lady*, 103.

3 Kleeman, Gracious Lady, 103.

4 Kleeman, *Gracious Lady*, 102–103.

5 Wedding guest interviewed by Kleeman in 1930s, and quoted in Ward, *Before the Trumpet*, 105.

6 Kleeman, *Gracious Lady*, 111.

7 Ward, *Before the Trumpet*, 52.

8 Kleeman, *Gracious Lady*, 111.

9 Kleeman, *Gracious Lady*, 118.

10 Kleeman, *Gracious Lady*, 111–112.

11 Kleeman, *Gracious Lady*, 111.

12 Kleeman, *Gracious Lady*, 121–124.

13 For details of FDR's birth, see Ward, *Before the Trumpet*, 109–110.

14 Ward, *Before the Trumpet*, 109–110.

15 Ward, *Before the Trumpet*, 110.

16 Sara Delano Roosevelt, Isabel Leighton, and Gabrielle Elliot Forbush, *My Boy Franklin* (New York: Ray Long & Richard R. Smith, 1933), 12.

17 Ward, *Before the Trumpet*, 111.

18 Quoted in Smith, *FDR*, 17.

19 Quoted in Ward, *Before the Trumpet*, 111.

20 Quoted in Kleeman, 126–127.

21 Peter Collier with David Horowitz, *The Roosevelts: An American Saga* (New York: Simon & Schuster, 1994), 101–102.

22 Quoted in Smith, *FDR*, 19.

23 Quoted in Kleeman, *Gracious Lady*, 153.

24 Quoted in Kleeman, *Gracious Lady*, 145.

25 Quoted in Kleeman. *Gracious Lady*, 146.

26 Quoted in Kleeman, *Gracious Lady*, 169.

27 Quoted in Kleeman, *Gracious Lady*, 142

28 Quoted in Kleeman, *Gracious Lady*, 138.

29 The Roosevelts' devotion was noted by the wife of artist Felix Moscheles, who spent several weeks at Springwood painting a portrait of Mr. James. Ward, *Before the Trumpet*, 125.

30 Kleeman, *Gracious Lady*, 146.

31 Ward, *Before the Trumpet*, 124–125.

32 April White, "The Divorce Colony," *Atavist*, December 2015, https://magazine.atavist.com/the-divorce-colony.

33 White, "The Divorce Colony."

34 Kleeman, *Gracious Lady*, 147.

35 Unless otherwise noted, these and other quotations and details are taken from Roosevelt, Leighton, and Forbush, *My Boy Franklin*.

36 Quoted in Kleeman, *Gracious Lady*, 26.

37 Roosevelt, Leighton and Forbush, *My Boy Franklin*, 20–21.

38 Quoted in Collier with Horowitz, *The Roosevelts*, 102.

39 Ward, *Before the Trumpet*, 144.

Chapter 8: Jennie's Dream Crumbles 1880–1886

1 Cornwallis-West, *Reminiscences*, 90.

2 Cornwallis-West, *Reminiscences*, 90–91.

3 Cornwallis-West, *Reminiscences*, 90–91.

4 Leslie, *Jennie*, 75.

5 "The Bill," unpublished manuscript of play written by Lady Randolph Churchill, Churchill Archives, BRDW IV/6.

6 Quoted in Martin, *Jennie*, vol. 1, 149.

7 Cornwallis-West, *Reminiscences*, 124.

8 Cornwallis-West, *Reminiscences*, 104.

9 Andrew Roberts, *Churchill: Walking with Destiny* (London: Allen Lane, 2018), 14.

10 Martin, *Jennie*, vol. 1, 149.

11 Lough, *My Darling Winston*, 2.

12 Leslie, *Jennie*, 70.

13 Cornwallis-West, *Reminiscences*, 102.

14 Cornwallis-West, *Reminiscences*, 98–99.

15 Simon Heffer, *The Age of Decadence: Britain 1880–1914* (London: Random House, 2017), 68.

16 Sebba, *Jennie Churchill*, 135.

17 Cornwallis-West, *Reminiscences*, 138.

18 Quoted in Robert Rhodes James, *Lord Randolph Churchill* (London: Weidenfeld & Nicolson paperback, 1995), 249.

19 Sebba, *Jennie Churchill*, 137.

20 Lady Walpurga Ehrengarde Helena von Hohenthal Paget, *Embassies of Other Days* (New York: George H. Doran Company, 1923), vol. 2, 415.

21 Frances, Countess of Warwick, quoted in Martin, *Jennie*, vol. 1, 187.

22 Cornwallis-West, *Reminiscences*, 104.

23 Cornwallis-West, *Reminiscences*, 136.

24 Cornwallis-West, *Reminiscences*, 135–137.

25 Martin, *Jennie*, vol. 1, 217.

26 Martin, *Jennie*, vol. 1, 162.

27 Sebba, *Jennie Churchill*, 145.

28 Churchill and Mitchell, *Jennie, Lady Randolph Churchill: A Portrait with Letters*, 143.

29 Churchill and Mitchell, *Jennie, Lady Randolph Churchill: A Portrait with Letters*, 147.

30 de Courcy, *The Husband Hunters*, 1–2.

31 Churchill, *My Early Life*, 3–4.

32 Quoted in Lough, *My Darling Winston*, 6.

33 Lough, *My Darling Winston*, 4.

34 Lough, *My Darling Winston*, 8.

35 Leslie, *Jennie*, 82.

36 Churchill, *My Early Life*, 13.

37 Churchill, *My Early Life*, 13.

38 Lough, *My Darling Winston*, 10.

39 Quoted in Eileen Quelch, *Perfect Darling: The Live and Times of George Cornwallis-West* (London: C. and A. Woolf, 1972), 60.

40 Quoted in Martin, *Jennie*, vol. 1, 206.

41 Shane Leslie, *Men Were Different: Five Studies in Late Victorian Biography* (London: Michael Joseph, 1937), 49.

42 Quoted in Leslie, *Men Were Different*, 42.
43 Quoted in Rhodes James, *Lord Randolph Churchill*, 311.
44 Cornwallis-West, *Reminiscences*, 141.
45 Cornwallis-West, *Reminiscences*, 141.
46 Cornwallis-West, *Reminiscences*, 143
47 Martin, *Jennie*, vol. 1, 228.
48 Martin, *Jennie*, vol. 1, 228.

Chapter 9: Churchills: Love and Death 1887–1895

 1 Cornwallis-West, *Reminiscences*, 142–144.
 2 Cornwallis-West, *Reminiscences*, 147.
 3 Cornwallis-West, *Reminiscences*, 145.
 4 Quelch, *Perfect Darling*, 58–59.
 5 Martin, *Jennie*, vol. 1, 277.
 6 Roy Jenkins, *Churchill: A Biography* (New York: Farrar, Straus and Giroux, 2001), 8.
 7 Rhodes James, *Rosebery*, 183.
 8 Martin, *Jennie*, vol. 1, 229.
 9 Sebba, *Jennie Churchill*, 155.
10 Lough, "The Inheritance of Winston Churchill."
11 Leslie, *Jennie*, 148.
12 Quoted in Sebba, *Jennie Churchill*, 165
13 Leslie, *Jennie*, 133.
14 Quoted in Churchill, *Lord Randolph Churchill*, vol. II, 440.
15 Quoted in Martin, *Jennie*, vol. 1, 279.
16 Lough, "The Inheritance of Winston Churchill."
17 Churchill and Mitchell, *Jennie, Lady Randolph Churchill: A Portrait with Letters*, 165.
18 Quoted in Sebba, *Jennie Churchill*, 189.
19 Leslie, *Men Were Different*, 73.
20 Quoted in Martin, *Jennie*, vol. 1, 321.
21 Quoted in Leslie, *Jennie*, 162.
22 Quoted in Sebba, *Jennie Churchill*, 193.
23 Sebba, *Jennie Churchill*, 192–193.
24 Leslie, *Men Were Different*, 68–75.
25 Leslie, *Jennie*, 108.
26 Quoted in Andrew W. Ellis, "What Killed Lord Randolph Churchill?," December 30, 2021, https://winstonchurchill.org/resources/myths/lord-randolph-churchill-maladies-et-mort.
27 Martin, *Jennie*, vol. 1, 322.
28 Lough, *My Darling Winston*, 20.
29 Quoted in Martin, *Jennie*, vol. 1, 240.

30 Quoted in Martin, *Jennie*, vol. 1, 240.

31 Quoted in Martin, *Jennie*, vol. 1, 256.

32 Lough, *My Darling Winston*, 62.

33 Lough, *My Darling Winston*, 34.

34 Quoted in Martin, *Jennie*, vol. 1, 257.

35 Leslie, *Jennie*, 153.

36 Lough, *My Darling Winston*, 78–79.

37 Lough, *My Darling Winston*, 78–79.

38 Lough, *My Darling Winston*, 80–81.

39 Quoted in Martin, *Jennie*, vol. 1, 317.

40 Quoted in Lough, *My Darling Winston*, 93.

41 Quoted in Leslie, *Jennie*, 165.

42 Martin, *Jennie*, vol. 1, 327.

43 Quoted in Leslie, *Jennie*, 168.

44 Leslie, *Men Were Different*, 78.

45 Quoted in Sebba, *Jennie Churchill*, 197–198.

46 Lough, *My Darling Winston*, 110–111.

47 Quoted in Quelch, *Perfect Darling*, 64.

48 Lough, *No More Champagne*, 35.

49 Lough, *My Darling Winston*, 123–124.

50 Lough, *My Darling Winston*, 128.

51 Sebba, *Jennie Churchill*, 210.

Chapter 10: Sara's "Dear, Dear Boy" 1890–1903

1 Roosevelt, Leighton, and Forbush, *My Boy Franklin*, 24–25.

2 Elliott Roosevelt, ed., *F.D.R.: His Personal Letters, The Early Years* (London: George. G. Harrap & Co. Ltd., 1949), 19–20.

3 Quoted in Ward, *Before the Trumpet*, 147.

4 Kleeman, *Gracious Lady*, 161.

5 Kleeman, *Gracious Lady*, 163.

6 Kleeman, *Gracious Lady*, 164–166.

7 Roosevelt, Leighton, and Forbush, *My Boy Franklin*, 35.

8 Roosevelt, Leighton, and Forbush, *My Boy Franklin*, 35.

9 Quoted in Ward, *Before the Trumpet*, 171.

10 Kleeman, *Gracious Lady*, 161.

11 All quotations from Ward, *Before the Trumpet*, 177–178.

12 Ward, *Before the Trumpet*, 182.

13 Roosevelt, ed., *F.D.R.: His Personal Letters, The Early Years*, 35.

14 Kleeman, *Gracious Lady*, 194–195.

15 Ward, *Before the Trumpet*, 181.

16 Roosevelt, ed., *F.D.R.: His Personal Letters, The Early Years*, 33.

17 Roosevelt Family Papers, Box 51, FDR Archives.

18 Kleeman, *Gracious Lady*, 196.

19 Roosevelt, ed., *F.D.R.: His Personal Letters, The Early Years*, 84.

20 Kleeman, *Gracious Lady*, 196.

21 Roosevelt Family Papers, Box 52, FDR Archives.

22 Roosevelt, Leighton, and Forbush, *My Boy Franklin*, 43.

23 Roosevelt, ed., *F.D.R.: His Personal Letters, The Early Years*, 105.

24 Kleeman, *Gracious Lady*, 208.

25 Kleeman, *Gracious Lady*, 203.

26 Quoted in Ward, *Before the Trumpet*, 211

27 Quoted in Ward, *Before the Trumpet*, 211.

28 Quoted in Ward, *Before the Trumpet*, 213.

29 Kleeman, *Gracious Lady*, 207.

30 Quoted in Ward, *Before the Trumpet*, 218.

31 Quoted in Ward, *Before the Trumpet*, 219.

32 All quotations from Ward, *Before the Trumpet*, 221.

33 Taddy was sent away to Florida, but he and Sadie remained officially married until 1910, though they were not always together. At some point, Taddy moved back to Forest Hills, New York, where he repaired automobiles. He never touched the Astor millions that his mother had left him, and most of his fortune went to the Salvation Army at his death in 1958. His father, Rosy Roosevelt, disowned him, and there is no evidence that Franklin ever spoke to Taddy after the latter left Harvard.

34 Kleeman, *Gracious Lady*, 209.

35 Roosevelt Family Papers, Box 52, FDR Archives.

36 Quoted in Ward, *Before the Trumpet*, 225.

37 Quoted in Ward, *Before the Trumpet*, 226.

38 Kleeman, *Gracious Lady*, 214.

39 https://www.measuringworth.com/dollarvaluetoday/?amount=120000&from=1900.

Chapter 11: Jennie: "No Wire Unpulled" 1895–1899

1 Cornwallis-West, *Reminiscences*, 278.

2 Martin, *Jennie*, vol. 2, 10.

3 https://www.uwyo.edu/numimage/currency.html.

4 Leslie, *Jennie*, 179.

5 Ralph Martin, *Jennie, The Life of the American Beauty Who Became the Toast–and Scandal–of Two Continents, Ruled an Age and Raised a Son–Winston Churchill–Who Shaped History* (Sourcebooks, 2007), 354.

6 Lough, *My Darling Winston*, 122–123.

7 Lough, *My Darling Winston*, 132.

8 Leslie, *Jennie*, 186–188.

9 Martin, *Jennie*, vol. 2, 58.

10 Lough, *My Darling Winston*, 130.

11 Lough, *My Darling Winston*, 130.

12 Lough, *My Darling Winston*, 131.

13 Leslie, *Jennie*, 189.

14 Roberts, *Churchill*, 34.

15 Lough, *My Darling Winston*, 133.

16 Martin, *Jennie*, vol. 2, 75.

17 Quoted in Lough, *My Darling Winston*, 138.

18 Winston S. Churchill, *Amid These Storms* (New York: Charles Scribner's Sons, 1932), 52.

19 Quoted in William Manchester, *The Last Lion: Winston Spencer Churchill*, vol. 1, *Visions of Glory, 1874–1932* (Boston: Little, Brown and Company, 1983), 225.

20 Quoted in Lough, *My Darling Winston*, 140.

21 Quoted in Lough, *My Darling Winston*, 232.

22 Quoted in Lough, *My Darling Winston*, 238.

23 Quoted in Lough, *My Darling Winston*, 201–222.

24 Quoted in Lough, *My Darling Winston*, 117.

25 Quoted in Lough, *My Darling Winston*, 257.

26 Quoted in Lough, *My Darling Winston*, 236.

27 Quoted in Lough, *My Darling Winston*, 159.

28 Quoted in Lough, *My Darling Winston*, 245.

29 Quoted in Lough, *My Darling Winston*, 241.

30 Quoted in Lough, *My Darling Winston*, 264.

31 Churchill, *My Early Life*, 137.

32 Manchester, vol. 1, *Visions of Glory*, 175.

33 Martin, *Jennie*, vol. 2, 60.

34 Cornwallis-West, *Reminiscences*, 301.

35 http://www.rvondeh.dircon.co.uk/incalmprose/ball.html.

36 http://www.rvondeh.dircon.co.uk/churchill2.html.

37 Leslie, *Jennie*, 214.

38 Greville, *Life's Ebb and Flow*, 89–95.

39 https://www.lrb.co.uk/the-paper/v37/n14/bee-wilson/throw-it-out-the-window

40 Cornwallis-West, *Reminiscences*, 278.

41 Cornwallis-West, *Reminiscences*, 279.

42 Cornwallis-West, *Reminiscences*, 279.

43 Martin, *Jennie*, vol. 2, 188.

44 Greville, *Life's Ebb and Flow*, 138.

45 Cornwallis-West, *Reminiscences*, 299.

46 Lough, *My Darling Winston*, 193.

47 Greville, *Life's Ebb and Flow*, 140.

48 Quoted in Lough, *My Darling Winston*, 243.
49 Manchester, vol. 1, *Visions of Glory*, 262.
50 Quoted in Lough, *My Darling Winston*, 324.
51 Quoted in Lough, *My Darling Winston*, 171.
52 Quoted in Lough, *My Darling Winston*, 173.

Chapter 12: Jennie Goes to War 1899–1901

 1 Cornwallis-West, *Reminiscences*, 308.
 2 Quoted in Manchester, vol. 1, *Visions of Glory*, 332.
 3 Quoted in Randolph S. Churchill, *Winston S. Churchill*, vol. 1, *Youth 1874–1900*, 449–450.
 4 https://winstonchurchill.org/publications/churchill-bulletin/bulletin -128-mar-2019/churchill-style-3/.
 5 Martin, *Jennie*, vol. 2, 205.
 6 *New York Times*, October 27, 1899.
 7 Quoted in Leslie, *Jennie*, 238.
 8 Cornwallis-West, *Reminiscences*, 317.
 9 Quoted in Leslie, *Jennie*, 234.
10 Quoted in Martin, *Jennie*, vol. 2, 209.
11 Cornwallis-West, *Reminiscences*, 317.
12 Cornwallis-West, *Reminiscences*, 324.
13 Cornwallis-West, *Reminiscences*, 327.
14 Quoted in Lough, *My Darling Winston*, 355.
15 Cornwallis-West, *Reminiscences*, 360.
16 Cornwallis-West, *Reminiscences*, 335.
17 Balsan, *The Glitter and the Gold*, 110.
18 Quoted in Churchill and Mitchell, *Jennie, Lady Randolph Churchill: A Portrait with Letters*, 173.
19 Quoted in Leslie, *Jennie*, 219.
20 Leslie, *Jennie*, 223.
21 Ethel Smyth, *What Happened Next?* (London: Longman, 1940), 285.
22 Quoted in Churchill and Mitchell, *Jennie, Lady Randolph Churchill: A Portrait with Letters*, 179.
23 Quoted in Lough, *My Darling Winston*, 342.
24 Quoted in Churchill and Mitchell, *Jennie, Lady Randolph Churchill: A Portrait with Letters*, 199.
25 Quoted in Churchill and Mitchell, *Jennie, Lady Randolph Churchill: A Portrait with Letters*, 201, 212.
26 Quoted in Churchill and Mitchell, *Jennie, Lady Randolph Churchill: A Portrait with Letters*, 215.
27 Quoted in Lough, *My Darling Winston*, 344.
28 Quoted in Leslie, *Jennie*, 250.

29 Quoted in Leslie, *Jennie*, 251.
30 Quoted in Churchill and Mitchell, *Jennie, Lady Randolph Churchill: A Portrait with Letters*, 221.
31 Quoted in Churchill and Mitchell, *Jennie, Lady Randolph Churchill: A Portrait with Letters*, 223.
32 Quoted in Churchill and Mitchell, *Jennie, Lady Randolph Churchill: A Portrait with Letters*, 223.
33 Quoted in Lough, *My Darling Winston*, 177.
34 WSC to LRC, April 6, 1897, Churchill Archives, CHAR 28/23/31.
35 Quoted in Lough, *My Darling Winston*, 296–298.
36 Quoted in Martin, *Jennie*, vol. 2, 180.
37 Quoted in Lough, *My Darling Winston*, 373.
38 Quoted in Lough, *My Darling Winston*, 377.
39 Quoted in Martin, *Jennie*, vol. 2, 256.
40 Quoted in Martin *Jennie*, vol. 2, 254.
41 Quoted in Lough, *My Darling Winston*, 387.
42 Quoted in Lough, *My Darling Winston*, 386.
43 Quoted in Manchester, vol. 1, *Visions of Glory*, 342.
44 Quoted in Jenkins, *Churchill*, 72.

Chapter 13: Sara Acquires a "Daughter" 1901–1904

1 Ward, *Before the Trumpet*, 226.
2 Quoted in Ward, *Before the Trumpet*, 244.
3 Quoted in Kleeman, *Gracious Lady*, 222.
4 Jan Pottker, *Sara and Eleanor: The Story of Sara Delano Roosevelt and her Daughter-in-Law, Eleanor Roosevelt* (New York: St. Martin's, 2004), 118.
5 SDR Diary Book No. 3, Roosevelt Family Papers Box 51, FDR Archives.
6 Roosevelt, Leighton, and Forbush, *My Boy Franklin*, 55–56.
7 Quoted in Kleeman, *Gracious Lady*, 228–229.
8 Quoted in Ward, *Before the Trumpet*, 246.
9 Quoted in Ward, *Before the Trumpet*, 250.
10 Ward, *Before the Trumpet*, 249.
11 Quoted in Ward, *Before the Trumpet*, 246–247.
12 Quoted in Ward, *Before the Trumpet*, 256–257.
13 Quoted in Ward, *Before the Trumpet*, 259.
14 Quoted in Kleeman, *Gracious Lady*, 233.
15 Roosevelt, Leighton, and Forbush, *My Boy Franklin*, 62–63.
16 Roosevelt, ed., *F.D.R.: His Personal Letters, The Early Years*, 517.
17 Roosevelt, ed., *F.D.R.: His Personal Letters, The Early Years*, 518.
18 Quoted in Ward, *Before the Trumpet*, 266, taken from *Hunting Big Game in the Eighties*, a book of letters from Elliott Roosevelt, edited by his daughter.

19 Quoted in Ward, *Before the Trumpet*, 272.
20 Quoted in Ward, *Before the Trumpet*, 278.
21 Quoted in Ward, *Before the Trumpet*, 286.
22 Quoted in Ward, *Before the Trumpet*, 289.
23 Eleanor Roosevelt, *The Autobiography of Eleanor Roosevelt* (New York: Harper & Brothers, 1961), 12.
24 Quoted in Ward, *Before the Trumpet*, 293.
25 Quoted in Blanche Wiesen Cook, *Eleanor Roosevelt*, vol. 1 (New York: Viking, 1992), 138.
26 Quoted in Cook, *Eleanor Roosevelt*, vol. 1, 132.
27 Quoted in Cook, *Eleanor Roosevelt*, vol. 1, 142–143.
28 Quoted in Kleeman, *Gracious Lady*, 239.
29 Quoted in Kleeman, *Gracious Lady*, 240.
30 Pottker, *Sara and Eleanor*, 106.

Chapter 14: The Ups and Downs of Churchill Marriages 1901–1912

1 Princess Daisy of Pless, *From My Private Diary* (London: John Murray, 1928), 84.
2 George Cornwallis-West, *Edwardian Hey Days: Or, a Little about a Lot of Things* (London: Putnam, 1930), 118.
3 Quoted in Lough, *My Darling Winston*, 382–383.
4 Cornwallis-West, *Edwardian Hey-Days*, 128.
5 Quoted in Leslie, *Jennie*, 254.
6 Cornwallis-West, *Edwardian Hey-Days*, 119.
7 Quelch, *Perfect Darling*, 81.
8 https://winstonchurchill.hillsdale.edu/great-contemporaries-sir-ernest -cassel-a-few-more-years-of-sunshine.
9 Pless, *From My Private Diary*, 99.
10 Celia Lee, ed., *Jean, Lady Hamilton, 1861–1941: Diary of a Soldier's Wife* (Yorkshire: Pen & Sword Military, 2020), 217.
11 Quoted in Lee, *Jean, Lady Hamilton*, 219.
12 Leslie, *Jennie*, 274.
13 Seymour Leslie, *The Jerome Connexion* (London: John Murray, 1964), 9.
14 Leslie, *Jennie*, 270.
15 Cornwallis-West, *Edwardian Hey-Days*, 132.
16 Quoted in Lough, *My Darling Winston*, 411.
17 Jenkins, *Churchill*, 148.
18 Quoted in Lough, *My Darling Winston*, 390.
19 Quoted in Lough, *My Darling Winston*, 391.
20 Peter Clarke, *Mr. Churchill's Profession* (New York: Bloomsbury, 2012), 56.
21 Quoted in Lough, *My Darling Winston*, 392.

22 Quoted in Lough, *My Darling Winston*, 414–415.

23 Quoted in Lough, *My Darling Winston*, 461.

24 Quoted in Martin, *Lady Randolph Churchill*, vol. 2, 227–228.

25 *The Spectator*, October 18, 1908, quoted in Lough, *My Darling Winston*, 488.

26 Quoted in Churchill and Mitchell, *Jennie, Lady Randolph Churchill: A Portrait with Letters*, 230.

27 Quelch, *Perfect Darling*, 82–83.

28 Quoted in Leslie, *Jennie*, 273.

29 Randolph S. Churchill, *Winston S. Churchill*, vol. 2: *Young Statesman, 1901–14* (Boston: Houghton Mifflin, 1967), 249.

30 Churchill, *Winston S. Churchill*, vol. 2, 249.

31 Lee, *Jean, Lady Hamilton*, 233.

32 Quoted in Lee, *Jean, Lady Hamilton*, 235.

33 Sonia Purnell, *Clementine, The Life of Mrs. Winston Churchill* (London: Viking, 2015), 35.

34 Quoted in Martin, *Jennie*, vol. 2, 319.

35 Quoted in Lough, *My Darling Winston*, 484.

36 Purnell, *Clementine*, 47.

37 Mary Soames, ed., *Speaking for Themselves, The Personal Letters of Winston and Clementine Churchill* (London: Doubleday, 1998), xiii, xx.

38 Quoted in Manchester, vol. 1, *Visions of Glory*, 401.

39 Quoted in Churchill and Mitchell, *Jennie, Lady Randolph Churchill: A Portrait with Letters*, 228.

40 Churchill Archives BRDW IV/ ½ Typescript of "Fabia."

41 Quoted in Churchill and Mitchell, *Jennie, Lady Randolph Churchill: A Portrait with Letters*, 233.

42 Quoted in Martin, *Jennie*, vol. 2, 334.

43 Campbell, Mrs. Patrick, *My Life and Some Letters* (New York: Dodd Mead, 1922), 307.

44 Quoted in Churchill and Mitchell, *Jennie, Lady Randolph Churchill: A Portrait with Letters*, 234.

45 Quoted in Churchill and Mitchell, *Jennie, Lady Randolph Churchill: A Portrait with Letters*, 235.

46 Quoted in Churchill and Mitchell, *Jennie, Lady Randolph Churchill: A Portrait with Letters*, 237.

47 Quoted in Leslie, *Jennie*, 301.

48 Quelch, *Perfect Darling*, 118.

49 Quoted in Martin, *Jennie*, vol. 2, 360.

50 Simon Heffer, ed., *Henry "Chips" Channon: The Diaries 1938–43* (London: Hutchinson, 2021), 288.

51 Quoted in Churchill and Mitchell, *Jennie, Lady Randolph Churchill: A Portrait with Letters*, 243.

Chapter 15: Sara Stays Close 1904–1913

1 Roosevelt, *The Autobiography of Eleanor Roosevelt*, 47.

2 Kleeman, *Gracious Lady*, 242.

3 Kleeman, *Gracious Lady*, 242.

4 Quoted in Ward, *Before the Trumpet*, 337.

5 Quoted in Kleeman, *Gracious Lady*, 244.

6 Roosevelt, ed., *F.D.R.: His Personal Letters, The Early Years*, 68.

7 Roosevelt, ed., *F.D.R.: His Personal Letters, The Early Years*, 20.

8 Roosevelt, ed., *F.D.R.: His Personal Letters, The Early Years*, 62.

9 Kleeman, *Gracious Lady*, 246.

10 Cook, *Eleanor Roosevelt*, vol. 1, 175.

11 Cook, *Eleanor Roosevelt*, vol. 1, 177.

12 Roosevelt, *The Autobiography of Eleanor Roosevelt*, 55.

13 https://measuringworth.com/dollarvaluetoday/?amount= 12000&from=1904.

14 SDR Diary Book No. 3, Roosevelt Family Papers Box 52, FDR Archives.

15 Pottker, *Sara and Eleanor*, 131.

16 SDR Diary, Roosevelt Family Papers Box 52, FDR Archives.

17 Geoffrey C. Ward, *A First-Class Temperament: The Emergence of Franklin Roosevelt* (New York: Harper & Row, 1989), 52.

18 Quoted in Pottker, *Sara and Eleanor*, 136.

19 Ward, *A First-Class Temperament*, 64.

20 Ward, *A First-Class Temperament*, 76.

21 Grenville Clark, "Franklin D. Roosevelt, 1882–1945: Five Harvard Men Pay Tribute to His Memory," in *Harvard Alumni Bulletin* 452 (April 28, 1945), 47.

22 Roosevelt, *The Autobiography of Eleanor Roosevelt*, 62.

23 Kleeman, *Gracious Lady*, 249.

24 Quoted in Pottker, *Sara and Eleanor*, 145.

25 Quoted in Pottker, *Sara and Eleanor*, 141.

26 Quoted in Pottker, *Sara and Eleanor*, 141.

27 Quoted in Joseph P. Lash, *Eleanor and Franklin: The Story of Their Relationship, Based on Eleanor Roosevelt's Private Papers* (New York: W. W. Norton, 1971), 163.

28 Quoted in Pottker, *Sara and Eleanor*, 143.

29 This story may be apocryphal, but it is well documented in Smith, *FDR*, 61, 653.

30 Kleeman, *Gracious Lady*, 252.

31 Quoted in Kleeman, *Gracious Lady*, 253.

32 Smith, *FDR*, 62.

33 Quoted in Pottker, *Sara and Eleanor*, 151.

34 Quoted in Pottker, *Sara and Eleanor*, 152.
35 Frances Perkins, *The Roosevelt I Knew* (New York: The Viking Press, 1946), 11.
36 Quoted in Lash, *Eleanor and Franklin*, 175.
37 Quoted in Kleeman, *Gracious Lady*, 257.
38 Quoted in Smith, *FDR*, 83.
39 Roosevelt, *The Autobiography of Eleanor Roosevelt*, 68.

Chapter 16: Jennie: "On the Wrong Side of the Ladder" 1912–1918

 1 Quoted in Lee, *Jean, Lady Hamilton*, 250.
 2 Manchester, vol. 1, *Visions of Glory*, 412.
 3 Quoted in Leslie, *Jennie*, 302.
 4 Quoted in Lough, *My Darling Winston*, 491–492.
 5 Quoted in Lough, *My Darling Winston*, 492
 6 Mary Soames, *Clementine Churchill* (London: Doubleday, 2002), 51.
 7 Soames, *Clementine Churchill*, 57.
 8 Purnell, *Clementine*, 45.
 9 Leslie, *Jennie*, 305.
10 *Daily Mail*, January 18, 1912.
11 *Daily Express*, May 27, 1912.
12 Quoted in Manchester, vol. 1, *Visions of Glory*, 403.
13 Quoted in David Stafford, *Oblivion or Glory* (New Haven, CT: Yale University Press, 2019), 4.
14 Manchester, vol. 1, *Visions of Glory*, 404.
15 Michael Shelden, *Young Titan: The Making of Winston Churchill* (New York: Simon & Schuster Paperbacks, 2014), 288.
16 Leslie, *Jennie*, 304.
17 Quoted in Lough, *No More Champagne*, 102–105.
18 Sir Edward Marsh, *A Number of People* (London: Heinemann, 1939), 154.
19 Quoted in Lough, *My Darling Winston*, 510.
20 Quoted in Lough, *No More Champagne*, 103–104.
21 Quoted in Lough, *My Darling Winston*, 519–520.
22 Quoted in Martin, *Jennie*, vol. 2, 364–365.
23 Quoted in Churchill and Mitchell, *Jennie, Lady Randolph Churchill: A Portrait with Letters*, 250.
24 Lady Randolph Churchill, *Small Talks on Big Subjects* (London: C. A. Pearson, 1916), 86.
25 Churchill, *Small Talk*, 111.
26 Sir Edward March, *A Number of People* (London: Heinemann, 1939), 154.
27 Lough, *No More Champagne*, 112.

28 Quoted in Lough, *My Darling Winston*, 523.
29 Quoted in Lough, *My Darling Winston*, 523.
30 Quoted in Leslie, *Jennie*, 321.
31 Quoted in Lough, *My Darling Winston*, 529.
32 Quoted in Lough, *My Darling Winston*, 529.

Chapter 17: Sara's Old-Fashioned Values 1913–1919

1 Kleeman, *Gracious Lady*, 259.
2 Roosevelt, *The Roosevelt Letters*, vol. 2, 170–171.
3 Roosevelt, *The Roosevelt Letters*, vol. 2, 170–171.
4 https://measuringworth.com/calculators/uscompare/relativevalue.php.
5 https://www.woodrowwilsonhouse.org/wilson-topics/wilson-and -race/.
6 Smith, *FDR*, 128
7 Elliott Roosevelt and James Brough, *An Untold Story: The Roosevelts of Hyde Park* (New York: G. P. Putnam's Sons, 1975), 82.
8 Quoted in Ward, *A First-Class Temperament*, 292.
9 David Michaelis, *Eleanor* (New York: Simon & Schuster, 2020), 136.
10 Pottker, *Sara and Eleanor*, 169.
11 Ward, *A First-Class Temperament*, 276.
12 James Roosevelt with Sidney Shalett, *Affectionately, F.D.R.* (New York: Hearst/Avon Division, 1959), 51.
13 Quoted in Pottker, *Sara and Eleanor*, 177.
14 Roosevelt, *The Roosevelt Letters*, vol. 2, 240.
15 Kleeman, *Gracious Lady*, 268.
16 Roosevelt, *The Roosevelt Letters*, vol. 2, 188.
17 Roosevelt, *The Roosevelt Letters*, vol 2, 207, 259.
18 Ward, *A First-Class Temperament*, 204.
19 Roosevelt, *The Roosevelt Letters*, vol. 2, 225–226.
20 Roosevelt and Brough, *An Untold Story*, 18.
21 Roosevelt and Brough, *An Untold Story*, 73.
22 Quoted in Lash, *Eleanor and Franklin*, 221.
23 Roosevelt, *The Roosevelt Letters*, vol. 2, 280.
24 Henry Brandon, "A Talk with an 83-Year-Old Enfant Terrible," *New York Times Magazine*, August 6, 1967.
25 Quoted in Cook, *Eleanor Roosevelt*, vol 1, 227.
26 Joseph P. Kennedy, unpublished diplomatic memoir, quoted in David Stafford, *Roosevelt and Churchill* (London: Little, Brown, 1999), xvi.
27 Quoted in Lash, *Eleanor and Franklin*, 226.
28 Pottker, *Sara and Eleanor*, 183.
29 Quoted in Pottker, *Sara and Eleanor*, 189.

30 Ward, *A First-Class Temperament*, 419.
31 Quoted in Pottker, *Sara and Eleanor*, 187.
32 Quoted in Pottker, *Sara and Eleanor*, 189.
33 Quoted in Lash, *Eleanor and Franklin*, 245.
34 Quoted in Pottker, *Sara and Eleanor*, 191.
35 Quoted in Pottker, *Sara and Eleanor*, 195.

Chapter 18: Jennie's "Best Foot Forward" 1918–1921

 1 Quoted in Sebba, *Jennie Churchill*, 304.
 2 Quoted in Martin, *Jennie*, vol. 2, 364.
 3 Quoted in Churchill and Mitchell, *Jennie, Lady Randolph Churchill: A Portrait with Letters*, 147.
 4 Martin, *Jennie*, vol. 2, 370.
 5 Leslie, *Jennie*, 303–304.
 6 Leslie, *Jennie*, 329.
 7 Quoted in Lough, *My Darling Winston*, 553.
 8 Lee, *Jean, Lady Hamilton*, 185.
 9 Quoted in Churchill and Mitchell, *Jennie, Lady Randolph Churchill: A Portrait with Letters*, 257.
10 Quoted in Churchill and Mitchell, *Jennie, Lady Randolph Churchill: A Portrait with Letters*, 261.
11 Asquith, Lady Cynthia, *Diaries 1915–1918* (London: Hutchinson, 1968), 445.
12 Quoted in Sebba, *Jennie Churchill*, 312.
13 Quoted in Lee, *Jean, Lady Hamilton*, 186.
14 Quoted in Sebba, *Jennie Churchill*, 312.
15 Lytton Strachey, *The Letters of Lytton Strachey* (London: Viking, 2005), 400.
16 Quoted in Quelch, *Perfect Darling*, 147.
17 Quoted in Martin, *Jennie*, vol. 2, 394.
18 Quoted in Martin, *Jennie*, vol. 2, 284.
19 Stafford, *Oblivion or Glory*, 88, 97, 136.
20 Quoted in Martin, *Jennie*, vol. 2, 393.
21 Stafford, *Oblivion or Glory*, 132.
22 Quoted in Sebba, *Jennie Churchill*, 315.
23 Quoted in Martin, *Jennie*, vol. 2, 400.
24 Quoted in Quelch, *Perfect Darling*, 148.
25 Quoted in Martin Gilbert, *Winston S. Churchill*, vol. 4, *World in Torment, 1916–22* (Hillsdale, MI: Hillsdale College Press/RosettaBooks, 2015), 602.
26 Soames, *Speaking for Themselves*, 292.
27 Quoted in Martin, *Jennie*, vol. 2, 401.

Chapter 19: Sara: "Our Dear Invalid" 1921–1931

1 Quoted in Ward, *A First-Class Temperament*, 578.
2 Roosevelt, *The Roosevelt Letters*, vol. 2, 415.
3 Kleeman, *Gracious Lady*, 276.
4 Quoted in Ward, *A First-Class Temperament*, 594.
5 Quoted in Pottker, *Sara and Eleanor*, 216.
6 Kleeman, *Gracious Lady*, 273.
7 Kathryn Smith, *The Gatekeeper* (New York: Touchstone, 2016), 60.
8 James Roosevelt with Bill Libby, *My Parents: A Differing View* (Chicago: Playboy Press, 1976), 28.
9 Roosevelt and Brough, *An Untold Story*, 165–167.
10 Kleeman, *Gracious Lady*, 281.
11 Roosevelt, *My Parents*, 61.
12 Quoted in Pottker, *Sara and Eleanor*, 231.
13 Roosevelt, *The Roosevelt Letters*, vol. 2, 463.
14 Quoted in Pottker, *Sara and Eleanor*, 207.
15 Quoted in Pottker, *Sara and Eleanor*, 238.
16 Roosevelt and Brough, *An Untold Story*, 191.
17 Roosevelt and Brough, *An Untold Story*, 192.
18 Roosevelt and Brough, *An Untold Story*, 227–228.
19 Roosevelt, *My Parents*, 29–31.
20 Roosevelt, *My Parents*, 79.
21 Quoted in Ward, *A First-Class Temperament*, 637.
22 Roosevelt, *My Parents*, 92–93.
23 Kleeman, *Gracious Lady*, 286.
24 Quoted in Pottker, *Sara and Eleanor*, 250.
25 Quoted in Pottker, *Sara and Eleanor*, 249.
26 Perkins, *The Roosevelt I Knew*, 48.
27 Kleeman, *Gracious Lady*, 288.
28 Perkins, *The Roosevelt I Knew*, 66.
29 Roosevelt and Brough, *An Untold Story*, 116.
30 Roosevelt and Brough, *An Untold Story*, 271.
31 Kleeman, *Gracious Lady*, 292.
32 Ward, *A First-Class Temperament*, 517, n. 4.
33 *New York Times*, February 26, 1933.

Chapter 20: Sara: America's Matriarch 1931–1941

1 Smith, *FDR*, 275.
2 Roosevelt and Brough, *An Untold Story*, 295.
3 Eleanor Roosevelt, *This I Remember* (New York: Harper & Brothers, 1949), 74–74.

4 Quoted in Pottker, *Sara and Eleanor*, 267.

5 Roosevelt, Leighton, and Forbush, *My Boy Franklin*.

6 *Time*, "National Affairs: *My Boy Franklin*," March 6, 1933.

7 Elliott Roosevelt and James Brough, *A Rendezvous with Destiny* (New York: G. P. Putnam's Sons, 1975), 21.

8 Roosevelt and Brough, *A Rendezvous with Destiny*, 21.

9 Doris Kearns Goodwin, *No Ordinary Time: Franklin and Eleanor Roosevelt: The Home Front in World War II* (New York: Simon & Schuster, 1994), 9.

10 Roosevelt and Brough, *A Rendezvous with Destiny*, 49.

11 Lash, *Eleanor and Franklin*, 515.

12 Michaelis, *Eleanor*, 326.

13 Equal Justice Initiative, "Antilynching Act Signed into Law," March 29, 2022, https://eji.org/news/antilynching-act-signed-into-law/.

14 Goodwin, *No Ordinary Time*, 197.

15 Roosevelt and Brough, *An Untold Story*, 289.

16 Kleeman, *Gracious Lady*, 320.

17 Roosevelt, *My Parents*, 31.

18 Roosevelt and Brough, *A Rendezvous with Destiny*, 149.

19 Smith, *FDR*, 434.

20 Roosevelt and Brough, *A Rendezvous with Destiny*, 233.

21 Smith, *FDR*, 434.

22 Roosevelt, *My Parents*, 31.

23 Roosevelt and Brough, *A Rendezvous with Destiny*, 69.

24 Quoted in Pottker, *Sara and Eleanor*, 328.

25 Quoted in Pottker, *Sara and Eleanor*, 329.

26 Roosevelt, *The Roosevelt Letters*, vol. 3, 383.

27 Ward, *A First-Class Temperament*, 9.

28 Quoted in Ward, *A First-Class Temperament*, 7.

Afterword: After Lives

1 Churchill, *My Early Life*, 5.

2 Sebba, *Jennie Churchill*, 328

3 Jenkins, *Churchill*, 7.

4 Roberts, *Churchill*, 30.

5 Pottker, *Sara and Eleanor*, 334.

6 Quoted in Pottker, *Sara and Eleanor*, 341.

7 Quoted in Pottker, *Sara and Eleanor*, 340.

8 Pottker, *Sara and Eleanor*, ix.

9 Pottker, *Sara and Eleanor*, x.

SELECTED BIBLIOGRAPHY

Thousands of books have been written about the Churchill and the Roosevelt families and the societies in which they operated. Here I have listed those I found most useful for this project. Because I was writing during the Covid lockdowns, when libraries and archives were usually closed, I had to rely on published collections of correspondence. I was fortunate that so much of the correspondence of the Roosevelt and the Churchill families has been published, and I am deeply grateful to collection editors, including Elliott Roosevelt, David Lough, Peregrine Churchill, and Mary Soames. I am also grateful to biographers, including Randolph Churchill, Martin Gilbert, Anne Sebba, Anita Leslie, Ralph Martin, Geoffrey C. Ward, Jean Edward Smith, Rita Halle Kleeman, and Jan Pottker, who quoted a great deal of primary material from which I could benefit.

Balsan, Consuelo Vanderbilt. *The Glitter and the Gold.* Maidstone: George Mann Books, 1973.

Brandon, Ruth. *The Dollar Princesses: Sagas of Upward Nobility, 1870–1914.* New York: Knopf, 1980.

Butler, Shannon. *Roosevelt Homes of the Hudson Valley: Hyde Park and Beyond.* Charleston, SC: The History Press, 2020.

Cannadine, David. *The Decline and Fall of the British Aristocracy.* New Haven, CT: Yale University Press, 1990.

Churchill, Peregrine, and Julian Mitchell. *Jennie, Lady Randolph Churchill: A Portrait with Letters.* London: Collins, 1974.

Churchill, Lady Randolph. *Small Talks on Big Subjects.* London: C.A. Pearson, 1916.

Churchill, Lady Randolph Spencer, ed. *The Anglo-Saxon Review: A Quarterly Miscellany*, 10 vols. London: John Lane, 1899–1901.

Churchill, Randolph S. *Winston S. Churchill*, vol. 1: *Youth 1874–1900.* London: Heinemann, 1966.

————. *Winston S. Churchill,* vol. 2: *Young Statesman 1900–1914.* London: Heinemann, 1967.

Churchill, Winston S. *Lord Randolph Churchill,* vol. I and II. London: Macmillan, 1906, *My Early Life.* London: Macmillan, 1930.

————. *Amid These Storms.* New York: Charles Scribner's Sons, 1932.

Clarke, Peter. *Mr. Churchill's Profession.* New York: Bloomsbury Press, 2012.

Collier, Peter, with David Horowitz. *The Roosevelts: An American Saga.* New York: Simon & Schuster, 1994.

Cook, Blanche Wiesen. *Eleanor Roosevelt,* vol. 1, *The Early Years: 1884–1933.* New York: Viking, 1992.

————. *Eleanor Roosevelt,* vol. 2, *The Defining Years: 1933–1938.* New York: Viking, 1999.

Cornwallis-West, George. *Edwardian Hey-Days: Or, a Little about a Lot of Things.* London: Putnam, 1930.

Cornwallis-West, Mrs. George. *The Reminiscences of Lady Randolph Churchill.* London: Edward Arnold, 1908.

Dallek, Robert. *Franklin D. Roosevelt: A Political Life.* New York: Viking, 2017.

De Courcy, Anne. *The Husband Hunters: Social Climbing in London and New York.* London: Weidenfeld & Nicolson, 2017.

Fielding, Daphne. *The Duchess of Jermyn Street: The Life and Good Times of Rosa Lewis of the Cavendish Hotel.* London: Eyre & Spottiswoode, 1964.

Ghaemi, Nassir. *A First-Rate Madness: Uncovering the Links Between Leadership and Mental Illness.* New York: Penguin Group, 2011.

Gilbert, Martin. *Churchill: A Life.* London: Heinemann, 1991.

Goodwin, Doris Kearns. *No Ordinary Time: Franklin and Eleanor Roosevelt: The Home Front in World War II.* New York: Simon & Schuster, 1994.

————. *Leadership in Turbulent Times.* New York: Simon & Schuster, 2018.

Greville, Frances Evelyn Maynard, Countess of Warwick. *Life's Ebb and Flow.* New York: William Morrow & Company, 1929.

————. *Discretions.* New York: Scribner's, 1931.

Hassall, Christopher. *Edward Marsh: Patron of the Arts: A Biography.* London: Longmans, 1959.

Heffer, Simon. *The Age of Decadence: Britain 1880–1914.* London: Random House, 2017.

Heffer, Simon, ed. *Henry "Chips" Channon: The Diaries 1943–57.* London: Hutchinson, 2022.

Higham, Charles. *Dark Lady: Winston Churchill's Mother and Her World.* London: Virgin Books, 2006.

Homberger, Eric. *Mrs. Astor's New York: Money and Social Power in a Gilded Age.* New Haven and London: Yale University Press, 2002.

Jenkins, Roy. *Churchill: A Biography.* New York: Farrar, Straus and Giroux, 2001.

Kehoe, Elisabeth. *Fortune's Daughters*. New York: Atlantic Books, 2004.

Kleeman, Rita Halle. *Gracious Lady: The Life of Sara Delano Roosevelt*. New York: D. Appleton-Century Company, 1935.

Layton, Thomas L. *The Voyage of the "Frolic": New England Merchants and the Opium Trade*. Palo Alto, CA: Stanford University Press, 1997.

Lash, Joseph P. *Eleanor and Franklin: The Story of Their Relationship, Based on Eleanor Roosevelt's Private Papers*. New York: W. W. Norton, 1971.

———. *Roosevelt and Churchill, 1939–1941: The Partnership That Saved the West*. London: André Deutsch, 1977.

Lee, Celia, and John Lee. *Winston and Jack: The Churchill Brothers*. London: Celia Lee, 2007.

Lee, Celia, ed. *Jean, Lady Hamilton, 1861–1941: Diary of a Soldier's Wife*. Yorkshire: Pen & Sword Military, 2020.

Lepore, Jill. *These Truths: A History of the United States*. New York: W. W. Norton, 2018.

Leslie, Anita. *The Remarkable Mr. Jerome*. New York: Henry Holt and Company, 1954.

———. *Jennie: The Life of Lady Randolph Churchill*. London: Hutchinson, 1969.

Leslie, Shane. *Men Were Different: Five Studies in Late Victorian Biography*. London: Michael Joseph, 1937.

———. *Long Shadows*. London: John Murray, 1966.

Lough, David. *No More Champagne: Churchill and His Money*. New York: Picador, 2015.

———. "The Inheritance of Winston Churchill." In *The Cambridge Companion to Winston Churchill* (Cambridge Companions to History), edited by Allen Packwood. Cambridge: Cambridge University Press, 2023.

Lough, David, ed. *My Darling Winston: The Letters between Winston Churchill and His Mother*. New York: Pegasus, 2018.

MacAllister, Ward. *Society as I Have Found It*. New York: Cassell, 1890.

Manchester, William. *The Last Lion: Winston Spencer Churchill*, vol. 1, *Visions of Glory, 1874–1932*. Boston: Little, Brown and Company, 1983.

———. *The Last Lion: Winston Spencer Churchill*, vol. 2, *Alone, 1932–1940*. Boston: Little, Brown and Company, 1988.

Mann, William J. *The Wars of the Roosevelts*. New York: Harper, 2016.

March, Sir Edward. *A Number of People*. London: Heinemann, 1939.

Martin, Ralph G. *Jennie: The Life of Lady Randolph Churchill*, vol. 1, *The Romantic Years: 1854–1895*. Englewood Cliffs, NJ: Prentice-Hall, 1969.

———. *Jennie: The Life of Lady Randolph Churchill*, vol. 2, *The Dramatic Years: 1895–1921*. Englewood Cliffs, NJ: Prentice-Hall, 1971.

Meacham, Jon. *Franklin and Winston: An Intimate Portrait of an Epic Friendship*. New York: Random House, 2003.

McCullough, David. *The Greater Journey: Americans in Paris*. New York: Simon & Schuster, 2012.

Michaelis, David. *Eleanor*. New York: Simon & Schuster, 2020.

Perkins, Frances. *The Roosevelt I Knew*. New York: The Viking Press, 1946.

Pottker, Jan. *Sara and Eleanor: The Story of Sara Delano Roosevelt and Her Daughter-in-Law, Eleanor Roosevelt*. New York: St. Martin's, 2004.

Primrose, Archibald Philip, Earl of Rosebery. *Lord Randolph Churchill*. London: Arthur J. Humphreys, 1906.

Purnell, Sonia. *Clementine: The Life of Mrs. Winston Churchill*. London: Viking, 2015.

Quelch, Eileen. *Perfect Darling: The Live and Times of George Cornwallis-West*. London: C. and A. Woolf, 1972.

Ridley, Jane. *Bertie, A Life of Edward VII*. London: Chatto & Windus, 2012.

Rhodes-James, Robert. *Churchill: A Study in Failure*. London: Weidenfeld & Nicolson, 1970.

——. *Rosebery: A Biography of Archibald Philip, Fifth Earl of Rosebery*. London: Weidenfeld & Nicolson, 1963.

Roberts, Andrew. *Churchill: Walking with Destiny*. London: Allen Lane, 2018.

Roosevelt, Eleanor. *This Is My Story*. New York: Harper & Brothers, 1937.

——. *This I Remember*. New York: Harper & Brothers, 1949.

——. *On My Own*. New York: Harper & Brothers, 1958.

——. *The Autobiography of Eleanor Roosevelt*. New York: Harper & Brothers, 1961.

Roosevelt, Elliott, ed. *The Roosevelt Letters*. vols. 1–3. London: George G. Harrap & Co. Ltd, 1949–1952.

Roosevelt, Elliott, and James Brough. *An Untold Story: The Roosevelts of Hyde Park*. London & New York: W. H. Allen, 1974.

——. *A Rendezvous with Destiny: The Roosevelts of the White House*. New York: G. P. Putnam's Sons, 1975.

Roosevelt, James, with Sidney Shalett. *Affectionately, F.D.R.* New York: Hearst/Avon Division, 1959.

Roosevelt, James, with Bill Libby. *My Parents: A Differing View*. Chicago: Playboy Press, 1976.

Roosevelt, Sara Delano, Isabel Leighton, and Gabrielle Elliot Forbush. *My Boy Franklin*. New York: Ray Long & Richard R. Smith, 1933.

Sebba, Anne. *Jennie Churchill: Winston's American Mother*. London: John Murray, 2007.

Seward, Desmond. *Eugénie: The Empress and Her Empire*. Stroud, Gloucestershire, UK: Sutton Publishing Limited, 2004.

Shelden, Michael. *Young Titan: The Making of Winston Churchill*. New York: Simon & Schuster Paperbacks, 2014.

Smith, Jean Edward. *FDR*. New York: Random House, 2007.

Smith, Kathryn. *The Gatekeeper: Missy LeHand, FDR, and the Untold Story of the Partnership That Defined a Presidency*. New York: Touchstone/Simon & Schuster, 2016.

Smyth, Ethel. *What Happened Next?* London: Longman, 1940.

Soames, Mary, ed. *Speaking for Themselves: The Personal Letters of Winston and Clementine Churchill*. London: Doubleday, 1998.

Soames, Mary. *Clementine Churchill*. London: Doubleday, 2002, rev. and updated.

Stafford, David. *Roosevelt & Churchill: Men of Secrets*. London: Little, Brown and Company, 1999.

———. *Oblivion or Glory: 1921 and the Making of Winston Churchill*. New Haven, CT: Yale University Press, 2019.

Ward, Geoffrey C. *Before the Trumpet: Young Franklin Roosevelt, 1882–1905*. New York: Harper & Row, 1985.

———. *A First-Class Temperament: The Emergence of Franklin Roosevelt*. New York: Harper & Row, 1989.

———. *Closest Companion: The Unknown Story of the Intimate Friendship Between Franklin Roosevelt and Margaret Suckley*. New York: Houghton Mifflin Harcourt, 1995.

Wharton, Edith. *The Age of Innocence*. New York: D. Appleton, 1920.

———. *The Custom of the Country*. New York: D. Appleton, 1913

Wharton, Edith, completed by Marion Mainwaring. *The Buccaneers*. New York: Viking Penguin, 1993.

Wilson, Theodore A. *The First Summit: Roosevelt and Churchill at Placentia Bay, 1941*, rev. ed. Lawrence: University Press of Kansas, 1991.

PHOTO CREDITS

Jennie Jerome Churchill Photos

Clara Jerome, Jennie's mother, raised her daughters to be genteel and accomplished. (Reproduced with the permission of Curtis Brown, London on behalf of Randolph S. Churchill. Churchill Archives Centre: RDCH 9-1-24)

Leonard Jerome, Jennie's reckless father, was known as "The King of Wall Street." (Reproduced with the permission of Curtis Brown, London on behalf of Randolph S. Churchill. Churchill Archives Centre: RDCH 9-1-24)

The Jerome Mansion on Madison Avenue boasted internal fountains, a three-story stable, and a private theater. (Museum of the City of New York)

From an early age, Jennie knew how to play to the camera. (Reproduced with permission of Curtis Brown, London on behalf of the Broadwater Collection © Broadwater Collection. Churchill Archives Centre, © The Broadway Collection: BRDW 1 Photo 2/4)

Jerome Park Racetrack attracted both Leonard's friends and Rosy Roosevelt. (Museum of the City of New York)

Mrs. Jerome and her three adult daughters (right to left): Vivacious Jennie overshadowed shy Leonie and dreamy Clara. (Bridgeman Images)

Edward, Prince of Wales: The heir to the throne welcomed American women to his "Marlborough House set." (Smith Archive/Alamy Stock Photo)

Lord Randolph Churchill, second son of the Duke of Marlborough: "instant chemistry." (Pictorial Press Ltd/Alamy Stock Photo)

Lord Randolph and Jennie: "a very dangerous affair." (History and Art Collection/Alamy Stock Photo)

Jennie, with two-year-old Winston, before the Irish exile. (Fremantle/Alamy Stock Photo)

Blenheim Palace: Magnificent and forbidding. (Print Collector/Getty Images)

Jennie with her sons Jack (left) and Winston, 1889. (Keystone Press/Alamy Stock Photo)

The devoted Mrs. Everest. (Fremantle/Alamy Stock Photo)

Jennie as Professional Beauty, with her diamond star. (Pictorial Press Ltd/Alamy Stock Photo)

Jennie, in riding outfit: "radiant . . . intense." (Granger Historical Picture Archive)

Lord and Lady Randolph Churchill in Japan, on the wretched round-the-world trip in 1895. (Fremantle/Alamy Stock Photo)

Jennie between Count Charles Kinsky (left) and Lord Dudley, two of her lovers. (Reproduced with the permission of Curtis Brown, London on behalf of Randolph S. Churchill. Churchill Archives Centre: RDCH 9/1/27)

Jennie as Empress Theodora at the Devonshire House Ball, 1897. (Lafayette Photography/Victoria and Albert Museum, London.)

Jennie's quarters on the Maine, *1899.* (Reproduced with permission of Curtis Brown, London on behalf of the Master, Fellows and Scholars of Churchill College, Cambridge © Master, Fellows and Scholars of Churchill College, Cambridge. Churchill Archives Centre: Papers of Peregrine Churchill. PCHL 8-6)

The Hon. George Cornwallis-West, "the best-looking man in England." (National Portrait Gallery, London)

Winston recruited his glamorous mother to help in the Oldham election campaign in October 1900. (Churchill Archives Centre, The Papers of Lady Soames MCHL 6/2/9)

Jennie, at fifty-six, could still dominate a party. (National Portrait Gallery, London)

Churchill, First Lord of the Admiralty, 1914, with inset of Clementine. (Fremantle/Alamy Stock Photo)

Jennie with grandson Peregrine. (Reproduced with permission of Curtis Brown, London on behalf of the Master, Fellows and Scholars of Churchill College, Cambridge © Master, Fellows and Scholars of Churchill College, Cambridge. Churchill Archives: Papers of Peregrine Churchill. PCHL 8-6)

At Bladon churchyard on July 2, 1921, Winston (left) and Jack lead the mourners. (Reproduced with permission of Curtis Brown, London on behalf of the Master, Fellows and Scholars of Churchill College, Cambridge © Master, Fellows and Scholars of Churchill College, Cambridge. Churchill Archives: Papers of Peregrine Churchill. PCHL 8-6)

Sara Delano Roosevelt Photos

Ten-year old Sara in China: Conventional upbringing in an exotic location. (Courtesy of the Franklin D. Roosevelt Library.)

A formal portrait of nineteen-year-old Sara captures her self-possession. (Courtesy of the Franklin D. Roosevelt Library.)

The five beautiful Delano sisters in 1883: (standing, left to right) Laura, Sara, Cassie, (sitting) Annie, and Dora. (Courtesy of the Franklin D. Roosevelt Library.)

Warren Delano, seen here with Sara and Annie, demanded unquestioning obedience. Sara idolized him. (Courtesy of the Franklin D. Roosevelt Library.)

From the moment of Franklin's birth in 1882, he had Sara's undivided attention. (Courtesy of the Franklin D. Roosevelt Library.)

Eleven-year-old Franklin was educated by private tutors, closely supervised by Sara. (Courtesy of the Franklin D. Roosevelt Library.)

As Franklin matured, his father James's health began to fail. (Courtesy of the Franklin D. Roosevelt Library.)

Forty-five-year-old Sara was a good-looking, very wealthy widow. (Courtesy of the Franklin D. Roosevelt Library.)

Sara Roosevelt realized that her son's fiancée, Eleanor, required a lot of guidance. (Courtesy of the Franklin D. Roosevelt Library.)

Sara stayed close to Franklin and his family during summers at Campobello. Anna (six) and James (five) grew to depend on her. (Courtesy of the Franklin D. Roosevelt Library.)

With Franklin at the helm, Sara pours tea for Eleanor and granddaughter Anna off Campobello. (Courtesy of the Franklin D. Roosevelt Library.)

As assistant secretary to the Navy during World War I, Franklin retreated to his childhood home frequently, despite Eleanor's discomfort there. (Bettmann/Getty Images)

Franklin's affair with Lucy Mercer nearly destroyed the Roosevelt marriage in 1918. (Historical/Getty Images)

By the time Franklin entered politics, he and his mother had remodeled Springwood into an impressive residence. (Courtesy of the Franklin D. Roosevelt Library.)

Sara with her son, granddaughter Anna, five grandsons, and two great-grandchildren on the porch of Springwood in 1931. Eleanor, standing behind Franklin, was a reluctant participant in family occasions. (Courtesy of the Franklin D. Roosevelt Library.)

On Franklin's victorious return to Springwood in 1932 as president-elect, Sara was beside him as he waved to neighbors. (Courtesy of the Franklin D. Roosevelt Library.)

Franklin's fiftieth birthday party, in 1932, was organized by his mother at Springwood. (Bettmann/Getty Images)

Anna, Eleanor, and Sara listen to Franklin's speech in 1936 at the Democratic nomination convention as he accepts to run for a second term. (Courtesy of the Franklin D. Roosevelt Library.)

Sara and her son read the congratulatory messages sent after his 1936 victory. (Courtesy of the Franklin D. Roosevelt Library.)

Sara Roosevelt and Mary McLeod Bethune, president of the National Association of Colored Women, at a luncheon at Sara's East 65th Street house. (New York Daily News Archive/Getty Images)

In June 1939, Sara hosted King George VI and Queen Elizabeth at Hyde Park. (Courtesy of the Franklin D. Roosevelt Library.)

Springwood, which evolved from a comfortable country house to a presidential mansion during FDR's lifetime, remained Franklin's beloved home and a monument to his mother. (Courtesy of the Franklin D. Roosevelt Library.)

Powerful Sons: Franklin D. Roosevelt and Winston S. Churchill at the Casablanca Conference in 1943. (Everett/Shutterstock)

INDEX

ABOUT THE AUTHOR

CHARLOTTE GRAY is one of Canada's best-known writers and the author of ten acclaimed books of literary nonfiction. Her most recent bestseller is *The Promise of Canada—150 Years: People and Ideas That Have Shaped Our Country*. Her bestseller *The Massey Murder: A Maid, Her Master, and the Trial That Shocked a Country* won the Toronto Book Award, the Heritage Toronto Book Award, the Canadian Authors Association Lela Common Award for Canadian History and the Arthur Ellis Award for Best Nonfiction Crime Book. It was shortlisted for the RBC Taylor Prize, the Ottawa Book Award for Nonfiction and the Evergreen Award, and longlisted for the BC National Award for Canadian Nonfiction. An adaptation of her bestseller *Gold Diggers: Striking It Rich in the Klondike* was broadcast as a television miniseries. An adjunct research professor in the department of history at Carleton University, Charlotte Gray is the recipient of the Pierre Berton Award for distinguished achievement in popularizing Canadian history. She is a Member of the Order of Canada and a Fellow of the Royal Society of Canada. Visit her at CharlotteGray.ca.